Study Guide

for Andersen and Taylor's

Sociology

Understanding a Diverse Society

Ninth Edition

Margie L. Kiter Edwards
University of Delaware

WADSWORTH
THOMSON LEARNING™

Australia • Canada • Mexico • Singapore • Spain • United Kingdom • United States

Acquisitions Editor: *Eve Howard*
Assistant Editor: *Analie Barnett*
Editorial Assistant: *Stephanie Monzon*

Ancillary Coordinator: *Rita Jaramillo*
Print Buyer: *Christopher Burnham*
Permissions Editor: *Robert Kauser*
Printer: *Globus Printing*

For more information, contact
Wadsworth/Thomson Learning
10 Davis Drive
Belmont, CA 94002-3098
USA

For more information about our products, contact us:
Thomson Learning Academic Resource Center
1-800-423-0563
http://www.wadsworth.com

International Headquarters
Thomson Learning
International Division
290 Harbor Drive, 2nd Floor
Stamford, CT 06902-7477
USA

UK/Europe/Middle East/South Africa
Thomson Learning
Berkshire House
168-173 High Holborn
London WC1V 7AA
United Kingdom

Asia
Thomson Learning
60 Albert Complex, #15-01
Singapore 189969

Canada
Nelson Thomson Learning
1120 Birchmount Road
Toronto, Ontario M1K 5G4
Canada

ISBN 0-534-58736-4

TABLE OF CONTENTS

Page

PREFACE

This study guide accompanies the second edition of *Sociology: Understanding a Diverse Society* by Margaret Andersen and Howard Taylor. Used as a supplement to the textbook, this guide can assist students in learning course material by highlighting core concepts, key people, principal theories, and relevant research on a variety of interesting topics in sociology.

Each chapter in the study guide begins with a set of questions to guide your reading by directing your attention to some of the most important issues to be covered in the corresponding chapter of the textbook. For each chapter, you should be able to: define and give an example of the key terms presented; identify the main contributions of key people, where listed; and apply each theoretical perspective to the topics discussed in the textbook. You can evaluate your comprehension of the material by completing the practice tests located at the end of each chapter in the study guide. Each practice test includes multiple choice, true-false, fill in the blank, and essay questions, followed by page number references and a detailed answer key.

Learn, grow, and imagine the possibilities.

CHAPTER 1
DEVELOPING A SOCIOLOGICAL PERSPECTIVE

BRIEF CHAPTER OUTLINE
What is Sociology?
Sociology: A Unique Perspective
Sociology in Practice
The Sociological Imagination
Revealing Everyday Life
Debunking in Sociology
Establishing Critical Distance
Discovering Unsettling Facts
The Significance of Diversity
Diversity: A Source of Change
Defining Diversity
Diversity in Global Perspective
The Development of Sociology
The Influence of the Enlightenment
The Development of Sociology in Europe
Classical Sociological Theory
The Development of American Sociology
Theoretical Frameworks in Sociology
Functionalism
Conflict Theory
Symbolic Interaction
Diverse Theoretical Perspectives

KEY TERMS (defined at page number shown and in glossary)

applied sociology 21	conflict theory 25
debunking 9	empirical 9
Enlightenment 17	functionalism 23
humanitarianism 17	issues 7
latent functions 24	manifest functions 24
organic metaphor 20	positivism 17
postmodernism 27	power 25
social action 20	Social Darwinism 20
social facts 18	social institution 5
social structure 7	sociological imagination 7
sociology 4	symbolic interaction theory 25
troubles 7	verstehen 19

KEY PEOPLE (defined at page number shown and in glossary)

Jane Addams 21	Peter Berger 9
Charles Horton Cooley 21	Auguste Comte 17
Oliver Cromwell Cox 22	Alexis de Tocqueville 17
Charles Darwin 20	W.E.B. Du Bois 22
Emile Durkheim 18	E. Franklin Frazier 23
Harriet Martineau 17	Karl Marx 19
George Herbert Mead 21	Robert Merton 24
C. Wright Mills 7	Robert Park 21
Talcott Parsons 24	Georg Simmel 13

Herbert Spencer 25
W.I. Thomas 21
Max Weber 19

William Graham Sumner 20
Lester Frank Ward 20
Florian Znaniecki 21

QUESTIONS TO GUIDE YOUR READING

1. What is the primary difference between sociology and other academic disciplines as frameworks for understanding human behavior?
2. What topics can be examined and explained using the sociological perspective?
3. What main tasks do professional sociologists engage in to accomplish their work?
4. Why can sociology be considered an empirical discipline?
5. What are the three major theoretical perspectives in sociology?

CHAPTER OUTLINE

I. WHAT IS SOCIOLOGY?

Sociology is the scientific study of human behavior and the social context in which it occurs.

- A. Sociology: A Unique Perspective
  1. Sociology differs from other social sciences in several ways.
     a. Psychology analyzes the behavior of individuals, while sociology examines groups or societies.
     b. Anthropologists study culture, often by investigating societies other than their own. They emphasize culture as the basis for society, whereas sociologists view culture as one part of a complex set of systems that comprise society.
     c. Political science is the study of politics, while economics investigates the production, distribution, and consumption of goods and services. These social sciences investigate a single **social institution**, or an established, organized system of social behavior with a recognized purpose. Sociology investigates multiple social institutions.
     d. Social work is an applied field that serves people in need. Sociology is a theoretical science that seeks to understand society as a whole, rather than provide services to particular individuals.
  2. The boundaries between the social sciences are not rigid and interdisciplinary research is often conducted.
- B. Sociology in Practice
  Sociologists engage in a variety of professional activities, including teaching, conducting research, debating public policy issues in the media, presenting expert testimony in courts and at government hearings, and providing information and assistance to community groups working toward social change.

II. THE SOCIOLOGICAL IMAGINATION

- A. **C. Wright Mills** (1916-1962) explored the concept of the **sociological imagination**, the ability to identify the societal patterns that influence individual and group life.
  1. Mills argued that it is necessary to understand the social and historical context to understand people's experiences.
  2. Mills distinguished personal troubles from social issues to clarify the process of developing a sociological imagination.
     a. **Troubles** are personal problems that are based in events or emotions in an individual's life.

2

<blockquote></blockquote>

     b. **Issues** affect large numbers of people and are based in the history and institutional arrangements of a society.

   3. This distinction is the basis of the difference between individual experience and **social structure**, defined as the organized pattern of social relationships and social institutions that constitute society.

   4. According to Mills, the task of sociology is to comprehend the personal and public dimensions of society.

B. <u>Revealing Everyday Life</u>

Sociology is an **empirical** discipline, where rigorous methods of research are used to investigate everyday life, and conclusions must be based on careful, systematic observations, rather than previous assumptions or "common sense."

C. <u>Debunking in Sociology</u>

   1. **Peter Berger** used the term **debunking** to refer to the role that sociology plays in looking beyond what is typically seen in everyday life. For example, sociology helps reveal situations present in schools in addition to the lessons presented in the classroom, including the effects of gender and social class on equity and the quality of public education.

   2. It is sometimes easier for sociologists to examine cultures other than their own because their thinking is less restricted by the common assumptions within the culture. For example, Westerners can more easily view the traditional Chinese custom of footbinding as bizarre than the Western practice of enhancing women's breasts by implanting silicone.

   3. Sociological researchers often find that common social beliefs are actually myths. Elaine Bell Kaplan's research on black teenage mothers in the United States indicates that the stereotypes about this group are inaccurate.

D. <u>Establishing Critical Distance</u>

   1. To see past cultural beliefs, sociologists must establish *critical distance*, or a certain detachment from the unquestioned engagement in everyday life.

   2. Some people can become detached from daily interactions more easily than others, particularly *marginal people,* because they share the dominant culture to some extent, but are blocked from full participation within it because of their status. Their unique position may help them maintain critical distance.

   3. **Georg Simmel** explored the role of the stranger within a group, who may provide unique insights because s/he is not limited by the group's assumptions and perspectives.

   4. Sociologists can develop critical distance by questioning the social forces that shape social behavior.

E. <u>Discovering Unsettling Facts</u>

   1. Sociological research often provides evidence of persistent problems in the United States, which challenges the common assumption that all people have an equal opportunity to succeed.

   2. Sociologists study a wide range of topics, including unusual groups and behaviors as well as common, everyday ones.

III. THE SIGNIFICANCE OF DIVERSITY

    A.   <u>Diversity: A Source of Change</u>

        1.   The United States is an increasingly diverse nation. By the year 2010, 38 percent of the population under 18 years old will be members of racial or ethnic minority groups.

        2.   Immigration, which is higher than at any time since the early 1900s, has become a critical social issue.

        3.   Cultural diversity is evident in the United States, where members of various groups share many cultural characteristics but also maintain some distinct patterns, such as language, religion, and family traditions.

    B.   <u>Defining Diversity</u>

        1.   *Diversity* is defined as the variety of group experiences that result from the different factors that shape how society is organized.

        2.   Although race, class, and gender are critical components of diversity in the United States, factors such as age, nationality, sexual orientation, and region of residence also influence people's experiences.

        3.   Understanding the complex process of diversity is necessary to analyze social institutions in the United States. For example, various groups have differential access to medical care, quality education, and economic resources.

        4.   Sociologists also explore how diverse groups respond to oppression and attempt to change society, noting how diversity can be a source of strength.

    C.   <u>Diversity in Global Perspective</u>

        1.   Nations are increasingly connected to each other in complex ways, making it necessary to use a global perspective to understand topics such as employment and immigration.

        2.   Comparing and contrasting the United States to other societies can also reveal patterns in your own society that would otherwise be invisible or easily taken for granted.

IV. THE DEVELOPMENT OF SOCIOLOGY

Sociology first emerged in western Europe in the 18th and 19th centuries, when rapid political and economic changes were occurring.

    A.   <u>The Influence of the Enlightenment</u>

        1.   The **Enlightenment**, known as the Age of Reason, strongly influenced the development of sociology. The Enlightenment's faith in the ability of human reason to solve society's problems by identifying natural social laws and processes was strongly linked to the development of modern science.

        2.   **Positivism**, a system of thought in which accurate observation and description is considered the highest form of knowledge, was another concept that emerged at this time and influenced the development of sociology.

        3.   **Humanitarianism,** based on the principle that human reason can successfully direct social action for the improvement of society, contributed to the emphasis on social reform in the discipline of sociology.

B.   The Development of Sociology in Europe
    1.   **Auguste Comte** (1798-1857), who first used the term *sociology*, believed that this discipline would become the "Queen of Sciences" because it studied the complex and changing systems of society.
    2.   **Alexis de Tocqueville** (1805-1859), author of *Democracy in America*, explored the democratic and egalitarian values in the United States, which he argued influenced social institutions and personal relationships. He believed that individualism made people self-centered and anxious about their position.
    3.   **Harriet Martineau** (1802-1876), a British author and sociologist who analyzed social customs in the United States, wrote *Society in America*. Martineau also wrote the first sociological research methods book, *How to Observe Manners and Morals*, which explored participant observation. She was a controversial, articulate feminist and abolitionist, who attacked slavery and the subservience of women in the United States.

C.   Classical Sociological Theory
    1.   **Emile Durkheim** (1858-1917) explored *social solidarity*, or the bonds that link members of a group, which he argued were based on belief systems.
        a.   Durkheim believed that the rituals of religion and other institutions reinforce the sense of belonging of group members.
        b.   Durkheim believed that members express social solidarity by condemning deviant behavior.
        c.   Durkheim discussed society *sui generis*, referring to his belief that society is a subject that should be studied separately from the total of individuals who comprise it.
        d.   Durkheim's work was the basis for *functionalism*, one of the major theories of sociology. He viewed society as an integrated whole, with each part contributing to the stability of the system.
        e.   Durkheim defined **social facts** as those social patterns that are *external* to individuals, such as customs and values. He argued that social facts are the proper subject of sociology.
    2.   **Karl Marx** (1818-1883) investigated the effects of capitalism, an economic system based on private property and profit, on individuals and societies.
        a.   Marx viewed capitalism as a system of relationships between the different social classes.
            1)   The capitalist class owns the *means of production*, or the system by which goods are produced and distributed.
            2)   Members of the working class sell their labor in exchange for wages.
            3)   Profit for the capitalist class is produced through exploitation of the working class.
        b.   Marx argued that virtually every social institution (e.g., family, education, law, religion) is shaped by economic forces.

        c.   It is an error to dismiss Marx's work on the basis of the political orientation of some of his followers. He produced an important body of work that identified class as a fundamental dimension of society.

   3.   **Max Weber** (1864-1920) argued that society has three basic, related dimensions: political, economic, and cultural.

        a.   Weber did not believe there could be a value-free sociology. Rather, he thought sociologists should acknowledge the influence of values and beliefs so that they would not interfere with their objectivity.

        b.   Weber believed that sociologists needed to use the technique of **verstehen**, or understanding social behavior from the point of view of those engaged in it. He believed sociologists need to develop some *subjective* understanding of how other people experience their world.

        c.   Weber defined **social action** as behavior to which people give meaning. It is the responsibility of sociologists to identify these meanings and the context in which behavior occurs.

D.   <u>The Development of American Sociology</u>

Although sociology in the United States developed from the foundations of the discipline begun in Europe, American sociology had some unique characteristics. Pragmatism, or a belief in practicality, led sociologists to value social planning. There was an emphasis on identifying the causes of social problems and developing strategies to improve them.

   1.   Sociology and Social Change

        a.   Early sociologists viewed society as an organism, a system of interrelated parts that work together. This is referred to as the **organic metaphor**.

        b.   **Social Darwinism** used Charles Darwin's theory of biological evolution to analyze social evolution or change.

            1)   **Herbert Spencer** (1820-1903) believed that societies evolve along a natural course; thus, he supported a *laissez-faire* (hands-off) approach to social change.

            2)   **William Graham Sumner** (1840-1910) claimed that "survival of the fittest" justifies inequalities in society.

        c.   **Lester Frank Ward** (1831-1914) advocated *social telesis*, or the idea that human intervention in the natural evolution of society would improve the social system and its problems.

        d.   **Applied sociology**, or the use of sociological research and theory in solving human problems, is based on the work of early activists who identified urbanization and industrialization as the cause of many social problems.

   2.   The Chicago School

        a.   Two key aspects of the *Chicago School* of sociology were an interest in how society shaped the mind and identity of individuals, and the use of social settings as human laboratories for research.

        b.   **Charles Horton Cooley** (1864-1929) believed that an individual's identity is based on his/her understanding of how others perceive them.

      c.   **George Herbert Mead** (1863-1931) extended Cooley's idea by investigating how individuals develop through the relationships they establish with others.

      d.   *Social psychology,* which studies the social basis of psychological behavior, developed at the University of Chicago at this time.

      e.   Some sociologists used Chicago as a laboratory to investigate social problems, including **W. I. Thomas** (1863-1947) and **Florian Znaniecki** (1882-1958), who studied Polish immigrants.

           1)   Thomas used immigrants' personal documents to examine their social relationships and feelings about their new lives.

           2)   Thomas identified the concept known as the *definition of the situation*: "If men define situations as real, they are real in their consequences." This principle argued that social influences were so great that people behave according to what they think is true, even with evidence to the contrary.

      f.   **Robert Park** (1864-1944) investigated how people of different races interact, as well as the sociological design of cities. He developed the concentric circle model of urbanization.

      g.   Although sexism prevented most female sociologists from achieving the same careers as men, **Jane Addams** (1860-1935) received a Nobel Peace Prize in 1931 for her work in the settlement house movement. One such facility was Hull House, which provided community services to its poverty-stricken residents.

      h.   Because female sociologists were usually excluded from university teaching positions, they often entered the applied field of social work.

3.   The Segregated Academy

African American sociologists have a long tradition of investigating Black communities, despite their historical exclusion from White universities.

      a.   **W.E.B. Du Bois** (1868-1963) was the first Black person to receive a doctorate from Harvard in any field.

           1)   With Isabel Eaton, DuBois wrote *The Philadelphia Negro*, one of the first empirical community studies to be published.

           2)   Du Bois noted that "the problem of the twentieth century is the problem of the color line."

           3)   Du Bois viewed sociology as a scientific, community-based, activist profession committed to social justice.

      b.   **Oliver Cromwell Cox**, another Black sociologist, analyzed racial prejudice, discrimination, and segregation in the United States. He was interested in the origins of capitalism and what is currently termed *world systems theory*, or theoretical explanations that use a global approach to understand the relationship between social systems, economic markets, and political structures.

        c.   **E. Franklin Frazier** (1894-1962) was the first Black person to be elected President of the American Sociological Association.

        d.   The sociological profession is more diverse than it has ever been, and the American Sociological Association has made a concerted effort to be more inclusive of diverse groups.

V.   THEORETICAL FRAMEWORKS IN SOCIOLOGY

Sociologists use theories to organize observations, produce logically related statements about observed behavior, and relate their observations to other data. Sociological theories use one of two basic approaches. *Macrosociological* theories, such as those developed by Durkheim, Marx, and Weber, seek to understand society as a whole. *Microsociological* theories, such as many developed in the Chicago School, focus on face-to-face interactions. The three major theoretical perspectives in sociology are functionalism, conflict theory, and symbolic interactionism.

    A.   <u>Functionalism</u>

        1.   **Functionalism** investigates how each part of society contributes to the stability of the whole system.

        2.   Functionalists emphasize stability and order in society, and believe that *disorganization* in the system leads to change. Because all parts of a society are related, a change in one part leads to changes throughout the society.

        3.   **Talcott Parsons** (1902-1979) identified the four principal functions of society as: adaptation to the environment, goal attainment, integration of members into harmonious units, and maintenance of basic cultural patterns.

        4.   **Robert Merton** (born 1910) realized that social practices can have consequences that are neither immediately apparent nor necessarily the same as their stated purposes.

            a.   Merton defined **manifest functions** as the stated and open goals of social behavior; e.g., reduce government spending by reforming welfare programs.

            b.   Merton defined **latent functions** as the unintended consequences of behavior; e.g., increasing homelessness by reducing welfare programs.

        5.   Critics of functionalism argue that the theory's view of society is too accepting of the status quo and understates the roles of power and conflict in society.

    B.   <u>Conflict Theory</u>

        1.   **Conflict theory** emphasizes the role of coercion in producing social order, noting that **power** is the ability to influence and control others.

        2.   Conflict theory, derived from the work of Karl Marx, views society as fragmented into groups that compete for social and economic resources.

        3.   Those groups with the most resources utilize their power to defend and maintain their advantages in society.

        4.   Conflict theorists view inequality as inherently unfair and believe that social change is the result of struggles between competing groups.

        5.   Critics of conflict theory argue that it overemphasizes inequality and social control and neglects shared values and public consensus.

    C.   <u>Symbolic Interaction</u>

        1.   **Symbolic interaction** theory views social interaction as the basis of society. It is used to investigate face-to-face interactions as a way of

identifying the subjective meanings that people give to objects, events, and behavior.

2. Symbolic interaction theorists argue that people behave based on what they *believe,* not just what is objectively true. They argue that society is *socially constructed* through human interpretation and that it is constantly modified through social interaction.

3. According to symbolic interaction theory, society is highly subjective because it exists in the imaginations of people, even though its effects are real.

4. Critics of social interaction theory argue that it overemphasizes the subjective basis of society and tends to ignore differences between groups in society.

D. <u>Diverse Theoretical Perspectives</u>
Sociological thought is diverse and includes additional theoretical frameworks.

1. *Feminist theory* analyzes the status of women in society by seeking knowledge to improve women's lives. Feminist scholars argue that traditional theoretical perspectives have distorted or ignored women's experiences, thereby providing an inadequate analysis of society.

2. *Exchange theory* argues that individual behavior is determined by the rewards or punishments people receive in daily interactions with others.

3. *Rational choice theory* argues that the choices people make are guided by reason, with society being seen as the sum of individual decisions and actions.

4. **Postmodernism** argues that society is reflected in the words and images, or *discourses*, that people use to represent behavior and ideas. Postmodernists typically engage in detailed analyses of film, music, literature, and other forms of culture.

5. Sociologists may draw from multiple theoretical perspectives to gain the greatest understanding of human behavior or social structures.

PRACTICE TEST

MULTIPLE CHOICE QUESTIONS.

1. Which of the following is **not** one of the main goals of sociology as a discipline?
   a. increase awareness about the ways that social institutions shape people's lives
   b. examine the common assumptions and beliefs underlying public opinion
   c. highlight the accomplishments of famous individuals to society and history
   d. analyze the influence of social change on people's experiences

2. Mills referred to the ability to identify the societal patterns that influence individual and group life as the:
   a. sociological structure.
   b. sociological imagination.
   c. debunking dynamic.
   d. naturalizing attitude.

3. Which of the following is **not** one of the primary professional activities engaged in by most sociologists?
   a. teaching information about society to students
   b. providing expert testimony on public policy issues
   c. consulting with community groups working toward change
   d. providing therapeutic counseling to individuals under stress

4. The shared problems experienced by groups of individuals subject to similar social, political, and economic circumstances are referred to as:
   a. troubles.
   b. issues.
   c. functions.
   d. myths.

5. The organized pattern of social relationships and social institutions that constitute society is:
   a. social structure.
   b. social function.
   c. sociological diversity.
   d. sociological imagination.

6. Sociology is an empirical discipline, which means that:
   a. conclusions about behavior must be based on careful, systematic observations.
   b. common sense is a reliable source of information for understanding behavior.
   c. research on human behavior must occur in its natural setting.
   d. All of the above statements are true.

7. One sociologist who studied teenage pregnancy in Black communities found that:
   a. most adolescent girls intentionally become pregnant and have a baby to become eligible for welfare benefits that make them economically self-sufficient.
   b. most adolescent girls who have a baby do not feel any stigma or shame about receiving welfare benefits because they believe the government owes them some assistance.
   c. most mothers of adolescent girls who have babies are disappointed by their daughters' pregnancies because they think it will limit their opportunities.
   d. most mothers of adolescent girls who have babies condone their daughters' early sexual behavior because they are happy that their daughters have boyfriends.

8. According to functionalist theory, the basis of social order is:
   a. coercion and competition.
   b. verstehen and debunking.
   c. consensus and cohesion.
   d. struggle and power .

9. Georg Simmel's main contribution to sociology was to provide insight into the role of:
   a. cultural products in shaping people's perceptions of reality.
   b. deviance in socializing people to behave responsibly.
   c. strangers in revealing group dynamics.
   d. children in creating stress within familes.

10. A study of African-American women revealed that many of them became mothers even though doctors told them that they carried the gene that can cause sickle-cell anemia. Many of the women believed the medical warnings were unreliable and had children anyway because personal beliefs, rather than objective facts, motivate human behavior. This case illustrates the principles of _____ theory.
   a. conflict
   b. functionalist
   c. social exchange
   d. symbolic interactionist

11. Which of the following "unsettling facts" about the United States is true?
   a. Half of all marriages formed now last less than two years.
   b. The rate of imprisonment is higher than in all other industrialized nations.
   c. The poverty rate among White citizens is higher than that of Asian immigrants.
   d. The gap between men's and women's average earnings is the same as it was in 1970.

12. Karl Marx argued that _____ was the core organizing element of modern societies.
   a. crime
   b. religion
   c. politics
   d. economics

13. The idea that human reason can direct social action for the improvement of society is:
   a. posivitism.
   b. postmodernism.
   c. humanitarianism.
   d. organicism.

14. Who was the prominent sociologist and community activist who received the first Ph.D. awarded to a Black person by Harvard University?
   a. Jane Addams
   b. Sophinista Breckenridge
   c. E. Franklin Frazier
   d. W.E.B. Du Bois

15. Emile Durkheim's research on social solidarity illustrates the principles of _____theory.
   a. conflict
   b. functionalist
   c. social exchange
   d. symbolic interactionist

16. Max Weber stated that sociologists should try to understand human behavior from the perspective of the people engaged in it. He referred to this concept as:
   a. debunking.
   b. wohnen.
   c. verstehen.
   d. application.

17. The concept of debunking refers to:
    a. making judgements about the beliefs and practices of the people being studied.
    b. questioning the taken-for-granted assumptions of social life.
    c. treating the people being studied as objects to avoid being biased.
    d. studying only people who are similar to you to avoid misunderstandings.

18. Social Darwinists such as Sumner suggested that:
    a. sociologists should use research to improve the quality of life for all citizens.
    b. social inequality is the result of the unequal distribution of economic resources.
    c. social inequality is rooted in biological processes such as adaptation.
    d. sociology is not a real science because it does not use objective research methods.

19. Joe was fired from his job because he repeatedly overslept and came to work late. This example illustrates the type of problem C. Wright Mills referred to as:
    a. deficiencies.
    b. troubles.
    c. issues.
    d. faults.

20. Two hundred men were laid off from their auto assembly jobs because the company closed the factory to cut costs. This example illustrates the type of problem C. Wright Mills referred to as:
    a. deficiencies.
    b. troubles.
    c. issues.
    d. faults.

21. Sociologists affiliated with the Chicago School of American sociology were:
    a. interested in how society shaped the mind and identities of individuals.
    b. committed to the application of sociological ideas to real social problems.
    c. involved in using social settings as laboratories for human research.
    d. All of the above are true.

22. Because of sex discrimination in academic settings, early female sociologists often worked as:
    a. nurses.
    b. secretaries.
    c. book editors.
    d. social workers.

23. Robert Merton realized that some social practices have consequences that are neither apparent nor consistent with their stated purpose. These unintended consequences of behavior are called _____ functions.
    a. mythical
    b. manifest
    c. latent
    d. covert

24. According to the 1999 Census, the largest number of immigrants to the United States now come from:
   a. South America.
   b. Eastern Europe.
   c. Africa.
   d. Asia.

25. The theoretical perspective that suggests society is reflected in the words and images that people use to represent behavior and ideas is called:
   a. feminism.
   b. functionalism.
   c. postmodernism.
   d. neodarwinism.

TRUE-FALSE QUESTIONS

1. The majority of professional sociologists work in applied settings, such as providing relief services to homeless people.

2. The boundaries between the social sciences are clear and rigid, making it unlikely that professionals from different disciplines would do research on the same topics.

3. Max Weber argued that the dynamics of any society could be fully understood by examining its most significant social institution, the economy.

4. During the Enlightenment period, scientific observation replaced religious dogma as the system of thought generally believed to be the highest form of knowledge.

5. In *How to Observe Manners and Morals*, sociologist Harriet Martineau argued that social activists' efforts to grant women the vote in the United States threatened the stability of the American family.

6. The term *sociology* was first coined by Auguste Comte, who thought that sociology would eventually become the "Queen of the Sciences."

7. Those aspects of diversity that have the most influence on structuring people's experiences in the United States today are gender, age, and religion.

8. The pioneers of American sociology at the University of Chicago identified industrialization as the main cause of the social problems they observed in U.S. cities.

9. W.I. Thomas' famous saying "If men define situations as real, they are real in their consequences," is referred to as the *irrational situation*.

10. Although racial discrimination was prevalent in sociology in earlier historical periods, the sociological profession has made great strides toward increasing the diversity of its membership.

FILL-IN-THE-BLANK QUESTIONS

1. Sociologist Georg Simmel suggested that a sociologist must have enough critical _____ from the group he or she is observing to be objective, but also be near enough to the group to share in their understanding of the situation.

2. Emile Durkheim conceptualized social _____ as those values, customs, and other patterns of behavior that are external to individuals and therefore, the proper subject of sociology.

3. Social _____ theorists argue that human beings consciously consider the costs and benefits of their actions before engaging in social behavior.

4. According to _____ scholars, the main problem with classical sociological theories is that they ignore or distort women's experiences and contributions.

5. Merton referred to the stated and open goals of human behavior as _____ functions.

ESSAY QUESTIONS

1. Distinguish between macrosociological and microsociological approaches to the study of society and human behavior. Give an example of a major theory that reflects each approach.
2. Explain why Emile Dukheim, a functionalist theorist, believed that deviant behavior had an important purpose in society. What positive functions does deviance serve for societies?
3. Define *diversity* and identify the three most influential aspects of diversity in the United States today. Explain why sociologists think it is important to understand diversity in society.
4. Use the principles of conflict theory to critique the functionalist perspective on social inequality.
5. According to Max Weber, what influence do social values have on sociological research? How did Weber suggest sociologists manage their own values while conducting scientific research?

ANSWERS TO PRACTICE TEST

Answers to Multiple Choice Questions

1. C. 4 Sociologists study a variety of individuals engaged in social interaction, but the goal of sociology is not to examine the unique contributions of famous people.
2. B. 7 The sociological imagination is a way of looking at society that reveals social patterns, while structure is the organized pattern of social relationships and social institutions that constitute society
3. D. 6 Few sociologists provide therapeutic counseling to individuals.
4. B. 7 Troubles are personal problems based in events or emotions in an individual's life, whereas issues affect large numbers of people and are based in the history and institutional arrangements of a society.

5.	A.	24	Social structure is the organized pattern of social relationships and social institutions that constitute society.
6.	A.	9	Empiricism demands that conclusions be based on careful, systematic observations, because common sense is unreliable. Research may occur in a variety of settings and be empirical.
7.	C.	10	Kaplan's research indicates that the common assumptions made about Black teenage mothers are myths. Her study showed that most of the mothers are disappointed and most of the girls feel shame about being pregnant and receiving welfare assistance.
8.	C.	26	Functionalist theorists emphasize stability, order, and cohesion, while conflict theorists emphasize coercion, competition, and power struggles.
9.	C.	11	Georg Simmel explored how the stranger in a group may provide unique insights into the group's structures and behaviors.
10.	D.	25	Symbolic interactionism is concerned with how people interpret information and the meanings people attach to situations.
11.	B.	11	The United States has the highest rate of imprisonment of all nations in the world; half of all marriages formed in the United States now will last less than 7.2 years; the poverty rate for Asian-Americans is higher than that of Whites; and the gap between men's and women's earnings has closed since 1970, although women with a college degree earn less on average than men without a college degree.
12.	D.	19	Marx theorized that societies could be understood by closely examining their economic organization.
13.	C.	17	Humanitarianism is the principle that human reason can successfully direct social action for the improvement of society.
14.	D.	22	W.E.B. Du Bois was awarded the first Ph.D. from Harvard University. E. Franklin Frazier was the first Black President of the American Sociological Association. Addams and Breckenridge were White.
15.	B.	18	Emile Durkheim's research was the basis for functionalist theory.
16.	C.	19	Verstehen refers to the ability to understand people's behavior from their perspective, while debunking refers to questioning taken-for-granted assumptions about social life.
17.	B.	9	Sociologists should avoid judging the people being studied and respect them as human beings, whether they are the same or different. Social life must be studied with an open mind to look beyond what is often assumed to be true.
18.	C.	20	Unlike most sociologists, Social Darwinists did not think sociology should be used to interfere with the "natural evolution" process. Theorists such as Sumner applied the principles of Darwin's theory of evolution, such as survival of the fittest, to human society.
19.	B.	7	According to Mills, troubles result from problems originating in individual emotions or conditions, such as being fired for oversleeping and arriving at work late.
20.	C.	7	According to Mills, issues result from problems originating in the social structure, such as economic recession and mass unemployment.
21.	D.	21	Sociologists affiliated with the Chicago School of American sociology were interested in how society shaped the mind and identities of individuals, and they used social settings as laboratories for human research to develop ways to solve social problems related to urbanization and industrialization.

22.	D.	22	Early female sociologists were usually excluded from faculty jobs, so they frequently entered the lower-paying field of social work.
23.	C.	24	Robert Merton called the unintended consequences of behavior latent functions, while the stated goals of behavior are manifest functions.
24.	D.	15	The largest number of immigrants to the United States now come from Asia.
25.	C.	27	Postmodernist studies provide a detailed analysis of images and words in film, music, and other forms of culture.

Answers to True-False Questions

1.	F.	6	Eighty percent of the members of the American Sociological Association list teaching as their primary work. Most direct services to people in need are provided by social workers.
2.	F.	5	The boundaries between the social sciences are not rigid and considerable interdisciplinary research is conducted on topics of mutual interest.
3.	F.	19	Karl Marx focused almost solely on the economy, while Max Weber thought that a complete sociological analysis must examine the interplay between economic, political, and cultural institutions.
4.	T.	17	
5.	F.	17	Harriet Martineau was an outspoken feminist and abolitionist who supported equal rights for women. Her book is a classic work on the research method known as participant observation.
6.	T.	17	
7.	F.	15	The most influential aspects of diversity in the United States today are race, class, and gender.
8.	T.	21	
9.	F.	21	Thomas and Thomas referred to this concept as the *definition of the situation*.
10.	T.	23	

Answers to Fill-in-the-Blank Questions

1.	distance	11
2.	facts	18
3.	exchange	27
4.	feminist	26
5.	manifest	24

CHAPTER 2
DOING SOCIOLOGICAL RESEARCH

BRIEF CHAPTER OUTLINE
The Research Process
> Sociology and the Scientific Method
> Developing a Research Question
> Creating a Research Design
> Gathering Data
> Analyzing the Data
> Reaching Conclusions and Reporting Results

The Tools of Sociological Research
> The Survey: Polls, Questionnaires, and Interviews
> Participant Observation
> Controlled Experiments
> Content Analysis
> Comparative and Historical Research
> Evaluation Research

Prediction, Sampling, and Statistical Analysis
> Prediction and Probability
> Sampling
> Statistics in Sociology
> The Use and Misuse of Statistics

Is Sociology Value-Free?
> Political Commitments and Sociological Research
> The Insider-Outsider Debate

Research Ethics

QUESTIONS TO GUIDE YOUR READING
1. What are the main sources of sociological research questions?
2. What is a research design? What are the major components included in the design?
3. What types of research methods do sociologists use to collect and analyze data?
4. What are the main advantages and disadvantages of each research method?
5. What are the common ethical dilemmas that sociologists might encounter while doing research?

KEY TERMS (defined at page number shown and in glossary)

concept 36	content analysis 45
controlled experiment 44	correlation 50
data 35	data analysis 39
deductive reasoning 33	dependent variable 36
empirical 32	evaluation research 46
generalization 41	hypothesis 35
independent variable 36	indicator 36
inductive reasoning 33	mean 50
median 50	mode 50
operational definition 36	participant observation 42
percentage 49	population 48
probability 47	qualitative research 35
quantitative research 35	random sample 49
rate 49	reliability 37

CHAPTER OUTLINE

I. **THE RESEARCH PROCESS**

Sociologists use a variety of techniques to collect data about research questions. Each of the research methods used requires rigorous observation and careful, logical analysis.

    A. Sociology and the Scientific Method

        1. Sociological research derives from the **scientific method**, originally defined by Sir Francis Bacon. The scientific method involves several steps in a research process, including observation, hypothesis testing, data analysis, and making generalizations.

        2. Science is **empirical**, meaning it is based on careful, systematic observation and the idea that a theory must be testable.

        3. Sociological insights can be achieved through two processes.

            a. **Deductive reasoning** derives specific conclusions from general principles.

            b. **Inductive reasoning** derives general conclusions from specific observations.

    B. Developing a Research Question

The first step in sociological research is to develop a research question, which may come from a variety of sources.

        1. Typically, developing a research question involves reviewing the existing, relevant research. Technological advances, including on-line databases, have made extensive resources available to researchers.

        2. A **replication study** repeats a prior investigation exactly, but on a different group of people or in a different time or place. This technique is an effective method for identifying social change.

        3. Sociological questions may come from the casual observation of behavior.

        4. Social policy or practical goals are often the source of research questions, such as the investigation of public assistance recipients and welfare reform.

        5. Sociological theory can be a source of research questions, because research is often developed to test existing theories.

    C. Creating a Research Design

A **research design** is the overall logic and strategy underlying the study. The research design, which is created after a research question has been developed, lays out a plan for investigating the research questions. The details of the research design, such as which technique to use to collect data, flow from the specific questions of the study.

        1. **Qualitative** research is somewhat less structured yet focused on a question being asked, is more interpretive, tends to have greater depth, and does not make extensive use of statistical methods.

        2. **Quantitative** research uses statistical methods to analyze numerical data.

3. Some research designs involve the testing of a **hypothesis**, or a prediction to be tested. Hypotheses are often formulated as "if-then" statements.

4. A research design includes a plan for how **data** will be collected. Quantitative data, such as census data, are numerical, while qualitative data are not; however, both forms of data can be logically interpreted and analyzed.

5. Sociological research investigates social **variables**, which are conditions or characteristics that can have more than one value, such as age or income.

6. Sociologists design research to test the influence of one variable on another.

   a. The **independent variable** is the one that the researcher wants to test as the presumed cause of something else.

   b. The **dependent variable** is the one upon which there is a presumed effect.

   c. Intervening influences, called intervening variables, can change the effect of an independent variable on a dependent variable.

7. Research designs may be cross-sectional or longitudinal.

   a. In a *cross-sectional study*, data from a single point in time are studied. This type of study may compare different groups of subjects in different locations.

   b. In a *longitudinal study*, data from two or more points in time are collected and compared. A longitudinal study is useful for measuring social change over time.

8. Sociological researchers study **concepts**, which are abstract characteristics or attributes that can potentially be measured, such as prejudice.

   a. Researchers must develop **operational definitions** of the concepts they study to specifically state how a concept is to be measured.

   b. Operational definitions are typically based on a series of **indicators**, which point to or reflect abstract concepts. An indicator is a measure of something real that corresponds in s useful way to a concept. For example, income is an indicator of social class.

   c. Sometimes indicators are combined into a single measure of an abstract concept to develop an *index*. One example is the Human Development Index, which measures human well-being.

9. Sociological research employs two statistical techniques for accuracy.

   a. The **validity** of a measurement is the degree to which it accurately measures or reflects a concept. To insure validity, researchers usually measure more than one indicator for a particular concept.

   b. A measurement is **reliable** if a repeat of the measurement gives the same result.

      1) Researchers may use measures that have proven sound in past studies; or they may employ various people to collect data to insure that subject's responses are not based on the personal characteristics of the interviewer.

    2) People may change their behavior in response to being studied, a phenomenon known as the *Hawthorne Effect*.

    3) Sociologists may use *unobtrusive measures* to study people without them being aware of it; however, these studies raise ethical issues concerning a subject's privacy. Research subjects are entitled to give their *informed consent*, which indicates their willingness to participate in a research study.

D. Gathering Data

  1. A large collection of data is known as a *data set* or a *database*. Examples include national crime statistics and the results of national opinion polls.

  2. After the research design is created, data collection occurs. Sociologists may gather original material, known as *primary data*; or use information that was already gathered and organized by another party, known as *secondary data*.

  3. There are many sources of raw data for sociologists to use in their research.

    a. The General Social Survey, an annual survey taken since 1972, is a survey of about 1500 people that solicits information about gender, race, education, income, and region on attitudes toward social issues.

    b. Sociologists frequently use the extensive database maintained by the United States Bureau of the Census to analyze data on United States residents. One issue concerning the use of census data is that some groups are more likely to be miscounted than others, resulting in the *census undercount problem*.

E. Analyzing the Data

  1. **Data analysis** is the process that sociologists use to organize the collected data and examine it for patterns and uniformities. The analysis may be quantitative (statistical) or qualitative, which depends upon the type of data collected.

    a. Coding is a process by which data are categorized and put into a form suitable for analysis.

    b. Data analysis is labor intensive but exciting, because it leads to discoveries about the data.

  2. Computers have greatly facilitated data analysis and have made data more accessible through the Internet.

F. Reaching Conclusions and Reporting Results

  1. The final stage in the research process involves reaching conclusions and reporting the results. Researchers try to draw conclusions from specific data and apply them to a broader population, a process known as **generalization**.

  2. An important part of research is sharing the results with others. Research results may be shared in classrooms, at professional conferences, and through the media, professional journals, and books.

  3. Research reports must: clearly state the methodology used and the results obtained; summarize relevant prior research; state the theory or theories that may have been tested; and specify what recommendations are being made.

4.   Research reports should also: state why and in what context the research is important; evaluate the overall quality of the data and results; discuss ethical issues raised by the research; and suggest what additional research on the topic is needed.

II.   THE TOOLS OF SOCIOLOGICAL RESEARCH

Many different research methods are used by sociologists, including survey research, participant observation, controlled experiments, content analysis, historical research, and evaluation research.

A.   <u>The Survey: Polls, Questionnaires, and Interviews</u>

1.   Surveys, which include questionnaires, interviews and telephone polls, are among the most commonly used tools of sociological research.

2.   Survey questions can be structured in two ways.

     a.   In a *closed-ended questionnaire*, people choose a reply from the list of possible answers, similar to a multiple choice test.

     b.   In an *open-ended questionnaire*, respondents can provide their own responses, similar to an essay question test.

3.   Questionnaires are typically distributed to large numbers of people. The *return rate* is the percentage of the questionnaires returned out of the total number distributed. A low return rate introduces possible bias in the results.

4.   Interviews may be conducted face to face, by telephone or by electronic mail.

5.   Using a survey to collect data has both advantages and disadvantages.

     a.   Surveys can include questions about a wide variety of topics and the results can be effectively analyzed to identify relationships among many different variables.

     b.   The disadvantages of surveys include the possibility that responses on closed-ended questions will not accurately reflect the opinions of the respondents, as well as the potential for respondents to use deception to conceal answers they believe might be offensive or controversial.

B.   <u>Participant Observation</u>

1.   In **participant observation**, the researcher becomes a member of the group they are studying and acts as both a subjective *participant* and an objective *observer*. Researchers who use this method, which is also known as *field research*, vary in the degree to which they participate in the group.

2.   In 1943, William F. Whyte published *Street Corner Society*, a book detailing the results of one of the first participant observation studies conducted in sociology. Whyte utilized the services of an *informant*, or person with whom the participant observer works closely to learn about the group. This study revealed that, contrary to popular opinion, urban gangs are highly organized mini-societies, with their own social hierarchy, morals, practices, and punishments.

3.   In 1976, Elijah Anderson published his participant observation field study of a bar in Chicago's South Side. He identified a status hierarchy among the men who frequented the bar, who ranked both themselves and others in the group.

4.   In 1985, Judith Rollins posed as a maid during her participant observation study of the relationships between Black domestic workers and their White employers.

5.   Participant observation research has produced some of the most valuable studies in sociology, but it has several disadvantages.
   a.   This method is time-consuming because the research may require years of data collection prior to reaching conclusions and reporting results.
   b.   The extensive note taking associated with this method creates a massive quantity of data that the researcher must organize and examine.
   c.   Participant observation research involves investigating small groups, which may make it difficult for the researcher to generalize the results.

C.   Controlled Experiments
1.   **Controlled experiments** are highly focused ways of collecting data and are especially useful for determining a pattern of cause and effect.
2.   To conduct a controlled experiment, two groups with similar subjects are created.
   a.   The *experimental group* is exposed to the factor that the researcher is examining.
   b.   The *control group* is not exposed to the factor that the researcher is examining.
3.   It is critical for all external influences to either be eliminated or *equalized* for both groups to establish cause (independent variable) and effect (dependent variable).
4.   Controlled experiments have been used to study many variables, including whether violent television programming and video games cause aggressive behavior in children; and whether there is a relationship between violence and pornography.
5.   Although experiments can clearly establish causation, they often occur in artificial environments that eliminate some elements of real life, making it difficult to determine how much the laboratory setting affected the results.

D.   Content Analysis
1.   **Content analysis** is a method of investigating society and social behavior by examining cultural artifacts such as magazines, television commercials, novels, biographies, soap operas, movies, and songs.
2.   Content analysis can measure cultural change and be used to indirectly determine how social groups are perceived.
   a.   Simonds (1988) applied content analysis to the "true confessions" in *True Story* magazine between 1920 and 1985. She found that stories about taboo subjects, such as pregnancy resulting from extramarital affairs, became increasingly frequent from the 1950s through the 1980s.
   b.   Children's books are often the subject of content analyses because they influence the development of young people. Researchers have been especially concerned with how the portrayal of Black Americans and women in children's books has changed over time.
3.   Content analysis has the advantage of being unobtrusive, yet it is limited to topics that are found in forms of mass communication. It does not reveal what people think about these images or how the images affect them.

E.   Comparative and Historical Research
  1.   In **comparative research**, sociologists examine how features in two or more societies shape social behavior, such as the relationship between poverty, employment patterns and the proportion of single parents. These studies are called *cross-cultural studies*, or investigations that compare different societies.
  2.   **Historical research** investigates social themes over time by examining the data in historical archives, which include government and church records, oral histories, and private diaries and letters.
  3.   Although comparative and historical research can provide important insight into long-term social changes, official records can be misleading, because they may be incomplete or misrepresent certain groups.
F.   Evaluation Research
  1.   **Evaluation research** assesses the effect of policies and programs on people in society. When the research is intended to produce policy recommendations, it is called policy research.
  2.   The evaluation of social policy can be controversial when there is disagreement about which indicators are appropriate measures of success, and there is often conflict during the research design stage.
  3.   *Market research* is a form of evaluation research where the sales potential of a product or service is determined by assessing customers' preferences.
III.   **PREDICTION, SAMPLING, AND STATISTICAL ANALYSIS**
A.   Prediction and Probability
  1.   The essence of science is prediction and explanation. Social, behavioral, and attitudinal characteristics can be measured and predicted within a margin of error.
  2.   A **probability** is the likelihood that a specific behavior or event will occur. For example, age is a good predictor of the chances of dying.
  3.   Probability statements reflect general patterns, but cannot predict with certainty that any specific person will adhere to the pattern.
B.   Sampling
  1.   A **population** is a relatively large collection of people (or other units) that a researcher studies and about which generalizations are made.
  2.   When a population is so large that it is impossible to include every member in the study, the researcher selects a **sample**, or subset of the population for the study.
  3.   If the sample is *representative* and large enough to overcome statistical abnormalities, the researcher can generalize the results from the sample to the entire group; however, if it is not representative, it is a *biased* sample.
  4.   To improve the likelihood of being representative, a sample should have the same overall composition as the population. A *sampling bias* is a deviation from an expected or proper value resulting from a systematic error in sampling procedure.
  5.   Sampling errors can lead to grossly inaccurate conclusions, as in the 1948 Presidential election. In that case, the Gallup poll incorrectly predicted Truman's defeat using a *quota sample*, which is a set number of people in a selection of key counties across the nation. Because

recent demographic changes were not reflected in the sample, an inaccurate prediction was made for that election.

    6.   The best way to insure that the sample is representative is to select it randomly. A **random sample** gives everyone in the group an equal chance of being selected.

    7.   At times, researchers deliberately *oversample* some respondents to collect enough data to conduct a detailed analysis of a particular subset of the population, such as Black Americans or gay and lesbian people.

    8.   The common media procedure of interviewing the "man on the street" is not scientific and therefore does not provide adequate results.

C.   <u>Statistics in Sociology</u>

    1.   Quantitative research is an important part of sociology and all sociologists must have at least basic quantitative skills to interpret research findings.

    2.   The main statistical tools researchers use are percentage, rate, mean and median.

          a.   A **percentage** is the same as parts per hundred.

          b.   A **rate** is the same as parts per some number, such as 10,000 or 100,000. A rate is meaningless without knowing the numerical base on which it is based.

          c.   A **mean** is the same as an average.

          d.   The **median** is the midpoint in a series of values arranged in a numerical order. In some cases the median is a better measure than the mean because the mean can be skewed by extremes at either end.

          e.   The **mode** is the value that appears most frequently in a set of data.

    3.   Sociologists can relate different variables to each other using the techniques of **correlation** and *cross-tabulation*.

          a.   **Correlation** is a widely used technique for analyzing the patterns of association between pairs of variables, such as income and education level. Correlation analysis indicates both the *direction* of the relationship between two variables and the *strength* of that relationship. The strength of the correlation is how closely the variables are associated or correlated, regardless of the direction of the correlation.

          b.   When interpreting correlation, it is important to realize that it is only an association and does not necessarily imply cause and effect. A *spurious correlation* exists when there is no meaningful causal connection between apparently associated effects. For example, the relationship between wife beating and watching the Super Bowl is spurious; the real correlation is between wife beating and alcohol consumption.

          c.   Another widely used method for analyzing sociological data is *cross-tabulation*, in which data are broken down into subsets for comparison, as illustrated in Table 2.1.

D.   <u>The Use and Misuse of Statistics</u>

    1.   Statistical information is easy to misinterpret, either willfully or accidentally.

2. "Fudging" is the term for tampering with or falsifying data. Fudging is not only a misuse of statistics and intellectual vandalism, but sometimes a criminal offense.

3. There are many types of statistical mistakes.

    a. *Citing a correlation as a cause* involves incorrectly assuming that an association between variables is a cause-effect relationship.

    b. *Overgeneralizing* beyond the population represented by the sample in the study is a misuse of statistics.

    c. *Building in bias* occurs when variables are presented to subjects in such a way that there is an increased probability the subject will select one response over other possible choices, whether or not such a response is accurate.

    d. *Faking data*, or making up information, is one of the worst misuses of data.

    e. *Using data selectively* misrepresents research findings by ignoring or minimizing those responses that fail to show an association between the researched variables, while reporting that portion of the study that supports the significance of the "findings."

4. Statistics are a numerical snapshot of reality and great care must be taken to avoid presenting them in a way that gives a distorted picture.

IV. IS SOCIOLOGY VALUE FREE?

Because sociological knowledge has an intimate connection to political values and social views, researchers must struggle to balance their own moral commitments against the need to be objective and open-minded.

A. Political Commitments and Sociological Research

1. Sometimes a political component is a valuable motivator to do research. For example, sociological research was *androcentric*, that is, centered on the experiences of men, until feminist scholars identified this limitation. This led to the development of new theories and concepts that transformed sociological thought.

2. Sociologists cannot be completely value-free, but researchers have an obligation to make their research as objective as possible.

3. To preserve objectivity, researchers must be free to ask questions without political constraints. The withdrawal of funding from research that raises controversy, such as in the study of sexual attitudes discussed in Box 2.2, violates scientific standards for open inquiry.

B. The Insider-Outsider Debate

1. No one will ever have another person's or group's experience, but if only insiders could understand the experience of a group, we would never be able to empathize with others or learn from their experiences.

2. Max Weber argued that sociologists could understand other people's perspectives through *verstehen*, a process in which the researcher imagines himself/herself in the place of their subject. This is an essential part of doing good research.

3. The insider-outsider debate has been especially important in studies about race.

4. Regardless of one's identity, doing research requires trust between the researcher and the study group.

V.   RESEARCH ETHICS

One of the most controversial studies in which serious ethical violations occurred was the Tuskegee Syphilis Study. From 1932 to the early 1970s, researchers infected 400 Black men with syphilis and left them untreated to study the effects of the disease on the Black population.

A.   Ethical considerations exist with all types of research, because research may require some degree of deception, or misleading respondents about the purpose of the study. The purpose is often revealed after completion of the study in a session called a *debriefing*.

B.   Most sociologists agree that deception is not unethical if no harm comes to the subject.
1.   Sociologists use pseudonyms (false names) or no names to protect respondents from being identified.
2.   The professional code of ethics is clear that if a research subject is at risk of physical, mental or legal harm, the subject must be informed of the rights and responsibilities of both the researcher and the subject.

C.   An important ethical dilemma emerges when sociologists study topics that violate laws.
1.   The law is not yet clear on whether sociologists must reveal the identities of their subjects or give their data to investigating authorities.
2.   Ethical dilemmas derive from two potentially conflicting research objectives, protecting the rights of individuals and guaranteeing the possibility of open scientific inquiry. This dilemma is particularly difficult when the topic is controversial or sensitive.

PRACTICE TEST

MULTIPLE CHOICE QUESTIONS

1.   The process of scientific thought by which sociologists derive general conclusions from specific observations is referred to as _____ reasoning.
a.   empirical
b.   inductive
c.   deductive
d.   dependent

2.   The last step in the research process is:
a.   developing a research question.
b.   creating a research design.
c.   collecting the data.
d.   reporting the data.

3.   When a sociologist repeats a prior investigation with a different group of subjects in a different time or place, it is referred to as a(n) _____ study.
a.   replication
b.   operational
c.   secondary
d.   independent

4. Correlation analysis delivers two types of information. The _____ of the correlation refers to how closely the two variables being analyzed are associated.
    a. code
    b. cause
    c. strength
    d. direction

5. A sociologist wants to know if racial prejudice in the United States has declined, increased, or stayed the same over the last fifty years. The best technique for investigating this topic is _____ research.
    a. experimental
    b. evaluation
    c. survey
    d. field

6. Characteristics that can have more than one value, such as age and income, are:
    a. rates.
    b. variables.
    c. hypotheses.
    d. generalizations.

7. Dr. Smith is conducting a participant observation study in a college dormitory. She observes how the residents interact with each other and asks them how they feel about their living situations. The type of data she is collecting is:
    a. qualitative.
    b. quantitative.
    c. predictive.
    d. secondary.

8. Dr. Jones decided to specifically measure the concept "social class" using the subjects' annual income. In this example, income refers to the _____ definition of the concept.
    a. conceptual
    b. operational
    c. professional
    d. correlational

9. A teacher thinks that gender may cause differences in her students' performance on math tests. In this example, gender is the _____ variable.
    a. independent
    b. indicator
    c. dependent
    d. deductive

10. A teacher thinks that gender may cause differences in her students' performance on math tests. In this example, test performance is the _____ variable.
    a. independent
    b. indicator
    c. dependent
    d. deductive

11. Drawing conclusions from specific data and applying them to a broader population is known as:
    a. fudging.
    b. analyzing.
    c. reasoning.
    d. generalizing.

12. Dr. Brown wants to know if the particular measure he is using accurately reflects the concept he is studying. He is interested in the _____ of the measure.
    a. generalizability
    b. objectivity
    c. reliability
    d. validity

13. The disadvantage(s) of using surveys to investigate people's opinions and attitudes is/are that:
    a. respondents may use deception to conceal answers that they believe may be offensive.
    b. this method of collecting data is especially time-consuming for the researcher.
    c. researchers can only study the views of a small number of people at one time.
    d. All of the above are disadvantages of using surveys.

14. According to the United Nations, the Human Development Index score is lowest for the population of which continent?
    a. Asia
    b. North America
    c. South America
    d. Africa

15. The research method that is especially useful for determining a pattern of cause and effect is:
    a. participant observation.
    b. controlled experiment.
    c. historical comparison.
    d. policy evaluation.

16. Dr. Lee wants to know how the portrayal of women in magazines has changed over the last 50 years. The most useful technique for her to use in this investigation is:
    a. field research.
    b. national survey.
    c. content analysis.
    d. program evaluation.

17. Research that examines social themes over time by investigating the data in archives, including government records, private diaries, and church records, is _____ research.
    a. comparative
    b. evaluation
    c. historical
    d. policy

18. When a researcher uses the results of data analysis to predict the likelihood that a specific behavior or event will occur, s/he is referring to the _____ of the behavior or event.
     a. probability
     b. possibility
     c. reliability
     d. validity

19. Dr. Wood selected his sample in such a way that everyone in the population he was studying had an equal chance of being included, resulting in a _____ sample.
     a. biased
     b. random
     c. democratic
     d. hypothetical

20. A researcher using correlational analysis found that as the youth unemployment rate goes up, youth participation in criminal activity increases. This reflects the _____ of the association.
     a. strength
     b. accuracy
     c. direction
     d. causality

21. To say that sociology is an empirical science means that the discipline:
     a. relies primarily on common sense to explain behavior.
     b. relies primarily on systematic observation and careful analysis to explain behavior.
     c. is strongly influenced by the researcher's own moral commitments and political agenda.
     d. All of the above statements are true.

22. The statistical tool used by researchers that is not skewed or distorted by extreme scores at either end is the:
     a. mean.
     b. mode.
     c. median.
     d. percentage.

23. The statement, "If a person drops out of high school, then s/he will be more likely to be unemployed," is an example of a(n):
     a. concept.
     b. variable.
     c. analysis.
     d. hypothesis.

24. Which of the following statements represents Max Weber's view on the insider/outsider debate?
   a. Scholars are not qualified to study people who are different from themselves in race, gender, and other social characteristics.
   b. Scholars cannot study people who are similar to themselves in race, gender, and other social characteristics because they will not be able to achieve scientific objectivity.
   c. Scholars can study people who are different from themselves in race, gender, and other social characteristics if they consciously try to see things from the group's perspective.
   d. None of the above statements accurately reflect Max Weber's perspective.

25. Which of the following potential ethical violations did Judith Rollins commit in her participant observation study on Black domestic workers and their White employers?
   a. Rollins took the role of an employer and interviewed Black women for the job of maid, but never intended to hire a maid.
   b. Rollins took the role of an employer, hired Black women as maids, and paid them without reporting their wages to the Internal Revenue Service, thereby breaking the law.
   c. Rollins took the role of a maid and organized other domestic workers to strike against their White employers, resulting in many maids losing their jobs.
   d. Rollins took the role of a maid and never revealed to the other maids or her employer that she was a researcher, thereby preventing them from giving informed consent to be studied.

TRUE-FALSE QUESTIONS

1. When researchers develop specific hypotheses from general theoretical principles, they are using the process of deductive reasoning.

2. Numerical data, such as those collected by the U.S. Census Bureau, are known as qualitative data.

3. In all cases, sociologists are ethically prohibited from conducting research without the informed consent of subjects.

4. Sociologists are required by federal law to identify specific individuals and hand over research data to investigators when a person or group they have studied is arrested for committing a crime.

5. Data collected by the United States Census Bureau accurately reflects the characteristics of the entire population of the nation.

6. In a controlled experiment, the control group is exposed to the independent variable and the experimental group is exposed to the dependent variable.

7. Sociologists have a variety of professional forums in which they can report the results of their research, including conferences, journals, and books.

8. Probability statements reflect general patterns, but cannot predict with certainty that a specific person will adhere to the pattern.

9.	Academic freedom refers to the idea that the government should restrict the ability of scholars to conduct research on sensitive or controversial topics to protect national security.

10.	In a closed-ended questionnaire, respondents must choose a response from a list of options provided by the researcher.

FILL IN THE BLANK QUESTIONS

1.	A _____ correlation exists when there is no meaningful causal connection between apparently associated events.

2.	The _____ is the value that appears most frequently in a data set.

3.	Operational definitions are typically based on a series of _____, which point to or reflect an abstract concept.

4.	After an experiment in which the researcher originally concealed the true purpose of the study, participants may engage in a _____, where the true purpose of the study is revealed.

5.	During a participant observation study, a sociologist may use the services of an _____, who is a person with whom the researcher works closely to learn about the group from an insider's perspective.

ESSAY QUESTIONS

1.	Describe four common statistical mistakes that researchers may make when analyzing or interpreting their data.

2.	You are a sociologist who is planning to collect data about the rate of alcohol consumption among college students. You need to create a research design to collect data that are both reliable and valid. Explain what steps you will take to accomplish this task.

3.	Your professor decides to investigate the effects of teaching methods on student performance. He decides to lecture in one section of his sociology class, and to combine lecture with group discussions and cooperative learning assignments in another section. Identify the independent and dependent variables, the hypothesis, and the research method being used for this study.

4.	Explain why the Tuskegee Syphilis Study violated the professional code of ethics that sociologists are obligated to follow when conducting research.

5.	Explain how sociologists may incorporate their own values into their research while also maintaining scientific objectivity.

ANSWERS TO PRACTICE TEST

Answers to Multiple Choice Questions

1. B. 33 Inductive reasoning derives general conclusions from specific observations, while deductive reasoning begins with a general theory and tests that theory through making specific observations.

2. D. 34 Developing a research question is the first step in the research process, followed by creating a research design, collecting and analyzing the data, and finally, reporting the results.

3. A. 34 Repeating a prior investigation with a different group of subjects or in a different time or place is a replication study.

4. C. 50 The direction of the correlation indicates in what way the variables are associated, while the strength of the correlation indicates how closely the variables are associated.

5. C. 42 Survey research is an efficient technique for assessing the attitudes and opinions of large numbers of people.

6. B. 36 Variables are conditions or characteristics that can have more than one value, such as age, years of education, and marital status.

7. A. 35 Qualitative data includes observations and interview transcripts, while quantitative data are numerical.

8. B. 36 An operational definition specifically details how a concept will be measured.

9. A. 36 The independent variable is the variable that the researcher is testing as the presumed cause of something else.

10. C. 36 The dependent variable is the variable upon which there is a presumed effect.

11. D. 41 Generalization is the ability to draw conclusions from specific data and apply them to a broader population

12. A. 37 The validity of a measurement is the degree to which it accurately measures or reflects a concept. A measurement is reliable if a repeat of the measurement gives the same result.

13. A. 42 People may not always answer survey questions truthfully, but data can be collected from a large number of people in a relatively short time period using this method.

14. D. 37 Africa has the lowest score on the Human Development Index.

15. B. 44 The controlled experiment is especially useful for determining a pattern of cause and effect.

16. C. 45 Content analysis can be used to measure cultural change, to study various aspects of culture as portrayed in forms of mass communication, and to indirectly determine how social groups, such as women, are perceived in a particular society.

17. C. 46 Historical research examines social themes over time by investigating the data in archives, including government and church records.

18. A. 47 Probability is the likelihood that a specific behavior or event will occur.

19. B. 49 Selecting a random sample is the best way to be certain that a sample is representative. This technique gives everyone in the population an equal chance of being chosen.

20.	C.	50	The direction of the association indicates in what way the variables are associated. In this case, the dependent variable goes up when the independent variable goes up.
21.	B.	32	Systematic observation and careful, rigorous analysis are required for research to be considered scientific or empirical.
22.	C.	50	The median is the midpoint in a series of values arranged in numerical value. The mean is an average, which can be skewed by extremes at either end of the range of values. The mode is the value that appears most frequently in a set of data. A percentage refers to the number of parts per hundred.
23.	D.	35	A hypothesis is a testable statement about how two variables are expected to be associated. It is often phrased as an if-then statement.
24.	C.	53	Weber thought that sociologists could study people different than themselves if they used tried to take the other people's perspective. He called this *verstehen*.
25.	D.	54	Using deception during research is potentially unethical; however, most Sociologists would not consider Rollin's behavior unethical because no one was harmed in this study.

Answers to True False Questions

1.	T.	33	Deductive reasoning involves the use of general theoretical principles to derive specific hypotheses for testing.
2.	F.	35	Numerical data, such as those collected by the Census Bureau, are quantitative data. Qualitative data are not numerical and cannot be analyzed using statistical techniques.
3.	F.	54	Sociologists may use unobtrusive measures to study people without them being aware of it in some cases. However, participants have a right to provide informed consent if they could experience possible physical, mental, or legal harm from being involved in the research study.
4.	F.	55	The law is not clear about whether, or when, sociologists may be required to share their data with authorities, but the researcher-subject relationship is not privileged.
5.	F.	38	The U.S. Census has an undercount problem in which racial-ethnic minorities are more likely than Whites to be undercounted, leading to an inaccurate count of some groups.
6.	F.	44	In a controlled experiment, the control group is not exposed to anything, while the experimental group is exposed to the condition that is being tested.
7.	T.	41	In addition to sharing research results in these forums, sociologists may also share their results in classrooms and through the media.
8.	T.	47	An example is that age is an excellent predictor of dying.
9.	F.	52	Academic freedom refers to preserving researchers opportunities to ask questions without political constraint, even when the topic is controversial.
10.	F.	42	In closed-ended questionnaires, respondents must choose from a list of possible answers, as in a multiple choice test. In an open-ended questionnaire, respondents can provide their own responses, as in an essay question test.

Answers to Fill in the Blank Questions

1. spurious   50
2. mode   50
3. indicators   36
4. debriefing   54
5. informant   43

CHAPTER 3
CULTURE

BRIEF CHAPTER OUTLINE
Defining Culture
      Characteristics of Culture
      Humans and Animals: Is There a Difference?
The Elements of Culture
      Language
      Norms
      Beliefs
      Values
Cultural Diversity
      Dominant Culture
      Subcultures
      Countercultures
      Ethnocentrism
      The Globalization of Culture
Popular Culture
      The Influence of the Mass Media
      Racism and Sexism in the Media
Theoretical Perspectives on Culture
      Culture and Group Solidarity
      Culture, Power, and Social Conflict
      New Cultural Studies
Cultural Change
      Culture Lag
      Sources of Cultural Change

QUESTIONS TO GUIDE YOUR READING
1. What are the five universal features of culture?
2. Why is language an essential feature of culture?
3. Why does cultural diversity contribute to both group solidarity and social conflict?
4. What is the difference between cultural relativism and ethnocentrism? Which approach do sociologists use in their attempts to understand culture?
5. What are the main sources of cultural change?

KEY TERMS (defined at page number shown and in glossary)

androcentrism 76	beliefs 68
counter-culture 75	cultural capital 83
cultural diffusion 85	cultural hegemony 83
cultural relativism 62	culture 60
culture lag 84	culture shock 84
dominant culture 72	ethnocentrism 76
ethnomethodology 68	folkways 67
global culture 77	language 64
law 68	mass media 78
material culture 60	mores 68
non-material culture 60	norms 67
popular culture 77	reflection hypothesis 81
Sapir-Whorf hypothesis 64	social sanctions 68

KEY PEOPLE (identified at page shown)

CHAPTER OUTLINE

I.   DEFINING CULTURE

    A.   It is difficult to understand the perception of our culture as "strange" by outsiders because we learn to accept the practices and beliefs of our culture as normal. Sociologists try to both know the culture as insiders and understand it as outsiders.

        1.   **Culture** is the complex system of meaning and behavior that defines the way of life for a given group of people.

        2.   Culture includes patterns of behavior (customs, habits, fashion) and ways of thinking (beliefs, values, knowledge, morals, language, laws).

            a.   **Material culture** consists of the objects created in a given society, including buildings, art, tools, toys, and print and broadcast media.

            b.   **Non-material culture** includes the norms, laws, ideas, and beliefs of a group of people.

    B.   <u>Characteristics of Culture</u>

        Certain features of culture are universal.

        1.   **Culture is shared**.

            a.   Culture is collectively experienced and agreed upon. The shared nature of culture makes society possible.

            b.   Within the United States, culture varies by region, age, gender, ethnicity, religion, class, and other social characteristics.

            c.   Despite these differences, certain symbols, language patterns, belief systems, and ways of thinking form a common American culture.

        2.   **Culture is learned**.

            a.   Cultural beliefs and practices are learned, even though they often seem perfectly natural to the members of the culture.

            b.   A person becomes a member of a culture through both the formal and informal transmission of culture. *Socialization* is the process of learning culture directly through instruction as well as indirectly through observation and imitation.

        3.   **Culture is taken for granted**.

            a.   Members of a culture seldom question their own culture; however, if a person becomes an outsider or establishes critical distance from typical cultural expectations, s/he may be able to examine the culture from a unique perspective.

            b.   Culture binds us together; however, lack of communication across cultures often has negative consequences.

        4.   **Culture is symbolic.**

            a.   **Symbols** are things or behaviors to which people give meaning, such as a flag or wedding band.

b.   The meaning attached to symbols depends on the cultural context in which they appear. For example, displaying a cross on a church has a different meaning than burning a cross on a front yard.

c.   Symbolic meanings guide human behavior. For example, many people have protested the display of a Confederate flag on the state capitol building in South Carolina, because the flag symbolizes racism and slavery.

5.   **Culture varies across time and place.**

    a.   Humans develop cultural solutions to adapt to the challenges posed by their particular physical and social environments.

    b.   **Cultural relativism** is the idea that something can be understood and judged only in relationship to the cultural context in which it appears. Practices that are accepted within certain cultures, such as body piercing, tattoos, and female circumcision, may be viewed negatively by members of other cultures.

    c.   Not only does culture vary from place to place, it also changes over time. Elements of prior cultural patterns combine with adaptations to new situations to form a complex, evolving system of culture.

C.   <u>Humans and Animals: Is There a Difference?</u>

    1.   The distinction between humans and animals is not as clear as people previously believed. For example, tool making was once considered a uniquely human activity, but it has been observed among animals, particularly chimpanzees.

    2.   Animals have developed systems of communication, with the most dramatic examples of language capability found among non-human primates. Washoe, a female chimpanzee, learned 160 standard signs in Ameslan, the American Sign Language system, and Koko, a female gorilla, learned 375 Ameslan signs. Koko also showed social development when she cared for a small kitten.

    3.   Scientists generally conclude that non-human animals lack the intelligence required to develop the elaborate symbol-based cultures common in human societies.

    4.   The interplay between biology and culture is complex. Cultural factors have a critical influence on human life, although biological and environmental limitations on human adaptations do exist.

II.   **THE ELEMENTS OF CULTURE**

Several elements of culture are of particular significance for societies: language, norms, beliefs, and values.

A.   <u>Language</u>

    1.   **Language** is a set of interrelated symbols and rules that provides a complex communication system.

    a.   The formation of human culture is made possible by language.

    b.   It is necessary to learn the language of a group to become accepted as a member. For example, when a person seeks to become a lawyer or a sociologist, it is necessary to learn the specialized, technical language of the group to function effectively and be accepted as a member.

     c.   Languages are fluid and dynamic. Linguistic changes develop in response to social change, as reflected by the number of new words and phrases created as computer use has increased.

  2.   Does Language Shape Culture?

     a.   The **Sapir-Whorf hypothesis** argues that language determines other aspects of culture because language provides the categories through which social reality is defined and constructed. Thus, language determines what people think and perceive because language forces them to perceive the world in certain terms.

     b.   According to the Sapir-Whorf hypothesis, speakers of different languages have different perceptions of reality. This can be seen in the way that speakers of different languages interpret time in various ways.

     c.   Recent critics do not think that language is as deterministic as Sapir and Whorf proposed, but there is general agreement that culture and language influence each other. For example, concepts of time in the United States are strongly linked to the Protestant work ethic.

  2.   Social Inequality in Language

     a.   Patterns of race, class, gender, and other forms of social inequality are reflected in language.

     b.   The labels given to various groups are used to convey certain attitudes and beliefs about those groups. Debates about the names given to certain groups in the United States have led to changes in the formal rules of language.

     c.   Power relationships between groups supply the social context for the connotations of language, and certain terms that were once acceptable may become defined as offensive. For example, "handicapped" has been replaced by "people with disabilities" in social and political discourse.

     d.   Language often reinforces the power structure in the United States. Women and members of racial and ethnic minorities are labeled, along with their behavior and practices, using words that have negative connotations; e.g., "Indian massacre."

     e.   Sexism in language, e.g., mankind, implies that the experiences of men reflect the experiences of all people. Likewise, terms such as "chairman" suggest that only men can hold this leadership position, and phrases like "woman doctor" suggest that the sex of the physician is something exceptional.

     f.   Language can reproduce racist and sexist thinking, but changing language may alter stereotypes by influencing how people think.

B.   <u>Norms</u>

  1.   **Norms** are the specific cultural expectations for how to behave in particular situations. Norms exist to govern every situation.

     a.   Sometimes norms are *implicit*, so they do not need to be spelled out for people to understand them, such as the norm that one must wait in line rather than barging in front of other people.

        b.   Norms are *explicit* when the rules governing behaviors are written down or formally communicated. There are specific sanctions for violations of specific norms, such as being removed from a non-smoking facility for lighting a cigarette.

2.   William Graham Sumner identified two types of norms.

        a.   **Folkways** are the general standards of behavior adhered to by a group, or the ordinary customs of different groups, such as fashion and etiquette.

        b.   **Mores,** the strict norms that control moral and ethical behavior, are often upheld by **laws**, which are the written set of guidelines that define right and wrong in a society.

3.   When a norm is violated, sanctions may be imposed on the violator. **Social sanctions**, which are mechanisms of social control that enforce norms, include both rewards and punishments.

        a.   Violations of folkways carry lighter sanctions than do violations of mores.

        b.   Negative sanctions may be mild or severe, ranging from ridicule to imprisonment and physical coercion.

        c.   Specific sanctions are not usually necessary, because people learn and follow the norms of their society.

4.   **Ethnomethodology** is a technique for studying human interaction that involves deliberately disrupting social norms and observing how individuals respond.

C.   Beliefs

1.   **Beliefs** are shared ideas held collectively by people within a given culture that form the basis for many norms and values. Beliefs can bind people in a society together.

2.   Beliefs provide a meaning system around which culture is organized, such as religion, mythology, science, or folklore.

3.   Sometimes beliefs are held so strongly that people are unable to tolerate ideas or experiences that contradict them.

4.   Sociologists study beliefs using various theoretical orientations. Each theory provides different insights into the significance of beliefs for human culture and society.

D.   Values

1.   **Values** are the abstract standards in a society or group that define ideal principles and provide a general outline for behavior.

2.   Values can be both a basis for cultural cohesion and a source of conflict. For example, conflict has developed over the topic of abortion in the United States.

3.   Values guide the behavior of people in society.

        a.   In the American Indian society known as Kwakiutl, wealthy chiefs would periodically give their possessions away to their followers and rivals in a practice called *potlatch*, reflecting this group's value of reciprocity.

        b.   In the United States, *conspicuous consumption*, which refers to consuming for the sake of displaying one's wealth, demonstrates a value opposite to that of the potlatch.

III. CULTURAL DIVERSITY

As societies develop and become more complex, different cultural traditions emerge. The more complex the society, the more likely its culture will be internally varied and diverse, as in the United States, where over eight percent of people are foreign born. Such cultural diversity creates a complex blend of cultural traditions. For example, the Native American Iroquois culture, with its emphasis on the principles of self-rule, federation, and representation, had a strong influence on the United States government.

A. Dominant Culture

    1.   The **dominant culture** is the culture of the most powerful group in society. It receives the most support from social institutions and constitutes the major belief system in that society.

    2.   A dominant culture need not be the culture of the majority of people. For example, in South Africa, Whites represent only 10 percent of the population, but dominate the country's laws and culture.

    3.   The "American" culture in the United States stems from middle-class values, habits, and economic resources. It is strongly influenced by television, the fashion industry, and Anglo-European traditions; and includes elements such as fast food and interest in professional sports.

    4.   There are heated political debates resulting from the increasing diversity of the United States. For example, 17 states have adopted laws designating English as the official state language. Opponents of such laws argue that the English-only movement represents an anti-immigration backlash and is based in growing hostility toward groups perceived as outsiders.

B. Subcultures

    1.   **Subculture** refers to the culture of a group whose values, norms, and behavior are noticeably different from those of the dominant culture.

    2.   Some subcultures physically retreat from the dominant culture, such as the Amish, while other subcultures co-exist within the dominant culture, such as the followers of the musical group, The Grateful Dead.

    3.   Sometimes subcultures are imposed on groups by excluding them from participation in the dominant group. Prohibiting a group from expressing its own culture may drive the culture underground, resulting in a *culture of resistance*, which challenges the dominant culture.

        a.   The Asian American community in California, historically forced to attend "Oriental Schools," developed a strong sense of solidarity.

        b.   "Race music," the precursor of rhythm and blues and later rock-and-roll, was created in response to the exclusion of Black musicians from the White-dominated music industry.

    4.   Subcultures also develop when new groups enter a society, such as the distinctive Puerto Rican subculture in the United States, which created the Salsa music now heard on mainstream radio stations.

C. Countercultures

    1.   **Countercultures** are subcultures created as a reaction against the values of the dominant culture. Nonconformity to the dominant culture, with practices that explicitly defy the dominant norms and values, may be the principal characteristic of counter-cultures.

2. "Women's communities," based on woman-centered, feminist social networks, relationships, and cultural activities, are an example of a counter-culture. Members may experience a sense of belonging in such groups that they do not experience in the dominant group.

3. Some counter-cultures directly challenge the dominant political system. An example of this type of counter-culture is the militia movement in the United States, whose members share a unique mode of dress, a common worldview, and a distinct style of life.

4. Counter-cultures may also develop around cultural pursuits, such as music. Rap music as a form of counter-cultural expression tells us about the experiences of young, urban African American men, who view and use rap as a mechanism for self-expression.

D. Ethnocentrism

1. **Ethnocentrism** is the habit of seeing things only from the perspective of one's own group. An ethnocentric view prevents people from understanding the world as it is experienced by others and can lead to negative conclusions about other cultures.

2. Although ethnocentrism may build group solidarity, it discourages understanding between groups.

   a. This problem is reflected in *nationalism*, the sense of identity that arises when a group exalts its own culture over all others and organizes politically and socially around this principle.

   b. Nationalist groups tend to be exclusionary, because they reject anyone who does not share their cultural experience and judge other cultures as inferior.

   c. In extreme form, ethnocentrism can lead to overt political conflict, war, or *genocide*, the mass killing of people based on their membership in a particular group. The brutality of the Hutus and Tutsis in Rwanda is an example of genocide, a process sometimes referred to as "ethnic cleansing."

3. **Androcentrism**, or modes of thinking that are centered only in men's experiences, is related to ethnocentrism. Feminist scholars and proponents of multicultural education have criticized knowledge based solely on the experience of White men, advocating multicultural education as a way to remedy ethnocentric and androcentric thinking.

E. The Globalization of Culture

1. The United States dominates the international mass culture through the influence of capitalist markets.

2. This diffusion of a single culture throughout the world is known as **global culture**, which combined with traditional cultural values, shapes the national culture of a specific society.

IV. **POPULAR CULTURE**

Popular culture includes the beliefs, practices, and objects that are part of daily traditions, including mass-produced, mass-marketed media that is shared by large audiences. Popular culture is distinct from *elite culture* or "high culture," which is shared by only a select group who can afford to participate in it. Thus, cultural tastes and participation in the arts is socially structured. Familiarity with different cultural forms stems from patterns of historical exclusion, as well as integration into networks that provide information about cultural products such as jazz, opera, and television.

A. The Influence of the Mass Media
  1. **Mass media** are those channels of communication that are available to wide segments of the population, including print and electronic media.
  2. The media strongly shape public information and attitudes, and television is an especially powerful force for transmitting cultural values in the United States.
  3. George Gerbner, a communication analyst, suggests television is the "national religion" of the United States, where leisure time for most Americans is dominated by watching TV. Gerbner argues that television generally portrays the most homogeneous view of culture and these images are resistant to change.
  4. The mass media have enormous power to shape public opinion. For example, because television news programs devote the largest amount of time to reporting crime stories, individuals' fear of crime is related to the time they spend watching television or listening to the radio.
  5. Commercial interests and producers' perceptions of what matters to the public determine what and how news is presented.

B. Racism and Sexism in the Media
  1. The mass media promote narrow definitions of who people are and what they can be. For example, the media communicate that only certain forms of beauty are culturally valued by treating characters differently according to their age, gender, race, and class.
  2. Music, films, books, and videos play a significant role in molding public consciousness, including upholding stereotypes about women.
  3. Cards, magazines, and computer software reinforce gender stereotypes by emphasizing physical appearance for women but competence and achievement for men.

V. **THEORETICAL PERSPECTIVES ON CULTURE**

The **reflection hypothesis** contends that the mass media reflect the values of the general population by trying to appeal to the most broad-based audience using characters with whom people will identify. However, media portrayals can also influence the values of those people who see them.

A. Culture and Group Solidarity
  1. Many sociologists have studied the relationship of culture to other social institutions. Classical theorist Max Weber examined the impact of culture on the formation of social and economic institutions. He argued that the Protestant faith rested on cultural beliefs, such as the work ethic and a need to display material success as a sign of religious salvation, that were compatible with modern capitalism.
  2. Many sociologists have examined how culture integrates members into society and social groups. Functionalists believe that norms and values create social bonds that attach people to society.
  3. Sociologists emphasize that non-material culture, including values, norms, and belief systems, has the ability to give people a sense of belonging and act as a major integrative force in society.

B Culture, Power and Social Conflict
  1. Conflict theorists have analyzed culture as a source of power in society that is dominated by economic interests. A few powerful groups are viewed as the major producers and distributors of culture.

2.   Conflict theorists view contemporary culture as produced within institutions that are based on inequality and capitalist principles. Thus, the cultural products most likely to be developed are those consistent with the values, needs, and interests of the most powerful groups, who have a strong interest in maintaining the status quo.

3.   **Cultural hegemony** refers to an excessive concentration of cultural power that leads to the pervasive influence of one culture throughout society. This process creates a homogeneous mass culture that reduces political resistance to the dominant culture.

4.   Those who produce cultural commodities in a capitalist society must constantly produce new needs to expand economic markets; thus, new fashions, music, and films are constantly available.

5.   Culture can be a source of political resistance, as illustrated by the American Indian Movement (AIM), which organized to reassert the independence of Native American cultures in the United States.

6.   **Cultural capital** refers to those cultural resources that are socially designated as being worthy, such as knowledge of elite culture. Groups that possess cultural capital have certain advantages. Pierre Bourdieu argues that members of the dominant class display their distinctive lifestyle to signal their importance to others, illustrating how culture contributes to reproducing social inequality.

C.   New Cultural Studies

1.   Symbolic interaction theory analyzes behavior in terms of the meaning people give to it. A relatively new interdisciplinary field known as *cultural studies* has emerged that builds on the insights of this theory.

2.   Cultural studies have been greatly influenced by postmodernism, which emphasizes the importance of material culture (such as film) in modern society. This approach directs researchers to view culture as a series of images that can be interpreted in multiple ways, depending on the viewpoint of the observer.

VI.   **CULTURAL CHANGE**
Culture is dynamic and develops as people respond to changes in their physical and social environments, despite social forces that attempt to maintain the status quo.

A.   Cultural Lag

1.   **Cultural lag** refers to the delay in making cultural adjustments to changing social conditions. Cultural lag is created when some parts of culture change more rapidly than others. Material culture generally changes more rapidly than nonmaterial culture.

2.   **Culture shock** is the feeling of disorientation that can occur when a person encounters a new or rapidly changing cultural situation.

B.   Sources of Cultural Change
The main sources of cultural change are changes in societal conditions, cultural diffusion, innovation, and the imposition of cultural change by outside groups.

1.   *Cultures change in response to changed conditions in society.*
Economic and population changes, as well as other social transformations, influence the development of culture. For example, cultural changes emerged as the Baby Boomers, or large number of children born after World War II, reached adulthood.

2. *Cultures change through cultural diffusion.*
   Cultural diffusion is the transmission of cultural elements from one society or culture to another. Cultural diffusion is swift and widespread due to the worldwide system of communication and transportation.
3. *Cultures change as the result of innovation.*
   The discovery and application of new knowledge, including technological developments such as the automobile and the personal computer, have led to dramatic changes in lifestyles.
4. *Cultural change can be imposed.*
   a. Change can occur when a powerful group imposes a new culture on a society. The dominant group may invade the society from outside or it may arise internally in a revolution.
   b. Cultural expression can be a form of political protest in which suppressed groups increase solidarity among members and attempt to establish a more powerful identity in the society.

PRACTICE TEST

MULTIPLE CHOICE QUESTIONS

1. Certain elements of Black urban street culture, such as rap music, have been fully integrated into the dominant American culture. This is an example of cultural:
   a. diffusion.
   b. innovation.
   c. oppression.
   d. lag.

2. The norms, laws, customs, ideas, and beliefs of a group of people constitute its _____ culture.
   a. popular
   b. material
   c. nonmaterial
   d. counter

3. Which of the following statements about culture is **false**?
   a. Cultural values are represented by symbols to which people attribute meaning.
   b. Culture is innate, or part of the basic instinctive patterns of human beings.
   c. Culture is fluid, so it changes as people adapt to emerging environmental and social conditions.
   d. Cultural beliefs and practices seem completely natural to members of the group.

4. The idea that something can be understood and judged only in relationship to the cultural context in which it appears is:
   a. cultural relativism.
   b. cultural hegemony.
   c. androcentrism.
   d. ethnocentrism.

5.   Which of the following is a uniquely human characteristic?
      a.   purposeful use of tools
      b.   intelligence required to develop symbol-based culture
      c.   formation of emotional attachments to other living creatures
      d.   ability to learn and use rudimentary language to communicate

6.   Which of the following is true about language?
      a.   It is essential for developing a complex culture.
      b.   It is fluid and dynamic, responding to social changes with linguistic changes.
      c.   It must be acquired for a person is to become accepted as a group member.
      d.   All of the above statements are true.

7.   The Sapir-Whorf hypothesis argues that language:
      a.   helps determine other aspects of culture because it provides the categories through which social reality is constructed.
      b.   single-handedly dictates people's perceptions of reality because people cannot perceive things for which they have no words.
      c.   is not necessary for acquiring the other social skills needed to participate in a group or society.
      d.   None of the above statements are true.

8.   Which of the following terms reflects social inequality in language?
      a.   Chairman
      b.   President
      c.   Director
      d.   Leader

9.   At the grocery store, people are expected to wait in line, rather than barge in front of other people, to pay for the items they are purchasing. This is an example of a:
      a.   value.
      b.   belief.
      c.   norm.
      d.   more.

10.   William Graham Sumner referred to food preparation techniques and standards of etiquette as:
      a.   mores.
      b.   folkways.
      c.   sanctions.
      d.   laws.

11.   There is a strict norm against incest in the United States. This morally offensive behavior may be severely punished. Therefore, incest is an example of a:
      a.   more.
      b.   folkway.
      c.   sanction.
      d.   belief.

12. Which of the following statements about sanctions is (are) true?
    a. Violations of folkways carry stricter sentences than violations of mores.
    b. Sanctions are mechanisms of social control that enforce norms.
    c. Sanctions involve punishments but not rewards.
    d. All of the above statements about sanctions are true.

13. The technique for studying human interaction by deliberately disrupting social norms and observing how individuals respond is known as:
    a. postmodernism.
    b. cultural studies.
    c. etiquette analysis.
    d. ehtnomethodology.

14. A shared idea held collectively by people within a given culture, such as cherishing democracy in the United States, is a:
    a. more.
    b. norm.
    c. belief.
    d. value.

15. An abstract standard that defines ideal principles within a given society, such as desiring individual freedom in the United States, is a:
    a. more.
    b. norm.
    c. belief.
    d. value.

16. When asked to identify famous Japanese people, respondents to Professor Akuto's survey named Yoko Ono (an American citizen), Bruce Lee (a Chinese film star) and Godzilla (a fictional character). This reflects:
    a. androcentrism.
    b. ethnocentrism.
    c. cultural relativism.
    d. cultural resistance.

17. The channels of communication that are available to very wide segments of the population, such as television news programs, are known as:
    a. mass media.
    b. inferior media.
    c. popular culture.
    d. elite culture.

18. Subcultures that are created as a reaction against the values of the dominant culture, such as the militia movement in the United States, are _____ cultures.
    a. symbolic
    b. material
    c. counter
    d. global

19. Which theoretical perspective views culture as a changing system that is socially constructed through the activities of social groups?
    a. conflict theory
    b. functionalist theory
    c. new cultural studies
    d. symbolic interaction theory

20. The theory that contends that the mass media reflect the values of the general population is known as the:
    a. mirror principle.
    b. reflection hypothesis.
    c. globalization process.
    d. mass socialization hypothesis.

21. The concentration of cultural power, or the pervasive and excessive influence of one culture throughout society is referred to as cultural:
    a. lag.
    b. capital.
    c. diffusion.
    d. hegemony.

22. The cultural resources that are socially designated as being worthy and that give advantages to those groups who possess them are known as cultural:
    a. lag.
    b. capital.
    c. diffusion.
    d. hegemony.

23. When Lisa, an American citizen, arrived in India, she felt disoriented because encountering such a different cultural situation led to cultural:
    a. shock.
    b. ignorance.
    c. hegemony.
    d. conflict.

24. Although we have the technology to develop more efficient, less polluting public transit systems, people's personal transportation habits have been difficult to change. This situation reflects the problem of cultural:
    a. lag.
    b. diffusion.
    c. ignorance.
    d. oppression.

25. A male college student wore a miniskirt to class. He was ridiculed by his classmates but did not receive any formal punishment. The student violated a:
    a. sanction.
    b. folkway.
    c. more.
    d. law.

TRUE-FALSE QUESTIONS

1. Sociologists agree that using ethnocentrism is the best way to fully understand and appreciate a culture other than their own.

2. The objects created by a given society, such as buildings, art, tools, and toys, are material culture.

3. Because culture is so critical to human survival, it is a stable, permanent system that does not change.

4. Because stereotypes are fundamental components of human thought, changing language to eliminate sexist or racist terms is not an effective way to change those stereotypes.

5. Cultural studies researchers argue that print, film, and electronic media have become increasingly important and influential sources of information in modern societies.

6. According to the Sapir-Whorf hypothesis, social inequality in language is justified because women are naturally inferior to men, and language reflects that fact.

7. Research indicates that individuals' fear of crime is directly related to the time that they spend watching television news programs.

8. Because participation in popular forms of culture is so expensive, it is usually restricted to high status groups.

9. According to Bourdieu, members of the dominant class display their distinctive lifestyle to indicate their social importance.

10. Nationalist movements focus on celebrating the indigenous culture of an oppressed group as a mechanism for building group solidarity and resisting the oppression.

FILL IN THE BLANK QUESTIONS

1. When someone is found guilty of murder in the United States, they are usually imprisoned. Imprisonment is an example of a _____.

2. Among residents of the United States who speak a language other than English at home, _____ is the most frequently used language.

3. According to _____ theory, culture serves the interests of powerful groups and is increasingly connected by economic monopolies.

4. According to _____ theory, culture provides coherence and stability in society and integrates people into groups.

5. When a tourist arrives in Hong Kong, s/he can get a Big Mac at McDonald's instead of having Chinese food. This reflects the development of a _____ culture.

ESSAY QUESTIONS

1. Explain why subcultures and countercultures develop and discuss what influence they have on the dominant culture. Identify specific examples of these groups in the United States.

2. Discuss the issue of social inequality in language, noting how language reinforces the current power structure in the United States. Provide specific examples to support your answer.

3. Explain how oppressed groups have used language to challenge stereotypes and promote positive self-images for members of their groups. Identify specific changes in language that have occurred in the United States.

4. Identify the four main sources of cultural change and provide an example of how each one has influenced behaviors or conditions in the United States.

5. Explain the statement, "Culture is symbolic." Give several examples of specific symbols used in the United States and discuss why their meanings vary according to the social context in which they appear.

ANSWERS TO PRACTICE TEST

Answers to Multiple Choice Questions

1.	D.	60	Diffusion and innovation are both sources of cultural change. Diffusion refers to the transmission of cultural elements from one group to another, while innovation refers to the discovery of new knowledge, such as technological advances.
2.	B.	60	Non-material culture includes the norms, laws, customs, laws, and beliefs of a group of people, while material culture includes the objects produced by the group, such as art, toys, and buildings.
3	B.	62	Culture is learned through socialization, thus it is not innate.
4	A.	62	Cultural relativism is the idea that something can be understood and judged only in relationship to its cultural context.
5.	B.	64	Some primates, such as Koko, have been observed using tools and rudimentary language, as well as developing emotional attachments; but the intelligence required to develop elaborate symbol-based cultures is a distinctly human characteristic.
6.	D.	64	Language is a set of symbols and rules which, when put together in a meaningful way, provides a complex communication system. It responds to social changes with linguistic changes, and must be acquired if a person is to become accepted as a group member.
7.	A.	64	The Sapir-Whorf hypothesis argues that language determines other aspects of culture since it provides the categories through which social reality is defined and constructed.
8.	A.	65	Social inequality in language is reflected in the term "chairman" because it suggests that only a man may hold the position.
9.	C.	67	Norms are the specific cultural expectations for how to behave in a given situation. Mores are strict norms governing moral behavior. Beliefs are collectively held ideas about what is right and wrong, and values are abstract ideals.
10.	B.	67	Folkways are norms governing customary practices, such as manners.
11.	A.	68	Mores are strict norms governing moral behavior, such as murder.

12.	B.	68	Sanctions are mechanisms of social control that enforce norms. They include rewards and punishments. The most severe sanctions are used for violations of mores.
13.	D.	68	Ethnomethodology helps reveal the normal social order by deliberately disrupting patterns of human interaction.
14.	C.	68	Beliefs are shared ideas held collectively by people within a given Culture, while values are ideal standards in a society.
15.	D.	69	Values are the abstract standards in a society or group that define ideal principles and provide a general outline for behavior.
16.	B.	76	Ethnocentrism is the habit of seeing things only from the point of view of one's group, while androcentrism is thinking centered only in men's experiences.
17.	C.	77	Popular culture is mass-produced and distributed, while elite culture is expensive and restricted to a few groups with high social status.
18.	C.	75	Counter-cultures are subcultures that are created to challenge the values of the dominant culture.
19.	D.	82	Symbolic interaction theory focuses on systems of meaning and people's interpretations of cultural symbols.
20.	B.	81	The reflection hypothesis contends that the mass media reflect the values of the general population.
21.	D.	83	Cultural hegemony refers to the pervasive and excessive influence of one homogeneous culture throughout society.
22.	B.	83	Cultural capital refers to the resources that are socially designated as being worthy and give advantages to the groups possessing them.
23.	A.	84	Culture shock can lead to disorientation and alienation.
24.	A.	84	Cultural lag occurs when there is a delay in adjustments to changes in society.
25.	B.	68	Violations of folkways involve relatively minor sanctions, while violations of mores, which are usually formalized in laws, receive the strictest sanctions.

Answers to True-False Questions

1.	F.	62	Sociologists advocate using cultural relativism to avoid being judgemental toward cultural practices in other societies.
2.	T.	60	
3.	F.	63	Not only does culture vary from place to place, it also changes over time as people adapt to changes in the environment and society.
4.	F.	65	Changes in language can, to some extent, change the way people think about certain groups, because what someone is called imposes a social identity on them.
5.	T.	83	
6.	F.	64	According to the Sapir-Whorf hypothesis, language provides the categories through which social reality is defined and constructed by people. The hypothesis does not suggest that inequality among social groups is innate or natural.
7.	T.	79	Television news programs devote the largest percentage of time to reporting stories about crime, and the more people watch these programs, the greater their fear of crime.

8.   F.   77   Popular culture is mass produced and distributed, while elite culture is expensive; therefore, popular culture is available to the largest number of people.

9.   T.   83   Bordieu views the appropriation of culture as one way groups maintain their social status.

10.   T.   85   Resistance to oppression often takes the form of a cultural movement, such as the development of Black Nationalism in the United States in the 1920s and 1970s.

Answers to Fill in the Blank Questions

1.   sanction   68
2.   Spanish   71
3.   conflict   82
4.   functionalist   82
5.   global   77

CHAPTER 4
SOCIALIZATION

BRIEF CHAPTER OUTLINE
The Socialization Process
Socialization as Social Control
Conformity and Individuality
Socialization and Self Esteem
The Consequences of Socialization
Theories of Socialization
Psychoanalytic Theory
Object Relations Theory
Social Learning Theory
Symbolic Interaction Theory
Agents of Socialization
The Family
The Media
Peers
Religion
Sports
Schools
Growing Up in a Diverse Society
Socialization Across the Life Cycle
Childhood
Adolescence
Adulthood and Old Age
Rites of Passage
Resocialization
The Process of Conversion
The Brainwashing Debate

QUESTIONS TO GUIDE YOUR READING
1. Why do sociologists consider socialization a form of social control?
2. What are the four main consequences of the life-long socialization process?
3. How does the socialization process vary by gender, race, ethnicity, and social class?
4. What are the primary agents of socialization in most societies?
5. What characteristics and expectations are associated with each of the main stages of the life course in the contemporary United States?

KEY TERMS (identified at page number shown)

adult socialization 111

ego 96

generalized other 101

identity 92

life course perspective 108

object relations theory 97

play stage 100

psychoanalytic theory 96

rites of passage 112

self-esteem 94

socialization 92

anticipatory socialization 112

game stage 100

id 96

imitation stage 100

looking-glass self 99

personality 92

peers 102

resocialization 114

roles 92

significant others 100

socialization agents 101

social learning theory 98   symbolic interaction theory 99
superego 96   taking the role of the other 100

KEY PEOPLE (identified at page shown)

Nancy Chodorow 97   Kenneth and Mamie P. Clark 94
Charles Horton Cooley 99   Erik Erikson 110
Sigmund Freud 96   Carol Gilligan 99
Lawrence Kohlberg 99   George Herbert Mead 99
Jean Piaget 98   Darlene Powell-Hopson and Derek Hopson 95

CHAPTER OUTLINE

Although people are fascinated by the notion of people raised with little to no human contact, most rumors of so-called feral children are not scientifically documented. One carefully documented case of a 12 year old boy found in a forest in Paris in 1800 indicates that despite intense attempts at education, Victor never acquired the speech or behavior typical of humans. A second case of a 13 year old girl who had been kept in nearly complete isolation in her California home was discovered in 1970. After intense language instruction and psychological treatment, she developed some verbal ability and showed progress in her mental and physical development, but in the 1980s, she was living in a home for mentally retarded adults.

I.   **THE SOCIALIZATION PROCESS**

Socialization is the process through which people learn the expectations of society, including social **roles**, the expected behavior associated with a given status in society. Socialization is the basis for **identity**, which is how a person defines him- or herself. It also establishes **personality**, which is the relatively consistent patterns of behavior, feeling, and beliefs in a given person. Socialization contributes to *internalization*, which occurs when behaviors and assumptions are learned so thoroughly that people no longer question them, but simply accept them as correct. People's lives are *socially constructed*, because the organization of society and the life outcomes of people within it are the result of social definitions and processes. What a person becomes is more a result of their social experiences than their innate, or inborn, traits. The socialization process varies by gender, race, ethnicity, and class.

A.   Socialization as Social Control

     1.   Socialization works as a mechanism of social control because once people accept the norms, values, and beliefs of their culture, they are likely to conform to social expectations.

     2.   Deviating from cultural expectations can lead to ridicule and other forms of peer pressure to conform.

B.   Conformity and Individuality

     1.   Despite the importance of social influences, human beings are individuals, not totally passive creatures who accept and conform to all social expectations at all times.

     2.   Conforming too much to the masculine or feminine gender role may create stress, which can lead to negative consequences such as depression for women and high-risk activities for men.

C.   Socialization and Self-Esteem

     1.   **Self-esteem** is the value a person places on his or her identity. This value is influenced by socialization, since the groups that surround us can influence our evaluation of our group as well as our evaluation of other groups.

2. The Clarks' classic study of African American children's preferences for Black or White dolls, conducted in the 1930s, revealed that most Black children preferred the White doll. Their research was cited in the landmark Supreme Court case, *Brown v. the Board of Education*, which ruled that segregation of public facilities was unconstitutional.

3. In a replication study during the 1980s, Powell-Hopson and Hopson found that providing positive reinforcement (rewards) reverses the doll selection trend, increasing the number of both Black and White children who select Black dolls. They concluded that reinforcement about being Black helps Black children develop a positive self-image.

4. In general, Black Americans have relatively high self-esteem compared to White Americans, because they use other Black people (who are likely to value being African American) as their reference group.

5. African Americans have a relatively low sense of *personal efficacy*, or the feeling of being an effective person. Research suggests this is due to the discrimination experienced by African American people.

6. Societal expectations can be contradictory. For example, a wealthy mother and a lower-income mother who choose to stay home to care for their children are evaluated differently in the United States.

D. The Consequences of Socialization

Socialization is a life-long process that affects how we think of ourselves and how we behave toward other people.

1. *Socialization establishes self-concepts:* self-esteem and identity are established through social experiences.

2. *Socialization creates the capacity for role-taking*: we are able to see ourselves as others see us.

3. *Socialization creates the tendency for people to act in acceptable ways:* we can understand social expectations and this creates some predictability in human behavior.

4. *Socialization makes people bearers of culture*: we have the opportunity to pass cultural expectations on to others.

II. **THEORIES OF SOCIALIZATION**

Several different theoretical perspectives have been used to explain the process of development, including psychoanalytic theory, object relations theory, social learning theory, and symbolic interaction. Each theory relies on unique assumptions about the effects of socialization on individual identity.

A. Psychoanalytic Theory

1. **Psychoanalytic theory**, rooted in the work of Sigmund Freud, argues that the unconscious mind shapes human behavior. Psychoanalysis can be used to discover the causes of psychological problems that exist deep within a patient's mind.

2. This theory suggests the human psyche is comprised of three parts.

    a. The **id** consists of deep drives and impulses, such as sexuality.

    b. The **superego** is the dimension of the self that represents the standards of society. Because social standards (superego) will always be in conflict with impulses (id), individuals develop defense mechanisms such as repression, avoidance, and denial.

    c. As the psychological component of common sense and reason, the **ego** balances the id and the superego.

3. "Freudian slips" are occasional slips of the tongue that apparently reveal an underlying state of mind.

4. Freud's theory is controversial and has been critiqued as being androcentric (male-centered). Questions have also been raised about the ability to generalize his findings beyond his non-representative sample of clients who underwent psychoanalysis.

5. Despite criticism, psychoanalytic theory is an influential and popular way to think about human behavior. It posits that the development of social identity is an inconsistent process characterized by dynamic tensions between strong instinctual impulses and social standards.

B. Object Relations Theory

1. **Object relations theory** places less emphasis on biological drives, arguing that the social relationships children experience determine the development of their adult personalities.

2. Developmental processes are believed to be largely unconscious. These processes include *attachment* to the primary caregiver and *individuation* (physical and emotional separation) from the caregivers.

3. Nancy Chodorow uses object relations theory to explain how gender shapes men's and women's personalities.
   a. The modern family has an *asymmetrical division of labor*, in which women "mother" and men do not.
   b. Because children identify with the same-sex parent, they individuate from mothers and fathers differently.

4. Despite criticism that Chodorow's theory is limited to traditional, nuclear families, it has been used effectively to analyze the experiences of Chicana mothers and daughters in large families and multi-generational households characterized by *familism*, where there is a high value on family unity and a high level of interaction with kin.

5. Chodorow's work has interesting practical implications. For example, if men acquired more mothering skills and participated more in daily caregiving, the result would be a society where men and women have less gender-stereotyped personalities.

C. Social Learning Theory

1. **Social learning theory** considers the formation of identity to be a learned response to social stimuli. Identity is viewed as the result of modeling oneself in response to reinforcement and encouragement from other people.

2. **Jean Piaget** believed that socialization and imagination have critical roles in learning. He stressed the significance of conscious, creative, and adaptive mental processes in social learning.
   a. Piaget argued that the human mind organizes experiences into mental categories called *schema*, through which individuals actively make sense of the world.
   b. Piaget noted that there are four stages of child development.
      1) *Sensorimotor stage*: children experience the world directly through the senses-- touch, taste, sight, and sound.
      2) *Preoperational stage*: children begin to use language and other symbols, cannot think in abstract terms, and begin to see things as others might see them.
      3) *Concrete operational stage*: children learn logical principles about the concrete world and prepare for more abstract forms of reasoning.

4) *Formal operational stage*: children are able to think abstractly and imagine alternatives to their reality.

3. Social learning theory suggests that behavior can be changed by altering the social environment, because children learn appropriate behavior through rewards and punishments.

4. Kohlberg elaborated on Piaget's work by developing a theory of moral development. He saw moral reasoning as a process occurring in several stages that are grouped into three levels.

    a. *Preconventional stage*: young children judge right and wrong in simple terms of obedience and punishment, based on their own needs and feelings.

    b. *Conventional stage*: adolescents develop moral judgement in terms of cultural norms, especially acceptance and following authority.

    c. *Postconventional stage*: people are able to consider abstract ethical questions, demonstrating maturity in moral reasoning.

5. Kohlberg argued that men, who are more concerned with authority, reach a higher level of moral development than women, because women remain more concerned with feelings and social opinions.

6. Carol Gilligan challenged Kohlberg's theory, arguing that men's moral development is not more mature than women's development; rather, women conceptualize morality differently than do men.

D. Symbolic Interaction Theory

1. According to **symbolic interaction theory**, people's actions are based on the meanings they attribute to things. These meanings emerge through social interaction. For example, as individuals learn roles, they assume the appropriate behavior and characteristics of the role.

2. For symbolic interactionists, the *self* is what we imagine we are, rather than an internal set of drives, instincts, and motives. This theory emphasizes that people make conscious, meaningful adaptations to their social environment.

3. Symbolic interactionists view the self as evolving over the life span; therefore, socialization is an ongoing process.

4. Charles Horton Cooley and George Herbert Mead greatly influenced the development of symbolic interactionism in sociology. These theorists viewed the self as developing in response to the expectations and judgements of other people in their social environments.

    a. Cooley developed the **looking-glass self** to explain how a person's conception of self develops through reflection about his/her relationships to others. This is a three-step process.

        1) We carefully note the reactions of others toward us.

        2) We develop an understanding of how others judge us.

        3) We develop feelings about ourselves based on the way we understand other people's perceptions of us.

    b. Mead agreed with Cooley that children are socialized as they respond to other people's attitudes toward them.

        1) Mead believed that the basis of all social interaction is social roles, or sets of expectations that govern a person's relationships with other group members and society.

2) **Taking the role of the other** is the process of imagining oneself from someone else's point of view. Self-awareness changes as people take on new roles.

3) Mead argued that there are three stages of childhood socialization, based on the child's developing ability to take on the role of the other.

    a) **Imitation stage**: children only copy the behavior of those around them, without the ability to take on the role of the other.

    b) **Play stage**: children begin to take on the roles of significant people in their environments. Of particular importance is taking on the role of **significant others**, or those with whom they have close relationships, such as their parents.

    c) **Game stage**: the child becomes capable of taking on multiple roles at the same time.

        (1) The roles are organized in a complex system that gives the child a more general, comprehensive view of the self.

        (2) The child understands how people are related to each other and to him or her.

        (3) At this stage, children acquire the **generalized other**, or the abstract composite of social roles and social expectations. Specifically, they develop an awareness of community values and general social expectations, which vary based on such factors as race, class, gender, and religion.

4) Mead believed that the self has two dimensions.

    a) The "I" is the active, creative, self-defining, unique part of the personality.

    b) The "me" is the passive, conforming self that reacts to others.

5) Mead believed that social identity is always changing and emerging, dependent on social situations. Stability is achieved as the individual learns to respond consistently to common situations.

III. **AGENTS OF SOCIALIZATION**

Socialization agents refer to individuals and groups who pass on social expectations, thereby influencing others both intentionally and unintentionally. Socialization often occurs in the context of social institutions, including the family, peers, the media, and religious, educational, and recreational institutions such as sports.

    A. <u>The Family</u>

        1. The family is the first source of socialization for most people. Within and across cultures, families are quite diverse.

2.   Researchers found that Japanese mothers speak to use objects as part of a ritual of social exchange in their interactions with their children, thereby emphasizing polite routines. American mothers focus on labeling things for their children. These different styles of interaction are interpreted as reflecting the beliefs and practices of each culture.

B.   The Media
1.   The media (including television, films, music, video games, radio, and print messages) are an increasingly important agent of socialization. In the United States, children spend more time, on average, with television than they do in school.
2.   Although there is extensive violence in the media, research has yielded conflicting results about the effects of televised violence on children. Both the images themselves and the broader social context in which children live must be considered, because the values and attitudes about violent behavior, along with observed violence, contribute to a child's behavior and attitudes.
3.   The media have also been criticized for portraying racist and sexist stereotypes.

C.   Peers
1.   **Peers** are those people with whom you interact on equal terms, such as friends, fellow students, and coworkers. Peer relationships vary among different groups.
2.   Peer interaction helps children learn concepts of self, gain social skills, and form values and attitudes.
3.   Members of minority groups frequently experience isolation and stress when they are "token" members of a dominant group, which often results in the formation of same-sex or same-race groups for support, social activities, and information-sharing.

D.   Religion
1.   Religious instruction greatly contributes to the identities children construct for themselves.
2.   Religious socialization influences the development of beliefs that guide adults in organizing their lives, including beliefs about the roles of men and women.

E.   Sports
1.   Through sports, men and women learn concepts of self and form ideas about gender differences.
2.   In interviews with male athletes, Messner identified sports as very important to male identity. He reported that playing or watching sports is often the context in which men develop relationships with their fathers, even when the father is otherwise absent or emotionally distant.
3.   Although sports were less significant in the formation of women's identity in the past, women are increasingly participating in sports. Traditionally, negative stereotypes of female athletes were a form of social control that reinforced traditional gender roles. Current research indicates that women who play sports develop a strong sense of bodily competence and self-confidence.

F. Schools
    1. The expectations encountered in schools vary for various groups of students. For example, teachers have different expectations for boys and girls and for students from different social class backgrounds.
    2. Negative appraisals are often *self-fulfilling prophecies*, because the expectations they create may become the basis for actual behavior, thereby affecting children's likelihood of success.
    3. Schools have a *hidden curriculum* that is composed of informal, often subtle, messages about social roles that are conveyed through classroom interaction and materials.
    4. Gender is especially relevant in the interactions of boys and girls when they are placed together in working groups. The results of Barrie Thorne's research on school-aged children suggests that gender has a "fluid" character; therefore, relationships between boys and girls can be improved by consciously discouraging gender separation in schools.
    5. Schools emphasize conformity to societal needs, such as respect for authority, punctuality, and conformity; however, students internalize these lessons differently.

IV. **GROWING UP IN A DIVERSE SOCIETY**
Socialization instills in us the values of the culture. It brings society into our self-definitions, our perceptions of others, and our understanding of the world. In a heterogeneous cultural system such as the United States, variation in social contexts creates vastly different social experiences. The on-going socialization process is structured by social factors such as race, ethnicity, class, gender, religion, regional background, sexual preference, and age.

V. **SOCIALIZATION ACROSS THE LIFE CYCLE**
Socialization begins at birth and continues throughout the lifespan. The **life course perspective** connects individuals, their roles, and their experiences to the social and historical context.

A. Childhood
During childhood, socialization establishes one's initial identity and values. Cultural experiences for children typically vary according to the sex of the child. For example, childhood play seems to encourage competition for boys and conversation for girls.

B. Adolescence
    1. Adolescence was not always recognized as a separate phase of life. It developed as a distinct stage when education was extended to people of all social classes.
    2. Erik Erikson stated that the central task of adolescence is the formation of a consistent identity. Conflict and confusion can arise as the adolescent moves between childhood and being an adult.
    3. Patterns of adolescent socialization vary significantly by race, gender, and social class. For example, youths from the upper- and middle-classes are more likely to base their friendships on shared activities and interests, and often change friendships as their activities change. Working-class youth are more likely to base their friendships on loyalty and stability.

C.   Adulthood and Old Age

    1.   **Adult socialization** is the process of learning new roles and expectations during adulthood. This process involves learning behavior and attitudes appropriate to specific situations and roles, such as being a college student.

    2.   Events such as marrying, childbearing, beginning a career, entering the military, and getting a divorce all transform an individual's identity.

    3.   Another part of learning new roles is **anticipatory socialization**, a process in which an individual learns the expectations associated with a role that s/he expects to enter in the future.

    4.   In the transition from an old role to a new one, individuals may vacillate between their old and new identities as they adjust to changed expectations. For example, *coming out*, or openly identifying oneself as gay or lesbian, is an example of a process that typically occurs in stages and creates a new sense of self.

    5.   Passage through adulthood involves many transitions, with one of the most difficult being the transition to old age. Part of the difficulty for aging Americans is the devaluing of the elderly in the United States.

D.   Rites of Passage

    1.   A **rite of passage** is a ceremony or ritual that marks the passage of an individual from one role to another. Rites of passage, including graduation ceremonies, weddings, and religious affirmations, define and legitimize abrupt role changes that begin or end each stage of life.

    2.   Sociologists note that contemporary American society does not have a formalized rite of passage marking the transition from childhood to adulthood. Consequently, the period of adolescence is often characterized by ambivalence and uncertainty.

VI.   RESOCIALIZATION

Resocialization is the process by which existing social roles are radically altered or replaced. It is especially likely when people enter institutional settings where the institution gains almost complete control over the individual, such as prisons and monastic orders. It often occurs when people enter hierarchical organizations, such as the military, that require them to respond to authority on principle, not out of loyalty. Resocialization may involve degrading new members physically and psychologically with the aim of breaking down and replacing their old identity.

A.   The Process of Conversion

    1.   A *conversion* is a far-reaching transformation of identity, often related to a significant change in religious or political beliefs.

    2.   *The Autobiography of Malcolm X* describes a personal conversion that spanned religious, political, and social convictions. Through his encounter with the Nation of Islam in prison, Malcolm X transformed his identity from a prisoner to that of a Black leader who analyzed racial oppression in the context of international capitalism.

B.   The Brainwashing Debate

    1.   Researchers have found that highly suggestible people, such as young adults who are socially isolated and drifting, are the most susceptible to cult influence. Despite the belief that people have to be de-programmed to get them out of cults, many leave on their own.

    2.   Forcible confinement and physical torture can be used as instruments of extreme resocialization.

3. The *Stockholm Syndrome* refers to a captive who is dependent on the captor and may come to identify with him or her under conditions of severe deprivation. Prisoners of war, hostages, and battered women may all experience this phenomenon.

PRACTICE TEST

MULTIPLE CHOICE QUESTIONS

1. The few rare individuals who were raised in extreme isolation from other human beings and later found, sometimes referred to as feral children, are:
   a. usually able to reach a similar level of development as their peers after several years of intense language instruction.
   b. never able to learn to speak the language of their culture because the capacity for learning language is only present during early childhood.
   c. always able to emotionally recover from such severe neglect after they undergo intensive psychological treatment.
   d. sometimes able to develop limited verbal ability and progress slightly in their physical and mental development after comprehensive training and treatment.

2. Most people accept the norms of their society as correct because:
   a. most social norms are derived from the Bible and it would be blasphemous to question a sacred text.
   b. people are innately motivated to desire similarity and seek conformity.
   c. people internalize social expectations so well that they no longer question them.
   d. most social norms are established by the government and people trust the government to act in their best interest.

3. According to the U.S. Bureau of the Census, the largest population of people age five years and younger is located in which region of the country?
   a. Northwest (including Washington and Oregon)
   b. Southwest (including California and New Mexico)
   c. Southeast (including Florida and Georgia)
   d. Northeast (including New York and Pennsylvania)

4. Which stage of the life course is characterized by tension, contradiction, and the task of establishing one's identity?
   a. childhood
   b. adolescence
   c. middle adulthood
   d. old age

5. Which of the following statements about socialization is (are) true?
   a. Socialization creates the tendency for people to act in deviant ways.
   b. Socialization makes it difficult for individuals to see themselves as others see them.
   c. Socialization takes place during childhood and adolescence but is complete by adulthood.
   d. None of the above statements about socialization are true.

6. Carol Gilligan's research on moral development indicates that:
   a. men reach a higher standard of moral reasoning than women because men are more concerned with authority.
   b. women reach a higher standard of moral reasoning than men because women are more concerned with relationships and other people's feelings.
   c. even though women and men define morality differently, neither women's nor men's moral reasoning is more mature.
   d. there are no differences between women and men in the ways that they define morality and respond to moral dilemmas.

7. According to Freud, the part of the personality that represents common sense and reason and helps balance the conflict between the other two components is the:
   a. superego.
   b. ego.
   c. me.
   d. id.

8. Which of the following statements about Freud's theory of development is (are) true?
   a. Freud's theory has been criticized for being gynocentric, or female-centered, because he only wrote about women's behavior.
   b. Freud's theory has been widely accepted because of its ability to be generalized to a large population.
   c. Freud's theory views identity as deeply rooted in the unconscious processes of the mind.
   d. All of the above are true.

9. Symbolic interaction theory views identity as developing:
   a. through interaction and conscious, meaningful adaptation to one's environment.
   b. from tensions between strong instinctual impulses and social standards.
   c. from a passive, learned response to social stimuli such as reinforcement.
   d. through the largely unconscious processes of attachment to, and separation from, one's caregivers.

10. Object relations theory views identity as developing:
    a. through interaction and conscious, meaningful adaptation to one's environment.
    b. from tensions between strong instinctual impulses and social standards.
    c. from a passive, learned response to social stimuli such as reinforcement.
    d. through the largely unconscious processes of attachment to, and separation from, one's caregivers.

11. Which theory considers the formation of identity to be a learned response to social stimuli such as encouragement from others?
    a. Mead's game theory
    b. Piaget's social learning theory
    c. Freud's psychoanalytic theory
    d. Chodorow's identification theory

12. According to Piaget, the preoperational stage of development is characterized by:
    a.   experiencing the world directly through the senses of taste, touch, and sound.
    b.   beginning to use language and other symbols but not thinking abstractly.
    c.   thinking abstractly and imaging alternatives to one's own reality.
    d.   learning logical principles about the concrete world.

13. According to Piaget, children are able to think abstractly and imagine alternatives to the reality in which they live in which of the following stages of development?
    a.   formal operational
    b.   concrete operational
    c.   preoperational
    d.   sensorimotor

14. Which of the following is **not** a component of the looking-glass self concept?
    a.   your perception of how you appear to other people
    b.   your beliefs about how other people perceive you
    c.   your feelings about how you are perceived by others
    d.   your beliefs about how you should treat other people

15. George Herbert Mead identified three stages of childhood. In which of the following stages do children typically begin to take on the roles of their significant others?
    a.   game
    b.   play
    c.   imitation
    d.   reflection

16. According to Mead, the abstract composite of social roles and social expectations that children acquire in the game stage is known as the:
    a.   attachment process.
    b.   significant other.
    c.   resocialization effect.
    d.   generalized other.

17. Through which source of socialization are boys and men best able to form both an appropriate masculine identity and socially acceptable bonds with other men?
    a.   religion
    b.   sports
    c.   media
    d.   family

18. Tara, a graduate student, interacts regularly and on equal terms with the other graduate students in her program. The other students are Tara's:
    a.   significant others.
    b.   generalized others.
    c.   models.
    d.   peers.

19. The informal and often subtle messages about social roles that are conveyed through classroom interaction and materials is called the:
    a. hidden curriculum.
    b. official curriculum.
    c. teacher effect.
    d. student bias.

20. Barrie Thorne's study of school-aged children indicates that gender:
    a. becomes less relevant in the interactions of boys and girls when they are grouped together in common working groups.
    b. is so central to the formation of identity that children should be grouped into boys-only and girls-only working groups to facilitate their development.
    c. has a "rigid" character that cannot be changed to improved gender relationships between boys and girls, who both benefit from gender separation.
    d. None of the above statements are true.

21. Research on adolescent socialization indicates that:
    a. working-class youth are more likely to base their friendships on shared activities and interests, so they change friends as their activities change.
    b. middle-class youth are likely to base their friendships on loyalty and stability.
    c. middle-class youth are more likely to base their friendships on shared activities and interests, so they change friends as their activities change.
    d. None of the above statements are true, because social class does not influence the development of friendship groups.

22. Elizabeth is a high school senior who wants to attend college, so she visits several college campuses, observes how college students dress, and begins to imitate their actions. Elizabeth is engaged in:
    a. resocialization.
    b. unsocialization.
    c. optimistic socialization.
    d. anticipatory socialization.

23. What metaphor did Cooley use to describe how individuals form their identities?
    a. undressing
    b. playing games
    c. looking in a mirror
    d. constructing a building

24. When military recruits enter boot camp, their heads are shaved, they are given identical uniforms, and they must subordinate their identities to the group. This process is:
    a. resocialization.
    b. unsocialization.
    c. optimistic socialization.
    d. anticipatory socialization.

25. The phenomenon whereby a hostage identifies with his or her captor is known as the:
   a.   Victimization Hypothesis.
   b.   Stockholm Syndrome.
   c.   Looking-Glass Self.
   d.   Imitation Stage.

TRUE-FALSE QUESTIONS

1.   According to Mead, the "I" is the component of self that is active, creative, and unique.

2.   Social influences affect human beings so strongly that most people become passive creatures who accept and conform to all social expectations.

3.   Nearly every adolescent in the United States completes the transition from childhood to adulthood by participating in a formalized rite of passage.

4.   In the 1980s, Powell-Hopson and Hopson found that regardless of the rewards provided, both Black children and White children consistently select White dolls.

5.   Compared to White Americans, African Americans have relatively high self-esteem but low personal efficacy.

6.   Social learning theory argues that behavior can be changed by altering the social environment, because children learn appropriate behavior through rewards and punishments.

7.   Most of the people who join cults have to be deprogrammed to be freed from the cult's influence, because they are rarely able to leave on their own.

8.   According to research conducted by Van Ausdale and Feagin, young children (ages three to five years old) do not understand the concepts of race and ethnicity well enough to use them as a basis for their concepts of themselves and other children.

9.   According to Chodorow, it is not possible for men to acquire mothering skills, even if they participate more in the daily care of their families, because mothering is an innate, unconscious process located deep in the mind, rather than a learned behavior.

10. The passage to old age in the United States is often difficult because Americans generally fear aging and devalue the elderly.

FILL IN THE BLANK QUESTIONS

1.   In the _____ stage of Mead's theory or socialization, children only copy the behavior of people around them, because they are not yet able to take the role of the other.

2.   The relatively consistent patter of behavior, feelings, and beliefs in a given person refers to his/her _____.

3.   During _____, individuals establish their initial identities and values, and the family is usually the most influential source of socialization.

4. A _____ is a far-reaching transformation of identity, often related to political or religious beliefs.

5. The main _____ agents in the United States are the family, peers, religion, sports, schools, and the media.

ESSAY QUESTIONS

1. Explain the statement, "our lives are socially constructed," and provide an example of how sexual identity would be explained using this perspective.
2. Discuss the practical implications of the Clark's and the Powell-Hopson's studies of Black and White children's doll preferences.
3. Explain why overconformity to gender roles is associated with negative mental and physical health consequences.
4. Identify the four primary stages of the life course in the United States and describe the main characteristics or expectations associated with each stage.
5. Explain how teachers' perceptions of gender and social class differently affect the school experiences of boys and girls and working-class and middle-class children.

ANSWERS TO PRACTICE TEST

Answers to Multiple Choice Questions

1.	D.	92	The few feral children who have been scientifically documented have suffered severe intellectual and physical developmental problems and were unable to achieve even a "normal" level of functioning.
2.	C.	92	Socialization is the process through which people learn and internalize the expectations of society; thus, most people accept them as correct.
3.	B.	109	As shown in Map 4.1, California and Texas have the largest populations of children ages five years old and younger.
4.	B.	110	According to Erikson, adolescence is a period characterized by contradiction in which individuals have the task of establishing their identities.
5.	D.	92	Socialization is a life-long process that establishes personality and self-concept, makes people bearers of culture, creates the tendency for people to act in acceptable ways, and creates the capacity for role-taking, or seeing ourselves as others see us.
6.	C.	99	Gilligan argues that women's moral reasoning should not be judged according to men's moral reasoning because men and women define morality differently.
7.	B.	96	According to Freud, the part of the personality which represents commonsense and reason and balances the conflict between the other two (the id and the superego) is the ego.
8.	C.	97	Freud's theory has been criticized for being androcentric, or male-centered, and for being limited in the ability to generalize to a larger population. His theory argues that development is the result of unconscious processes of the mind.
9.	A.	99	Symbolic interaction theory views individuals as active participants in the creation of meanings who consciously adapt to the social environment. Psychoanalytic theory views personality as the result of tensions between unconscious processes and social standards. Social

learning theory views development as a response to social stimuli. Object relations theory argues that young children's relationships with their caregivers determine adult development.

10. D. 97 According to object relations theory, the largely unconscious processes of attachment and individuation strongly affect adult personality development.

11. B. 98 Social learning theory, associated with Piaget, considers the formation of identity to be a learned response to social stimuli. Chodorow's analysis of the role of gender in personality development is based on object relations theory. Freud's psychoanalytic theory focused on unconscious mental processes. Mead's theory of role taking is based on symbolic interaction theory.

12. B. 98 According to Piaget, children experience the world only through the senses at the sensorimotor stage. They use language but cannot think abstractly at the preoperational stage. At the concrete operational state, children learn logical principles about the concrete world.

13. A. 98 According to Piaget, children are able to think abstractly and imagine alternatives to the reality in which they live in the formal operational stage of development.

14. D. 99 In Cooley's looking-glass self concept, individuals note the reactions of others toward them. They understand how others judge them and develop feelings about themselves based on their perceived evaluations from others. Cooley's concept does not address how people feel about how they treat others.

15. B. 100 George Herbert Mead identified three stages of childhood. In the play stage, children typically take on the roles of significant people in their environment. Taking the role of the other is the process of imagining oneself from the point of view of another. In the game stage of Mead's theory, children develop an awareness of community values and general social expectations. The "I" is the active, creative, self-defining, unique part of the personality. The "me" is the passive, conforming self that reacts to others.

16. D. 100 According to Mead, the abstract composite of social roles and social expectations which children acquire in the game stage is termed the generalized other.

17. B. 104 Messner's research on former athletes indicates that sports are very important in the development of masculine identity and the formation of male relationships.

18. D. 103 Individuals with whom a person interacts on equal terms, such as friends, fellow students, and co-workers, are peers.

19. A. 105 The informal and often subtle messages about social roles that are conveyed through classroom interaction and materials is called the hidden curriculum.

20. A. 105 Gender becomes less relevant in the interactions of boys and girls when they are grouped together in common working groups. Gender has a "fluid" character, and relationships between boys and girls can be improved through conscious changes that discourage gender separation.

21. C. 110 Patterns of adolescent socialization vary significantly with race, gender, and social class. Middle- and upper-class youth are likely to base their friendships on shared activities and interests and change their

friendships as their activities change. Working-class youth are likely to base their friendships on loyalty and stability.

22. D. 112 The learning of expectations associated with a role one expects to enter in the future is anticipatory socialization.

23. C. 100 Cooley compared the process of development to viewing one's reflection in a mirror. Mead compared socialization to playing a game where you learn social rules and practice social roles.

24. A. 114 The process whereby existing social roles are radically altered or replaced is resocialization. Resocialization often occurs when one enters a hierarchical institution such as the military.

25. B. 115 The phenomenon of a captive identifying with the captor, which has been found among some hostages, prisoners of war, and battered women, is termed the Stockholm Syndrome.

Answers to True-False Questions

1. T. 101 The self has two dimensions. The "I" is the active, creative, self-defining part. The "me" is the passive, conforming part. According to Mead, there is a balance between the I and the me.

2. F. 94 We are all unique to some extent, and some people resist the expectations society has of them; however, most people conform, although to differing degrees.

3. F. 113 There is no universal, formalized rite of passage marking the transition from childhood to adulthood in the United States; consequently, adolescence is characterized by ambivalence and uncertainty.

4. F. 95 In the 1980s, Powell-Hopson and Hopson found that rewards can help Black children and White children to select a Black doll.

5. T. 95 Overall, African Americans have relatively high self-esteem compared to White Americans because they use other African Americans as their reference group.

6. T. 99

7. F. 115 Many people leave cults on their own and do not require deprogramming to be freed of the cult's influence.

8. F. 107 Young children are aware of racial and ethnic differences and use these concepts to form perceptions of themselves and other people.

9. F. 98 According to Chodorow's work on gender, if men were to acquire more mothering skills and participate more in the daily care of their family, the result would be a society where men and women had less gender-stereotyped personalities.

10. T. 112

Answers to Fill in the Blank Questions

1. imitation 100
2. personality 92
3. childhood 108
4. conversion 114
5. socialization 101

CHAPTER 5
SOCIETY AND SOCIAL INTERACTION

BRIEF CHAPTER OUTLINE

What is Society?
> Microanalysis and Macroanalysis
> Groups
> Statuses
> Roles

Theories About Analyzing Social Interaction
> The Social Construction of Reality
> Ethnomethodology
> Impression Management and Dramaturgy
> Social Exchange
> Interaction in Cyberspace

A Study in Diversity: Forms of Nonverbal Communication
> Touch
> Paralinguistic Communication
> Kinesic Communication
> Use of Personal Space

Interpersonal Attraction and the Formation of Pairs
> Proximity
> Mere Exposure Effect
> Perceived Physical Attractiveness
> Similarity

Social Institutions and Social Structure
> Social Institutions
> Social Structure

What Holds Society Together?
> Mechanical and Organic Solidarity
> Gemeinschaft and Gesellschaft

Types of Societies: A Global View
> Industrial Societies
> Postindustrial Societies

QUESTIONS TO GUIDE YOUR READING
1. What is the difference between macroanalysis and microanalysis?
2. What are the four main types of nonverbal communication?
3. Which social factors are most important in determining to whom individuals will be attracted and with whom they will form relationships?
4. What are the major institutions in society and what purposes do they serve?
5. What are the six types of societies found in the world and how do sociologists distinguish among the types?

KEY TERMS (defined at page number shown and in glossary)

achieved status 121	ascribed status 121
collective consciousness 137	cyberspace interaction 127
division of labor 138	ethnomethodology 125
gemeinschaft 138	gesellschaft 138
group 120	impression management 125
master status 122	mechanical solidarity 137

organic (contractual) solidarity 137
role 122
role strain 123
social interaction 120
social structure 136
status 121
status set 121

proxemic communication 132
role conflict 122
social institution 135
social organization 120
society 120
status inconsistency 121

KEY PEOPLE (identified at page number shown)
Elijah Anderson 129
Harold Garfinkle 125
E.T. Hall 132
W.I. Thomas 124

Emile Durkheim 120
Erving Goffman 125
Arlie Hochschild 123

CHAPTER OUTLINE

I.   WHAT IS SOCIETY?

Human interaction is guided by social forces and humans shape the social institutions that exist in society. Human **society** is a system of social interaction that includes both culture and social organization. Culture refers to people's general way of life, including norms, customs, beliefs, and language. Members of a society view themselves as distinct from other societies, maintain social ties through interaction, and have a high degree of interdependence. **Social interaction** refers to meaningful behavior between two or more people. Interaction involves communication, or the conveyance of information to other people. Durkheim viewed society as an organism, or something composed of different parts that work together to create a unique whole, such as the human body. Sociologists try to use the sociological imagination to picture society as a whole, while also investigating its parts and the complex relationships among the parts.

A.   Microanalysis and Macroanalysis

  1.   *Microanalysis* refers to the technique sociologists use to investigate the *microlevel* of society, or the patterns of social interaction that are relatively small, less complex, and less differentiated. For example, this approach could be used to study interpersonal attraction and the formation of couples and friendship groups.

  2.   *Macroanalysis* refers to the technique sociologists use to comprehend society as a whole, including how it is organized and how it changes. *Macrolevel* sociology investigates patterns of social interaction that are vast, complex, and highly differentiated. For example, this approach is useful for studying social problems such as poverty.

  3.   **Social organization** describes the order established in social groups. This order brings regularity and predictability to human behavior.

B.   Groups

  1.   Sociologists define a **group** as a collection of individuals who interact and communicate with each other, share goals and norms, possess a subjective awareness of themselves as a distinct social unit, and feel a sense of "we" or belonging to the group.

  2.   In sociological terms, not all social units are groups.

    a.   *Social categories* are people who are categorized together based on one or more shared characteristic, such as teenagers, teachers, and millionaires.

    b.   *Audiences* are comprised of all of the people who are simultaneously watching the same program or performance.

        c.   *Formal organizations* are highly structured social groupings that form to pursue a set of shared goals. This includes formal associations, such as the PTA, and bureaucracies, such as business corporations.

C.   Statuses

1. **Status** is an established position or rank in a social structure that carries with it a degree of prestige, or social value. A person's occupation is one example of a status.
2. Typically, a person has many statuses simultaneously. A **status set** is the complete set of statuses occupied by a person at a given time. Each status is associated with a different level of prestige.
3. **Status inconsistency** occurs when a person's several statuses are associated with significantly different amounts of prestige. For example, recent immigrants who were professionals in their home countries but are forced into jobs with little status in the United States experience status inconsistency.
4. There are two ways by which a person receives a particular status.
   a. **Achieved statuses** are those attained by independent effort, such as occupational and educational statuses.
   b. **Ascribed statuses** are those automatically assigned to a person at birth, such as race. These statuses are sometimes ambiguous, as in the case of biracial individuals. Although biological sex is ascribed, gender status is a social construct, because regardless of genetic characteristics, gender appropriate behavior is learned, not innate.
   c. Class status includes both ascribed and achieved components. For example, upper-class membership is more likely if one's parents are wealthy (ascribed status) *and* if one works in a high-paying occupation (achieved status).
5. A **master status** is a dominant status for an individual that overrides all other features of a person's identity. It may be imposed by others (e.g. criminal) or voluntarily chosen by the individual (e.g. mother). Because master statuses override other identities, they may be the basis for stereotypes, as in the case of someone who has a disability.

D.   Roles

1. A **role** is the expected behavior or collection of expectations associated with a particular status. A *role set* includes all of the roles occupied by a person at a given time.
2. **Role conflict** occurs when two or more roles have contradictory expectations. For example, Hochschild identified the problem of the "second shift," which refers to women who are employed outside of the household but still expected to fulfill traditional expectations at home.
3. **Role strain** is a condition in which a single role brings conflicting expectations. For example, first-generation college students may experience role strain if their parents expect them to live at home and continue a traditional family role, while choosing the best college may require leaving home and thinking independently.
4. Although role conflict and role strain are experienced at the individual level, their origins are societal, because they originate in the social expectations rooted in specific roles.

II. ANALYZING SOCIAL INTERACTION

Sociologists analyze social interaction through different theoretical frameworks and perspectives, including social exchange theory and symbolic interaction theory, from which the social construction of reality, ethnomethodology, and impression management perspectives are derived.

A. The Social Construction of Reality
1. The principle of *the social construction of reality*, central to symbolic interaction theory, argues that our perception of what is real is determined by the subjective meaning that we attribute to an experience. Things do not have their own intrinsic meaning; rather, people subjectively impose meaning on things.
2. As a result of the social construction of reality, we see what we want to see. In fact, people sometimes attribute certain meanings to things when it benefits them to perceive it that way, even if the perception seems to be contrary to fact.
3. W.I. Thomas coined the phrase *definition of the situation* to refer to the idea that *situations defined as real are real in their consequences*. Through the process of defining the situation, people adjust their attitudes and perceptions based on the context in which they find themselves. For example, researchers found that the way physicians define emergency room patients has important consequences for how the patients are treated. In one study, older patients were examined less thoroughly before being pronounced dead than were younger patients. .
4. Understanding the social construction of reality allows us to gain insight into the social significance of race and gender. Race and gender have meaning because we choose to give them meaning, which may change our behavior toward different individuals.

B. Ethnomethodology
1. **Ethnomethodology** is a technique for studying human interaction by deliberately disrupting social norms and observing how individuals attempt to restore normalcy.
2. Because many norms that influence social behavior are not conscious, it is impossible to identify all of them simply by asking people to list them. Thus, ethnomethodologists suggest that the technique of normative violations is an effective strategy for identifying norms. For example, an ethnomethodologists might disrupt "normal" interactions, such as demanding to pay more for a product than its listed price.

C. Impression Management and Dramaturgy
1. **Impression management**, labeled by Erving Goffman, is a process by which people control how others perceive them by willfully attemping to manipulate other peoples' impressions of him or her.
2. Goffman's theory is sometimes referred to as the *dramaturgy model* of interaction because we present different "selves" to other people in different settings. This approach analyzes interaction by assuming that all participants are actors on a stage in the drama of everyday life.
3. Even when we define ourselves as "individuals," our behavior is shaped by social forces. For example, a teacher's behavior when s/he returns graded papers is influenced by his/her relationship with the students and by the students' performance on the papers.

D. Social Exchange Theory
1. The *social exchange model* of social interaction argues that interactions are determined by the rewards or punishments that we receive from other people. For example, receiving approval in a relationship increases the probability that interaction will continue.
2. People often assess situations in terms of rewards and punishments. If the reward for an interaction exceeds the punishments for it, a potential for *social profit* exists and the interaction is likely to continue. If the rewards are less than punishments, however, the interaction produces a social loss or negative profit and will be less likely to continue.
3. Because social exchange tends to encourage conformity and discourage deviance, it is a force for cohesion in society.
4. Rewards include tangible gains, such as gifts, recognition, and money, as well as subtle rewards, such as smiles and hugs.
5. Punishments include both subtle gestures, such as a frown, and extreme behaviors, such as public humiliation, beating, and banishment.
6. Exchange theory has been used to understand racist and sexist attitudes. For example, stereotypes that are rewarded by one's group tend to persist, while those that are punished tend to change.

E. Interaction in Cyberspace
1. *Cyberspace interaction* occurs when people interact and communicate with each other using a personal computer to access "chat rooms," computer bulletin boards, and e-mail.
2. Through virtual reality, what the individual perceives to be real is created by and on the computer. When two or more people share a virtual reality experience, they are engaged in **cyberspace interaction.**
3. Cyberspace interaction differs from face-to-face interaction because a person is free to become a different self by interacting via a virtual self that may have a different gender, for example, than one's real self.
4. Goffman's principle of impression management and dramaturgy can be applied to cyberspace interaction because a person can present him- or herself as having any set of characteristics, thereby controlling the impression the other person receives. For example, what one becomes during chatroom interaction is a direct outgrowth of that interaction, because it is the interaction process that produces the reality.
5. Cyberspace interaction and the anonymity connected with it represent a new kind of social relationship, which may not transfer well into a face-to-face interaction.
6. There is an evolving *cyberculture*, with its own norms, language, set of beliefs, and practices, including: encouraging a new identity while engaging in cyberspace interaction; permitting or encouraging certain negative forms of interaction, such as aggression, intolerance, and exclusion; and maintaining a "frontier mentality," or sense that virtual interaction is a new frontier in our society.

III. **A STUDY IN DIVERSITY: FORMS OF NONVERBAL COMMUNICATION**
Social interaction includes both verbal and nonverbal communication. *Verbal interaction* consists of spoken and written language, whereas *nonverbal interaction* is conveyed by touch, tone of voice, gestures, body postures, eye contact, and facial expressions. The meanings of nonverbal communication are strongly dependent upon

race, ethnicity, social class, and gender. Scientists classify nonverbal communication into four types: tactile, paralinguistic, kinesic, and proxemic.

A.   Touch

    1.   *Tactile communication* involves any conveyance of meaning through touch, whether positive (embracing) or negative (hitting).

    2.   The meanings associated with tactile communication vary by cultural context and social characteristics such as gender. For example, as children, girls tend to be touched tenderly and protectively while boys are touched more roughly. As adults, women are generally more likely to touch and hug as an expression of emotional support, whereas men touch and hug more often to assert power or to express sexual interest.

B.   Paralinguistic Communication

    1.   *Paralinguistic communication* is the component of communication that is conveyed by the pitch and loudness of the speaker's voice, its rhythm, emphasis, and frequency, and the frequency and lengths of hesitations.

    2.   The meaning of paralanguage varies by cultural context and ethnicity. For example, Japanese people regard silent periods during conversations as opportunities to collect their thoughts, while Americans avoid such periods with small talk. Americans often consider paralinguistics to be a small part of communication, while the Japanese consider them more important than verbal communication.

    3.   The formal grammar of some languages, such as Chinese, includes paralinguistic elements.

    4.   *Nonverbal leakage* refers to an individual's emotions and feeling being revealed by paralinguistic slips despite the person's attempts to conceal them. For example, when a person is lying, the pitch of his or her voice is slightly higher than when that same person is telling the truth.

C.   Kinesic Communication

    1.   *Kinesic communication* involves gestures, facial expressions, and body language, which form a crucial part of nonverbal communication. These forms are gender related and reflect patterns of dominance in society.

    2.   Meanings conveyed by kinesis usually vary by cultural context, ethnicity, and gender. For example, avoiding eye contact is a sign of respect in some cultures; making eye contact can be evaluated as a sign of sexual interest or hostility in other cultures and subcultures.

    3.   Certain modes of kinesic communication, however, are identical across genders and different cultures. For example, the facial expressions for anger, happiness, sadness, and disgust are recognized in all cultures, as are many hand gestures, including "stop," "good-bye," and "OK."

D.   Use of Personal Space

    1.   *Proxemic communication* refers to the amount of space present between interacting individuals. Generally, the more friendly a person feels toward someone, the closer he or she will stand.

    2.   According to Hall, each individual has a *proxemic bubble* that represents our personal 3-dimensional space. We feel threatened and may take evasive action when people we do not know enter our proxemic bubble. This largely unconscious process is illustrated by a typical person's behavior in an elevator, where s/he usually attempts to protect his/her bubble and stay outside of other people's bubbles.

3. Proxemic interaction varies by gender and ethnicity. The proxemic bubbles of different groups have different sizes, and people from different groups may experience difficulty when they interact if they are not aware of cultural differences in the use of personal space.

IV. **INTERPERSONAL ATTRACTION AND THE FORMATION OF PAIRS**

The formation of human pairings, including romantic couples and friendship groups, has a strong social structural component; that is, patterned by social forces. Humans have a strong need for *affiliation*, or a desire to be with other people, and women generally reveal this tendency more than men. The affiliation tendency is similar to *imprinting*, which is a phenomenon observed in newly hatched animals. These animals attach themselves to the first living creature they encounter, regardless of species. In humans, infant attachment is a more complex and changeable process that is influenced more by social factors. Interpersonal attraction is a nonspecific, positive response toward another person that can be understood using sociological principles.

A. Proximity
    1. Because we are more likely to meet and become attracted to people that we live or work near, proximity strongly affects relationship formation.
    2. In a study of friendships among recruits at a police academy, proximity in seating had a stronger effect than all other factors, including race, socioeconomic background, age, religion, and nationality.

B. Mere Exposure Effect
    1. The *mere exposure effect* refers to the fact that the more you see someone, the more you like him or her.
    2. This effect even occurs when a person only sees someone in a photograph. The initial response of the viewer can determine how much liking will increase with exposure to additional photographs. If you start out liking the pictured person, exposure will increase the liking; however, if you start out disliking the person, the amount of dislike tends to remain about the same. Furthermore, "overexposure" can result when a photograph is seen too often and the viewer becomes "saturated" with the pictured person.

C. Perceived Physical Attractiveness
    1. The attractions we feel toward people of either gender are based on our perceptions of their physical attractiveness. Perceived physical attractiveness is an important dimension of human interaction.
        a. Adults react more leniently to the bad behavior of an attractive child than to the same behavior of an unattractive child.
        b. Teachers evaluate cute children of either gender as "smarter" than unattractive children with identical academic records.
        c. In studies of mock jury trials, attractive male and female defendants receive lighter sentences on average than do unattractive defendants convicted of the same crime.
    2. Although standards of attractiveness vary across cultures and among subcultures within the same society, there is considerable agreement within a culture about who is attractive.
    3. Studies of dating patterns among college students show that the more attractive one is, the more likely one will be asked to go on a date; however, there are two important exceptions to the pattern.
        a. The *movie star effect* refers to those persons regarded as "exceptionally" attractive being asked out for dates slightly less often than those rated as somewhat less attractive.

| b. | Physical attractiveness predicts only the early stages of a relationship. Other factors, such as religion, political attitudes, and social class background are better predictors of how long a relationship will last. |

    D.   <u>Similarity</u>

1. With few exceptions, people are attracted to others who are similar in socioeconomic status, race, ethnicity, religion, perceived personality traits, and general attitudes and opinions.
2. For long-term heterosexual and homosexual relationships, including both friends and lovers, people mostly prefer a great deal of similarity.
3. The less similar a heterosexual relationship is with respect to race, social class, age, and educational aspirations (how far in school the person wants to go), the quicker the relationship is to end.
4. Although people tend to date within their own race, nationality, or ethnicity, many interracial couples enjoy long-lasting relationships. For interracial couples, similarities in characteristics other than race, including social class background, religion, age, and educational aspirations, tends to predict how long the relationship will last.
5. Most romantic relationships end, with one person wanting to break it off and the other wanting to continue it. On college campuses, relationships tend to end most frequently during school breaks.

V.   SOCIAL INSTITUTIONS AND SOCIAL STRUCTURE

    A.   <u>Social Institutions</u>

1. A **social institution** is an established and organized system of social behavior with a recognized purpose. Institutions are organized to meet various needs in society.
2. Institutions cannot be directly observed, although their impact and structure can be studied. Specific schools are organizations where learning occurs, while at the broadest level, education is a social institution that includes all schools, as well as the norms, values, and beliefs that guide education at the societal level.
3. The major institutions in society include: family, education, work and the economy, politics (or state), religion, and health care. There are other institutions as well, such as the mass media and organized sports.
4. Functionalist theorists have identified the purposes of institutions.
   a. The *socialization of new members of the society* is a primary function of the family and education, although religious organizations and the mass media contribute to this function.
   b. The *production and distribution of goods and services* is the responsibility of the economic and political institutions.
   c. *Replacement of the membership* is achieved through the family and other heterosexual pairings, although the government establishes policies that influence membership replacement.
   d. The *maintenance of stability and existence* is achieved through the government, law enforcement agencies, and the military.
   e. *Providing the members with an ultimate sense of purpose* involves virtually all institutions because commonly held purposes, values, and assumptions are evident in diverse institutions. This commonality helps members maintain a common sense of purpose.

5.	Functionalists see societal needs as universal, although societies do not fill these needs in the same way or through the same institution.

6.	Conflict theorists argue that social institutions do not provide for all social members equally. Institutions affect individuals differently because they grant more power to some social groups than to others. Generally, the lower one's social class, the less one's political power, wealth, influence, and prestige. Additionally, racial and ethnic minorities and women generally occupy lower social status than do men and dominant group members.

B.	Social Structure

1.	**Social structure** refers to the organized pattern of social relationships and social institutions that together comprise society.

2.	Social structural analysis is a way of looking at society in which sociologists analyze the patterns in social life that reflect and produce social behavior.

3.	Social class distinctions are an example of a social structure. For example, class shapes many social interactions as well as the access that different groups have to social resources.

4.	Social structures form invisible patterns that can be identified by using the sociological imagination.

5.	Marilyn Frye uses the metaphor of a birdcage to describe the concept of social structure. Just as a birdcage is a network of wires, society is a network of micro and macro structures that holds society together, sometimes oppressing certain groups.

## VI.	WHAT HOLDS SOCIETY TOGETHER?

A.	Mechanical and Organic Solidarity

1.	Emile Durkheim argued that people in a society have a **collective consciousness**, or a body of common beliefs that that give people a sense of belonging and a feeling of moral obligation to its demands and values. Collective consciousness develops from participation in the common activities of social institutions.

2.	According to Durkheim, there are two different kinds of social solidarity.

a.	**Mechanical solidarity** occurs when individuals play similar roles within the society. It is found in less complex societies, such as Native American groups prior to European conquest. Durkheim argued that collective consciousness was strongest in such societies; however, they are rare today due to the global trend of increasing complexity and interrelatedness.

b.	In societies with **organic solidarity** (also called contractual solidarity), individuals play a great variety of different roles and social unity is based on role differentiation and shared interdependence, as in the U.S. and other industrialized societies. Such societies have a complex **division of labor**, or the systematic interrelatedness of different tasks.
Within any division of labor, tasks become distinct from each other, yet they are woven together as a whole.

3.   Unlike societies characterized by organic solidarity, societies characterized by mechanical solidarity manifest tensions among competing groups, often due to divisions based on gender, race, and class. It is also more difficult to identify a uniform set of values that guides the entire social order.

B.   Gemeinschaft and Gesellschaft

1.   **Gemeinschaft**, a German word that means "community," refers to a society in which there is a sense of "we" feeling among members, a moderate division of labor, strong personal ties and family relationships, and a sense of personal loyalty. Social control is largely achieved through the sense of belongingness that members share.

2.   **Gesellschaft**, a German word for "society," refers to a society in which there is increasing importance on less intimate, more instrumental, secondary relationships. There is a reduced sense of personal loyalty to the total society, an elaborate division of labor, and a somewhat diminished role of the nuclear family. Social control is partly achieved through mechanisms external to the individual, such as the police.

3.   Social solidarity is weaker in a gesellschaft society than in a gemeinschaft society because gesellschaft societies are more likely to experience class conflicts and racial-ethnic divisions that reduce internal cohesiveness.

VII.   **TYPES OF SOCIETIES: A GLOBAL VIEW**

Over time and across different cultures and continents, societies are distinguished by different forms of social organization that evolve from both the relationship of the society to its environment, and from the processes that the society develops to meet basic human needs. Societies differ in many critical ways, including size, population, and resource base. Contemporary societies are increasingly global, with highly evolved systems of social differentiation and inequality, particularly along class, gender, racial, and ethnic lines. Sociologists distinguish six types of societies based on the complexity of their social structure, the amount of overall cultural accumulation, and the level of their technology. These types, listed in Table 5.1, include: *foraging*, *pastoral*, *horticultural*, *agricultural*, *industrial*, and *postindustrial*. Although examples of every type can be found today, all but the most isolated societies are moving toward the industrial and postindustrial stages of societal development.

A.   Industrial societies

1.   An *industrial society* uses machines and other advanced technologies to produce and distribute goods and services. The "industrial revolution," accompanied by the growth of science, brought advances in farming techniques, medical developments, and other technological advances that led to the development of industrial societies.

2.   Industrial societies rely upon a highly differentiated labor force and the intensive use of capital and technology. Large formal organizations (bureaucracies) and institutions with a high division of labor (economy and work, government and politics) are of critical importance in holding industrial societies together.

3. Industrial societies use a cash-based economy that pays wages for labor performed in factories, while household labor remains unpaid. This situation introduced the family-wage economy, in which families become dependent on wages to support themselves, but work within the family becomes increasingly devalued. Because men are viewed as the primary breadwinners, an increasing wage gap between men and women develops.

4. Industrial societies tend to be highly productive and have a large working class of industrial laborers. With industrialization, the population becomes increasingly urbanized, immigration is common, economic activities move outside of the family, and other institutions, such as schools, become increasingly important.

5. Although industrialization brought many benefits to the United States. It also produced some of the nation's most serious social problems, including pollution, overdependence on consumer goods, widespread wage inequality and job dislocation, and urban crime and crowding.

B. Postindustrial Societies

1. *Postindustrial societies* such as Japan and the United States are an emerging type of society characterized by economic dependence on the production and distribution of services, information, and knowledge.

2. The transition to a postindustrial society strongly influences the character of social institutions. For example, education and science become critically important, and workers without technical skills may find themselves in low-pay, unskilled work or permanent joblessness.

3. The U.S. is in transition from an industrial to a postindustrial society. Although manufacturing jobs are still a major segment of the labor force, they are in decline. Most workers are employed in the service sector of the economy, in which they participate in the delivery of services and information rather than the production of material goods.

4. Postindustrial societies are increasingly dependent on the global economy as more manufacturing occurs in less technologically developed societies. Global poverty and inequality are increasing.

PRACTICE TEST

MULTIPLE-CHOICE QUESTIONS

1. According to social _____ theory, people may conform to others' expectations even when they disagree with them because they wish to maximize the rewards and minimize the punishments they receive from social interaction.
   a. solidarity
   b. exchange
   c. disruption
   d. construction

2. The sociological term that refers to behavior involving communication between two or more people is social:
   a. interaction.
   b. impression.
   c. institution.
   d. linguistics.

3. The technique that sociologists use to investigate large patterns of social interaction and to comprehend society as a whole is:
   a. ethnomethodology.
   b. dramaturgy.
   c. microanalysis.
   d. macroanalysis.

4. Which type of status do individuals gain through personal effort, such as educational attainment?
   a. ascribed
   b. achieved
   c. shared
   d. master

5. Which of the following statements about groups is (are) true?
   a. A group is a collection of individuals who interact and communicate with each other.
   b. Group members possess a subjective awareness of themselves as a distinct social unit.
   c. Group members share a sense of belonging or "we" feeling.
   d. All of the above statements are true.

6. A highly structured social grouping that forms to pursue a set of shared goals is a(n):
   a. social category.
   b. social institution.
   c. formal organization.
   d. audience.

7. Kim is a recent immigrant who holds a college degree. She was a well-respected nurse in Korea, but she speaks limited English and is not licensed to practice nursing in the United States. She currently works as a maid, a job that carries little prestige. She is experiencing:
   a. status inconsistency.
   b. status dysfunction.
   c. role conflict.
   d. role strain.

8. Sociologists refer to those statuses that are automatically assigned to a person at birth, such as race, as:
   a. created.
   b. ascribed.
   c. achieved.
   d. secondary.

9. Mark was born with Cerebral Palsy, a physical disability that impedes his speech and mobility. Other people perceive Mark's disability as a dominant status that overrides all other features of his identity. For Mark, having a disability is a(n) _____ status.
   a. inconsistent
   b. master
   c. organic
   d. mechanical

10. Your boss asked you to work this weekend, you need to study for a test, and your mother expects you to come home for a family celebration. You are experiencing role:
   a. strain.
   b. conflict.
   c. disruption.
   d. dysfunction.

11. According to research on interpersonal attraction and couple formation,
   a. there is considerable evidence that opposites attract.
   b. the more you see someone, the more you like them.
   c. characteristics such as race and class have little influence on your selection of dating partners.
   d. All of the above statements are true.

12. W.I. Thomas coined the phrase _____ to refer to the idea that if people define things as real, then they are real in their consequences.
   a. normative disruption
   b. impression management
   c. social construction of reality
   d. definition of the situation

13. According to ethnomethodologists,
   a. social interaction is determined primarily by the rewards and punishments we receive from other people.
   b. interpersonal attraction is determined primarily by biological and chemical processes located within the human nervous system.
   c. the most effective technique for identifying social norms is disrupting social settings.
   d. the most effective technique for identifying social norms is directly asking people to identify them.

14. Which of the following observations about cyberspace interaction is **false?**
   a. It is supported by a set of beliefs, language, and practices that encourage creating alternative identities.
   b. It has resulted in the formation of a new subculture in society.
   c. It eliminates the opportunity to develop intimate, long-term relationships.
   d. It provides greater anonymity than do most other forms of social interaction.

15. The social positions, networks of relationships, and institutions that hold a society together and shape people's experiences make up:
   a. a status system.
   b. an organization.
   c. the social structure.
   d. the division of labor.

16. When Emily's mother asked her how she performed on her sociology test, she told her that she received a C even though she failed the test. Her mother knew that Emily was lying because the pitch and loudness of her voice betrayed her. This reflects:
    a. proxemic communication.
    b. kinesic communication.
    c. tactile communication.
    d. paralinguistic communication.

17. Harry is sexually attracted to Joanne so he stands very close to her when they talk. His behavior reflects a form of _____ communication.
    a. proxemic
    b. kinesic
    c. tactile
    d. paralinguistic

18. Tactile communication refers to the:
    a. pitch and volume of our voices when we speak.
    b. touching we do while we interact with other people.
    c. distance we maintain between ourselves and other people.
    d. facial expressions and gestures we exhibit while talking to other people.

19. According to functionalist theorists, the purpose of the economic institution is to:
    a. replace members of society.
    b. socialize new members of society.
    c. maintain stability and existence.
    d. produce and distribute goods and services.

20. Emile Durkheim referred to the shared body of beliefs that give people a sense of belonging and a feeling of moral obligation to society's demands and values as:
    a. normative consensus.
    b. social conformity.
    c. cultural homogeneity.
    d. collective consciousness.

21. According to Durkheim, less complex, more homogeneous societies in which individuals play similar roles within the society are held together by _____ solidarity.
    a. secondary
    b. primary
    c. mechanical
    d. organic

22. A(n) _____ society uses machines and other technologies to produce and distribute goods, relies on a highly differentiated labor force, and uses a cash-based economy.
    a. post-industrial
    b. industrial
    c. agricultural
    d. foraging

23. Joe notices that some boys he would like to be friends with frequently play basketball after school. Although he is not that interested in sports, Joe talks excitedly about the upcoming championship playoffs when he is with the boys so that they will invite him to join their group. According to Erving Goffman, Joe is practicing:
    a. social deception.
    b. impression management.
    c. normative disruption.
    d. interpersonal manipulation.

24. Erving Goffman's _____ model is based on the idea that members of society interact with each other in different settings as if they are actors on a stage.
    a. ethnomethodology
    b. impressionistic
    c. dramaturgy
    d. exchange

25. Which of the following statements about social institutions is true?
    a. They are complex structures that exist for explicit purposes.
    b. They are loosely organized and temporary by nature.
    c. Like individuals, they can be directly observed.
    d. Microanalysis is the most useful technique for studying them.

TRUE-FALSE QUESTIONS

1. Microanalysis refers to the technique sociologists use to investigate patterns of social interaction that are relatively small, less complex, and less differentiated.

2. An audience is comprised of all people nationwide or internationally who watch the same program or performance.

3. Marilyn Frye compares the concept of social structure to a birdcage because she views both birdcages and society as havens that protect vulnerable groups from harm.

4. A gesellschaft society is held together by organic solidarity.

5. Because master statuses often override an individual's other components of identity, they are often the basis for prejudice and stereotypes.

6. Role conflict and role strain are rooted in the individual's mind and do not have any societal origins.

7. It is not possible to establish close, long-term relationships through cyberspace interaction because face-to-face communication is necessary to establish intimacy.

8. Although all humans have a strong need for affiliation, or a desire to be with other people, women generally reveal this tendency more than men.

9. Research indicates that perceptions of physical attractiveness influence how people are evaluated and treated, with attractive children being viewed as "smarter" and more attractive adult defendants receiving lighter sentences for their crimes.

10. Social solidarity is generally stronger in a gesellschaft society than in a gemeinschaft society because the extensive racial and ethnic diversity found in gemeinschaft societies often promotes tension and social divisions.

FILL IN THE BLANK QUESTIONS

1. Role _____ occurs when a single role consists of conflicting expectations.

2. Social _____ describes the order established in groups at any level and helps bring regularity and predictability to human behavior.

3. When a person rolls his or her eyes to indicate disbelief or frowns to indicate disappointment, s/he is using _____ communication to convey information.

4. Because they are very knowledgeable about Church doctrine and express a commitment to high moral standards, members of the clergy are highly respected. The prestige associated with this occupation reflects its _____ in society.

5. A(n) _____ society is economically dependent on the production and distribution of services, information, and technology.

ESSAY QUESTIONS

1. Describe the basic principles of social exchange theory and explain how this theory can be used to understand the persistence of sexist and racist attitudes.
2. Describe the basic principles of symbolic interaction theory and explain how this theory can be used to understand status differences between hair stylists and their clients.
3. Compare and contrast gesellschaft and gemeinschaft societies in terms of their social organization, division of labor, degree of heterogeneity, and mechanisms of social control.
4. Identify four negative consequences of industrialization and the corresponding social problems that have developed in the United States since industrialization occurred.
5. Apply Goffman's principle of impression management to the phenomenon of cyberspace interaction and explain how the rituals of cyberculture contribute to the specific ways that individuals behave when engaged in cyberspace interaction.

ANSWERS TO PRACTICE TEST

Answers to Multiple Choice Questions

1. B. 126 The social exchange model of social interaction suggests that when an interaction elicits approval, it is more likely to be repeated than an interaction that incites disapproval.
2. A. 120 Behavior involving communication between two or more people is Referred to as social interaction.
3. D. 120 The technique that sociologists use to investigate large patterns of social interaction and comprehend society as a whole is macroanalysis. Microanalysis is used to study social interaction in small groups.

4.	B.	121	Ascribed statuses, such as race and biological sex, are present at birth. Achieved statuses are gained through individual effort, such as educational attainment.
5.	D.	120	A group is a collection of individuals who interact and communicate with each other. Group members share goals and norms, and members possess a "we" feeling.
6.	C.	120	Social organization brings regularity and predictability to human behavior and describes the order established in social groups at any level. A social category refers to people who are categorized together based on a shared characteristic. An audience includes all of the people watching a program or performance. A social institution is an established and organized system of behavior with a recognized purpose.
7.	A.	121	Status inconsistency occurs when several statuses held by one person are associated with significantly different amounts of prestige. Role conflict occurs when the expectations of multiple roles conflict, while role strain occurs when one role has conflicting expectations.
8.	B.	121	Statuses that are automatically assigned to a person at birth, such as race, are ascribed. Achieved statuses are gained through effort.
9.	B.	122	The dominant status for an individual, which overrides all other features of the person's identity, is a master status.
10.	D.	122	Role conflict occurs when multiple roles have contradictory expectations, while role strain occurs when a single role includes conflicting expectations.
11.	B.	134	Proximity and shared social characteristics such as race and class increase the likelihood of attraction and relationship formation.
12.	D.	124	W.I. Thomas argued that situations defined as real are real in their consequences. This concept is known as the definition of the situation.
13.	C.	125	Because many norms are unconscious, asking people to identify them is not a useful strategy. Disrupting social situations reveals the norms.
14.	C.	127	Cyberspace interaction occurs when people interact and communicate with each other through use of a personal computer. People can develop long-term, intimate relationships in cyberspace.
15.	C.	136	Social structure consists of the social positions, networks of relationships, and institutions that hold a society together.
16.	D.	130	Paralinguistic communication is conveyed by the pitch and loudness of the speaker's voice, as well as its rhythm, emphasis, and frequency.
17.	A.	132	The amount of distance maintained between people engaged in social interaction is referred to as the proxemic bubble.
18.	B.	130	Tactile communication refers to physical touch, including positive (such as hugging) and negative (such as hitting) forms of touching.
19.	D.	136	Functionalist theorists argue that all social institutions fulfill specific purposes. The economy produces and distributes goods and services, the political institution maintains stability and order, the family replaces membership, and families and schools socialize members.
20.	D.	137	Collective consciousness gives people a sense of belonging and feeling of obligation to the society's norms and values.
21.	C.	137	Organic solidarity would typically be found in more diverse, complex societies, while mechanical solidarity would characterize more homogeneous gemeinschaft societies.
22.	B.	139	In agricultural societies, livelihood depends on large-scale patterns of

agriculture; in foraging societies, economic sustenance depends on hunting and gathering. Post-industrial societies rely on complex technology and produce primarily information and services.

23.	B.	125	Impression management is a process by which a person consciously manipulates other people's perceptions of him or her.
24.	C.	125	The dramaturgy model analyzes people's behavior in different settings.
25.	A.	135	Social institutions are well established, highly organized systems of social behavior that have recognized purposes in society. Although they cannot be directly observed, they can be studied using macroanalysis.

Answers to True-False Questions

1.	T.	120	Microanalysis refers to the technique that sociologists use to investigate patterns of social interaction that are relatively small.
2.	T.	121	Social categories and audiences are types of social units that do not fit the criteria necessary to be defined as groups.
3.	F.	137	Frye uses the metaphor of a birdcage to describe social structure as an oppressive network that confines and exploits some social groups.
4.	T.	138	A gesellschaft society is held together by organic solidarity.
5.	T.	122	A person who has AIDS, for example, has a master status.
6.	F.	122	Role strain and role conflict are experiencd by individuals but have societal origins.
7.	F.	127	Although cyberspace interaction makes anonymity and the assumption of false identity possible, people can develop long-term, intimate relationships through chat rooms and e-mail.
8.	T.	133	
9.	T.	134	
10.	F.	138	Social solidarity is stronger in gemeinschaft societies, which are more homogeneous. Greater diversity in gesellschaft societies can cause conflict and social divisions that undermine solidarity.

Answers to Fill in the Blank Questions

1.	strain	123
2.	organization	120
3.	kinesic	131
4.	status	121
5.	post-industrial	139

CHAPTER 6
GROUPS AND ORGANIZATIONS

BRIEF CHAPTER OUTLINE
Types of Groups
> Dyads and Triads: Group Size Effects
> Primary and Secondary Groups
> Reference Groups
> In-Groups and Out-Groups
> Social Networks
> The Small World Problem

Social Influence
> The Bystander Intervention Problem
> The Asch Conformity Experiment
> The Milgram Obedience Studies
> Groupthink
> Risky Shift

Formal Organizations and Bureaucracies
> Types of Organizations
> Bureaucracy
> Bureaucracy's Other Face
> Problems of Bureaucracy
> The McDonaldization of Society
> New Global Organizational Forms: The Japanese Model

Diversity: Race, Gender, and Class in Organizations
Functionalist, Conflict, and Symbolic Interaction: Theoretical Perspectives

QUESTIONS TO GUIDE YOUR READING
1. What characteristics do sociologists consider necessary for a collection of individuals to be considered a group?
2. Why do sociologists consider the size of a group important, and in what ways does the size of a group influence people's behavior?
3. What are the three main types of organizations identified by sociologists, and on what basis are organizations classified?
4. What influence do race, class, and gender have on the development of social networks for individuals from diverse groups?
5. How does bureaucracy serve positive functions for organizations but also encourage the development of problems within the organization?

KEY TERMS (defined at page number shown and in glossary)

attribution theory 152	bureaucracy 161
dyad 149	expressive needs 150
formal organization 159	group 148
group size effect 149	groupthink 157
instrumental needs 150	primary group 150
reference group 151	risky shift 158
secondary group 150	social network 153
status generalization 155	total institution 161
triad 149	triadic segregation 149
voluntary organization 159	

KEY PEOPLE (identified at page number shown)

Solomon Asch 155	Charles Horton Cooley 150
Erving Goffman 161	I.L. Janis 157
Stanley Milgram 155	Thomas F. Pettigrew 152
George Ritzer 164	Georg Simmel 149
James Stoner 158	W.I. Thomas 152
Max Weber 161	Philip Zimbardo 154

CHAPTER OUTLINE

Jury deliberations and verdicts reveal the influences of status, race, and gender, as do the other segments of society. Many lawyers believe that jury selection is the most important part of a trial, since choosing jurors means choosing a verdict. Trial consultants trained in sociological techniques are sometimes hired for juror analysis, which includes more than identifying the likely bias of a given juror. Juries are **groups**, and groups behave differently than individuals. Predictions can be made about who will become the most influential jury member. Factions form, which often influence deliberations and verdicts. Studies have shown that jury verdicts correlate not just with evidence, but also with jury composition, including its racial-ethnic and gender composition. Groups are subject to social influences, and understanding these influences can be essential to understanding a process like the operation of social justice. Analyzing the nature of groups is a step toward understanding how groups interact to form society.

I. **TYPES OF GROUPS**

A **group** is a collection of individuals who interact with each other, share goals and norms, and have a subjective awareness as "we." Certain gatherings are not groups, but may be *social categories*, such as truck drivers, or *audiences*, such as persons watching a movie. By examining a group more closely, we are able to identify characteristics that reliably predict trends in the behavior of the group, and even in the behavior of individuals within the group.

A. Dyads and Triads: Group Size Effects
1. Georg Simmel investigated the effects of size on groups, noting that the difference between a **dyad** (a group of two people) and a **triad** (a group of three people) creates entirely different group dynamics.
2. **Triadic segregation** refers to the tendency for triads to segregate into a pair and an isolate, or a *coalition* of a dyad against an isolate. This may place the isolate in an advantageous position because it creates the potential for initiating a coalition with either member of the dyad.
3. Simmel identified **group size effects** and noted that triads are *unstable* social groupings, whereas dyads are relatively stable.

B. Primary and Secondary Groups
1. Charles Horton Cooley introduced the concept of a **primary group**, or a group consisting of intimate, face-to-face interaction and relatively long-lasting relationships. For example, the family is a primary group that has a strong influence on an individual's personality and identity.
2. **Secondary groups** are larger in membership, less intimate, and less long-lasting. They tend to be less significant in people's emotional lives. In times of crisis or high stress, some secondary groups can take on the characteristics of primary groups, as when a community experiences a natural disaster.

3.   Primary and secondary groups generally serve different needs, although the distinction is not rigid. The difference between the groups is less in why they form than in how strongly the participants feel about each other and how dependent they are on the group for identity.

    a.   Primary groups serve **expressive** or socioemotional needs, such as intimacy, companionship, and emotional support. Primary groups are an important source of social control, and they have a strong influence on individual preferences as well as religious and political affiliations.

    b.   Secondary groups serve **instrumental** or task-oriented needs.

C.   <u>Reference Groups</u>

1.   **Reference groups** are those to which you may or may not belong, but that you use as a standard for evaluating your values, attitudes, and behaviors. Reference groups are generalized versions of role models.

2.   Imitation of reference groups can have both positive and negative effects. Identification with reference groups can strongly affect self-evaluation and self-esteem.

    a.   The representation of racial and ethnic groups in society may have a striking positive or negative effect on children who are acquiring their lifetime set of group affiliations.

    b.   A multicultural and pluralistic educational program may help students develop positive self-esteem.

D.   <u>In-Groups and Out-Groups</u>

1.   W.I. Thomas identified a distinction between in-groups and out-groups.

    a.   *In-group* members, such as families and college fraternities, are favored with liking and trust.

    b.   *Our-group* members are frequently regarded with suspicion.

2.   **Attribution theory** is the principle that *dispositional attributions* are made about others under certain conditions.

    a.   Thomas F. Pettigrew's summary of research on attribution theory indicates that individuals commonly generate a significantly distorted perception of the motives and capabilities of other people's acts based on whether that person is an in-group or out-group member.

    b.   These misperceptions are *attribution errors*, or errors made in attributing causes for people's behavior to their membership in a particular group, such as a racial group.

    c.   Attribution error has several dimensions, which tend to favor the in-group over the out-group.

        1)   Observing improper behavior by an out-group member, onlookers are likely to attribute the deviance to the *disposition*, or perceived "true nature," of the wrong-doer. This nature is viewed as genetically determined.

        2)   When the same behavior is exhibited by an in-group member, the act is commonly perceived as a result of the *situation* of the wrong doer, not his/her disposition.

        3)   If an out-group member performs in an exceptional way, it is often attributed to good luck or the individual is viewed as "exceptional."

4) An in-group member who performs in the same positive way is given credit for a valued disposition.
    d. We generally perceive people in our in-group positively and those in out-groups negatively. Attribution errors commonly occur between racial groups and between men and women.

E. Social Networks

1. A **social network** is a set of links between individuals or between other social units, such as bureaucratic organizations or entire nations. Individual membership in several groups provides links between groups and groups overlap.

2. Research indicates that people get jobs, especially high-paying, prestigious jobs, via personal networks more often than through formal job listings, want ads, or placement agencies.

3. One's family usually forms the first social network in a person's life. One's adult networks include neighborhood and professional contacts, as well as associations formed in fraternal, religious, occupational, and volunteer groups. Networks are influenced by race, class, and gender.

F. The Small World Problem

1. Research into the *small world problem* indicates that networks make the world much smaller than commonly thought.

2. One study of Black national leaders revealed that they form a closely knit network that is considerably more dense than that of the longer-established White leadership.

    a. When considering only personal acquaintances, not indirect links involving intermediaries, one-fifth of the entire national Black leadership is included.

    b. Reasons for this include the relatively small nationwide numbers of Black leaders and the sense of "family" that often exists among influential African Americans nationwide.

II. SOCIAL INFLUENCE

The influences of our youth extend to adulthood. For example, the choices of political party and religious affiliation correlate strongly with those of one's parents. Philip Zimbardo labeled the "Not-Me Syndrome" as the situation where individuals believe that some people conform to group behavior but "not me." Sociological research reveals gaps between what people think they will do and what they actually do.

A. The Bystander Intervention Problem

1. *Bystander intervention studies* examine the dynamics of when and how people come to the aid of someone in trouble.

2. In a situation where a person on the street is in danger, the more bystanders there are observing the episode, the less likely that any of them will call for the police or an ambulance.

3. One example of **group size effect** is that the failure of bystanders to offer help correlates directly with an increase in group size.

B. The Asch Conformity Experiment

1. Solomon Asch designed an experiment showing that even simple objective facts cannot withstand the distorting pressure of group influence. Rather mild social pressure was sufficient to cause an astonishing rise in the number of wrong answers participants gave.

2. Individuals accorded higher status tend to have more influence on small groups than those of lesser status. **Status generalization** occurs when the status hierarchy in a society has a measurable effect on behavior within a closed group.

C. The Milgram Obedience Studies

    1. Stanley Milgram's research reveals the personal dilemma caused by a conflict between conscience and authority.

    2. Milgram designed an experiment to test his subject's behavior when given a command by an authority figure to perform a task which the subject found reprehensible. Subjects believed that they were administering an increasingly powerful set of electric shocks to another subject.

    3. In Milgram's original study, 65 percent of the volunteer subjects obeyed the researcher and believed they administered shocks of 450 volts from the shock machine. Gender, race, class, and ethnic differences had no detectable effect on subjects' compliance rates.

    4. Milgram's interest in group conformity occurred when people were trying to understand why members of Hitler's army in Nazi Germany engaged in brutality toward Jews during World War II.

D. Groupthink

    1. **Groupthink**, described by I. L. Janis, is the common (although not inevitable) tendency for group members to reach a consensus opinion, even if that decision is stupid.

    2. Janis investigated presidential decisions, which are often based on group discussions with advisors. He discovered that horrible decisions were made by groups of very intelligent people.

    3. Janis argued that the process of groupthink occurred under specific conditions where the groups:

        a. possess *an illusion of invulnerability*, by which they believe that members are so talented that any group decision will succeed.

        b. develop *a falsely negative impression of those who are antagonists to the group's plans*, which results in an underestimation of their strength and power.

        c. *discourage dissenting opinions*, and view dissent as disloyalty, thereby prohibiting serious discussion and examination of alternative strategies.

        d. develop *an illusion of unanimity*, so that despite the personal reservations of some group members, there is a prevailing sense that the entire group is in complete agreement.

E. Risky Shift

    1. **Risky shift**, also known as *polarization shift*, is another group phenomenon that helps explain why the products of groupthink are frequently calamities. Risky shift is the tendency for groups to weigh risk differently than individuals.

    2. James Stoner, the first to identify risky shift, presented subjects with descriptions of situations involving risk, such as switching jobs. After subjects discuss in groups how much risk individuals should take in hypothetical situations, there is generally some type of shift in subjects'

responses, in one direction or another, about what is considered reasonable risk.

      3.   The risky shift is probably caused by *deindividuation*, which is the sense that one's self has merged with a group. In terms of risk taking, people feel that responsibility, and possibly blame, is borne not only by the individual but by the group. Deindividuation is a *group-size effect*, because it increases with the number of people in a group.

III.   FORMAL ORGANIZATIONS AND BUREAUCRACIES

A **formal organization** is a large, secondary group, highly organized to accomplish a complex task and achieve goals in an efficient manner. Organizations may consist of an array of other organizations, such as the federal government, which is comprised of thousands of other organizations. Although an organization is ultimately a collection of people, organizations develop routinized practices and cultures that may be reflected in symbols, values, rituals, and norms. Organizations tend to be persistent, but are also responsive to the social environment. For example, organizations such as rape crisis centers can be tools for innovation by changing the way that victims are treated by police and hospital personnel, and by advocating legal changes.

    A.   <u>Types of Organizations</u>

Sociologists classify formal organizations into three categories that are distinguished by their types of membership affiliation: normative, coercive, and utilitarian.

      1.   Normative organizations are those that people join to pursue goals that they personally consider worthwhile. Through joining, they obtain personal satisfaction and possibly prestige but no monetary reward.

          a.   Service and charitable organizations such as the PTA, the National Organization for Women (NOW), and the NAACP (National Association for the Advancement of Colored People) are also called **voluntary organizations.**

          b.   Gender, class, race, and ethnicity structure who joins which voluntary organizations. Because membership in some organizations is expensive, lower-income persons cannot afford to join them. Many racial-ethnic minority groups have formed their own voluntary organizations, partly due to their historical exclusion from traditionally White voluntary organizations.

      2.   Coercive organizations such as prisons and mental hospitals are characterized by membership that is largely involuntary.

          a.   Erving Goffman described coercive organizations as **total institutions**, or organizations cut off from the rest of society where residents are subject to strict social control over all aspects of their lives.

          b.   Individuals placed in total institutions are frequently subjected to what Goffman called "degradation ceremonies" or *mortification of the self*, which are actions by the staff to make inmates surrender their former identities.

      3.   Utilitarian organizations are large organizations, either for profit (e.g., Microsoft) or nonprofit (e.g., colleges), that individuals join for specific purposes, such as monetary reward. Joining is usually voluntary.

    B.   <u>Bureaucracy</u>

      1.   A **bureaucracy** is a type of formal organization characterized by an authority hierarchy, a clear division of labor, explicit rules, and

impersonality. The federal government, Disney, and IBM are examples of formal organizations that have developed into huge bureaucracies.

2. Max Weber identified the *ideal type* bureaucracy, a model rarely seen in reality but that defines the typical characteristics of this social form.

    a. There is a *high degree of division of labor and specialization* with clearly defined responsibilities and privileges.

    b. There is a *hierarchy of authority* that is often depicted in a complex organizational chart, which is a diagram identifying the position of each participant in the chain of command.

    c. Detailed *rules and regulations*, designed to handle virtually all situations and problems, govern the activities of a bureaucracy.

    d. Establishing efficient *impersonal relationships* is important because social interaction in a bureaucracy is supposed to be guided by instrumental criteria, such as organizational rules, rather than by social or emotional criteria.

    e. *Career ladders* are created within bureaucracies where job candidates are supposed to be hired and promoted on the basis of their qualifications.

    f. *Efficiency* is important to coordinate the activities of a large number of people who are pursuing organizational goals.

C. Bureaucracy's Other Face

1. In addition to the formal structure of a bureaucracy, an *informal structure* exists, which includes social interactions in bureaucracies that ignore, change, or otherwise bypass the formal structure and rules of the organization. This condition is referred to as *bureaucracy's other face*, or the informally evolved culture that evolves over time as a reaction to the formality and impersonality of the bureaucracy.

2. Bureaucracy's other face can also be seen in the workplace subcultures that develop. Sometimes, the informal culture becomes exclusionary, thereby increasing some workers' feelings of isolation.

3. Sexual harassment can become an aspect of the informal culture of the workplace. Sexual harassment often occurs when someone in a higher status position within the organization makes unwanted sexual overtures toward someone in a relatively lower status position.

4. The informal norms that develop within a bureaucracy may cause worker productivity to increase or decrease, dependent upon the norms and how they are informally enforced. In the Hawthorne Studies, researchers found that workers who produced too much or too little each day were informally "punished" by coworkers.

D. Problems of Bureaucracies

1. Several problems, including the risky shift in work groups and the development of groupthink, develop from the nature of the complex bureaucracy.

2. Additional problems in bureaucracies include *organizational ritualism* and the potential for alienation among those within the bureaucracy.

    a. Ritualism refers to workers' rigid adherence to rules, regardless of whether their behavior accomplishes the purpose for which the rule was originally designed.

        1) The 1986 explosion of the Space Shuttle *Challenger* was caused by a problem with the "O-ring" gasket on

the solid fuel booster rockets, which NASA managers and engineers were aware of as a potential problem

2) Such rigid group conformity within an organizational setting can lead to deviant behavior being redefined, or socially constructed, so that it is perceived as normal.

b. Alienation is characterized by the individual becoming psychologically separated from the organization and its goals, and may result in increased turnover, tardiness, absenteeism, and overall dissatisfaction with the organization.

E. The McDonaldization of Society

1. George Ritzer used the term the *McDonaldization of society* to describe the phenomenon whereby the principles that characterize fast food organizations increasingly dominate more aspects of U.S. society.

2. Ritzer identified four dimensions of the McDonaldization process: efficiency, calculability, predictability, and control.

a. *Efficiency* means that things move from start to completion in a standardized, streamlined way, often with machines or customers doing work once done by an employee.

b. *Calculability* means there is an emphasis on the quantitative aspects of products sold, such as size, cost, and time of production, rather than the quality of products.

c. *Predictability* is the assurance that products will be exactly the same, regardless of where or when purchased.

d. *Control,* the primary organizational principle of McDonaldization, refers to the reduction of people's behavior, both customers and workers, to a series of machine-like actions. People are carefully monitored in these organizations.

3. McDonaldization brings many benefits, such as greater availability of goods and services to a wider portion of the population and instantaneous service and convenience to a public with less free time. Further, there is predictability and familiarity in the goods bought and sold, and standardization of pricing and uniform quality of the goods.

4. McDonaldization also has some disadvantages, such as a danger of dehumanization and threat of loss of creativity as humans accept increasingly standardized products and services.

5. Ritzer's theory is based on Weber's prediction that human behavior would be increasingly guided by rational systems, that is, rules, regulations, and formal structures, rather than by abstract values.

F. New Global Organizational Forms: The Japanese Model

1. At one time, managers in the U.S. used *Theory X* to guide their behavior. Theory X was based on a belief that workers do not care about the organization, but only about their personal needs, therefore will only work when they are rigidly monitored and controlled.

2. *Theory Y* suggests that people have a desire to work and be responsible but become passive and irresponsible because of their experience within the organization. Management's task is to organize things so that people can accomplish their personal goals while also furthering the organization's goals.

3. There has been increasing interest in *Theory Z*, which is the organizational form used by many Japanese corporations and recently

adopted by some U.S. companies. This approach is based on long-term employment, interpersonal trust, and close personal relationships.

4. Research indicates that there is less alienation and greater solidarity among workers in firms that practice more participatory management, compared to workers where power rests completely with management.

IV. DIVERSITY: RACE, GENDER, AND CLASS IN ORGANIZATIONS

The hierarchical structuring of positions within organizations, which concentrates power and influence in the hands of a few individuals at the top, reflects the inequality in race, gender, and class relations evident throughout society. Traditionally, the most powerful positions are held by White men of upper social class status. The glass ceiling effect creates an invisible barrier that prevents women and minorities from gaining access to higher ranks of management.

The greater the involvement of the federal government in a given industry, the more favorable jobs and earnings are for Black men and women and White women. In most organizations, White men are more likely to receive promotions than African Americans, Hispanics, Native Americans, and women workers with the same education. Kanter found that "token" employees comprise a small percent of the employees hired and are viewed as representing all minorities or women, making it difficult for them to gain credibility in the organization and increasing the stress they experience. Social class plays a similar role in determining people's place within organizations, because middle and upper class employees tend to make higher wages and salaries and receive more promotions than people of lower social class status. Thus, social class stratification produces differences in the opportunities and life chances of individuals.

V. FUNCTIONALIST, CONFLICT, AND SYMBOLIC INTERACTION: THEORETICAL PERSPECTIVES

All three major sociological perspectives are concerned with the analysis of formal organizations and bureaucracies. The functionalist perspective argues that certain positive functions, called *eufunctions*, characterize bureaucracies and contribute to the overall unity of the bureaucracy. The bureaucracy exists to accomplish these eufunctions, such as efficiency, control, impersonal relations, and the chance for the individual to develop a career in the bureaucracy.

The conflict perspective, which is the basis for Theory X, argues that the hierarchical or stratified nature of the bureaucracy encourages conflict among the individuals within it, which interferes with the smooth and efficient running of the bureaucracy.

The symbolic interaction perspective, which underlies Theories Y and Z, stresses the role of the self in any group, especially how the self develops as a product of social interaction.

PRACTICE TEST

Multiple Choice Questions

1. Which of the following statements about juries is (are) true?
   a. As groups, juries behave differently than do the individual members who comprise each jury.
   b. Sociologists can make educated predictions about who will become the most influential member in a jury.
   c. A jury verdict correlates with the racial-ethnic and gender composition of the jury.
   d. All of the above statements are true.

2. A group is a collection of individuals who:
   a. regularly interact with each other.
   b. share a subjective sense of "we."
   c. share norms and goals.
   d. All of the above are features of groups.

3. Simmel identified the tendency for triads to separate into a pair and an isolate as triadic:
   a. aggregation.
   b. segregation.
   c. alignment.
   d. isolation.

4. A group consisting of intimate, face-to-face interaction and relatively long-lasting relationships, such as a family, is a(n):
   a. intimate aggregate.
   b. secondary group.
   c. primary group.
   d. social category.

5. Which of the following statement about secondary groups is (are) true?
   a. They serve primarily instrumental or task-oriented needs.
   b. They generally have fewer members than do primary groups.
   c. They tend to have long-lasting, powerful influences on the members' personality development and self-concept.
   d. All of the above statements are true.

6. Although James has never met or interacted with a professional athlete, he reveres major league baseball players and uses them as a standard for determining his own values about physical fitness and good sportsmanship. For James, professional athletes represent a _____ group.
   a. secondary
   b. reference
   c. primary
   d. ideal

7. Because of *attribution error*, when people observe an *in-group* member behaving in an exceptional manner, they attribute the behavior to the:
   a. person's good luck.
   b. person's good disposition or "true nature."
   c. situation in which the behavior occurs.
   d. None of the above are true.

8. When a person is prejudiced toward a particular out-group and observes a member of that group behaving in a positive, non-stereotypical manner, the observer will probably:
   a. dismiss his/her prejudice about the out-group because s/he realizes that the stereotype is based on inaccurate information.
   b. retain his/her original prejudice because s/he will assume that the behavior was a special exception to the person's usual behavior.
   c. attempt to become a member of the out-group so that s/he can better understand the members' perspectives and experiences.
   d. consult members of his/her in-group about the observation to evaluate the new information more objectively.

9. The set of links between individuals or other social units, such as bureaucratic organizations or entire nations, are referred to as:
    a. social networks.
    b. social organizations.
    c. formal organizations.
    d. dispositional networks.

10. The tendency for group members to reach a consensus opinion, even if the decision is stupid, is referred to as:
    a. polarization.
    b. generalization.
    c. groupthink.
    d. attribution.

11. In his *risky shift* experiments, Stoner found that Americans are _____ to take greater risks as members of a group than as individuals, while Japanese people are _____ to take greater risks as members of a group than as individuals.
    a. less likely, more likely
    b. less likely, less likely
    c. more likely, less likely
    d. more likely, more likely

12. The Marriot Corporation now provides the same food to students and staff at over 500 college campuses across the U.S. The predictability and uniformity associated with these meals is due to the process known as the:
    a. Bureaucratization of society.
    b. McDonaldization of society.
    c. Monopolization of society.
    d. Ritualization of society.

13. A large, secondary group, highly organized to accomplish a complex set of tasks and achieve goals in an efficient manner is a(n) _____ organization.
    a. formal
    b. informal
    c. coercive
    d. total

14. According to Max Weber's ideal type, which of the following is (are) typical of a bureaucracy?
    a. extensive, detailed lists of rules and procedures
    b. cooperative, non-hierarchical management styles
    c. low degree of division of labor and specialization
    d. All of the above are typical characteristics of a bureaucracy.

15. The informally evolved culture that develops over time as a reaction to the formality and impersonality of bureaucracy represents:
    a. McDonaldization of society.
    b. bureaucracy's other face.
    c. the bystander intervention problem.
    d. social network density.

16. NASA experts proceeded with the *Challenger* launch despite numerous signs of potential danger. This illustrates which problem common to bureaucracies?
    a. ritualism
    b. alienation
    c. rate busting
    d. rationalization

17. When individuals become psychologically separated from a bureaucratic organization and its goals, often resulting in increased turnover, tardiness, and absenteeism, the problem of _____ is occurring.
    a. ritualism
    b. alienation
    c. rate busting
    d. rationalization

18. According to George Ritzer, the *McDonaldization* of society is characterized by an increasing emphasis on the:
    a. quality of the products created.
    b. degree of autonomy provided to the workers.
    c. range of choice provided to the customers.
    d. quantity of the products created.

19. According to Theory Y:
    a. people are passive and irresponsible by nature.
    b. people are responsible and have a desire to be creative.
    c. people will only work when they are rigidly monitored and controlled.
    d. management's sole task is to further the organization's goals at any cost.

20. Which of the following statements about organizational diversity is true?
    a. White women are more likely than White men and Black men and women with the same education to receive promotions within the organization.
    b. "Token" employees, hired to increase minority and female representation in organizations, generally report high levels of job satisfaction.
    c. White federal employees (both male and female) are twice as likely to be dismissed from their jobs as their Black coworkers.
    d. The most powerful positions in organizations are generally held by White men of upper social class status.

21. Status _____ occurs when the status hierarchy in a society has a measurable effect on behavior within a closed group.
    a. tokenism
    b. segregation
    c. alignment
    d. generalization

22. The symbolic interaction perspective:
   a.   assumes that people hate their jobs and try to avoid working and taking responsibility.
   b.   stresses the role of the self in any group, especially how the self develops as a product of social interaction
   c.   argues that bureaucracies exist to accomplish positive functions such as efficiency, control, and impersonal relations.
   d.   All of the above statements are true.

23. Sociologists classify formal organizations into three categories that are distinguished by their types of membership affiliations, including:
   a.   isolates, dyads, triads.
   b.   collectives, bureaucracies, and total institutions.
   c.   primary groups, secondary groups, and bureaucracies.
   d.   normative organizations, coercive organizations, and utilitarian organizations.

24. Which of the following characteristics increases the likelihood that groupthink will occur?
   a.   falsely positive impressions of those who are antagonistic to the group's plans
   b.   an illusion of invulnerability
   c.   an illusion of disunity
   d.   All of the above contribute to groupthink.

25. The Black sorority known as the Deltas is a(n) _____ organization whose members voluntary join the organization primarily for personal fulfillment.
   a.   total
   b.   coercive
   c.   utilitarian
   d.   normative

TRUE-FALSE QUESTIONS

1. The size of a group has relatively little effect on how members of the group behave.

2. In times of crisis or high stress, such as a natural disaster, some secondary groups can take on the characteristics of primary groups.

3. A triad is an unstable social grouping, whereas dyads are relatively stable.

4. An individual is more likely to go streaking, or run nude in a public place, when he or she is alone than when he or she is part of a group.

5. Identification with reference groups has strong positive effects on self-evaluation, but rarely has negative effects on self-esteem.

6. A total institution is a charitable organization such as NOW or the NAACP, that people voluntary join because they support the organizations' goals.

7. In his study of conformity, Milgram found that the class, race, and ethnicity of the subjects significantly influenced whether they would comply with the request to administer shocks during the experiment.

8.   Choices of political party and religious affiliation correlate strongly with those of one's parents.

9.   Informal norms within a bureaucracy are almost always beneficial to management because they usually contribute to increased productivity.

10.   Research indicates that people get high-paying, prestigious jobs through formal job listings, want ads, and placement agencies more often than through personal networks.

FILL IN THE BLANK QUESTIONS

1.   Risky shift is caused partly by _____, a process in which a person perceives his or her own identity as merging with the group.

2.   A _____ group is a group to which you may or may not belong, but that you use as a standard for evaluating your values, attitudes, and behaviors.

3.   The _____ Experiment showed that mild social pressure, especially from high status individuals, is sufficient to cause many people to give wrong answers on objective tests.

4.   Theory _____, which views workers as irresponsible and concerned only about their own needs, lies behind the classical Western bureaucracy.

5.   Theory _____, an organizational form often used in Japanese corporations, places considerable emphasis on interpersonal trust and the establishment of primary group relationships within the organization.

ESSAY QUESTIONS

1.   Provide evidence to support George Ritzer's argument that modern society resembles fast-food organizations such as McDonald's.
2.   Use the principles of attribution theory to explain why racial prejudice persists.
3.   Explain how group size contributes to the *bystander intervention problem*.
4.   Identify the four specific conditions that tend to promote *groupthink* according to Janis, and give an example of a situation in which groupthink produced a poor decision.
5.   Identify the six characteristics of bureaucracy according to Weber and explain how each feature supports the goals of bureaucratic organizations.

ANSWERS TO PRACTICE TEST

Answers to Multiple Choice Questions

1.	D.	147	Juries are groups, and groups behave differently than individuals. Predictions can be made about who will become the most influential jury member, and jury composition is related to the verdict rendered.
2.	D.	148	A group is a collection of individuals who interact with each other and share goals and norms. A group also has a subjective awareness of "we," which is an essential characteristic of a group. Truck drivers and audiences are examples of social categories, rather than groups.
3.	B.	149	A triad is an unstable group with a tendency to segregate into a pair (a dyad) and an isolate, resulting in triadic segregation.

4.	C.	150	According to Cooley, a group consisting of intimate, face-to-face interaction and relatively long-lasting relationships is a primary group. It generally consists of fewer members than a secondary group and is concerned primarily with meeting members' socioemotional needs.
5.	A.	150	Secondary groups serve instrumental needs.
6.	B.	151	Reference groups are those to which you may or may not belong, but that you use as a standard for evaluating your values, attitudes, and behaviors. They may have both positive and negative influences on behavior.
7.	B.	153	Attribution errors include the following: If an in-group member performs in an exceptional way, they are given credit for a valued disposition. Also, when observing improper behavior by an out-group member, onlookers are likely to attribute the deviance to the disposition of the wrong doer. If an out-group member performs in an exceptional way, it is often attributed to good luck or the individual is viewed as "exceptional." When observing improper behavior by an in-group member, onlookers are likely to attribute the behavior to the situation of the wrong doer.
8.	B.	153	If an out-group member behaves in an exceptional way, the person is perceived an an exception to the rule or as exceptionally lucky.
9.	A.	153	A set of links between individuals or between other social units, such as bureaucratic organizations or entire nations, is a social network. Social network membership varies by gender, race, and class.
10.	C.	157	Janis argues that groupthink results from an illusion of invulnerability, a falsely negative impression of those who are antagonistic toward the group's plans, discouragement of dissenting opinion, and an illusion of unanimity.
11.	C.	158	The risky shift can occur in either direction, depending on the group's cultural values.
12.	B.	164	Ritzer identified four dimensions of the McDonalidization process: efficiency, calculability, predictability, and control.
13.	A.	159	A large, complex secondary group highly organized to accomplish a task and achieve goals in an efficient manner is a formal organization.
14.	A.	161	A bureaucracy is a type of formal organization characterized by an authority hierarchy, clear division of labor, explicit rules, and impersonality.
15.	B.	162	The informally evolved culture that develops over time as a reaction to the formality and impersonality of the bureaucracy is bureaucracy's other face.
16.	A.	163	Problems that may develop from the nature of bureaucracy include alienation, ritualism, and groupthink. The Challenger accident reflects workers' and managers' rigid adherence to rules, or ritualism.
17.	B.	164	Alienation may be widespread in organizations where individuals have little control over their work and engage in repetitive tasks.
18.	D.	165	McDonaldization stresses quantity over quality and involves control over both workers and customers.
19.	B.	167	According to Theory Y and Theory Z, management should encourage personal development while furthering the organization's goals.
20.	D.	168	Patterns of race and gender discrimination in hiring and promotions persist in organizations and jobs reflect differences in workers' class status.

21.	D.	165	Status generalization is reflected in the fact that people of higher status generally have greater influence over the behavior of people of lower status.
22.	B.	169	Symbolic interactionism is concerned with self-identity and views the self as a product of social interaction, as noted in Table 6.1. This perspective underlies Theories Y and Z.
23.	D.	159	People join normative organizations voluntarily to pursue personal fulfillment and utilitarian organizations for rewards such as wages. Membership in coercive organizations is usually involuntary.
24.	B.	157	Groupthink typically occurs in groups with falsely negative impressions of those who are antagonists to the group's plans, an illusion of invulnerability, and an illusion of unanimity.
25.	D.	160	People join organizations such as sororities for personal satisfaction.

Answers to True-False Questions

1.	F.	149	Simmel discovered that group size influences group behavior, which is reflected in both the bystander intervention problem and triadic segregation.
2.	T.	150	
3.	T.	149	Simmel showed that a triad is an unstable grouping that tends to separate into a dyad and an isolate.
4.	F.	158	Individuals are more likely to take risks such as streaking when they are in groups because they experience deindividuation, or the merging of the self with the group.
5.	F.	152	Reference groups can have both positive and negative influences on an individual's self-evaluation and self-esteem.
6.	F.	161	Goffman referred to coercive organizations such as prisons and mental hospitals as total institutions. People do not usually join these organizations voluntarily.
7.	F.	155	Milgram did not detect any significant effects of race, class, or gender on the subjects' behavior.
8.	T.	150	Primary groups such as the family have a powerful influence on people's behavior and values throughout their lives.
9.	F.	162	The informal norms that develop as a result of bureaucracy's other face often lead to exclusion and reduced productivity.
10.	F.	153	Research indicates that people get jobs, especially high-paying, prestigious jobs, via personal networks rather than through formal job listings, want ads, and placement agencies.

Answers to Fill in the Blank Questions

1.	deindividuation	158
2.	reference	151
3.	Asch Conformity	155
4.	X	167
5.	Z	167

CHAPTER 7
SEXUALITY AND INTIMATE RELATIONSHIPS

BRIEF CHAPTER OUTLINE
Is Sex Natural?
The Sexual Revolution
       Scientific Studies of Sex
       Sex and Social Change
Contemporary Sexual Attitudes and Behavior
       Changing Sexual Values
       Sexual Practices of the American Public
Sex: Diversity, Social Organization, and the Global Context
       The Influence of Race, Class, and Gender
       A Global Perspective on Sexuality
Sexuality and Sociological Theory
       Sex: Functional or Conflict-Based?
       The Social Construction of Sexual Identity
       Understanding Gay and Lesbian Experience
Sex and Social Issues
       Birth Control
       New Reproductive Technologies
       Abortion
       Pornography
       Teenage Pregnancy
       Sexual Violence

QUESTIONS TO GUIDE YOUR READING
1.   What are the primary differences between the biological determinism and social constructionist perspectives of sexuality?
2.   What does research indicate about the sexual values and practices of people living in the United States?
3.   What are sexual politics and what consequences do they have for people according to their gender, race, ethnicity, and social class?
4.   How do race and class structure people's access to, and use of, reproductive technology such as contraception, abortion, and in vitro fertilization?
5.   What are the most prevalent forms of sexual violence in the United States and around the world?

KEY TERMS (defined at page number shown and in glossary)

coming out 192	compulsory heterosexuality 192
eugenics 196	heterosexism 194
homophobia 193	minority group 195
queer theory 193	script 177
sexology 178	sexual orientation 191
sexual politics 182	sexual scripts 177
sexual revolution 178	social constructionist perspective 190

KEY PERSONS (identified at page number shown)

Havelock Ellis 179	Sigmund Freud 178
William Masters and Virginia Johnson 180	Alfred Kinsey 179
Edward Laumann 185	Janet Lee 187

CHAPTER OUTLINE

Controversy frequently develops concerning subjects related to sexuality. While some people argue that sexual permissiveness is common in the United States, others argue that the society is not sexually free enough. Stereotypes about people of diverse sexual orientations are common, and individuals who are suspected of engaging in "deviant" sexual behavior may be subject to violent attacks. Sexuality is a complex social phenomenon and sexual behavior and attitudes are socially influenced. Like other forms of social behavior, the expression of human sexuality is structured by social institutions.

I. **IS SEX NATURAL?**

    A. *Sexuality is socially defined and patterned.*

        1. Behavior that appears to be natural is usually that which is accepted by cultural customs and sanctioned by social institutions.

        2. Sexuality creates intimacy between people and is an important part of our social identity.

    B. The social and cultural basis of sexuality is apparent in a number of ways.

        1. *Human sexual attitudes and behavior vary in different cultural contexts.*

            a. Culture affects whether we define certain sexual behaviors as normal or deviant.

            b. If sex were purely natural behavior, sexual behavior would be uniform across societies, but it is not. Sexual behaviors considered normal in one society may be seen as peculiar in another. For example, the Hijras of India are a religious community of men who are born male but think of themselves as neither men nor women. Their identity can be understood only within the cultural context of Hinduism.

        2. *Sexual attitudes and behavior change over time.*

            a. Public opinion polls show that young people are more permissive in their sexual values than were young people in the past, although tolerance of casual sex has declined somewhat in recent years.

            b. Sexual behavior has changed dramatically when one uses a long-term historical perspective. For example, most teenagers now have sexual intercourse in their mid-teens.

        3. *Sexual identity is learned.*

            a. Like other forms of social identity, sexual identity is acquired through socialization and the ongoing relationships we have with other people.

            b. Learning about sex is part of the socialization process, which includes learning sexual norms.

                1) Sexual socialization takes place at a very early age, before young people become sexually active.

                2) Children acquire "sexual" **scripts**, or learned performances that are the basis for later adolescent and adult behaviors, through role-taking, such as playing doctor.

                3) **Sexual scripts** teach us what is appropriate behavior for our gender, such as norms about marriage.

        4. *Social institutions channel and direct human sexuality.*

       a.   Social institutions such as religion and family define some forms of sexual experience as more legitimate than others, thus granting heterosexual people more institutional privileges than gay men and lesbian women.

       b.   Laws direct sexuality into socially legitimate forms by defining some forms of sexual behavior as lawful and others as criminal.

       c.   Sex is influenced by the economic institutions of society through the use of sex for marketing products and the sale of sexual services.

       d.   Although sexuality is generally considered a private matter, governments routinely intervene in people's sexual lives. State-supported agencies may exert influence on sexuality and reproduction. For example, poor women and women who receive welfare have very high rates of sterilization.

       e.   Public policies regulate sexuality and reproductive behaviors. Government decisions about funding abortions and about which reproductive technologies to endorse influence the choices of birth control technology available to men and women. Government funding, or lack thereof, for sex education can influence how people understand sexuality.

II.   **THE SEXUAL REVOLUTION**

The **sexual revolution** refers to the widespread changes in men's and women's roles and a greater public acceptance of sexuality as a normal part of social development. The movement originates in social and historical changes in the late 19th and early 20th centuries, but its effects were most obvious in the late 20th century.

A.   Scientific Studies of Sex

The development of **sexology**, which is the scientific study of sex and sexuality, brought profound changes to our understanding of sexuality.

    1.   The Influence of Freud

       a.   Freud's message that the formation of sexual identity is a basic part of personality development and his analysis of sexuality continue to influence people's understanding of sexuality.

       b.   Freud presented a developmental model of sexuality, arguing that sexual expression began in childhood and developed over the life cycle in several stages. He argued that the *libido*, or sexual energy, was the driving force behind all activities.

       c.   Much of Freud's interpretation of women's sexuality was based on the assumption that men are more sexual and psychologically mature than women, which has been criticized by feminist theorists.

    2.   Havelock Ellis (1859-1939) was one of the most influential early sexologists.

       a.   He believed that sexual dysfunction was the result of psychological, not organic, problems.

       b.   His work was strongly influenced by the sexist assumptions of his time and he regarded any sexual behavior other than heterosexual, monogamous sexuality as "sexual deviance."

    3.   The Kinsey Reports

       a.   Alfred Kinsey published the first major national surveys of sexual behavior in the U.S. in the 1940s and 1950s.

        b.   His study was limited by its reliance only on White respondents and interviewers. Self-report information about sexual habits is notoriously unreliable; however, the Kinsey reports were still informative in describing sexual behavior.

        c.   Kinsey's studies reported the rates of premarital intercourse, the variety of sexual activities of younger couples, and the proportion of the U.S. population that was homosexual.

        d.   When the Kinsey studies were done, widespread societal changes were taking place in the sexual practices and beliefs of the U.S. public. Overall, Kinsey reported a weakening of sexual taboos and a more permissive sexual atmosphere.

4.   The Masters and Johnson Studies

        a.   Masters and Johnson's research explored physiological sexual responses (i.e. heart rate, orgasm) and is the most extensive, thorough study of human sexual response ever done.

        b.   Masters and Johnson initially used prostitutes as subjects, but the majority of their data was collected from White, middle and upper class, married couples.

        c.   These studies dispelled many prevalent myths about sexuality, especially the myth that women and men experienced sex in radically different ways. They asserted that both women and men had a right to sexual pleasure.

        d.   More contemporary studies of sexuality have investigated the social dimensions of sexual behavior, rather than its physiological character.

B.   <u>Sex and Social Change</u>

1.   Many of the changes associated with the sexual revolution have been changes in women's behaviors, which have narrowed the differences in the sexual experiences of women and men.

2.   The sexual revolution has been strongly influenced by political movements in recent years, especially feminism and the gay rights movement.

C.   **Sexual politics** refers to the link that exists between sexuality and power and between sexuality and race, class, and gender oppression. It is reflected in personal relationships, when one person is powerless or is defined as the property of someone else, in the sexual exploitation of women in society, through high rates of violence against women, in the cultural use of women as sex objects, and by exploiting women's work.

1.   The gay and lesbian liberation movement has challenged gender role stereotypes and sexual oppression, resulting in profound changes in the way we understand homosexuality. Some scholars propose that homosexuality is one of several alternatives for happy, intimate social relationships.

2.   The work of feminist and gay and lesbian activists has had a profound impact on how sociologists and the public think about sexuality and human relationships.

D.   The Internet has introduced new forms of sexual relationships, including cybersex and stimulation through on-line chatrooms.

E.   The sexual revolution has produced more commercialized sex, in which sex is defined as a commodity and women are portrayed in demeaning ways.

III. CONTEMPORARY SEXUAL ATTITUDES AND PRACTICES

Overall, Americans are more sexually liberal today and there is greater tolerance for diverse sexual lifestyles and practices than in the past.

A. Changing Sexual Values

1. Sexual attitudes vary by issue (e.g., a person may be more liberal about one topic than another) and change over time. Whereas 21 percent of Americans approved of premarital sex in 1969, 55 percent of people approve today.

2. There are significant gender differences among young people on many topics regarding their sexual behavior, including reasons for their first sexual experience.

3. Sexual attitudes are shaped by race, age, education and religious identification, reflecting the importance of social and political systems within society on developing sexual meaning systems.

B. Sexual Practices of the American Public

1. Most surveys investigate sexual attitudes because self-report data about sexual practices are unreliable.

2. Laumann and colleagues' survey of sexual practices in the U.S., conducted in the early 1990s, reveals several things.

   a. *Young people are becoming sexually active earlier.*

   b. *The proportion of young people who are sexually active has increased, particularly among young women. The largest increase is among White teenagers with higher family incomes.*

   c. *Having only one sexual partner in one's lifetime is rare.*

   d. *A significant number of people have extramarital affairs.*

   e. *A significant number of people are lesbian or gay. The social stigma associated with being gay or lesbian causes underrepresentation.*

   f. *For those who are sexually active, sex is relatively frequent. Age and marital status are the most significant predictors of the frequency of sex, with married and cohabiting people in their 20s having sex the most often.*

   g. *People are not very well informed about sex.*

IV. SEX: DIVERSITY, SOCIAL ORGANIZATION, AND THE GLOBAL CONTEXT

Patterns of sexuality reflect the social organization of society.

A. The Influence of Race, Class, and Gender

Race, class, and gender are linked in various stereotypes about sexuality and form a context in which sexual relationships are formed.

1. Sexual behavior follows gendered patterns that stem from definitions of masculinity and femininity in the culture.

2. Cultural definitions of what is sexually appropriate differ significantly for women and men, resulting in a "double standard."

   a. Women are more likely than men to have their first sexual experience with someone with whom they are romantically involved.

   b. For men, sexuality is frequently associated with power.

   c. Janet Lee's research reveals that women in various cultural contexts may define menstruation differently.

3. Sexual politics are tied to race and class relations in society.

        a.   Sexual stereotypes of different racial-ethnic groups and social classes illustrate how sexuality is linked to systems of oppression. Poor women and women of color are the group most vulnerable to sexual exploitation.

        b.   Class, race, and gender hierarchies have historically been justified by claims that people of color and women are sexually promiscuous and uncontrollable.

        c.   Sexual abuse is often part of men's behavior in national conquests, such as the abuse of American Indians by Whites.

        d.   Advertising commonly utilizes and reinforces condescending images based on gender, race, and class.

B.   A Global Perspective on Sexuality

    1.   Cross-cultural studies show that sexual norms develop within cultural meaning systems and vary across cultures. Significant cross-cultural differences exist in jealousy and tolerance for homosexuality.

    2.   As the world has become more globally connected, an international sex trade has flourished, linking economic development, world poverty, tourism, and the subordinate status of women in many societies.

        a.   The *international sex trade*, sometimes referred to as the "traffic in women," refers to the use of women worldwide as sex workers in an institutional context where sex is a commodity used to promote tourism, cater to business and military men, and support a huge nightclub industry.

        b.   The international sex trade has been strongly implicated in the spread of AIDS worldwide and the exploitation of women in countries where they have limited economic opportunities.

V.   **SEXUALITY AND SOCIOLOGICAL THEORY**
Sociological theory provides an analytical framework to examine the connection of sexuality to social institutions and current social issues.

  A.   Sex: Functional or Conflict-Based?

    1.   Functionalist theory views sexuality in terms of how it contributes to the stability of social institutions, such as the family.

    2.   Conflict theorists view sexuality as part of the power relations and economic inequality in society. Thus, sex is associated with power and sexual relations are linked to other forms of subordination and exploitation, including race, class, and gender inequality.

    3.   Both functionalism and conflict theory are macrosociological theories that are used to analyze sexuality in terms of the overall social organization of society.

  B.   The Social Construction of Sexual Identity

The *social construction perspective*, rooted in symbolic interaction theory, interprets sexual identity as learned, not inborn. Therefore, culture and society shape sexual experiences through social approval and social taboos.

    1.   Biology and Sexual Identity

        a.   Sociologists believe that social experiences are more significant in shaping sexual identity than biology.

        b.   LeVay claims to have identified anatomical differences in the brains of deceased homosexual and heterosexual men. Critics have questioned the validity of his research based on the limited sample size and ambiguous methodology used to identify the sexual orientation of the subjects.

      c.   Public beliefs about the biological cause of homosexuality are stronger than the current scientific evidence supports.

      d.   Sociological research suggests that social influences interact with biological influences in the creation of various dimensions of identity, including sexual identity.

2.   The Social Basis of Sexuality

      a.   From a social constructionist perspective, one's sexual identity develops through social experiences and is constructed over the life course, making a variety of different sexual identities possible, all of them learned through the socialization process.

      b.   From a social constructionist perspective, no form of sexual identity is considered more normal than any other form.

            1)   *Heterosexuals* are those who are sexually attracted to members of the other sex.

            2)   *Homosexuals* are those who are sexually attracted to members of the same sex.

            3)   *Bisexuals* are those who are sexually attracted to members of both sexes.

      c.   **Sexual orientation** is how individuals experience sexual arousal and pleasure.

      d.   **Compulsory heterosexuality**, a concept developed by Adrienne Rich, is the idea that heterosexual identity is not a choice. Rich argues that institutions define heterosexuality as the only legitimate form of sexual identity and enforce it through social norms and sanctions, including peer pressure, socialization, law, economic policies and even violence.

      e.   In societies where cultural supports for multiple forms of sexual identity are strongest, distinctions between heterosexual and homosexual behavior may not be so rigid.

      f.   **Coming out**, the process of defining oneself as gay or lesbian, is a series of events and redefinitions in which a person comes to see herself or himself as having a gay identity. A person's sexual identity may change over time, which indicates that identity is created over the life course, rather than being innate.

C.   <u>Understanding Gay and Lesbian Experiences</u>

1.   *Queer theory* is a new social science perspective that interprets various dimensions of sexual identity as evolving over the life course.

2.   In the United States, **homophobia**, which is the fear and hatred of homosexuality, permeates the culture.

      a.   This learned attitude is reflected in prejudiced attitudes and overt hostility and violence directed toward people suspected of being gay.

      b.   Myths about gay people include the belief that they cannot control their sexuality and that they are mostly wealthy White men who work in artistic or personal services jobs.

3.   **Heterosexism** refers to the institution of heterosexuality as the only legitimate sexual orientation, which is reflected in the unequal distribution of privileges to people presumed to be heterosexual. Businesses and communities rarely recognize the legal rights of those in homosexual relationships, although this is changing.

4. Gay and lesbian people primarily receive social support for the formation and continuation of their relationships from other people in the gay community.

5. The absence of institutionalized roles for lesbians and gays affects the roles they adopt in relationships. Gay and lesbian couples are more likely than heterosexual couples to both be employed and to establish egalitarian relationships.

6. In the U.S., gays and lesbians are a **minority group**, which refers to a group whose members have similar characteristics (or at least are perceived to have similar characteristics) and are treated with prejudice and discrimination. Because gays and lesbians have been denied equal rights and are singled out for negative treatment by dominant groups, they are a minority group. Like other minority groups, they have organized to advocate for their rights.

VI. SEX AND SOCIAL INSTITUTIONS
A. Birth Control
1. The availability of birth control is less controversial now than in the past, yet it is still mostly men who continue to define laws and make scientific decisions about what types of birth control will be available.

2. Unmarried people were not given the legal right to birth control in the United States until 1972. Heated public policy controversy remains about young people's access to birth control.

3. Class and race relations have shaped birth control policy. For example, a declining birth rate among White upper and middle class families in the early 20th century was accompanied by a fear that immigrants and poor people would overpopulate the society.

4. **Eugenics** sought to apply scientific principles of genetic selection to "improve" the offspring of the human race.
   a. The eugenics movement was explicitly racist and class-based and rooted more in social stereotypes than in scientific fact.
   b. Proponents of eugenics argue that the inferior genetic composition of some groups is responsible for social problems such as crime.

B. New Reproductive Technologies
1. While new reproductive technologies have increased sexual freedom, they have also raised social policy questions. Surrogate mothering, in vitro fertilization, and new biotechnologies such as gene splicing, cloning and genetic engineering may remove biological parents from the reproduction process.

2. Issues of class, race and gender are related to new reproductive technology in many ways. One obvious issue is accessibility, because typically only the upper class can afford expensive new technology.

C. Abortion
1. Abortion is one of the most controversial policy issues in the U.S. Public support for abortion has remained relatively constant over the last 20 years, with the majority of the public believing it should be legal in certain circumstances.

2. The right to abortion was first established by constitutional law in 1973, but the Supreme Court has allowed states to impose some restrictions on this right.

3.   Data on abortions show it occurs across social groups but certain patterns by age, race, and religion are evident. The abortion rate in the U.S. has declined somewhat since 1980.

4.   Research demonstrates that abortion rights activists and anti-abortion activists hold different views about sexuality and the roles of women.

D.   <u>Pornography</u>

1.   There is little consensus about the acceptability and effects of pornography. Debate often centers on the unclear legal definition of obscenity.

2.   Communities in which outlets for pornography appear are often economically vulnerable and their residents frequently organize unsuccessfully to oppose it. Their failure illustrates the power of different social groups to control their environments.

3.   Public agitation over pornography has divided into those who think it is solidly protected by the first amendment, those who want it strictly controlled, those who think it should be totally banned for moral reasons, and those who think it must be banned because it harms women.

4.   There is little evidence to support the assertion that exposure to non-violent pornography increases sexual promiscuity.

E.   <u>Teenage Pregnancy</u>

1.   Each year, one-half million teenage girls have babies in the United States. The U.S. has the highest rate of teen pregnancy in the world, although levels of teen sexual activity around the world are roughly comparable.

2.   Teenage pregnancy and motherhood are strongly correlated with poverty, lower educational attainment, and health problems for both the mothers and their babies.

3.   Although an increasing number of teenagers appear to be using birth control, many delay using contraception until several months after they become sexually active.

F.   <u>Sexual Violence</u>

1.   The women's movement has been successful in identifying and raising public awareness about the problems of rape, incest and other forms of sexual coercion and violence.

2.   Sexual violence is a form of power relations that is shaped by the social inequality between men and women.

3.   One common but underreported form of sexual coercion is *date rape*, which occurs when a woman is forced to have unwanted sexual relations with someone she knows. Date rape is especially common on college campuses.

4.   Black, Hispanic, and poor women are more likely to be victimized by some forms of violence, indicating that violence is tied to the social status of diverse groups.

PRACTICE TEST

MULTIPLE CHOICE QUESTIONS

1. Sociologists generally agree that sexual identity:
   a. develops in early childhood and changes little over one's lifetime.
   b. is the driving force behind all human activities.
   c. is biologically or genetically determined at birth.
   d. None of the above statements are true.

2. According to Vasquez, men who disdain sports, work in personal service occupations such as hairdresser, or dress in ways considered feminine are at risk for assault because they engage in:
   a. compulsory heterosexuality.
   b. homosexuality.
   c. gender betrayal.
   d. sexual violation.

3. The sexual revolution in the United States contributed to which of the following?
   a. increased use of birth control
   b. greater public acceptance of sex as a normal part of social development
   c. increased percentage of people who have sexual intercourse before marriage
   d. All of the above are true.

4. The scientific study of sex and sexuality is:
   a. eugenics.
   b. sexology.
   c. anatomy.
   d. genderology.

5. Which theorist argued that sexual expression begins in childhood and develops over the life course through several stages of psychosexual development?
   a. Sigmund Freud
   b. Havelock Ellis
   c. Alfred Kinsey
   d. Janet Lee

6. The first major national surveys of sexual behavior in the United States in the 1940s and 1950s were published by:
   a. Alfred Kinsey.
   b. Havelock Ellis.
   c. Sigmund Freud.
   d. Virginia Johnson.

7. The researcher who conducted a 1990 study investigating the genetic basis of homosexuality by comparing the brains of deceased men was:
   a. William Masters.
   b. Sigmund Freud.
   c. Alfred Kinsey.
   d. Simon LeVay.

8. According to the Masters and Johnson studies of sexual behavior in the United States:
   a. men and women experience sex and sexual pleasure in radically different ways.
   b. any sexual behavior other than heterosexual, monogamous sexuality is "sexual deviance."
   c. men are more sexually and psychologically mature than women.
   d. None of the above statements are consistent with their research findings.

9. Young children learn what is appropriate sexual behavior for people of their gender from sexual:
   a. activities.
   b. politics.
   c. scripts.
   d. revolutions.

10. According to Laumann and colleagues' study of sexual practices in the United States:
    a. a large percentage of Americans have sexual intercourse before marriage.
    b. Americans are very well informed about sex.
    c. relatively few Americans have extramarital affairs.
    d. All of the above statements are true.

11. Which of the following is **not** one of the new forms of technology that has removed the necessity of biological parents from reproduction?
    a. cloning
    b. selective abortion
    c. genetic engineering
    d. gene splicing

12. Which of the following statements about teenage pregnancy is (are) true?
    a. Teen pregnancy is strongly correlated with poverty, low educational attainment, and increased health problems for both the mother and her baby.
    b. The United States has the higher rate of teenage pregnancy than any other industrialized country.
    c. An increasing number of teenagers are using birth control, but they often delay using contraception until several months after they become sexually active.
    d. All of the above statements are true.

13. Conflict theorists view sexuality and sexual relations as:
    a. linked to other forms of subordination that associate sex with power.
    b. contributing to the stability of social institutions such as the family.
    c. natural behavior that manifests itself similarly across societies.
    d. None of the above statements are consistent with conflict theory.

14. According to the Gallup Poll, more than half of all Americans believe that abortion should be:
    a. illegal in all circumstances.
    b. legal in all circumstances.
    c. legal only in certain circumstances.
    d. completely unregulated by the government.

15. Sexual politics in the United States are reflected in:
    a.   the exploitation of women as prostitutes.
    b.   high rates of interpersonal violence among heterosexual couples.
    c.   the advertising industry's use women as sexual objects.
    d.   All of the above are reflections of sexual politics.

16. Sexual _____ refers to how individuals experience sexual arousal and pleasure.
    a.   identity
    b.   orientation
    c.   script
    d.   association

17. According to the social constructionist perspective, which of the following identities are learned through the process of socialization?
    a.   heterosexuality
    b.   homosexuality
    c.   bisexuality
    d.   All sexual identities are learned according to this perspective.

18. Adrienne Rich argues that institutions define heterosexuality as the only legitimate form of sexual identity and enforce this definition through social norms and sanctions. She refers to this concept as:
    a.   compulsory heterosexuality.
    b.   double standard.
    c.   coming out.
    d.   pervasive homophobia.

19. Coming out:
    a.   refers to the process of publicly defining oneself as gay or lesbian.
    b.   occurs at a single moment in time when an individual recognizes that he or she has a gay identity.
    c.   rarely poses psychological or social difficulties for the individual completing the process.
    d.   All of the above statements are true.

20. Defining heterosexuality as the only legitimate sexual orientation and granting certain privileges to those presumed to be heterosexual is defined as:
    a.   sexual scripting.
    b.   double standard.
    c.   heterosexism.
    d.   homophobia.

21. A common but underreported form of sexual violence on college campuses today is:
    a.   genital mutilation.
    b.   date rape.
    c.   female infanticide.
    d.   body piercing.

22. The 1995 report concerning non-marital pregnancy in the United States that was presented to Congress by a group of sociologists provided evidence that:
    a.   the majority of out-of-wedlock births are to Black women.
    b.   unmarried couples experiencing a pregnancy today are just as likely to marry as similar couples twenty-five years ago.
    c.   poorly educated men and women are less likely than better educated men and women to marry but not less likely to have children.
    d.   All of the above statements about pregnancy outside marriage are true.

23. Eugenics refers to the:
    a.   development of reproductive technology that allows previously infertile couples to have children.
    b.   application of scientific principles of genetic selection to efforts aimed at "improving" the human species.
    c.   scientific study of human sexual response and behavior.
    d.   development of medical technology that improves people's sensitivity to sexual stimulation and heightens their sexual pleasure.

24. Which of the following statements about abortion is (are) true?
    a.   Prior to 1973, only married women had a legal right to abortion in the U.S., but after 1973, unmarried women were granted the same right.
    b.   The abortion rate has increased steadily since 1973 when the U.S. Supreme Court issued a new decision concerning abortion rights.
    c.   Black women are more likely than White women to have abortions.
    d.   All of the above are true.

25. The birth control pill:
    a.   is a widely used form of contraception in the United States.
    b.   was approved by the Food and Drug Administration (FDA) in 1950.
    c.   has always been legally available to women regardless of their marital status.
    d.   All of the above statements are true.

TRUE-FALSE QUESTIONS

1.   Social institutions, including the family, religion, and the law, define some forms of sexual experience as more legitimate than other forms.

2.   Poor women and women who receive welfare have a very high rate of sterilization.

3.   Women are more likely than men to have their first sexual experience in the context of a romantic relationship.

4.   Proponents of eugenics blame social problems such as crime on the structural arrangements in society that prevent some groups from having equal access to education and jobs.

5.   Nearly half of the states in the U.S. have hate crime laws that include crimes committed against people because of their sexual orientation.

6.   Most sociological research concerning sexuality relies on self-reported data about sexual practices because survey data about sexual attitudes is so unreliable.

7. A major factor contributing to the spread of AIDS worldwide is the international sex trade, which includes the sale of sex to promote tourism.

8. Although advertisers commonly utilized condescending and degrading images of women in the past, significant changes have occurred since the sexual revolution that ended this practice.

9. American men report having sexual intercourse for the first time at a considerably younger age than do American women.

10. Most states in the U.S. now grant homosexual couples the right to legally register their union and receive the same benefits as heterosexual married couples.

FILL IN THE BLANK QUESTIONS

1. The pervasive fear and hatred of homosexuality in American society is referred to as _____.

2. Sexual _____ teach us what is appropriate behavior for our gender, such as norms about marriage.

3. Because gay and lesbian people are perceived to have a similar characteristic that serves as the basis for denying them equal rights in society, sociologists categorize them as a _____ group.

4. The Supreme Court granted people the legal right to _____ in the 1973 Supreme Court case, *Roe v. Wade*.

5. The _____ are a religious community of men in India who are born male but come to define themselves as neither men nor women.

ESSAY QUESTIONS

1. Explain how the Internet has introduced new forms of sexual relations into society and discuss the potential consequences of cybersex for people who engage in it.
2. Explain how Janet Lee's research on menstruation illustrates the significance of cultural expectations on women's experiences of physiological processes.
3. Explain why the *international sex trade* is flourishing in countries such as Thailand.
4. Summarize the findings of LeVay's research into the biological basis of homosexuality and identify the three main criticisms that scholars have raised about this study.
5. Compare and contrast how functionalist and conflict theorists' views of sex and sexuality in the United States.

ANSWERS TO PRACTICE TEST

Answers to Multiple Choice Questions

1. D. 176 Sexual identity is one component of self-identity. It continues to develop over one's life course, rather than being fixed at birth, and is constructed within one's cultural and social context.
2. C. 193 Men and women who do not conform to strict social definitions of

masculinity and femininity are perceived as engaging in gender betrayal, which increases the likelihood that they will be victims of hate crimes according to Carmen Vasquez.

3.   D.   181   The widespread changes in men's and women's roles, a greater public acceptance of sexuality as a normal part of social development, an increase in the use of birth control, and an increase in the incidence of premarital sex for men and women are all consequences of the sexual revolution.

4.   B.   178   Sexology, the scientific study of sex and sexuality, brought profound changes to our understanding of sexuality.

5.   A.   178   Freud presented a development stage model of sexuality and argued that sexual expression begins in childhood.

6.   A.   179   Kinsey published the first national surveys of sexual behavior in the in the United States in the 1940s and 1950s.

7.   D.   190   LeVay concluded that there are anatomical differences in homosexual and heterosexual men's brains, thus, there is a genetic basis for sexual orientation. His study was widely criticized for its small sample and unclear methodology.

8.   D.   180   Masters and Johnson found that men and women experience sex and sexual pleasure in similar ways. Ellis viewed only heterosexual, monogamous sex as normal. Freud viewed men as more sexually and psychologically mature than women.

9.   C.   177   Sexual scripts teach us what is appropriate sexual behavior for people of our gender. Children practice these scripts through play.

10.   A.   185   According to Laumann and colleagues' recent study, young people are becoming sexually active earlier, Americans are not very well informed about sex, a significant number of people have extramarital affairs, and few people have just one sexual partner in their lifetimes.

11.   B.   196   Genetic engineering, cloning, and gene splicing allow scientists to create new life in a laboratory without sexual activity occurring between a man and a woman.

12.   D.   199   Teenage pregnancy rates in the U.S. are higher than other industrialized nations and are correlated with low educational attainment, joblessness, poverty, and maternal and infant health problems.

13.   A.   189   Conflict theorists view sexuality as intertwined with race, class, and gender inequality and the power relations in society. Functionalist theorists view sexuality in terms of how it contributes to the stability of society.

14.   C.   197   According to national polls, 59 percent of Americans think abortion should be legal in certain circumstances (see figure 7.4).

15.   D.   182   Sexual politics are reflected in the sexual exploitation of women in society, high rates of violence against women, and treatment of women as sexual objects, which are consequences of the link between power and sexuality, race, class, and gender oppression according to feminists.

16.   B.   191   How individuals experience sexual arousal and pleasure is their sexual orientation. Sexual orientation is generally classified as heterosexual, homosexual, or bisexual.

17.   D.   190   All sexual identities are learned through the process of socialization according to social constructionists.

18.   A.   192   Adrienne Rich argues that institutions define heterosexuality as the

only legitimate form of sexual identity and enforce it through social norms and sanctions. This concept is *compulsory heterosexuality*.

19.	A.	192	Coming out is the process of publicly defining oneself as gay or lesbian and involves a series of events and redefinitions in which a person comes to see himself or herself as having a gay identity. It is often a difficult process for the individual.
20.	C.	194	Heterosexism refers to the institutionalized practice of granting certain rights only to heterosexual people and presuming that heterosexuality is the only legitimate form of sexual identity.
21.	B.	200	Date rape is forced, unwanted sexual relations with someone whom the victim knows, and is common on college campuses. Genital mutilation and infanticide are more common in other countries than in the U.S., and body piercing is a voluntary activity, not a form of sexual violence.
22.	C.	201	This report indicates that the majority of non-marital births are to White women, teenagers have a disproportionate number of non-marital births, and unmarried couples are less likely to marry today than in the past when facing a pregnancy. Lower-educated and lower-income people are less likely to marry, but not less likely to have children.
23.	B.	196	Eugenics sought to apply scientific principles of genetic selection to "improve" the offspring of the human race.
24.	C.	197	Black and Hispanic women are more likely than White women to have abortions. The 1973 Supreme Court case, *Roe v. Wade*, made abortion legal regardless of a woman's marital status. The abortion rate in the U.S. declined somewhat during the1990s.
25.	A.	196 .	The availability of birth control in the U.S. is less debated now than in the past. The birth control pill, a widely used form of contraception in the U.S., was approved by the FDA in 1960 but did not become legally available to unmarried women until 1972.

Answers to True-False Questions

1.	T.	177	Sexual scripts teach us what is appropriate behavior for our gender.
2.	T.	178	Poor women and welfare recipients have a high rate of sterilization.
3.	T.	179	Freud argued that the libido, or sexual energy, was the driving force behind all human activities.
4.	F.	196	Proponents of eugenics blame social problems on the presumed inferior genetic makeup of some groups.
5.	T.	195	Twenty-two states and the District of Columbia have hate crime laws including crimes motivated by the sexual orientation of the victim.
6.	F.	185	Most sociological surveys investigate sexual attitudes because self-reported data about sexual practices is unreliable.
7.	T.	189	The international sex trade contributes to the spread of AIDS.
8.	F.	183	There is more commercialized sex today. Sex is defined as a commodity and advertisers use men an women to sell products.
9.	F.	185	Sexual activity among older male and female teenagers is quite common. Both men and women are likely to have sexual intercourse before marriage and to have more than one partner in their lifetimes.
10.	F.	195	Unlike most states, Vermont passed a law allowing gay and lesbian couples to marry in 2000; however, the U.S. Congress passed a law in 1996 allowing states the right not to recognize same-sex marriages.

Answers to Fill in the Blank Questions

1.	homophobia	193
2.	scripts	177
3.	minority	195
4.	abortion	197
5.	Hijras	176

CHAPTER 8
DEVIANCE

BRIEF CHAPTER OUTLINE
Defining Deviance
      Sociological Perspectives on Deviance
      Biological Explanations of Deviance
      Psychological Explanations of Deviance
Sociological Theories of Deviance
      Functionalist Theories of Deviance
      Conflict Theories of Deviance
      Symbolic Interaction Theories of Deviance
Forms of Deviance
      Mental Illness
      Social Stigmas
Deviance in Global Perspective

QUESTIONS TO GUIDE YOUR READING
1. Why do sociologists emphasize the social context in understanding deviant behavior?
2. What is the *medicalization of deviance* and why do sociologists find it problematic?
3. How do social movements influence changes in the classification and management of certain behaviors as deviant?
4. How do race, class, and gender shape perceptions of, reactions to, and participation in deviant behavior?
5. What are the main forms of deviance and how are they classified by sociologists?

KEY TERMS (defined at page number shown and in glossary)

KEY PEOPLE (identified at page number shown)

CHAPTER OUTLINE
From a sociological perspective, any deviance, including cannibalism, resides not in the act itself but in the social context in which it occurs. Social attitudes and beliefs contribute to the number of people who violate specific norms, as well as the way in which society's members respond to deviance.

I. DEFINING DEVIANCE

Sociologists define **deviance** as behavior that is recognized as violating expected rules and norms. Sociological understandings of deviance stress social context, not individual behavior, recognizing that established rules and norms are socially created, rather than morally decreed or individually imposed. All groups do not judge all behaviors similarly, and some groups have more power than others to define behaviors as deviant.

A. Sociological Perspectives on Deviance
   1. Sociologists distinguish between formal and informal deviance.
      a. *Formal deviance* is behavior that breaks laws or official rules, such as crime. There are formal sanctions, such as fines and imprisonment, for violations of formal deviance.
      b. *Informal deviance* is behavior that violates customary norms, such as body piercing.
   2. The Context of Deviance
      a. Behavior that is deviant in one circumstance may be normal in another, or behaviors may be ruled deviant only when performed by certain people.
      b. The definition of deviance can also vary over time, which is reflected in the criminalization of date rape.
   3. Emile Durkheim argued that deviance is "functional" for society.
      a. Because the social order is threatened by deviance, judging and punishing deviant acts confirms general social standards. Thus, public executions and publicized trials reinforce the social order and inhibit future deviance.
      b. Deviance helps define normal behavior and produces social solidarity by integrating people into society. This was illustrated by the social support the public showed for stoning two adulterers in Afghanistan in 1996.
   4. The Influence of Social Movements
      a. Perceptions of deviance may be influenced by *social movements*, or networks of groups that organize to support or resist changes in society, such as reducing the social acceptance of smoking.
      b. Groups such as MADD (Mothers Against Drunk Driving) have changed public perceptions of drunk driving. Both legal penalties and social stigmas for drunk drivers have increased.
      c. Social movements such as the gay and lesbian movement can organize to remove the deviant label from certain behaviors, such as homosexuality.
      d. *Moral entrepreneurs* are people who organize a social movement to reform how a behavior is perceived and managed by society.
         1) Moral reformers in the 1920s, known as "child savers," campaigned for juvenile offenders to receive rehabilitation, not punishment.
         2) Modern moral entrepreneurs who are "tough on crime" advocate more severe punishments for juvenile offenders.
   5. Deviance as Social Behavior
      a. Certain widespread behaviors, even illegal ones, are often not considered deviant and are seldom punished.

     b.   Sometimes the majority of a population may engage in deviance, even extreme deviance, such as the Nazi Holocaust.

     c.   People commonly think that deviance is irrational behavior, but it may be a positive adaptation to a situation. For example, in a society where profit and material affluence are prized, selling drugs may be seen as a way to achieve the American dream.

     d.   Deviant behavior often occurs or increases because of the social support it receives from the group in which it develops. This may include cheating in school, where students know it is wrong but assume that everyone does it.

     e.   Some behavioral patterns defined as deviant are similar to normal behavior. For example, a business executive may spend all of his extra income on alcohol but not be defined as deviant.

     f.   Sociologists who study deviance understand it in the context of social relationships and social arrangements and argue that it is not just weird, pathological, or irrational behavior.

B.   <u>Biological Explanations of Deviance</u>

    1.   Early biological explanations of crime were often linked to racist and sexist explanations of group differences and tended to be popular during periods of widespread social change.

    2.   Lombroso is credited with the introduction of scientific measurement in the study of crime and deviance; however, racism and sexism were evident in his ideas.

    3.   Wilson and Herrnstein argue that there may be a biological predisposition to crime. They assert that crime is usually committed by people with low IQs and psychological impairments that prevent them from deferring gratification or resisting the impulse to commit crime.

    4.   Biological theories generally ignore deviant acts committed by middle and upper class people, such as embezzlement.

    5.   Sociologists criticize biological theories for oversimplifying and distorting the social processes that influence the development and labeling of deviance.

C.   <u>Psychological Explanations of Deviance</u>

    1.   Psychological explanations for deviance emphasize individual factors as the underlying cause of deviant behavior. Sociologists argue that these explanations overlook the context in which deviance is produced.

    2.   According to sociologists, the **medicalization of deviance** refers to the popularity of explanations of deviant behavior that interpret deviance as the result of individual pathology or sickness. This approach emphasizes the physical or genetic roots of deviant behavior.

     a.   Although alcoholism has medical consequences, the social relationships, social conditions, and social habits of alcoholics must be altered to change their behavior.

     b.   Attention Deficit Disorder (ADD) seems to have physiological causes, but there may also be environmental origins for this behavior, including the overstimulation of modern life.

     c.   Sociologists are critical of the medicalization of deviance for ignoring the effects of social structures on the development of deviant behavior.

II. SOCIOLOGICAL THEORIES OF DEVIANCE

A. Functionalist Theories of Deviance

Functionalist theory interprets all parts of society, including deviance, as contributing to the stability of the whole. Deviance, for example, creates social cohesion, clarifies society's norms, and affirms the collective identity of the group when those who are defined as deviant are punished.

1. Durkheim: The Study of Suicide

   a. Durkheim viewed deviance as functional for society because it produces solidarity among society's members.

   b. Durkheim increased social knowledge through his analysis of suicide, in which he criticized psychological interpretations of suicide and instead developed sociological explanations that emphasized the role of social structure in producing deviance.

   c. Durkheim investigated causes of suicide related to time and place, rather than emotional stress, and identified the importance of social attachments in preventing or producing deviant behavior such as suicide.

   d. Durkheim analyzed three types of suicide: anomic suicide, altruistic suicide, and egoistic suicide.

      1) **Anomie** is the condition which exists when social regulations in a society breakdown so that people exist in a state of relative normlessness. **Anomic suicide** occurs when the disintegrating forces in society make individuals feel lost or all alone. For example, suicides by students on college campuses are often traced to feelings of loneliness and hopelessness. In contrast, the low incidence of suicide among Navajos, which is unusual among American Indians, may be related to Navajo cultural values that strongly integrate members into the group.

      2) **Altruistic suicide** occurs when there is excessive regulation of individuals by social forces. For example, the suicides of Buddhist monks who protested the Vietnam War were altruistic.

      3) **Egoistic suicide** occurs when people feel totally detached from society. For example, the high rate of suicide among elderly (75-84 years old) men in the United States, who often have lost work roles and have weakened ties to family and community, may be egoistic. Likewise, the higher rates of suicide for unmarried persons may reflect their weaker social integration compared to married persons.

   e. Durkheim's concept of anomie has implications beyond suicide. Although anomie is reflected in how individuals feel, its origins are in society, where there may be unclear or conflicting norms. Anomie is related to a variety of social problems, including juvenile delinquency.

2. Merton: Structural Strain Theory
   a. Merton's **structural strain theory** traces the origins of deviance to the tensions caused by the gap between cultural goals and the means people have to achieve those goals.
   b. Societies are characterized by both *culture* and *social structure*.
      1) Culture establishes goals for both people and society.
      2) Social structure provides, or fails to provide, the means for people to achieve these goals.
      3) When the means are out of balance with the goals, deviance is likely to occur.
   c. Merton categorized individuals by how they adapt to social systems.
      1) *Social conformists* accept the goals and means.
      2) *Innovators* accept the goals but not the means. They develop creative, although illegitimate, means to achieve the goals set by society, such as theft.
      3) *Ritualists* accept the means but not the goals. They engage in socially legitimate behavior, but have no sense of purpose or direction, such as many bureaucrats.
      4) *Retreatists* accept neither the goals nor the means and include skid row alcoholics and hard core drug addicts.
      5) The *politically rebellious* reject the goals and the means of society, but substitute other goals and means.
   d. Cloward and Ohlin elaborated on Merton's theory, arguing that deviance results from *both* being blocked from legitimate means for achieving goals *and* having accessibility to illegitimate means. This theory helps explain the rise of organized crime in the United States during the 1920s.
3. Social Control Theory
   a. Social control theory, developed by Travis Hirschi, posits that deviance occurs when an individual's or group's attachment to social bonds is weakened.
   b. This theory assumes there is a common value system within society and breaking one's allegiance to that value system is the source of social deviance.
   c. This theory can be used to explain men's higher crime rate, because men appear to be socialized to be more aggressive and take more risks than women.
4. Functionalism: Strengths and Weaknesses
   a. Functionalists emphasize that social structure, not just individual motivation, produces deviance. Although individuals choose to behave in a deviant manner, they make their choices from among socially structured options. What appears to be dysfunctional behavior may actually be functional for society.
   b. Critics of functionalism argue that it does not explain how norms of deviance are established and does little to explain why some behaviors are defined as normative and others as illegitimate.

     1) Functionalists tend to overlook the injustices that labeling someone as deviant can produce.

     2) Functionalists rarely consider the different effects that the administration of justice has for various groups.

B. Conflict Theories of Deviance

  1. *Conflict theory* emphasizes the unequal distribution of power and resources in society.

    a. Conflict theory sees the dominant class as controlling societal resources and using its power to create values and belief systems that support its power.

    b. This theory posits that the economic organization of capitalist societies produces deviance and crime.

    c. **Elite deviance** (or corporate crime) refers to the wrongdoing of wealthy and powerful individuals and organizations.

    d. Due to the social class of people who commit *white-collar crime*, most elite deviance provokes little public reaction.

    e. According to conflict theory, the ruling groups in society develop mechanisms to protect their interests, such as the law.

    f. This theory emphasizes the significance of **social control**, or the process by which groups are brought into conformity with dominant social expectations.

    g. *Social control agents* are those who regulate and administer the responses to deviance, such as police and health workers.

    h. When powerful groups hold stereotypes about other groups, the less powerful people are frequently assigned deviant labels.

  2. Conflict Theory: Strengths and Weaknesses

    a. The strength of conflict theory is its insight into the significance of power relationships for the definition, identification, and handling of deviance.

    b. Critics argue that laws protect most people, not just the wealthy. Although conflict theory offers a powerful analysis of the origins of crime, it is less effective in explaining other forms of deviance, such as delinquency among middle class adolescents.

C. Symbolic Interaction Theories of Deviance

Symbolic interaction theory argues that people behave as they do because of the meanings people attribute to situations.

  1. W.I. Thomas and the Chicago School

    a. Thomas explained deviance as a *normal response to the social conditions in which people find themselves.*

    b. He used *situational analysis* to understand deviant behavior within its social framework. For example, he explained delinquency as a result of the social disorganization brought on by slum life and urban industrialism.

  2. Differential Association Theory

    a. **Differential association theory**, developed by Edwin Sutherland, interprets deviance as learned through interaction with others.

    b. This theory offers a powerful explanation for how deviance is culturally transmitted and how people pass on deviant expectations through the social groups in which they interact.

c.   Critics of differential association theory argue that it tends to blame deviance on the values of particular groups.

3.   Labeling Theory

   a.   **Labeling Theory** interprets the responses of others as the most significant factor in understanding how deviant behavior is created and sustained.

   b.   A *label* is the assignment of a role to a person by a powerful social institution. Labeling theory shows how those with the power to label an act or a person as deviant impose sanctions.

   c.   Labeling theory identifies three types of deviance.

      1)   **Primary deviance** is the actual violation of a norm or law, such as cheating on a test.

      2)   **Secondary deviance** is the behavior that results from being labeled deviant. Reiman argues that the prison system socializes prisoners into a career of deviance.

      3)   **Tertiary deviance** occurs when the deviant accepts the deviant role, but rejects the stigma associated with it, as when lesbians or gays proudly display their identity.

4.   Deviant Identity

   a.   **Deviant identity** is the definition a person has of himself or herself as deviant.

   b.   The formation of a deviant identity involves a process of social transformation that occurs over time and results from the person who was labeled as deviant taking on a personal identity consistent with the label.

5.   Deviant Careers

   a.   **Deviant career** is the sequence of movements people make through a particular subculture of deviance.

   b.   Within deviant careers, people are socialized into new roles and may have to demonstrate their commitment to superiors.

   c.   Social responses and labeling may be seen as a rite of passage, thereby reinforcing one's commitment to a deviant career.

6.   Deviant Communities

   a.   **Deviant communities** are groups that are organized around a particular form of deviance, such as Alcoholics Anonymous.

   b.   Joining a deviant community can shut one off from conventional society and solidify a deviant career.

   c.   Some deviant communities, such as Al Anon, are organized specifically to provide support to those presumed to be in deviant categories.

7.   The Problem with Official Statistics
Official rates of deviance are produced by people in the social system who define, classify, and record only certain behaviors as deviant; thus, the death of one person may be classified as a "suicide" while the similar death of another person may be classified as an "accident."

8.   Labeling Theory: Strengths and Weaknesses

   a.   The strength of labeling theory is its recognition that social definitions about presumably deviant behavior have powerful social effects.

   b.   Two problems with labeling theory are that it neglects to explain why deviance occurs in the first place, and it fails to

126

explain why officials define some behaviors as deviant or criminal, but not others.

III. FORMS OF DEVIANCE

The sociology of deviant behavior has focused heavily on subjects like mental illness, social stigmas, and crime. Race, class, and gender structure these different forms of deviance.

A. Mental Illness

1. Sociological explanations of mental illness examine the social systems in which mental illness is defined, identified, and treated.

2. Sociologists have found that persons from the lower classes, women, and racial minorities are more likely to be labeled mentally ill.

a. It may be that the stress associated with being lower-income, a woman, or a member of a racial minority contributes to increased rates of mental illness.

b. It may be that some behavior that is labeled mental illness for some groups is tolerated in others, or defined as "eccentric."

c. Mental illness as a cause of homelessness is not as pervasive as is popularly believed; however, the stress of homelessness may produce mental illness.

B. Social Stigmas

1. A **stigma** is an attribute that is socially devalued and discredited, such as a physical disability.

2. A physical disability can become the **master status** for a person, or the characteristic that overrides all other features of their identity.

3. According to Erving Goffman, people with stigmas are perceived as having a *spoiled identity* that is inferior to the presumed norm.

4. Stigmatized individuals may attempt to hide their stigmas by "passing," or trying to appear like members of the non-deviant majority, such as gay men who "stay in the closet" rather than reveal themselves as gay.

5. The term **hate crime** is used to refer to crimes (such as physical assault) committed against members of stigmatized groups.

IV. DEVIANCE IN GLOBAL PERSPECTIVE

Crime and deviance increasingly cross national borders. Technological developments that have eased communication and transportation for legitimate business activities have also enabled illegal activities to thrive. For example, many nations participate in the international drug trade as consumers (the United States), major drug producers (Columbia), and conduits for drug traffic (Mexico).

PRACTICE TEST

Multiple Choice Questions

1. Which of the following statements about deviance is (are) true?

a. Sociological definitions of deviance emphasize social context rather than individual behavior.

b. Biological definitions of deviance recognize that not all groups perceive or judge deviance in the same ways.

c. Medical definitions of deviance recognize that established rules and norms are socially created, rather than morally decreed or individually imposed.

d. All of the above statements are true.

2. Behavior that breaks laws or official rules is _____ deviance.
   a. elite
   b. formal
   c. informal
   d. situational

3. Networks of groups, such as MADD and SADD, that develop to support or resist changes in society through organized activities constitute social:
   a. rebels.
   b. conformists.
   c. movements.
   d. structures.

4. Biological theories of deviance generally:
   a. overemphasize how many deviant acts are committed by middle and upper class people.
   b. exaggerate or distort the influence of economic and political systems on the classification and labeling of deviance.
   c. stress the influence of genetic intelligence and psychological impairments on the tendency to commit crimes and other deviant acts.
   d. stress that some forms of deviance are functional for society because they reinforce social norms.

5. Criminologist Joel Best argues that crimes such as "wilding" and "road rage" are completely:
   a. random acts of violence.
   b. patterned, predictable social phenomena.
   c. unrelated to the class, race, ethnicity, age, and other social characteristics of the perpetrators and victims.
   d. exaggerated by the media and not really that "horrible."

6. The condition that exists when social regulations break down in a society and people exist in a state of relative normlessness is:
   a. crime.
   b. anomie.
   c. altruism.
   d. deviance.

7. The type of suicide that occurs when people feel detached from society, which characterizes many suicides among elderly men in the U.S., is _____ suicide.
   a. egoistic
   b. anomic
   c. altruistic
   d. egalitarian

8. According to Robert Merton, individuals who accept both the goals and means of their society are:
   a. conformists.
   b. innovators.
   c. retreatists.
   d. ritualists.

9. Sutherland interprets deviant behavior as learned through interaction with others, the basic assumption of _____ theory.
    a.   social labeling
    b.   social control
    c.   deviant contact
    d.   differential association

10. When the deviant person accepts the deviant role but rejects the stigma associated with it, as when gay men proudly display their sexual identity, _____ deviance occurs.
    a.   primary
    b.   secondary
    c.   tertiary
    d.   elite

11. The sequence of movements people make through a particular subculture of deviance, which involves socialization into new roles, is their deviant:
    a.   career.
    b.   identity.
    c.   stigma.
    d.   community.

12. Merton classifies individuals who accept the goals of society but substitute illegitimate means for achieving them, such as prostitutes, as:
    a.   conformists.
    b.   innovators.
    c.   retreatists.
    d.   ritualists.

13. Bureaucrats who engage in socially legitimate behavior but have no overall purpose other than conformity to the rules are classified by Merton as:
    a.   conformists.
    b.   innovators.
    c.   retreatists.
    d.   ritualists.

14. Which theory explains crime as the result of economic inequality among groups and the inability of the poorest groups to access power and other resources?
    a.   symbolic interaction theory
    b.   functionalist theory
    c.   conflict theory
    d.   control theory

15. Criminal acts, such as embezzlement, that are committed by persons of high social status in the context of their occupations, are _____ crimes.
    a.   inside
    b.   personal
    c.   organized
    d.   white-collar

16. Functionalist theory posits that:
    a. social structure, not just individual motivation, produces deviance.
    b. people choose whether or not to behave in a deviant manner.
    c. what appears to be dysfunctional behavior may be functional for society.
    d. All of the above are basic assumptions of functionalist theory.

17. Which theory of deviance assumes there is a common value system within society and that deviance is the result of breaking one's allegiance to those values?
    a. symbolic interactionist theory
    b. social control theory
    c. social conflict theory
    d. social labeling theory

18. When a single characteristic overrides all other features of an individual's identity, such as a physical disability, it is referred to as a(n):
    a. differential status.
    b. elite identity.
    c. master status.
    d. deviant identity.

19. Deviant _____ maintain their own values, norms, and symbolic systems that promote their identity as a group.
    a. labels
    b. victims
    c. institutions
    d. communities

20. W.I. Thomas argued that juvenile delinquency was brought on by the social disorganization of slum life and urban industrialism, reflecting his assertion that:
    a. poor individuals are genetically predisposed to delinquent or criminal behavior.
    b. deviance is an irrational response to the development of capitalism.
    c. deviance is a normal response to the social conditions in which people find themselves.
    d. adolescents are psychologically impaired.

21. Which of the following groups of people suffer higher rates of *reported* mental illness?
    a. men
    b. women
    c. White people
    d. upper-class people

22. When a criminal is convicted, he is formally and publicly labeled a wrongdoer, thereby restricting his future options. This labeling process therefore produces _____ deviance.
    a. primary
    b. secondary
    c. tertiary
    d. cultural

23. Which role do nations such as the United States play in the international drug trade?
    a. conduits for drug traffic
    b. major drug producers
    c. major drug consumers
    d. money laundering locations

24. The actual violation of a norm, such as cheating on a test, is _____ deviance.
    a. primary
    b. secondary
    c. tertiary
    d. binary

25. A deviant _____ develops when a person undergoes a process of social transformation in which a new self-image and new public definition of the person as deviant emerges.
    a. identity
    b. career
    c. value
    d. role

TRUE-FALSE QUESTIONS

1. Labeling theory assumes there is a common value system within society and breaking one's allegiance to that value system is the main cause of deviant behavior.

2. Sociologists do not define binge drinking as deviant behavior because it is so common among young adults on college campuses.

3. Conflict theorists are critical of the medicalization of deviance because this approach ignores the effects of social structure on the development, definition, and treatment of deviant behavior.

4. According to Robert Merton, those individuals who reject both the norms and values of the society, such as hard-core drug addicts, are retreatists.

5. Functionalist theory views the dominant class as controlling societal resources and using its power to create values and belief systems that support that power.

6. Labeling theorists accept that the official rates of deviant behavior, such as suicide and deaths from AIDS, accurately reflect the actual incidence of such behavior.

7. A disproportionate amount of mental illness is found among racial minorities in the United States.

8. Mental illness is the primary cause of homelessness in the United States.

9. Durkheim suggested that altruistic suicide occurs when there is excessive regulation of individuals by social forces.

10. The northeast region of the United States has the highest suicide rate in the country.

FILL IN THE BLANK QUESTIONS

1. Goffman referred to an attribute that is socially devalued and discredited, such as a physical disability, as a social _____.

2. Body piercing is a good example of _____ deviance, a behavior that violates customary norms in society.

3. Stigmatized individuals, such as gay people, may attempt to hide their stigma by _____, or trying to appear the same as members of non-deviant groups, such as heterosexuals.

4. Teenage suicide, which is strongly linked to personal feelings of loneliness and to the breakdown of social regulations, is an example of _____ suicide.

5. Because men are less likely than women to be embedded in caring social relationships, men are more prone to _____ suicide.

ESSAY QUESTIONS

1. Compare and contrast how functionalist and conflict theorists would explain the issue of prostitution.
2. Identify the three types of suicide according to Emilie Durkheim, and use his analysis to explain why suicide rates are higher in Alaska and the Midwestern region of the United States than in other parts of the country.
3. Critique Wilson, Herrnstein, and Murray's study of the role of genes and IQ in criminal behavior using a sociological perspective on deviance.
4. Use labeling theory to explain why criminals in the U.S. have such high rates of recidivism and why prison does not seem to act as a deterrent to committing crime.
5. Explain why women, people in poverty, and racial minorities have higher rates of reported mental illness than do men, upper and middle class people, and White people.

ANSWERS TO PRACTICE TEST

Answers to Multiple Choice Questions

1.	A.	207	The sociological definition of deviance stresses social context rather than individual behavior. Biological and psychological explanations of deviance do not generally recognize that some groups have more power to judge behaviors as deviant, or that established rules and norms are socially created, rather than morally decreed or individually imposed.
2.	B.	206	Behavior that breaks laws or official rules is formal deviance.
3.	C.	208	Networks of groups that organize to support or resist changes in society are social movements. These movements can alter our perceptions, definitions, and treatment of deviance.
4.	C.	211	Biological theories of deviance and crime stress internal, genetic factors as the primary cause of deviant behavior, thus oversimplifying or distorting the social processes that influence the development and labeling of deviance.
5.	B.	210	Best argues that school shootings and road rage are horrible events; but rather than being random, they are patterned behaviors subject to the same social forces as other behavior in society.
6.	B.	213	Anomie develops when social regulations break down, leaving people

			in a state of relative normlessness that makes them feel lost or alone.
7.	A.	214	Egoistic suicide occurs when people feel detached from society and lack sufficient social bonds.
8.	A.	215	According to Robert Merton, individuals who accept both the goals and the means of society are conformists.
9.	D.	219	Differential association theory, developed by Edwin Sutherland, is associated with symbolic interactionism. It explains deviance as learned through interaction with others.
10.	C.	220	When the deviant accepts the deviant role but rejects the stigma associated with it, such as when lesbians or gays proudly display their identity, it is called tertiary deviance. Primary deviance occurs when an individual commits a deviant act. Secondary deviance results from the label attached to the deviant, whether or not s/he engages in deviance.
11.	A.	221	The sequence of movements people make through a particular subculture of deviance that involves socialization into new "occupational" roles is a deviant career.
12.	B.	215	According to Merton, innovators accept the goals of society but create alternative, often illegitimate, means to achieve those goals.
13.	D.	215	Ritualists engage in socially legitimate behavior without any sense of purpose. Retreatists reject both the goals and the means of society and become social pariahs, while the politically rebellious replace both the goals and the means of society with alternative goals and means.
14.	C.	217	Marx, a conflict theorist, argued that the hierarchical economic organization of capitalist societies produces deviance.
15.	D.	217	Elite deviance is committed primarily by high status professionals within the workplace. It is also referred to as white-collar crime.
16.	D.	216	Functionalist theory supports all of these assumptions.
17.	B.	216	According to social control theory, people internalize norms because of their attachment to social bonds and allegiance to a shared value system; thus, deviance is produced when social bonds are weakened and allegiance to those values is broken.
18.	C.	225	A physical disability, for example, can become a master status when other people see the disability as overriding all other features of identity for the person who has a disability.
19.	D.	222	Deviant communities, such as Alcoholics Anonymous, are organized around the deviance, and may socially isolate members from the larger society.
20.	C.	219	W.I. Thomas used situational analysis to understand deviant behavior within social frameworks. He saw deviance as resulting from particular social conditions.
21.	B.	223	Women, poor people, and racial minorities have the highest reported rates of mental illness and suffer from more serious disorders.
22.	B.	221	Secondary deviance results from being labeled as deviant. Even if an individual never engaged in deviant behavior, s/he may partially accept the role and subsequently behave in accordance with the label.
23.	C.	228	In the international drug trade, the United States and Australia are major drug consumers, Mexico and China are conduits for drug traffic, Columbia is a major drug producer, and Nigeria and Switzerland are sites for money laundering.
24.	A.	220	Primary deviance refers to engaging in deviant behavior, such as cheating on a test.

25.   A.   221   According to labeling theory, deviance is not just something one does, but something one becomes; thus, people who regularly engage in deviant behavior develop a deviant identity.

Answers to True-False Questions.

1.   F.   216   Social control theory assumes there is a common value system in society and breaking one's allegiance to that value system is the source of deviant behavior.

2.   F.   209   Although binge drinking is common, and sometimes encouraged, on college campuses, sociologists define it as deviant behavior because it violates expected rules and norms in society.

3.   T.   212   Sociologists criticize the medicalization of deviance for ignoring the effects of social structure on the development of deviant behavior.

4.   T.   215   According to Merton, retreatists such as hard-core drug addicts reject both the goals and the means; thus, they are viewed as social pariahs.

5.   F.   217   Conflict theorists emphasize the unequal distribution of economic resources and power in society to explain deviance.

6.   F.   222   Labeling theorists do not accept official statistics as accurate reflections of the actual incidence of deviant behavior such as suicide; rather, they see official statistics as reflecting social judgements about deviance.

7.   T.   223   Research indicates that women, poor people, and racial minorities suffer from higher rates of reported mental illness and more serious disorders than do men, wealthy people, and Whites.

8.   F.   213   Mental illnesses are less pervasive among homeless people than is popularly believed.

9.   T.   214   Altruistic suicide occurs when there is excessive regulation of individuals by social forces. An example of this is suttee, the Hindu practice of burning a woman with her deceased husband.

10.   F.   224   Suicide rates are highest in less densely populated states located in the far Midwestern region of the United States (see Map 8.1).

Answers to Fill in the Blank Questions

1.   stigma   225
2.   informal   207
3.   passing   226
4.   anomic   213
5.   egoistic   214

CHAPTER 9
CRIME AND CRIMINAL JUSTICE

BRIEF CHAPTER OUTLINE
Crime and Deviance
Types of Crime
>   Measuring Crime
>   Youth Gangs and Crime
>   Personal and Property Crime
>   Elite and White-Collar Crime

Crime and Organization
>   Organized Crime
>   State-Organized Crime
>   Organizational Crime and Deviance

Race, Class, Gender, and Crime
>   Race, Class, and Crime
>   Gender and Crime

Police, Courts, and the Law
>   The Policing of Minorities
>   Race and Sentencing
>   Prisons: Deterrence or Rehabilitation?
>   Courts, the Law, and Minorities
>   The Law and Social Change

Globalization and Crime

QUESTIONS TO GUIDE YOUR READING

1.   What are the two main sources of data that sociologists use to assess the prevalence of crime in the United States?
2.   What are the main similarities and differences between crimes committed by individual citizens, organized groups, government officials, and corporate employees?
3.   How do race, class, and gender systematically influence the commission of, and victimization by, crime in the United States?
4.   How has the law been used to reduce social injustices against minority groups in the United States?
5.   What kinds of crimes are especially likely to cross national borders today, and why?

KEY TERMS

crime 232

de facto segregation 248

elite crime 235

law 247

organizational crime and deviance 237

property crimes 234

state-organized crime 236

criminology 232

de jure segregation 248

index crimes 233

money laundering 250

personal crimes 234

racial profiling 243

victimization 233

CHAPTER OUTLINE

>   Crime is not simply a series of random acts, but a set of patterned and highly predictable phenomena. Race, social class, and gender play important roles in the occurrence of, and responses to, crime in the United States.

I. **CRIME AND DEVIANCE**

The concept of deviance in society is broad, encompassing many forms of behavior, both legal and illegal and ordinary and unusual. **Crime** is a form of deviance that violates specific criminal laws. **Criminology** is the study of crime from a social science perspective.

II. **TYPES OF CRIME**

In addition to violent crimes such as assault, there are other types of crime, such as embezzlement and gambling.

   A. Measuring Crime

   1. One type of crime data is provided by police departments to the Federal Bureau of Investigation (FBI), which publishes the data annually in the *Uniform Crime Reports*. These data show that crime overall has increased in the United States over the last twenty-five years.

   2. A second type of crime data measures **victimization**. These data are derived from surveying people about whether they have ever been the recipient of a criminal act. These surveys suggest that crime has been decreasing over the last twenty years.

   3. One-half to two-thirds of all crimes are *underreported*. Victims of forcible rape are especially unlikely to report the crime to police because they are often upset, embarrassed, or afraid.

   4. Police departments probably overestimate the occurrence of crimes because budget allocations depend on the incidence of crime.

   5. The *Uniform Crime Report* stresses **index crimes**, which are mostly "street" crimes such as robbery and drug dealing that are committed mainly by lower-income people, resulting in a biased picture that does not reflect "elite" crimes such as embezzlement.

   B. Youth Gangs and Crime

   1. Youth gangs have always been present in American cities, but today's gangs are more likely to be profit-oriented, engage in more serious crimes, and have unprecedented access to firearms.

   2. Sociologists such as Thrasher and Jankowski have noted that urban youth gangs are comprised of a group of young adults who create familial-like bonds, engage in criminal acts, protect their "turf" or territory, and require new members to undergo an initiation ritual such as engaging in a serious fight.

   3. Crimes committed by youths are usually termed juvenile delinquency. Juvenile offenders are classified in categories such as vagrancy, promiscuity, truancy, and incorrigibility, resulting in unequal treatment for juveniles depending on their race, ethnicity, class, and gender.

   C. Personal and Property Crime

   1. **Personal crimes** are classified by the *Uniform Crime Reports* as violent or non-violent crimes directed against people, including murder, aggravated assault, forcible rape, and robbery.

   2. **Property crimes** involve the theft or alteration of property without the threat of bodily harm and include burglary, auto theft, and arson.

   3. Although not listed in the FBI's serious crime index, *victimless crimes* are illicit activities in which there is no complainant, including illegal drug use, gambling, and prostitution.

   D. Elite and White-Collar Crime

   1. **Elite crime** refers to criminal activities by persons of high social status who commit their crimes in the context of their occupation.

2. Elite crimes, which include embezzlement and involvement in illegal stock manipulation, are also called white-collar crimes.

3. Despite their substantial financial cost to society, elite crimes generate little public concern and are the least prosecuted form of criminal activity.

III. **CRIME AND ORGANIZATION**

    A. Organized Crime

        1. *Organized crime* is committed by organized groups and typically involves the provision of illegal goods and services to others.

        2. Organized crime syndicates are often based on racial or ethnic membership, as well as family and kinship ties.

        3. Criminal industries such as drug trafficking and illegal gambling are typically organized along the same lines as legitimate businesses, with senior partners, workers, and clients.

        4. Organized crime in America has been resistant to attempts to control or eliminate it and continues to flourish despite media exposure and congressional investigations.

    B. State-Organized Crime

    State-organized crime is crime committed by state officials in the pursuit of their jobs as government representatives. An example of such crime is that the Central Intelligence Agency (CIA) sought assistance from mob criminals with a 1972 assassination attempt against Cuban president Fidel Castro.

    C. Organization Crime and Deviance

        1. **Organizational crime and deviance** is wrongdoing that occurs within the context of a formal organization and is sanctioned by the norms and operating principles of the organization.

        2. Individuals within an organization may participate in criminal behavior with little awareness that their actions are illegitimate.

        3. This form of activity is embedded in the routine activities of organizations and represents the *normalization* of deviance.

        4. An example of this type of deviance is that Beech Nut baby foods sold colored sugar water advertised as apple juice. The pursuit of higher profits led to organizational crime.

        5. Although organizations may be fined for violations, individuals are rarely punished for participation in organizational deviance.

IV. **RACE, CLASS, GENDER, AND CRIME**

    A. Race, Class, and Crime

        1. Arrest rates are strongly correlated with social class and poor people are more likely than others to be arrested for crimes.

            a. People who are economically deprived often see no alternative to crime so they commit more crimes than do others.

            b. Law enforcement is concentrated in lower-income and minority areas, so residents of these communities are under greater scrutiny and their crimes are more likely to be detected.

            c. When poor people are accused of crimes, they are more likely to be prosecuted, convicted, and sentenced to prison.

        2. There is also a strong correlation between race and crime.

            a. Although racial-ethnic minorities comprise 15 percent on the U.S. population, over one-third of people arrested for property crimes and nearly one-half of those arrested for violent crimes are members of minority groups.

b. African Americans and Hispanics are more than twice as likely to be arrested as Whites; however, Native Americans and Asian Americans have relatively low arrest rates.

c. Police discretion is greatest when dealing with minor offenses and discretion is strongly influenced by class and racial judgements, leading to increased arrests based on police perceptions of minorities as troublemakers.

d. Black and Latino juvenile offenders are treated more severely than their White peers in the justice system due to stereotypes held by prosecutors, judges, and other court personnel.

B. Gender and Crime

1. Despite some increases, the number of women arrested for crimes is relatively small compared to men, perhaps because they are socialized into less risk-taking roles.

2. Women most often commit crimes that seem to be extensions of their gender roles, including fraud, embezzlement, and prostitution.

3. Increases in women's criminal activity may be due to increased employment in jobs with opportunities for crimes, changing role expectations for women, and their continuing disadvantaged status in society.

4. Women are less likely to be victimized by crime than men; but Black women are more likely than White women to be victimized, and divorced, separated, and single women are more likely to be victimized than married women.

5. Women's fear of crime increases with age, although the likelihood of victimization decreases with age. For all women, victimization by rape is probably the greatest fear.

a. Over 100,000 rapes are reported to the police annually, although officials estimate that this probably reflects only 1 out of every 4 rapes committed.

b. Crimes of *family violence* such as spouse abuse illustrate the disadvantaged status of women in society.

V. **POLICE, COURTS, AND THE LAW**

One basic function of the state is the administration of justice. The most striking fact that stands out from sociological research on the legal system in the United States is the unequal treatment that different groups encounter when they enter it.

A. The Policing of Minorities

1. The police, along with the military, embody the state's right to use coercive force.

2. Minority communities are policed more heavily than are White neighborhoods, where police presence is generally reassuring.

3. Because police are more likely to use excessive, and even deadly, force against minority suspects, police presence in minority neighborhoods is often a terrifying experience.

4. **Racial profiling** refers to police officers' use of race alone as the criterion for deciding whether to stop and detain someone on suspicion of committing a crime.

B. Race and Sentencing

1. Upon arraignment, bail is set higher for African Americans and Latinos than for Whites, and minorities have less success in plea bargaining

2. Once at trial, minority defendants are found guilty more often than White defendants, and African American defendants receive longer sentences than do White Americans for property and violent crimes, especially when the victim is White.

3. There is strong evidence that the death penalty is applied unevenly based on race. After the Supreme Court declared this penalty discriminatory in 1972, there was a ban on executions, but the Supreme Court later upheld the death penalty in 1987.

C. Prisons: Deterrence or Rehabilitation?

1. In the late 1990s, over 5 million people were under correctional supervision (in jail, on probation, or on parole) in the U.S.

2. Racial minorities comprise more than half of the federal and state male prisoners in the U.S.

3. The U.S. and Russia have the highest rates of incarceration in the world, and the U.S. incarceration rate is rapidly increasing.

4. The privatization of prisons is a new trend in the U.S., where some prisons are now operated by private, for-profit companies.

5. A major reason for the growth in incarceration is the increased enforcement of drug offenses and the introduction of mandatory sentencing.

6. The number of women in prison is increasing at a faster rate than for men, although the numbers of women in prison are relatively small by comparison.

7. Women in prison face unique problems, in part because they are in a system designed for men and run mostly by men. One in four women entering prison is pregnant or has just given birth, and eighty percent of women entering prison are mothers.

8. If incarceration successfully deterred crime, then increasing the risk of imprisonment would lower the rate of crime; but this has not occurred in the case of drug offenses.

9. There is little evidence that the criminal justice system deters or rehabilitates offenders. In fact, sociologists Jeffrey Reiman contend that prisons socialize inmates into a career of crime rather than reducing crime, and reinforce a public image of crime as a threat from the poor and from minority groups.

D. Courts, the Law, and Minorities

1. The court system is a pivotal part of social control. Each state has its own guidelines and procedures for its court system, and the federal system has a specific hierarchical structure that determines which cases shall be heard at which level.

2. The role of all courts is to interpret and enforce the **law**, or the written guidelines that determine what is defined as right and wrong in society.

3. The specific role of the court system has been argued extensively. Social scientists debate whether the judiciary determines social values and imposes them on the public, or reacts to social pressures and enforces already existing values.

4. There is evidence that social factors such as the status of defendants and the wishes of powerful parties do sometimes influence the outcome of court decisions; however, appealing to the court system is also a primary avenue of recourse available to oppressed groups seeking justice.

5.	The overrepresentation of racial minorities as defendants and continuing problem of underrepresentation of minorities on juries contributes to an unjust court system.

E.	The Law and Social Change
1.	The landmark Supreme Court case, *Brown v. Board of Education of Topeka, Kansas* (1954) outlawed **de jure segregation**, or the legal segregation of public facilities such as schools and buses, thereby transforming race relations in the United States.
2.	**De facto segregation**, or segregation in practice, has persisted in the labor market, housing, and education.
3.	One area in which the courts have been influential in overtly directing social change has been in matters of equal opportunity.
a.	Affirmative Action is a legal principle designed to remedy past racial and gender discrimination by providing access to the benefits and opportunities historically reserved for White men.
b.	The 1963 Equal Pay Act mandated that employers provide equal wages to men and women when they perform equal work.
c.	The 1964 Civil Rights Act forbid discrimination in employment procedures and opportunities.
4.	The courts also make decisions that affect seemingly private aspects of life, including women's rights to contraception and abortion and equal legal protection for lesbians and gays.

## VI.	GLOBALIZATION AND CRIME
Crime now crosses international borders. The illegal drug trade and terrorism are two examples of the globalization of crime. International networks, such as the globalization of banking, have facilitated the development of other kinds of crimes as well, such as **money laundering**, a practice involving depositing cash gotten illegally into foreign banks to convert it into legal tender.

PRACTICE TEST

Multiple Choice Questions

1.	According to functionalist theory, crime results primarily from:
a.	institutions that have the authority to label people as criminals.
b.	individual genetic deficiencies and psychological impairments.
c.	structural strains within society and a need to clarify norms.
d.	class inequality that produces competition for social resources.

2.	Deviance is behavior that is recognized as violating:
a.	social norms.
b.	cultural practices.
c.	individual attitudes.
d.	personal beliefs.

3. The written set of guidelines that determine what is defined as right and wrong in society is the:
    a. government.
    b. ideology.
    c. democracy.
    d. law.

4. Which of the following factors increases the likelihood that a woman will engage in criminal behavior?
    a. experiencing sexual, emotional, or physical abuse
    b. being economically disadvantaged in the labor market
    c. being employed in a job that presents opportunities for financial gain through illegal means
    d. All of the above factors increase women's participation in crime.

5. According to the FBI, _____ crimes are assaults and other malicious acts directed against stigmatized groups such as gays and lesbians and racial minorities.
    a. psychotic
    b. random
    c. elite
    d. hate

6. Wrongdoing that occurs within the context of a formal organization and is sanctioned by the norms and operating principles of the organization, as in the case of Beech Nut selling colored water and labeling it as apple juice, constitutes:
    a. personal deviance.
    b. white-collar crime.
    c. organizational deviance.
    d. state-organized crime.

7. When members of the Central Intelligence Agency (CIA) sought assistance from members of the mob in an assassination attempt against Cuban president Fidel Castro, they committed:
    a. personal deviance.
    b. organizational deviance.
    c. white-collar crime.
    d. state-organized crime.

8. The FBI's *Uniform Crime Report* stresses what it calls _____ crimes, which are largely "street" crimes of a serious nature, such as robbery.
    a. elite
    b. index
    c. minority
    d. community

9. The crimes that women are most likely to commit include:
    a. sexual harassment and molestation.
    b. arson and armed robbery.
    c. fraud and embezzlement.
    d. assault and murder.

10. According to crime data derived from victimization surveys, crime has:
   a.   decreased over the last twenty years.
   b.   increased over the last twenty-five years.
   c.   stayed about the same for the last two decades.
   d.   It is not possible to assess whether crime has increased, decreased, or stayed the same from this data.

11. Criminology is the:
   a.   set of data collected by the FBI to assess the prevalence of crime in the U.S.
   b.   scientific study of the genetic causes of criminal behavior.
   c.   scientific study of the social causes and patterns of criminal behavior.
   d.   term used by the FBI to refer to crimes for which there is no complainant.

12. Criminal acts that are committed by persons of high social status in the context of their occupations, such as embezzlement, are defined as _____ crimes.
   a.   insider
   b.   personal
   c.   organized
   d.   white-collar

13. Ramiro Martinez's investigation of homicide among Latinos indicates that:
   a.   a higher poverty rate is strongly correlated with a higher homicide rate.
   b.   educational attainment is the strongest predictor of homicide for Latinos.
   c.   immigration to the U.S. weakens the importance of religion for Latinos, leading to participation in immoral behavior such as murder.
   d.   All of the above statements are supported by Martinez's research.

14. Which theory posits that social institutions such as prisons produce, rather than lessen, crime through their power to label deviance?
   a.   symbolic interaction theory
   b.   functionalist theory
   c.   conflict theory
   d.   naming theory

15. Compared to a lower-class youth, a middle-class youth who is convicted of the same offense is more likely to be:
   a.   fined.
   b.   sent to jail.
   c.   sent to reform school.
   d.   released into the custody of their families.

16. The 1954 Supreme Court case, *Brown v. Board of Education of Topeka, Kansas* stated:
   a.   it is illegal to pay men and women different wages for doing the same work.
   b.   executions should be stopped because the death penalty is discriminatory toward racial minorities.
   c.   racially segregating public facilities such as schools and buses is illegal.
   d.   states cannot pass laws that deny gays and lesbians equal protection under the law as provided by the Fourteenth Amendment to the Constitution.

17. The 1996 Supreme Court case, Romer v. Evans, stated that:
    a.   it is illegal to pay men and women different wages for doing the same work.
    b.   executions should be stopped because the death penalty is discriminatory toward racial minorities.
    c.   racially segregating public facilities such as schools and buses is illegal.
    d.   states cannot pass laws that deny gays and lesbians equal protection under the law as provided by the Fourteenth Amendment to the Constitution.

18. Which of the following crimes are classified as *personal crimes*?
    a.   larceny, auto theft, and arson
    b.   gambling and prostitution
    c.   assault, forcible rape, and murder
    d.   embezzlement and tax violations

19. Which of the following crimes are classified as *property crimes*?
    a.   larceny, auto theft, and arson
    b.   gambling and prostitution
    c.   assault, forcible rape, and murder
    d.   embezzlement and tax violations

20. Members of which of the following groups are most likely to be victimized by robbery and physical assault in the United States?
    a.   Black men
    b.   Black women
    c.   White men
    d.   White women

21. Which of the following nations has the highest rate of incarceration in the world?
    a.   Mexico
    b.   England
    c.   Australia
    d.   United States

22. Which of the following statements about rape in the U.S. is (are) true?
    a.   Over 100,000 rapes are reported to the police annually, yet rape is considered one of the most frequently underreported crimes.
    b.   Rape is a personal crime committed primarily by men suffering from sexual dysfunction or mental illness.
    c.   White women are more likely than Black women to be victimized by rape.
    d.   All of the above statements about rape are true.

23. Which of the following statements about policing in the United States is true?
    a.   There is ample evidence that police officers perceive Black and Hispanic men as "threats," regardless of what the men are actually doing.
    b.   Police officers are more likely to use excessive and deadly force against White suspects than against Black or Hispanic suspects.
    c.   Police officers are more likely to arrest and charge middle-class people than lower-income people because middle-class people consistently pay their fines, thereby generating more revenue for police departments.
    d.   Citizens cannot sue police departments even if they think that the police have stopped, detained, or arrested them because of their racial or ethnic status.

24. The increase in incarceration in the United States over the last twenty years is due to:
    a. increases in the number of female offenders.
    b. introduction of minimum mandatory sentences for drug crimes.
    c. more rigorous enforcement of laws pertaining to drug offenses.
    d. All of the above have contributed to increases in the prison population.

25. The rate of victimization by violent crime, including rape and aggravated assault, is highest for individuals at which annual income level?
    a. less than $15,000
    b. $15,000 to $35,000
    c. $35,000 to $75,000
    d. over $75,000

TRUE-FALSE QUESTIONS

1. Most factory workers, such as those employed by Beech Nut who labeled colored water as apple juice, are aware that their behavior is criminal but engage in such organizational deviance because they have strong loyalty to the company.

2. Because of extensive government investigations and considerable media exposure, organized crime networks in the United States lost most of their power and control over illegal businesses during the last twenty years.

3. Over sixty percent of the individuals arrested for arson, vandalism, and prostitution are White.

4. The privatization of prisons has been beneficial for prisoners, who are housed in safer, cleaner, less crowded facilities than are prisoners housed in state-operated facilities.

5. There is strong evidence that prisons serve a rehabilitative purpose for criminals, because more than half of the individuals incarcerated for drug offenses receive drug treatment while in prison.

6. There is little evidence that imprisonment deters crime, because there has been a marked increase in drug law enforcement but no significant decrease in drug use.

7. The majority of women in prison are mothers whose children are placed in foster care, left with relatives, or put up for adoption when their mothers are incarcerated.

8. Despite federal laws prohibiting racial segregation in public facilities, there is considerable racial segregation in housing, education, and employment today.

9. People convicted of killing White victims are three times more likely than people convicted of killing Black victims to get the death penalty.

10. Asian American men are the fastest growing minority group in U.S. prisons.

FILL IN THE BLANK QUESTIONS

1. Racial _____ refers to the common policing practice of using race as the sole criterion for stopping and detaining someone on suspicion of committing a crime.

2. Crime committed by youths is usually referred to as juvenile _____, which is categorized and punished using a different set of rules than those applied to adult offenders.

3. The financial success of _____ crime depends upon monopolistic control of criminal activities such as prostitution, infiltration of legitimate businesses such as garbage removal, and dependence upon violence for enforcement.

4. The _____ of prisons raises serious questions for social policy because, in the interest of operating a profitable center, prison managers may treat prisoners less humanely.

5. Many criminologists advocate _____ "victimless" crimes such as gambling and narcotics addiction to allow police to devote more time to investigating and enforcing serious personal and property crimes.

ESSAY QUESTIONS
1. Using a functionalist perspective, explain the purpose of prisons.
2. Using a conflict perspective, explain why Black men have higher rates of arrest and imprisonment than do White men.
3. Using symbolic interaction theory, explain why prisons tend to produce, rather than lessen, crime.
4. Explain why there is inconsistency between the *Uniform Crime Reports* and victimization survey data concerning the prevalence of crime in the United States.
5. Discuss how oppressed groups have used the law to combat social injustices and identify several major court cases that have supported greater racial and gender equality.

ANSWERS TO PRACTICE TEST

Answers to Multiple Choice Questions
1. C. 232 The sociological definition of deviance stresses social context, not individual behavior, recognizes that not all behaviors are judged similarly by all groups and that some groups have the power to judge behaviors as deviant more than other groups, and recognizes that established rules and norms are socially created, rather than morally decreed or individually imposed.
2. A. 232 Deviance is behavior that violates social rules and norms.
3. D. 247 The law is the written set of guidelines that states what society defines as right and wrong.
4. D. 241 Women's criminal behavior has increased as they work in jobs that provide opportunities to commit crime. Women who commit crimes are more likely to be poor and to have been victims of abuse.
5. D. 234 Hate crimes are personal crimes directed at members of stigmatized groups, including gays and lesbians, racial minorities, and people with disabilities.

6.	C.	237	Beech Nut employees engaged in organizational deviance that was tied to the company's pursuit of higher profits.
7.	D.	236	State-organized crime is committed by state officials in pursuit of their jobs as government representatives.
8.	B.	233	Index crimes are mostly street crimes, so the Uniform Crime Reports distort the prevalence of crime in the U.S. because these statistics do not include elite crimes.
9.	C.	240	Fraud, embezzlement, and shoplifting are crimes that are consistent with women's social roles.
10.	A.	233	Fewer people report being a victim of a crime today than 20 years ago.
11.	C.	232	Psychologists, sociologists, and political scientists contribute to the scientific study of crime, known as criminology.
12.	D.	235	White-collar crimes are also called elite crimes.
13.	B.	238	Martinez did not examine the influence of religious values on Latino homicide. His research indicates that educational attainment, not high poverty rate, is the most significant predictor of homicide.
14.	A.	232	Symbolic interaction theory argues that institutions produce crime through labeling people as criminals (See Table 9.1).
15.	D.	234	Judges are more likely to release middle-class youth to their families and to send lower-income youth to jail.
16.	C.	248	*Brown v. Board of Education of Topeka, Kansas* transformed race relations in the U.S. by prohibiting de jure (legal) segregation.
17.	D.	248	*Romer v. Evans* strengthened legal protection for gays and lesbians.
18.	C.	234	Personal crimes are crimes directed against people, such as assault.
19.	A.	234	Property crimes involve theft of, or changes to, property, such as arson.
20.	A.	240	Figure 9.3 shows that Black men have the highest rate of victimization.
21.	D.	245	Figure 9.4 shows that the United States and Russia have the highest incarceration rates in the world.
22.	A.	241	Rape is one of the most underreported crimes. Officials estimate that only 1 in 4 rapes are reported. Black and Latina women, poor women, young women, and unmarried women are the most likely to be victimized by rape. Rape is a crime of aggression.
23.	A.	243	The police perceive racial minorities as a greater threat than Whites and are more likely to use excessive and deadly force against racial minority suspects. Minority citizens can, and have, sued police for racial profiling and other forms of discrimination.
24.	D.	246	Drug offenders account for the steady increase in the prison population in the United States. Greater enforcement of drug laws and the establishment of mandatory sentences for drug offenses have increased both the male and female prison populations.
25.	A.	239	Figure 9.2 shows that people with annual incomes of less than $15,000 have the highest victimization rate.

Answers to True-False Questions

| 1. | F. | 237 | Most workers who participate in organizational deviance with little awareness that their behavior is illegitimate because it is sanctioned by the norms and routine operating principles of the organization. |
| 2. | F. | 236 | Organized crime in the United States has been resistant to attempts to control or eliminate it. |

3.	T.	239	Victimization by crime is correlated with social class (Table 9.2).
4.	F.	246	Private prisons have higher rates of violence than do state-operated prisons, and may reduce services to achieve a profit.
5.	F.	246	Only 20% of people imprisoned for drug offenses receive drug treatment while incarcerated.
6.	T.	246	Drug law enforcement has increased but there has been relatively little decrease in drug use.
7.	T.	246	Eighty percent of women in prison are mothers, and 85% of them have sole custody of their children.
8.	T.	248	De jure segregation (legal segregation) is prohibited, but de facto segregation (segregation in practice) persists.
9.	T.	244	The race of both the perpetrator and the victim influences the likelihood that a convicted killer will be sentenced to death.
10.	F.	245	Asian American men have the lowest incarceration rate. Hispanics are the fastest growing minority in American prisons.

Answers to Fill in the Blank Questions

1.	profiling	243
2.	delinquency	234
3.	organized	236
4.	privatization	246
5.	decriminalizing	249

CHAPTER 10
CLASS

BRIEF CHAPTER OUTLINE
Social Differentiation and Social Stratification
>   Forms of Stratification: Estate, Caste, and Class
>   Defining Class

Why Is There Inequality?
>   Karl Marx: Class and Capitalism
>   Max Weber: Class, Status, and Party

Functionalism and Conflict Theory: The Continuing Debate
>   The Functionalist Perspective on Inequality
>   The Conflict Perspective on Inequality

The Class Structure of the United States
>   Layers of Social Class
>   Class Conflict
>   The Distribution of Wealth and Income

Diverse Sources of Stratification
>   Race and Class
>   Gender and Class
>   Age and Class
>   Class and Cultural Diversity

Class Consciousness
Social Mobility: Myths and Realities
>   Defining Social Mobility
>   The Extent of Social Mobility

Poverty
>   Who Are the Poor?
>   Explanations of Poverty
>   Homelessness
>   Welfare

QUESTIONS TO GUIDE YOUR READING
1. What is the difference between a caste system and a class system, and which system characterizes the United States?
2. How is an individual's social class position determined in the United States?
3. How do race, ethnicity, gender, and age intersect with social class as mechanisms of stratification?
4. How severe is class inequality, and how common is social mobility, in the United States?
5. According to functionalist and conflict theories, what are the primary causes of, and solutions to, poverty in the United States?

KEY TERMS (defined at page number shown and in glossary)

poverty line 276
social class 256
social mobility 274
socioeconomic status (SES) 267
status attainment 261
underclass 264

prestige 262
social differentiation 254
social stratification 254
status 254
Temporary Assistance to Needy Families 282
wealth 266

KEY PEOPLE (identified at page number shown)
Herbert Gans 260
Karl Marx 257
William Julius Wilson 264

Oscar Lewis 278
Max Weber 258

CHAPTER OUTLINE
I.   **SOCIAL DIFFERENTIATION AND SOCIAL STRATIFICATION**

Status refers to a socially defined position in a group or a society. **Social differentiation** is the process by which different statuses in any group, organization, or society develop. **Social stratification** is a relatively fixed, hierarchical arrangement in society by which groups have different access to resources, power, and perceived social wealth. Social stratification is universal, since all societies rank individuals and groups. Systems of stratification, however, vary cross-culturally.

A.   Forms of Stratification: Estate, Caste, and Class
  1.   In an **estate system**, which is found mostly in agricultural societies, the elite have total control over societal resources, including property.
  2.   In a **caste system**, status is *ascribed*, or assigned to an individual at birth. Such a system typically prevents free association and movement between classes. Examples include the *apartheid* system of South Africa, the "Jim Crow" laws in the United States from the end of slavery to the 1960s, and the traditional caste system of India.
  3.   In class systems, there is a possibility of changing one's status over time, because class is partially based on *achieved status*, which is earned as wealth and other social resources are acquired or lost. Despite this possibility, most Americans experience little change in class during their lifetimes.

B.   Defining Class
  1.   **Social class** (or **class**) is the social structural position that groups hold relative to the economic, social, political, and cultural resources of society.
  2.   Max Weber identified **life chances** as the opportunities that people in a particular class have in common, such as access to jobs, health care, housing, and education.
  3.   Social class is strongly related to political and social attitudes (wealthy persons in the U.S. are more typically Republican than Democratic) and friendships (which are usually formed within class groups).
  4.   Because social class is a structural phenomenon that cannot be directly observed, sociologists measure it by using *indicators*, or measurements that assess a concept.
  5.   Sociologists use income, education, occupation, and place of residence to measure social class. These indicators tend to be related, because a person with a quality education and good job tends to earn a higher income and live in a wealthier neighborhood.

II. **WHY IS THERE INEQUALITY?**
    A.   <u>Karl Marx: Class and Capitalism</u>
        1.   Karl Marx (1818-1883), who analyzed the class system under capitalism, defined classes in terms of their relationship to the **means of production**, or the system by which goods are produced and distributed.
        2.   Marx identified two primary social classes under capitalism:
            a.   the *capitalist class* owns the means of production, and
            b.   the *working class* labors for wages.
            c.   Within these classes are the *petty bourgeoisie*, or small business owners and managers, who identify with the capitalists; and the *lumpenproletariat*, who become the permanently poor underclass.
        3.   Marx predicted that *class struggles* would occur because capitalists would continue to exploit workers for profit; but he did not foresee the emergence of a large middle class.
    B.   <u>Max Weber: Class, Status, and Party</u>
        1.   Max Weber (1864-1920) argued that there were three dimensions to stratification: class (the economic dimension), status or prestige (the cultural and social dimension), and party (the political dimension).
            a.   *Class* refers to how much access an individual or group has to the material goods of society. It can be measured by income, property, and other financial assets.
            b.   *Status* is the social judgement or recognition given to a person or group.
            c.   *Party* is the ability to impose one's will on others, even in the face of opposition. It is also reflected in one's ability to negotiate through social institutions, such as the criminal justice system.
        2.   Weber noted that a person can rank high on one or two dimensions of stratification and low on another.
        3.   Marx and Weber both recognized the importance of the economic basis of stratification and the significance of class in determining life chances.

III. **FUNCTIONALISM AND CONFLICT THEORY: THE CONTINUING DEBATE**
    A.   <u>The Functionalist Perspective on Inequality</u>
        1.   Functionalist theory views society as an interdependent system of institutions and emphasizes cohesion, cooperation, and stability.
        2.   Social inequality motivates people to fill different positions in society that are needed for the survival of the whole.
        3.   Herbert Gans argued that poverty is functional because it contributes to social stability and benefits the wealthy both economically and socially. For example, the lower class is a source of cheap labor, the poor purchase used goods that no one else wants, and poor people provide the wealthy with a chance to view themselves as charitable.
    B.   <u>The Conflict Perspective on Inequality</u>
        1.   Conflict theory, based largely on the work of Karl Marx, views society as a system held together by tension, competition, and coercion.

2. Groups vary in resources, and the most powerful groups are able to maintain their advantage and convince others that their unequal privilege is legitimate.

3. Conflict theorists argue that the consequences of inequality are negative, because the talents of people from less powerful groups are largely wasted because of blocked opportunities.

4. Implicit in the argument of each perspective is criticism of the other perspective.

IV. THE CLASS STRUCTURE OF THE UNITED STATES

Social class is the common position or rank that groups hold in a status hierarchy, measured by variables such as income, occupation, and educational attainment. **Social attainment** is the process whereby people end up in a particular position in the stratification system, influenced by such factors as class origins, educational level, and occupation. **Socioeconomic status (SES)**, or an individual's position in the stratification system, is measured in the United States primarily by three variables: income, occupational prestige, and education. *Income* is the amount of money a person receives in a given period of time. The **median income** is the midpoint of all household incomes in a particular society. In 1998, the median income in the U.S. was $38,885.

Prestige is the value assigned to people and groups by others. **Occupational prestige** is the subjective evaluation people give to jobs. In the U.S., the most prestigious occupations include Supreme Court justice, physician, professor, and lawyer. The occupations of electrician, newspaper columnist, insurance agent, and police officer are in the middle range. Those occupations with the lowest prestige rankings include maid, farm laborer, janitor, and garbage collector. These rankings reflect social judgements about the value of these jobs to society, rather than the worth of people who hold these jobs. Occupational prestige is strongly related to the amount of education required by the job. **Educational attainment** is typically measured as years of formal education. Generally, one's class increases as education level increases.

A. Layers of Social Class

1. The *upper class*, also called *elites* in Marxist terms, constitute a very small proportion of people who control vast amounts of wealth and property in the United States. The majority of their wealth is inherited.

   a. Even members of the elite who are considered "self-made" usually inherited significant assets.

   b. The *nouveau riche* are those in the upper class with newly acquired wealth, such a owners of dot.com companies.

2. The *upper-middle class* includes those with high incomes and high social prestige, such as well-educated professionals and business executives.

3. The *middle class* is probably the largest group in the U.S. This class includes those who are clustered around the median income, such as white collar workers, many skilled craftspeople, and self-employed persons. Most Americans identify themselves as middle class.

4. The *lower-middle class* includes workers in the skilled trades and low-income bureaucratic workers.

5. The *lower class* is comprised primarily of poor and displaced people who have little formal education and are often unemployed or working for minimum wage. People of color and women are overrepresented in this class. Contrary to popular belief, forty percent of the poor work and ten percent work year-round and full-time.

6. The *underclass* refers to people who are likely to be permanently unemployed and dependent on public assistance or crime for economic support. Sociologist William Julius Wilson argues that major economic changes have left many people, especially minorities, in vulnerable positions, thereby intensifying the problems of urban poverty.

B. Class Conflict

    1. Rather than defining social class in terms of a hierarchy, or "ladder," conflict theorists view class in terms of the relationship of various classes to each other and to the larger system of economic productivity.

        a. According to these sociologists, classes compete with each other and the capitalists, or elites, exploit and dominate other classes.

        b. The position of the middle class, or the *professional-managerial* class (including managers, supervisors, and professionals) is unique because members have substantial control over other people, especially in the workplace, but have minimal control over the economic system.

    2. Conflict theory suggests that as capitalism progresses, more members of the middle class will be pushed out of managerial jobs into working class jobs. Although the middle class has not been eliminated as Marx predicted, the classes have become more polarized, and many members of the middle class have experienced downward social mobility.

C. The Distribution of Wealth and Income in the United States

    1. Class inequality in the U.S. is enormous and has intensified as elites have gained more power and greater control over wealth.

    2. Sociologists distinguish between wealth and income.

        a. **Wealth** is the monetary value of everything one owns. It is calculated by adding all financial assets, such as stocks, bonds, property, insurance, and investments, and subtracting debts, resulting in the amount of one's *net worth*. Wealth is cumulative and can be passed on to the next generation.

        b. **Income** is the amount of money brought into a household from various sources, including wages, investments, income, and dividends, during a given period.

    3. The distribution of wealth in the U.S. provides evidence of significant class inequality.

        a. Since 1970, the top fifth of the U.S. population has received a larger share of total income than has the bottom fifth.

        b. From 1989 to 1997, the national share of wealth held by the top one percent of the population in the U.S. grew from 37.4 percent to 39.1 percent.

    4. Many factors have contributed to the declining fortunes of the lower and middle classes in the U.S., including the elimination of many government jobs, economic downsizing, and an uneven distribution of benefits through the tax structure.

    5. At all income, occupational, and educational levels, Black families have lower levels of wealth than similarly situated White families. Because the advantages of wealth accumulate over time, providing equality of opportunity in the present has not addressed differences in class status between Black and White Americans.

V.   DIVERSE SOURCES OF STRATIFICATION

Race, class, and gender are overlapping systems of stratification that people experience simultaneously.

A.   Race and Class

1.   The middle class structure among African Americans has historically existed separately from the White class structure and continues to do so, especially because of persistent residential segregation.

2.   Recently, the middle classes of both African Americans and Latinos have expanded, with increased access to education and middle class occupations, such as teacher and doctor, for people of color.

3.   The *myth of the model minority* reflects a stereotype based on the belief that a minority group member must adopt dominant group values to succeed. Asian Americans are often stereotyped this way because of their presumed educational achievement, hard work, and thrift, but there are high rates of poverty among some Asian American groups.

B.   Gender and Class

1.   The majority of American women work in low-prestige, low-wage occupations; and measured by their own incomes and occupations (rather than their husbands'), would be considered working class.

2.   Class differences between women are important because women are not a monolithic group.

3.   Women's class status is especially clear after divorce, when women's incomes typically drop but men's incomes increase.

C.   Age and Class

1.   Being born in a particular generation can have a significant influence on one's life chances. For example, today the age group that is most likely to be poor are children.

2.   A decline in the rate of poverty among the elderly occurred from 1970 to the present, reflecting the greater affluence of older people today.

D.   Class and Cultural Diversity

1.   The unequal distribution of economic resources is a quantitative index of class.

2.   Cultural practices and values, such as friendships, leisure habits, language, and dress, are strongly influenced by social class.

3.   Individuals become more aware of the culture of their own class when they are in a setting different from their own background.

4.   The dominant culture supports White middle-class values and lifestyles more than those of any other class, which may make it difficult for people from other social class backgrounds to comfortably participate in middle-class settings such as universities.

VI.   CLASS CONSCIOUSNESS

Class consciousness refers to people's perception that a class structure exists and the feeling of shared identification with one's class and others who share the same life chances. **False consciousness**, a concept developed by Karl Marx, refers to the existence of a specific type of class consciousness among subordinate classes, who tend to internalize the views and belief systems of the dominant class that justify inequality. Class consciousness varies among the different classes. The elite, who hold institutional power, are a cohesive group who are protective of their common interests. In the United States, the working class is more class conscious than is the middle class. The myth that the U.S. is a classless society supports inequality. The most important determinant of where one sees oneself in the class system is whether one does mental or manual labor, the main feature that distinguishes the middle from the working class.

VII. **SOCIAL MOBILITY: MYTHS AND REALITIES**
   A. Defining Social Mobility
       1. **Social mobility** refers to a person's movement over time from one class to another.
           a. *Intergenerational* mobility occurs between generations, such as when a child achieves significantly more or less than his or her parents.
           b. *Intragenerational* mobility occurs within a single generation, such as when an individual gains or loses a substantial amount of wealth during his or her lifetime.
       2. Societies differ in the amount of social mobility permitted.
           a. In *closed class systems*, movement from one class to another is virtually impossible.
           b. In *open class systems*, placement in the class system is based on achievement and may change over time.
   B   The Extent of Social Mobility
       1. Most people remain in the same class as their parents, because the privileges and disadvantages of class reproduce themselves.
       2. Mobility is strongly influenced by education. Many of the recent gains in social class by African Americans have been associated with increases in educational attainment.
       3. Two-earner families have been able to maintain middle-class status primarily because wives are working longer hours today.
       4. The rate of social mobility in the United States is significantly less than the "American dream" implies. Mobility can occur in two directions.
           a. **Upward mobility** often requires the individual to distance himself/herself from the community of origin.
           b. **Downward mobility** is becoming more common, as the middle class experiences a decline due to structural changes in the economy.

VIII. **POVERTY**
   The **poverty line**, which is the federal government's official definition of poverty, is the amount of money required to support the basic needs of a household. In 1998, the official poverty line for a family of four was $16,036.
   A. Who Are the Poor?
       1. In 1998, about 35 million people, or 12.7 percent of the U.S. population, were poor. The majority of poor people are White, but racial minorities are overrepresented among the poor relative to their total population.
       2. The **feminization of poverty** refers to the increasing proportion of the poor who are women and children as a result of the increase in single-female headed households, continued wage inequality between men and women, and federal budget cutbacks in support programs.
       3. Eighty percent of the poor live in metropolitan areas, particularly inner cities, which contain the most racially segregated neighborhoods.
   B. Explanations of Poverty
       1. Blaming the Victim: The Culture of Poverty

        a.   Some persons blame the poor for being poor and argue that individual motivation and ability will allow anyone to succeed in the United States.

        b.   The **culture of poverty** argument, developed by Oscar Lewis, views poverty as a way of life that is transmitted across generations.

        c.   Contrary to popular opinion, cycling in and out of poverty is more common than intergenerational welfare dependency, and most of the able-bodied poor do work, but they earn wages at or below the poverty line.

    2.   Structural Causes of Poverty

        a.   Most sociologists argue that poverty is caused by complex economic and social changes such as the *restructuring of the economy*, which has resulted in reduced earning power and increased unemployment, especially for the working class.

        b.   Most new jobs being created today offer low wages and no benefits, and are primarily filled by women.

        c.   The *status of women in the family and the labor market* has contributed to the overrepresentation of women among the poor. For example, the financial effects of divorce and the limited availability of affordable child care contribute to the feminization of poverty. Additionally, wages in the U.S. are based on the **family wage system**, which assumes that men are the primary breadwinners and are therefore paid higher wages than women who work, even though men are no longer the mainstay of family income.

C.   Homelessness

    1.   Although it is difficult to estimate the number of homeless persons, there is little doubt that homelessness has substantially increased in recent years, with families now comprising the largest segment of the homeless population.

    2.   Several factors contribute to homelessness today, including domestic violence, eroding work opportunities, and reductions in federal spending for housing and other social service programs.

D.   Welfare

    1.   Welfare reform resulted in the elimination of the Aid to Families with Dependent Children (AFDC) program in 1996, which significantly reduced financial assistance to the poor.

    2.   The **Temporary Assistance to Needy Families** (TANF) program was established through the 1996 Personal Responsibility Act, reflecting a shift from welfare to "workfare."

    3.   Sociological research has challenged many myths about welfare, including the stereotype that poor people do not want to work and prefer long-term welfare dependency as a way of life.

PRACTICE TEST

MULTIPLE CHOICE QUESTIONS

1. A relatively fixed, hierarchical arrangement in society by which groups have different access to resources, power, and perceived social wealth is:
    a. status system.
    b. social mobility.
    c. social stratification.
    d. culture of poverty.

2. Social differentiation refers to the:
    a. assignment of class position according to one's sex.
    b. systematic inequalities between nations that result from differences in wealth, power, and prestige in the international economy.
    c. process whereby the most talented individuals, who perform the jobs that are most important in a society, receive the greatest rewards.
    d. process by which different statuses in any group or society develop.

3. Marx identified two primary social classes under capitalism, the:
    a. capitalists and the middle class.
    b. capitalists and the working class.
    c. working class and the lumpenproletariat.
    d. elites and the petty bourgeoisie.

4. According to Max Weber, the three dimensions of stratification are:
    a. class, status, and party.
    b. power, party, and prestige.
    c. race, class, and gender.
    d. economic, political, and religious.

5. Herbert Gans argued that poverty is functional for society because it contributes to social stability in which of the following ways?
    a. The poor purchase used goods that no one else wants to buy.
    b. The poor allow the wealthy to view themselves as charitable.
    c. The poor provide a source of cheap labor.
    d. All of the above are ways that poverty is functional for society.

6. In the United States, socioeconomic status (SES) is measured primarily by three variables, which are:
    a. income, prestige, and political affiliation.
    b. income, occupation, and education
    c. occupation, education, and religious affiliation.
    d. occupation, wealth, and consciousness.

7. Which of the following occupations have the highest prestige ranking in the United States?
    a. lawyer and physician
    b. janitor and maid
    c. nurse and police officer
    d. secretary and cashier

8.   In the United States, those who become upper class through independent effort and have newly acquired wealth are the:
      a.   capitalists.
      b.   Ivy League.
      c.   nouveau riche.
      d.   old money elites.

9.   Those persons who are most likely to be permanently unemployed and dependent on public assistance or crime for economic support are located in the _____ class.
      a.   lower
      b.   under
      c.   working
      d.   criminal

10.   The vast majority of Americans identify themselves as _____ class.
      a.   working
      b.   middle
      c.   upper
      d.   None of the above, because most Americans do not define themselves as belonging to any particular class.

11.   According to conflict theorists, those who have substantial control over other people, especially in the workplace, but have minimal control over the economic system, are the _____ class.
      a.   upper-elite
      b.   working-laborer
      c.   welfare-dependent
      d.   professional-managerial

12.   The amount of money brought into a household from various sources, such as wages, investments, and dividends, during a given period refers to a person's:
      a.   wealth.
      b.   income.
      c.   surplus.
      d.   value.

13.   The monetary value of everything a person owns, including including property, stocks, bonds, and insurance, refers to a person's:
      a.   wealth.
      b.   income.
      c.   surplus.
      d.   value.

14.   The middle class has recently expanded for which of the following groups?
      a.   African Americans
      b.   Native Americans
      c.   Asian Americans
      d.   None of the above are true, because no racial or ethnic minority group in the United States has undergone an expansion of the middle class.

15. The age group most likely to be poor in the United States is:
    a. children under age 18.
    b. elderly people over age 65.
    c. adults age 21 to 40.
    d. adults age 41 to 60.

16. The myth of the model minority, which is based on the assumption that a minority group member must adopt dominant group values to succeed, has been most frequently applied to which racial-ethnic minority group in the United States?
    a. Hispanic Americans
    b. African Americans
    c. Native Americans
    d. Asian Americans

17. When an individual moves from one class to another in his or her own lifetime, it is referred to as _____ mobility.
    a. universal
    b. professional
    c. intragenerational
    d. intergenerational

18. According to _____ theory, upward mobility is available to individuals in the U.S. if they are motivated to acquire extended education and skills.
    a. conflict
    b. feminist
    c. functionalist
    d. symbolic interaction

19. The most important determinant of where an individual in the U.S. sees himself or herself in the class system is whether s/he:
    a. does mental or manual labor.
    b. graduates from high school.
    c. owns or rents a home.
    d. is single or married.

20. Class _____ refers to people's perceptions that a class structure exists and that they share identification with their class.
    a. status
    b. system
    c. conflict
    d. consciousness

21. Oscar Lewis argued that poverty is a way of life for the poor that is transmitted from one generation to the next. His view is known as the:
    a. restructuring of the economy.
    b. deindustrialization of society.
    c. familial dependency model.
    d. culture of poverty.

22. Measured by their own incomes and occupations (rather than by their husbands'), most women in the United States belong to the _____ class.
    a. middle
    b. working
    c. upper
    d. under

23. The largest segment of the homeless population in the United States today is:
    a. adult men.
    b. adult women.
    c. runaway adolescents.
    d. families with children.

24. Which of the following statements about welfare (public assistance) is true?
    a. The poor do not want to work.
    b. The poor prefer to remain on welfare as a way of life.
    c. Recipients generally remain welfare dependent throughout their adult lives.
    d. Higher levels of welfare benefits can hasten the recipient's exit from poverty.

25. The assumption that men are the breadwinners for families contributes to men typically being given higher compensation for their jobs than women, which supports the:
    a. estate system.
    b. family wage system.
    c. model minority system.
    d. slave mentality.

TRUE-FALSE QUESTIONS

1. The majority of poor people in the United States live in isolated rural areas.

2. White families are more likely than Black families to prepare their daughters for paid employment and less likely to stress marriage as a primary goal.

3. The estate system of stratification is found primarily in agricultural societies.

4. According to Max Weber, a person's position in the stratification system is almost solely determined by the type of job s/he holds and the income associated with that job.

5. The majority of upper class people in the United States acquire their wealth through independent efforts, such as establishing a successful business.

6. Most individuals in the United States move up in social class compared to their parents.

7. Occupational prestige in the United States is strongly related to the amount of education required for the job.

8. Approximately 25 percent of poor people in the United States are employed.

9. "Median income" refers to the minimum amount of income that a family needs to earn to support their basic needs, such as housing, food, and clothing.

10. The feminization of poverty refers to the increased percentage of poor women who received welfare benefits after the passage of the 1996 Personal Responsibility and Work Opportunity Act.

FILL IN THE BLANK QUESTIONS

1. According to Marx, _____ consciousness develops when subordinate classes internalize the views and belief systems of the dominant class, which justify inequality.

2. Karl Marx referred to members of the permanently poor underclass as the _____.

3. The United States is a(n) _____ class system because social mobility is permitted and an individual's placement in the system may change over time.

4. The dominant culture of the United States supports _____ class values and lifestyles more than those of any other class.

5. In the United States, an individual's position in the stratification system is usually measured by three variables: income, _____, and occupational prestige.

ESSAY QUESTIONS

1. Define *life chances* and explain how social class contributes to differences in life chances for people living in the United States.
2. Using a conflict perspective, explain why the consequences of class inequality for society are negative.
3. Using a functionalist perspective, explain why class inequality is functional for society.
4. Explain why differences in wealth between Black and White Americans persist despite an expansion of the Black middle class.
5. Explain what sociologists mean by the "cultural dimension" of social class. Discuss how several aspects of this dimension vary for the working class and the middle class.

ANSWERS TO PRACTICE TEST

Answers to Multiple Choice Questions

1. C. 254 Social stratification refers to the relatively fixed, heirarchical arrangement in society by which groups have different access to resources, power, and perceived social wealth.
2. D. 254 Social differentiation is the process by which different statuses in any group, organization, or society develop.
3. B. 257 Acccording to Marx, the two primary classes under capitalism are the capitalist class (also called elites) and the working class.
4. A. 258 According to Weber, the three dimensions of stratification are class, status, and party (the term Weber used for power).
5. D. 260 According to Gans, poverty contributes to social stability, and is therefore functional, because poor people buy used goods that no one else wants, the poor provide a source of cheap labor (which benefits wealthy employers by increasing their profits), and the poor provide an opportunity for the wealthy to feel charitable (when they contribute to organizations such as the Salvation Army).

6.	B.	262	Income, occupational prestige, and education tend to be related in the United States, so that high prestige jobs usually require high levels of education and provide high incomes. In the United States, sociologists measure socioeconomic status by these three variables.
7.	A.	262	Nurses and police officers are in the middle range of occupational prestige in the U.S.; lawyers, physicians, and professors are in the high range; and farm laborers, maids, and janitors are in the low range.
8.	C.	263	The nouveau riche are those people who have newly acquired wealth and have entered the upper class through independent effort, including successful Internet executives in the United States.
9.	B.	264	The underclass is comprised of people who are likely to be permanently unemployed and dependent on public assistance or crime for economic support.
10.	B.	264	The vast majority of Americans identify themselves as middle class, and this group tends to be less class conscious than either the upper or the working class.
11.	D.	264	The professional-managerial class has substantial control over people, especially in the workplace. According to conflict theorists, however, this group does not own the means of productions and therefore has minimal power in the economic system
12.	B.	266	Income is defined as the amount of money brought into a household from various sources, including wages, investments, and dividends, during a given period.
13.	A.	266	Wealth is the total monetary value of all one's assets, including stocks, bonds, property, and insurance. Wealth is cumulative and can be passed on to future generations.
14.	A.	264	There has been an expansion of the middle class for both African-Americans and Latinos in the U.S., primarily due to increased education levels and entrance into professional occupations.
15.	A.	272	Today, the age group in the United States that is most likely to be poor is children under age 18.
16.	D.	271	Asian Americans have often been stereotyped by the myth of the model minority.
17.	C.	274	Intragenerational mobility occurs when an individual's class status changes over his or her lifetime. Intergenerational mobility occurs when an individual's class changes from his or her parents' class. Social mobility occurs less frequently than is commonly believed.
18.	C.	260	Functionalist theorists view upward mobility as possible for those who acquire education and job skills, while conflict theorists believe there is blocked mobility in the system because the lower and working classes are not provided with the same opportunities as other classes.
19.	A.	274	The most important determinant of one's class identification in the U.S. is whether one does manual or mental labor.
20.	D.	273	Class consciousness refers to the perception that a class structure exists and the feeling of shared identification with one's class.
21.	D.	278	Oscar Lewis developed identified the culture of poverty to refer to his thesis that poverty is a way of life for the poor that is transmitted from one generation to the next.
22.	B.	271	Most women would be considered working class by their own incomes and occupations. The majority of women work in low-status, low-wage jobs despite having educational levels comparable to men.

23. D. 280 Homelessness has increased in recent years, and families are the largest segment of the homeless population today.
24. D. 281 Higher levels of welfare benefits can hasten an individual's exit from poverty because additional funds can be used for child care so that the recipient can get a job or get the training required to be hired. The public perception of welfare recipients is based primarily on myths.
25. B. 279 The family wage system is based on the assumption that men are the family breadwinners. This belief contributes to men typically being paid higher wages than women, despite evidence that men are no longer the mainstay of family income in the United States.

Answers to True-False Questions

1. F. 277 Eighty percent of poor people live in metropolitan areas, and the poor are disproportionately concentrated in racially-segregated inner-cities.
2. F. 275 Black families are more likely than White families to prepare their daughters for paid employment, and less likely to stress marriage as a primary goal.
3. T. 255 In the estate system of social stratification, which is found mostly in agricultural societies, the elite have total control over social resources.
4. F. 258 Marx viewed social stratification almost solely in terms of economics, while Weber identified three important dimensions of stratification – class, status, and party.
5. F. 262 Most of the wealth owned by the upper class is inherited.
6. F. 275 Most individuals in the U.S. occupy the same class position as do their parents.
7. T. 262 Occupational prestige is strongly related to the amount of education required by the job. For example, physicians have high prestige while janitors have low prestige in the United States.
8. F. 278 Forty-one percent of poor people in the U.S. work, but many of them remain below the poverty line because of low wages.
9. F. 262 Median income, the midpoint of all household incomes in a society, is $38,885 in the U.S. The minimum amount of income needed to support the household members' basic needs is referred to as the poverty line. The poverty line for a family of four in the U.S. is $16,036.
10. F. 277 The feminization of poverty refers to the fact that an increasing proportion of the poor are women and children. *Fewer* women with children received welfare benefits after the passage of welfare reform legislation in 1996.

Answers to Fill in the Blank Questions

1. false 274
2. lumpenproletariat 257
3. open 275
4. middle 273
5. education 267

CHAPTER 11
GLOBAL STRATIFICATION

BRIEF CHAPTER OUTLINE
Global Stratification
> Rich and Poor
> First, Second, and Third Worlds
> The Core and Periphery
> Race and Global Inequality

Consequences of Global Stratification
> Population
> Health
> Education
> Gender

Theories of Global Stratification
> Modernization Theory
> Dependency Theory
> World Systems Theory

World Poverty
> Measuring World Poverty
> Who Are the World's Poor?
> Women and Children in Poverty
> Poverty and Hunger
> Causes of World Poverty

The Future of Global Stratification

QUESTIONS TO GUIDE YOUR READING
1. How do sociologists measure the wealth of nations, and how reliable is this measure for industrialized and non-industrialized nations?
2. Which measure of world stratification combines levels of development and the political orientation of the country, and how are countries classified according to this model?
3. Using power as the main dimension of stratification in the world system, how are countries classified, and which countries are located in each position?
4. How can sociologists use the Human Poverty Index to assess the standard of living in countries around the world, and what does the index indicate about the world's poor?
5. What are the three main theories of global stratification, and what are the main criticisms of each theoretical perspective?

KEY TERMS (defined at page shown and in glossary)

I.   GLOBAL STRATIFICATION

Worldwide, there are not only rich and poor individuals, but there are also rich and poor countries. There is a **global system of stratification** in which units are countries; thus, nations cannot be seen independently of economic and social processes that link them together in a world-based economy.

A.   <u>Rich and Poor</u>

The global stratification system has several dimensions, one of which is wealth.

1.   One of the most common ways to measure the wealth of nations is to use the **annual per capita gross national product (per capita GNP).**

a.   The per capita GNP measures the total volume of good and services produced by a country each year, divided by the size of the population.

b.   Per capita GNP is only reliable in countries that are based on a cash economy. The measure is less reliable for poorer countries and may underestimate the wealth of countries at the lower end of the economic scale.

c.   The per capita GNP of the United States, the tenth richest nation in the world using this measure, was $28,240 in 1998.

2.   The inequality between rich and poor nations is increasing. Most of the wealthy countries are predominantly urban, industrialized countries in Western Europe. The world's poorest countries are mostly in Eastern and Central Africa.

3.   Not all people in poor countries are poor and not all people in rich countries are rich. On average, people in the poor countries are much worse off than people in the rich countries.

4.   In a world with nearly six billion people, over half of the world's population live in the poorest 45 countries.

B.   <u>First, Second and Third Worlds</u>

1.   Another dimension of world stratification combines levels of development with political orientation. This classification system, used during the Cold War, does not account for recent world changes.

a.   **First-world countries** consisted of industrialized, capitalist countries with market-based economies and democratically elected governments. They included the United States, New Zealand, Australia, Japan, and countries in Western Europe.

b.   **Second-world countries** were socialist countries with state-managed economies and Communist governments. They included the former Soviet Union, China, Eastern Europe, Cuba, and North Korea.

c.   **Third-world countries** were the remaining countries that were poor, underdeveloped, largely rural, and had increasing levels of poverty. They had farming economies and mostly autocratic governments.

164

2. Although this system of classification is still used to refer to richer and poorer nations, the collapse of the Soviet Union and change in governments in Eastern Europe led to transformations in the Second World nations.

C. The Core and Periphery
  1. Another dimension of stratification in the world system is **power**, or the ability of a country to exercise control over other countries.
  2. Using power as a dimension, the countries of the world can be classified based on their position in the world economic system.
    a. **Core countries** such as the U.S. and Japan are largely the same as the developed countries of the first world. They control and profit the most from the world system.
    b. **Semiperipheral countries** such as Spain and Turkey surround the core countries, both structurally and geographically. They are semi-industrialized countries that extract profits from the poor countries and pass them on to the core countries.
    c. **Peripheral countries** such as Haiti are the largely agricultural, poor countries of the world, with little power or influence in the world system. They often have important resources that are exploited by the core countries.

D. Race and Global Inequality
  1. The rich core countries that dominate the world system are largely European, in addition to the United States and Japan. In Europe and the U.S., the majority of the population is White.
  2. The poor countries of the world, mostly in Asia, Africa, and South America, have populations comprised primarily of people of color.
  3. There are enormous differences in lifestyle and life chances between nations in predominantly White and predominantly Black populations.
  4. People of color in nations in Africa and Latin America have long been exploited by imperialism and colonialism as cheap sources of labor.

II. **CONSEQUENCES OF GLOBAL STRATIFICATION**
  A. Population
    1. More than 60 percent of the people in the world live in mostly rural countries where the average income is less than $760 per year. These countries have the highest birth and death rates.
    2. The richest countries of the world contain only 15 percent of the world's population. Many of these urban countries are experiencing population declines because fertility rates are low.
    3. Rapid population growth caused by high fertility rates can cause significant differences in the quality of life across countries. This growth produces a large proportion of economic dependents in society, which strains public services such as schools and hospitals.
    4. Rich countries with declining birth rates experience a shortage of workers, who must be imported from other countries. The aging population found in these countries strains retirement programs.
    5. Scholars disagree about the exact relationship between rate of population growth and economic development; however, in general, fertility rates are affected by levels of industrialization. As countries develop, fertility levels decrease and population growth levels off.

B. Health
    1. There are significant differences in the basic health standards of countries depending on their position in the global stratification system.
    2. Higher income countries have lower childhood death rates, high life expectancy, fewer children born underweight, clean water, and access to adequate sanitation.
    3. In low-income countries, the problems of poor sanitation, contaminated water, high childhood death rates, and low life expectancy are closely related.

C. Education
    1. In high-income countries, education is nearly universal; literacy and school attendance are taken for granted.
    2. The percent of elementary-age children in school is significantly lower in middle and lower income nations; however, even in poor areas, education is improving.
    3. Much education, including basic literacy and math skills, occurs informally; that is, in family settings or religious congregations. This type of education does not help most people develop the skills and knowledge needed to function successfully in the modern world.

D. Gender
    1. Poverty is usually experienced more by women than men in society.
    2. Women in wealthier countries have better health and education than women in poorer countries.
    3. The **gender development** index measures gender inequality in terms of life expectancy, educational attainment, and income, revealing the relative well being of women in different nations around the world.

III. **THEORIES OF GLOBAL STRATIFICATION**

Sociological explanations of world stratification generally fall into three camps. One sociological approach emphasizes the market forces within and between countries, arguing that each country rises and falls according to its own efforts, resources, and energies. This *market-oriented approach* encompasses several specific theories. It is the most common orientation of the world development organizations that seek to help poor countries become more developed.

A. Modernization Theory
    1. **Modernization theory**, an early version of the market-oriented approach, views the economic development of a country as a worldwide process involving nearly all countries that have been affected by technological change.
    2. Based largely on functionalist theory and the work of Max Weber, this perspective argues that a country becomes more "modernized" by technological development. Modernization theory views economic development as a process by which traditional societies become more complex and differentiated.
    3. Modernization theory views countries as poor because they have poor attitudes and poor institutions; thus, proponents of this theory recommend development as the solution to poverty.
        a. In the traditional stage, countries are poor, people lack a work ethic, and people do not save or invest.
        b. As development begins, people begin to save and value hard work and efficiency.

        c.   After several more stages, the population becomes mass consumers and the country is fully modern, industrialized, and highly differentiated.

    4.   Modernization theory has been criticized for: not explaining the development or lack thereof all nations; blaming countries for being poor; and arguing that government should not make economic decisions or develop policies that restrict business or free trade.

B.   Dependency Theory

    1.   **Dependency theory** focuses on the processes and results of European colonization and imperialism.

    2.   Derived from the work of Karl Marx and supported by Andre Bunder Frank, dependency theory arguing that the poverty of low-income countries is a result of their exploitation by powerful countries.

    3.   **Neocolonialism** is a form of international control of poor countries by rich countries, without direct political or military involvement. In this process, rich industrialized nations set prices for raw materials produced by poor countries at very low levels so that the poor countries are unable to accumulate enough profit to industrialize.

    4.   **Multinational corporations**, who buy resources and labor in the countries with the lowest prices, play an important role in keeping dependent nations poor.

    5.   Critics of dependency theory argue that some colonies, such as Hong Kong, have done well economically. Critics also emphasize that it is not clear that the involvement of multinational corporations always impoverishes nations or increases their dependency.

C.   World Systems Theory

    1.   **World systems theory** argues that there is a world economic system that must be understood as a single unit, not in terms of individual countries or groups of countries.

    2.   A global system of stratification has developed based on historical and strategic imbalances in the economic system.

    3.   This theory, derived from conflict theory and most closely associated with the work of Immanuel Wallerstein, sees the world as divided into three groups of interrelated nations.

        a.   Core countries are the rich, powerful, capitalistic countries that control the world system.

        b.   Semiperipheral countries occupy an intermediate position in the world.

        c.   Peripheral countries are poor, largely agricultural, and manipulated by core countries that extract resources and profits from them.

    4.   World systems theory focuses on the economic interconnection of countries worldwide and the **new international division of labor**, which recognizes that products are now produced globally.

    5.   World systems theory describes a **commodity chain**, or a network of production and labor processes by which a product becomes a finished commodity.

    6.   Critics of this theory argue that it is not clear that the world system always works to the advantage of core countries and to the detriment of peripheral countries.

IV. WORLD POVERTY

A. <u>Measuring World Poverty</u>

1. The definition of poverty in the United States identifies **relative poverty**, or the amount of income considered necessary to maintain a suitable standard of living.

2. **Absolute poverty** is the situation in which human beings do not have enough money for basic survival. The United Nations defines world poverty in three ways.

   a. World poverty is defined as the situation in which individuals live on less that $365 per year. By this definition, there are 13 billion people, or approximately one in five people, in poverty.

   b. The United Nations also defines extreme poverty as the situation in which people live on less than $275 per year. There are 600 million people at or below this level of poverty.

   c. The United Nations uses the **Human Poverty Index** to indicate the degree of deprivation of a population in four dimensions of life: health and life expectancy, knowledge, economic well being, and social inclusion.

B. <u>Who are the World's Poor?</u>

1. Using the United Nations definition of world poverty, of the 1.2 billion people in poverty, almost half live in South Asia, mostly in the countries of India, Pakistan and Bangladesh.

2. There are some differences in the nature of poverty in different areas of the world. In Asia, population growth has left many people without sustainable employment. In sub-Saharan Africa, the poor live in marginal areas where poor soil, erosion, continuous warfare, and political instability have created extremely harsh conditions.

C. <u>Women and Children in Poverty</u>

1. There is no country in the world in which women are treated as well as men. The disproportionate burden of poverty carried by women in many poor countries is referred to as **double deprivation**.

   a. The United Nations Commission on the Status of Women estimates that women constitute almost 60 percent of the world's population, perform two-thirds all working hours, receive one-tenth of the world's income, and own less than one percent of the world's wealth.

   b. In poor countries, women suffer greater health risks than do men because fertility rates are higher in poor countries and women spend a greater part of their lives pregnant, nursing and raising small children. Furthermore, women suffer because of traditional cultural norms, such as feeding men before women, that increase women's rates of malnutrition and anemia.

2. Children are also hit particularly hard in poor countries, where they do not have the luxury of a childhood or an education.

   a. Children are required to work to help the family by performing domestic chores, working as beggars, laboring in sweatshops, or being sold into prostitution by their families.

   b. In poor countries, families feel they must have more children for their survival, yet more children perpetuates poverty.

        c.   Homeless children are another problem in the very poor areas of the world. These children survive through begging, selling drugs, stealing, and engaging in prostitution.

    D.   <u>Poverty and Hunger</u>
        1.   Each day 30,000 people die as a consequence of chronic, persistent hunger, and malnutrition stifles physical and mental development.
        2.   Although the food supply around the world is plentiful, food is not distributed to those who need it, resulting in hunger and starvation.

    E.   <u>Causes of World Poverty</u>
        1.   Poverty is not necessarily caused by too rapid population growth, although high fertility rates and poverty are related.
        2.   Poverty is not caused by an unmotivated, lazy population; in fact, people in poor countries work very hard to survive.
        3.   Poverty is a result of a number of tragic causes, including: a history of unstable government; collapsed economies that are in debt; and changes in the world economic system.

V.   THE FUTURE OF WORLD STRATIFICATION

In some areas of the world, particularly East Asia, but also in Latin America, many countries have shown rapid growth and have emerged as developed countries. In **newly industrialized countries** (NICs) such as Korea, Malaysia, Thailand, Taiwan, and Singapore, governments have invested in social and economic development and individuals have saved and invested. Despite these changes, some nations are facing enormous economic and social problems, including ethnic hatred leading to mass genocide, government collapse, bankruptcy, and plummeting standards of living. The continued growth of capitalism may assist some countries, although wealth may not filter down to the people at lower social levels. Capitalist expansion will also place some countries, which are suffering from years of neglect, at a further disadvantage.

PRACTICE TEST

MULTIPLE CHOICE QUESTIONS

1.   Which of the following measures the total volume of goods and services produced by a country each year?
    a.   annual commodity product
    b.   annual human poverty index
    c.   annual global economic index
    d.   annual per capita gross national product

2.   Most of the wealthy countries are located in which part of the world?
    a.   Western Europe
    b.   Eastern Europe
    c.   South America
    d.   South Africa

3.   The United States and Japan are examples of _____ countries.
    a.   First-world
    b.   second-world
    c.   peripheral
    d.   semiperipheral

4. Nations that are poor, underdeveloped, and largely rural with economies based on farming have been classified as _____ countries.
    a. core
    b. first-world
    c. second-world
    d. third-world

5. Using power as the main dimension of stratification in the world system, the partly industrialized nations of Spain and Turkey would be classified as _____ countries.
    a. core
    b. peripheral
    c. semiperipheral
    d. underdeveloped

6. Using power as a dimension of world stratification, most of the countries of Western Europe would be classified as _____ countries.
    a. underdeveloped
    b. semiperipheral
    c. peripheral
    d. core

7. Those largely agricultural countries with little power or influence in the world system, but often with important resources that are exploited by rich countries, are classified as _____ countries.
    a. core
    b. modern
    c. peripheral
    d. semiperipheral

8. Of the industrialized nations, _____ has the highest rating on the human poverty index; that is, it is the poorest of the industrialized nations.
    a. Japan
    b. Russia
    c. Sweden
    d. Australia

9. Approximately what percent of the world's population lives in the poorest countries of the world?
    a. 5 to 15 percent
    b. 20 to 30 percent
    c. 50 to 60 percent
    d. 70 to 80 percent

10. The most common orientation for understanding poverty and global stratification among world development organizations is the _____ approach.
    a. imperialist-colonialism
    b. normative-explanatory
    c. domestic-oriented
    d. market-oriented

11. Modernization theory focuses on the:
    a. role of neocolonialism in controlling and exploiting poor countries to prevent them from accumulating enough wealth to become industrialized.
    b. development of a country as a multistage process involving nearly all countries around the world that have been affected by technological change.
    c. contribution of multinational corporations to maintaining poverty in dependent nations by keeping wages low.
    d. economic interconnection of countries worldwide and the emergence of an international division of labor whereby products are produced globally.

12. Based on the work of Karl Marx, _____ theory asserts that the poverty of low-income countries is a result of their exploitation by the rich, powerful countries.
    a. dependency
    b. modernization
    c. world systems
    d. global production

13. The relative well being of women in countries around the world is measured by the:
    a. sex ratio.
    b. feminization rate.
    c. double jeapordy index.
    d. gender development index.

14. Under _____, rich industrialized nations set prices for raw materials produced by poor countries at very low levels so that the poor countries are unable to accumulate much profit and continue to be dependent on the rich countries.
    a. imperialism
    b. neocolonialism
    c. commodification
    d. peripheralization

15. A network of production and labor processes by which a product becomes a finished, saleable item is the:
    a. commodity chain.
    b. assembly process.
    c. industrial system.
    d. production phase.

16. Which of the following is a dimension of deprivation used to calculate the human poverty index?
    a. social inclusion
    b. life expectancy
    c. knowledge
    d. All of the above are dimensions of deprivation.

17. The United Nations identifies the situation in which individuals live on less than $275 per year as _____ poverty.
    a. relative
    b. double
    c. extreme
    d. world

18. The reason(s) that women in poor countries experience double deprivation is that they:
    a. perform only one-third of all working hours.
    b. constitute only half of the world's population.
    c. consume less food and suffer more malnutrition than do men.
    d. All of the above contribute to double deprivation.

19. Sociologists generally agree that people who suffer from chronic hunger:
    a. cannot purchase adequate food because they are not motivated to work enough to earn sufficient wages to support themselves and their families.
    b. experience malnutrition that may stifle mental and physical growth but rarely die as a result.
    c. cannot secure enough food because they live in countries that are so overpopulated that the demand is far greater than the available food supply.
    d. None of the above are accurate explanations for chronic hunger today.

20. In which of the following regions has poverty substantially increased since 1987?
    a. Africa
    b. South Asia
    c. Eastern Europe
    d. Poverty has increased in all of the above regions of the world.

21. The richest countries in the world have about _____ percent of the world's population.
    a. 15
    b. 25
    c. 50
    d. 75

22. Countries that have shown rapid growth and recently emerged as developed countries, including Korea, Malaysia, Thailand, Taiwan, and Singapore, are referred to as:
    a. Newly Dependent Countries (NDCs).
    b. Economically Revised Nations (ERNs).
    c. Newly Industrialized Countries (NICs).
    d. Urbanized Industrializing Nations (UINs).

23. Which of the following is a dimension of the gender development index?
    a. educational attainment
    b. home ownership
    c. family size
    d. All of the above are dimensions of this index of gender inequality.

24. Children in poor countries around the world contribute to their own and their families' survival by:
    a. begging.
    b. engaging in prostitution.
    c. working for wages in factories.
    d. All of the above are ways that poor children make economic contributions.

25. Of the following industrialized nations, which country has the highest rate of child poverty?
    a. United Kingdom
    b. United States
    c. Israel
    d. Italy

TRUE-FALSE QUESTIONS

1. One of the main problems that rich countries with declining birth rates experience is a shortage of workers.

2. The formal education of young children is nearly universal today.

3. Women outlive men in all countries, although the longevity gap between men and women is greatest in the least developed countries.

4. Modernization theory is derived from conflict theory and views traditional societies as poor because they have been colonized and otherwise exploited by rich countries.

5. World systems theory argues that the poverty of low-income countries is a result of having poor institutions and poorly motivated individuals who do not save or invest money.

6. Dependency theory views the world as divided into three groups of interrelated nations -- core countries, semiperipheral countries, and peripheral countries.

7. The populations of the poorest countries in the world are largely rural and comprised mainly of people of color.

8. According to a global classification system used during the Cold War, socialist countries with a Communist based government and state managed economy are categorized as first world countries.

9. Much of the basic education provided to people in poor countries occurs in informal settings such as the family and religious congregations.

10. In low-income countries, sanitation and water supply problems are strongly correlated with childhood death rates and adult life expectancy.

FILL IN THE BLANK QUESTIONS

1. The condition that people develop when they cannot acquire enough food to meet the body's minimum requirement of vitamins, minerals, and protein is _____.

2. In a _____ system of stratification, the units are countries rather than individuals.

3. In the United States, the poverty level is determined by the yearly income for a family of four that is considered necessary to maintain a suitable standard of living, which reflects the concept of _____ poverty.

4. The situation in which human beings do not have enough money for basic survival is referred to as _____ poverty.

5. Countries with high _____ rates face the challenge of having too many children and not enough adults to provide for them, which strains public services such as schools and hospitals.

ESSAY QUESTIONS

1. Explain why the classification system that categorizes countries as First World, Second World, and Third World is not as useful today as it was during the Cold War.
2. Use the concepts of the *commodity chain* and the *new international division of labor* to explain how clothing is produced.
3. Discuss how population characteristics are related to poverty levels around the world, specifically identifying how rich and poor nations differ on each relevant characteristic.
4. Compare and contrast how modernization theory and dependency theory view poverty, and identify the solutions each theory poses for reducing poverty in low-income nations.
5. Explain why women around the world bear a larger share of the burden of poverty, and identify several social changes that could reduce this *double deprivation*.

ANSWERS TO PRACTICE TEST

Multiple Choice Questions

1.	D.	290	One of the most common ways to measure the wealth of nations is by using the annual per capita gross national product (per capita GNP), which measures the total volume of goods and services produced per year. This measure is only reliable for cash-based economies.
2.	A.	291	Most of the wealthy countries are in Western Europe.
3.	A.	292	First world countries consist of the industrialized, capitalist nations such as the U.S., Japan, Australia, and the countries of Western Europe.
4.	D.	293	Third World countries are poor, underdeveloped, and largely rural.
5.	C.	293	Semiperipheral countries such as Spain, Turkey, and Mexico surround the core countries, both structurally and geographically, and are semi-industrialized.
6.	D.	293	Core countries, such as those wealthy countries in western Europe, control and profit the most from the world system. They rank highest on the power dimension of global stratification.
7.	C.	293	Those countries with little power or influence in the world system, but often with important resources that are exploited by the core countries, are peripheral countries.
8.	B.	304	Figure 11.6 indicates that of the industrialized nations, Russia has the highest rating on the human poverty index.
9.	C.	295	The poorest countries comprise 3.6 billion people, over half of the world's population. These countries have the highest birthrates and the highest death rates in the world
10.	D.	297	The market-oriented approach to understanding global stratification encompasses several specific theories. It is the most common orientation of world development organizations that seek to help poor countries become more developed. It is explanatory because

it describes why things are as they are, and it is normative because it suggests the way things should be.

11.   B.   297   Modernization theory represents the early version of the market-oriented approach. It focuses on the economic development of a country as a world-wide process involving nearly all countries that have been affected by technological change.

12.   A.   299   Dependency theory, based on the work of Karl Marx, argues that the poverty of low-income countries is a result of their exploitation by the powerful countries.

13.   D.   297   The gender development index compares women's well being using three dimensions of deprivation relative to men: life expectancy, educational attainment, and income.

14.   B.   300   In neocolonialism, rich industrial nations set wages and prices for raw materials produced by poor countries at very low levels so the poor countries are unable to accumulate enough profit to industrialize.

15.   A.   302   A network of production and labor processes by which a product becomes a finished, saleable item is the commodity chain.

16.   D.   304   The four dimensions of the human poverty index are knowledge, life expectancy, social inclusion, and economic well being.

17.   C.   303   The situation in which individuals live on less than $275 per year is extreme poverty. Six hundred million people live at or below this level. World poverty is the situation in which individuals live on less than $365 per year. Relative poverty is the amount of income that a family in the U.S. needs to maintain a suitable standard of living.

18.   C.   305   The disproportionate burden of poverty carried by women in poor countries is double deprivation. Women constitute 60 percent of the world's population, perform two-thirds of work hours, are more likely to suffer from malnutrition, and experience greater illness and death associated with pregnancy, birth, and childrearing.

19.   D.   307   Poor people are motivated to acquire food and other necessities; in fact, they work hard to survive. There is enough food to feed the world's population, but food is not distributed in such a way that it reaches all of the people who need it. In addition to causing widespread malnutrition, chronic hunger kills 30,000 people each day.

20.   D.   304   Despite an overall decrease in the proportion of people living in poverty since 1987, poverty has increased in Africa, Latin America, South Asia, eastern Europe, and Central Asia.

21.   A.   295   The richest countries have about 15 percent of the world's population, and population growth occurs at a slower rate than it does in poor countries due to declining fertility rates.

22.   C.   308   Newly industrialized countries such as Korea, Malaysia, Thailand, Taiwan, and Singapore have shown rapid growth and emerged as developed countries.

23.   A.   297   The three dimensions of the gender development index are education, income, and life expectancy.

24.   D.   306   Children in poor countries beg, engage in prostitution, and labor for wages to survive. They do not have the luxury of education.

25.   B.   306   Of the industrialized countries, Russia has the highest child poverty rate, followed by the United States, where over 25 percent of children live in poverty (see Figure 11.7).

Answers to True-False Questions

1.	T.	295	
2.	F.	296	In high-income countries, education is nearly universal, but in poor countries, school attendance is low and most basic education occurs in informal settings such as the family and religious congregations.
3.	T.	305	Women outlive men in most countries, although there is a smaller longevity gap in the least developed countries.
4.	F.	299	Dependency theory is derived from conflict theory and views poverty as the result of neocolonialism and the expansion of capitalism
5.	F.	297	Modernization theory argues that poverty is the result of having poorly developed institutions, low technological development, and unmotivated populations who do not save or invest money.
6.	F.	301	World systems theory views the world as divided into three groups of interrelated nations: core, semiperipheral, and peripheral countries.
7.	T.	294	The countries that suffer a poor standard of living, have low levels of education and high death rates, and are generally at the bottom of the world stratification system are comprised of predominantly people of color.
8.	F.	293	According to a global classification system used during the Cold War, countries with a Communist based government and state managed economy, such as the former Soviet Union, were second world countries.
9.	T.	297	
10.	T.	296	

Answers to Fill in the Blank Questions

1.	malnutrition	307
2.	global	288
3.	relative	303
4.	absolute	303
5.	fertility	295

CHAPTER 12
RACE AND ETHNICITY

BRIEF CHAPTER OUTLINE
Race and Ethnicity
  Ethnicity
  Race
  Minority and Dominant Groups
Racial Stereotypes
  Stereotypes and Salience
  The Interplay Between Race, Gender, and Class Stereotypes
Prejudice, Discrimination and Racism
  Prejudice
  Discrimination
  Racism
Theories of Prejudice and Racism
  Social Psychological Theories of Prejudice
  Sociological Theories of Prejudice and Racism
Diverse Groups, Diverse Histories
  Native Americans
  African Americans
  Latinos
  Asian Americans
  Middle Easterners
  White Ethnic Groups
Patterns of Racial and Ethnic Relations
  The Role of Minority Culture
  Assimilation and Pluralism
  Colonialism
  Segregation and the Urban Underclass
  The Relative Importance of Class and Race
Attaining Racial Equality: The Challenge
  Racial-Ethnic Conflict: A Global Problem
  Civil Rights
  Radical Social Change
  Affirmative Action: Race-Specific versus Color-Blind Programs for Change

QUESTIONS TO GUIDE YOUR READING
1. What characteristics do minority groups typically possess, and which groups would be defined as minority groups in the United States according to this definition?
2. What is the difference between prejudice and discrimination, and how do both concepts support inequality among the various racial and ethnic minority groups in society?
3. How do class and gender intersect with race and ethnicity in the differential treatment of diverse groups in the United States?
4. What evidence exists to support the assertion that race is a socially constructed category rather than a biologically determined category?
5. How and why are the histories and experiences of racial and ethnic minority groups in the United States similar in some ways, yet unique in other ways?

KEY TERMS (defined at page number and in glossary)

affirmative action 343

authoritarian personality 327

contact theory 327

discrimination 323

dominative racism 324

ethnocentrism 321

institutional racism 326

prejudice 320

racial formation 317

racialization 315

residential segregation 324

scapegoat theory 327

stereotype 318

urban underclass 3338

assimilation 327

aversive racism 324

cultural pluralism 338

domestic colonialism 338

ethnic group 314

gendered racism 329

minority group 318

race 316

racial and ethnic stratification 314

racism 324

salience principle 319

segregation 338

stereotype interchangeability 32

victimization perspective 336

KEY PEOPLE (identified at page number)

Hubert Blalock Jr. 334

Malcolm X 341

Thomas Pettigrew 325

Robert Blauner 338

Robert Park 337

William Julius Wilson 328

CHAPTER OUTLINE

Along with gender and social class, race is an integral part of social institutions and has fundamental importance in structuring human social interaction. **Racial and ethnic stratification**, or inequality between racial-ethnic groups in society, rests on privileges and disadvantages that accrue to persons based on their membership in different racial and ethnic groups.

I.   **RACE AND ETHNICITY**

A.   Ethnicity

1.   An **ethnic group** is a social category of people who share common cultural characteristics such as language, religion, and customs.

2.   Ethnic groups have a consciousness of their common cultural bond.

3.   Ethnic groups develop because of their unique historical and social experiences, which become the basis for the group's *ethnic identity*, or the definition the group has of itself as sharing a common cultural bond.

4.   Ethnic groups can develop a stronger or weaker ethnic identity at different points in time. Prejudice and hostility from other groups often strengthens ethnic identity and unity.

B.   Race

1.   Like ethnicity, race is a socially constructed category. Societies assign people to races not by logic and fact, but based on opinion and social experiences.

a.   The categories used to presumably divide groups into races are not fixed; they vary from society to society and over time.

b.   The biological characteristics that have been used to define different racial groups vary both within and between groups.

c.   The biological differences that are presumed to define different racial groups seem somewhat arbitrary, for example, skin color rather than hair color or eye color.

        d.   Different groups use different criteria to define racial groups. For example, a light-skinned Black person, especially if s/he is of high socioeconomic status, is considered White in Brazil.

    2.   A **race** is a group treated as distinct in society on the basis of certain characteristics, some of which are biological, that have been assigned social importance.

    3.   Races are singled out for differential and unfair treatment when they are socially defined as being biologically and/or culturally inferior to the dominant group.

    4.   **Racialization** is a process whereby some social category such as social class or nationality takes on what are perceived in the society to be race characteristics. For example, Adolph Hitler labeled Jews, a religious ethnic group, as a race.

    5.   **Racial formation** is the process by which a group comes to be defined as a race through support from official institutions such as the law and schools. For example, despite having varied backgrounds, Latinos are defined as a "race" in the United States.

  C.   <u>Minority and Dominant Groups</u>

    1.   Not all racial and ethnic groups are minorities; for example, Irish Americans are not now minorities, although they once were in the U.S.

    2.   A **minority group** is any distinct group in society that shares common group characteristics and is forced to occupy low status in society because of prejudice and discrimination.

        a.   A group may be a minority on the basis of ethnicity, race, sexual preference, age, or class status.

        b.   A minority group is not necessarily a numerical minority; for example, Blacks in South Africa under the *apartheid* system of government were a numerical majority but a social minority.

    3.   The group that assigns a racial or ethnic group to subordinate status in society is a *dominant group* or *social majority*.

    4.   A racial or ethnic group typically has the following characteristics:

        a.   It possesses characteristics that are popularly regarded as different from those of the dominant group.

        b.   It suffers prejudice and discrimination by the dominant group.

        c.   Membership is frequently ascribed rather than achieved, although either form of status can be the basis for being identified as a minority.

        d.   Members feel a strong sense of solidarity or "we feeling."

        e.   Marriages typically, although not always, occur between members of the same group.

II.   RACIAL STEREOTYPES

  A.   <u>Stereotypes and Salience</u>

    1.   A **stereotype** is an oversimplified set of beliefs about members of a social group or social stratum that is used to categorize individuals of that group. They are presumed to describe the "typical" member of the group. When based on race or ethnicity, they are called racial-ethnic stereotypes.

    2.   The categorization of people into groups and the subsequent application of stereotypes are based on the **salience principle**. Salience implies that we categorize people on the basis of what initially appears prominent and obvious about them, such as skin color, gender, and age.

B.   <u>The Interplay Between Race, Gender and Class Stereotypes</u>
1.   Among **gender stereotypes**, or those based on a person's gender, the stereotypes about women are more likely to be negative than those about men. Many gender stereotypes are cultural stereotypes that are conveyed and supported by the media.
2.   *Social class stereotypes* are based on assumptions about one's social position.
3.   The principle of **stereotype interchangeability** holds that stereotypes, especially negative ones, are often interchangeable from one targeted group to another. For example, ethnic jokes often interchange groups as the butt of the humor, but stereotype the groups in the same ways; eg., as lazy and inept.

III.   **PREJUDICE, DISCRIMINATION, AND RACE**
A.   <u>Prejudice</u>
1.   **Prejudice** is the evaluation of a social group, and individuals within that group, based on conceptions about the social group that hold together despite facts that contradict it. Prejudice involves both prejudgment and misjudgment.
2.   Prejudices are usually defined as negative evaluations.
   a.   A prejudiced person will have negative attitudes about a member of an *outgroup*, or any group other than one's own.
   b.   A prejudiced person will have positive attitudes about someone simply because they are in one's *ingroup*, or any group one considers one's own.
3.   Prejudice based on race or ethnicity is called *racial-ethnic prejudice*. *Gender prejudice* is a negative evaluation of someone based on gender, and *class prejudice* is a negative evaluation of someone solely on the basis of social class.
4.   Prejudice is revealed in **ethnocentrism**, or the belief that one's group is superior to all other groups.
5.   Racial and ethnic prejudice has a marked effect on how jurors view defendants and how people vote.
6.   Stereotypes and prejudices are learned and internalized through the socialization process. Primary socialization through family and peers is especially important. Secondary socialization, including the media, may also contribute to prejudice.

B.   <u>Discrimination</u>
1.   **Discrimination** is overt negative and unequal treatment of the members of some social group solely because of their membership in that group.
   a.   *Racial-ethnic discrimination* is the unequal treatment of a person on the basis of race or ethnicity.
   b.   The unfair and negative treatment of women relative to men of the same social class and racial-ethnic group is *gender discrimination*.
   a.   If one is both a woman and a racial-ethnic minority, one often faces the *double jeopardy effect*, in which the discriminatory effects of race and gender combined operate.
2.   Prejudice (an attitude) and discrimination (a behavior) do not always occur together, as evidenced in LaPierre's classic sociological study of prejudice and discrimination against Asian people in the 1930's.

3. Discrimination against the nation's minorities takes several forms. For example, the income gap between Whites and Blacks has remained virtually unchanged since 1967. Additionally, real estate agents selectively show houses to prospective buyers of different races.

4. Although housing discrimination is illegal in the United States. **residential segregation**, or the spatial separation of racial and ethnic groups into different residential areas, continues to be a reality.

C. Racism

1. **Racism** is the perception and treatment of a racial or ethnic group, or member of that group, as intellectually, socially, and culturally inferior to one's own group. Racism includes both attitudes and behaviors.

2. Individuals may engage in two forms of racism:

   a. **Dominative racism** is overt and exists in both individual and institutional forms. It includes racial slurs and assaults.

   b. **Aversive racism** is subtle, covert behavior such as avoiding interaction with members of other racial groups.

3. **Institutional racism** is negative treatment and oppression of one racial or ethnic group by society's existing institutions based on the presumed inferiority of the oppressed group.

   a. Institutional racism occurs when dominant groups have the economic and political *power* to subjugate the minority group, even if they do not have the explicit intention of being prejudiced or discriminatory against others.

   b. Institutional racism is evident in the criminal justice and educational systems of the United States. For example, Blacks and Latinos are systematically assigned to lower tracks in school than are White students with the same test scores.

IV. **THEORIES OF PREJUDICE AND DISCRIMINATION**

A. Social Psychological Theories of Prejudice

1. The **scapegoat theory** argues that historically, members of the dominant group in the United States have harbored various frustrations in their desire to achieve social and economic success. This frustration results in anger and aggression being directed toward minority groups.

2. Another social psychological theory focuses on the personality traits of prejudiced individuals. The **authoritarian personality** is characterized by a tendency to rigidly categorize other people, submit to authority, rigidly conform, be very intolerant of ambiguity, and be inclined to superstition.

B. Sociological Theories of Prejudice and Racism

Current sociological theory focuses on explaining the existence of racism in its various forms.

1. **Functionalist theory** argues that social stability requires the assimilation of racial-ethnic minorities and women. **Assimilation** is a process by which a minority becomes socially, economically, and culturally absorbed within the dominant society. How rapidly a group assimilates into a society will depend partly on its unique history and the group members' desire to assimilate.

2. **Symbolic Interaction theory** examines the role of social interaction in reducing racial and ethnic hostility and the social construction of race and ethnicity.

a. **Contact theory** argues that interaction between Whites and minorities will reduce prejudice on the part of both groups if three conditions are met.
   1) The contact must be between individuals of equal status.
   2) The contact between equals must be sustained.
   3) Social norms favoring equality must be agreed upon by the participants.

b. Symbolic interaction theory is also the basis for understanding race and ethnicity as socially constructed categories. People are assigned to racial and ethnic groups based on the meanings that their physical and/or cultural characteristics have been assigned in a racially stratified society.

3. **Conflict theory** assumes that class-based conflict is an inherent part of social interaction. Therefore, class inequality must be reduced to lessen racial and ethnic conflict in society. **Gendered racism** theory, a variety of conflict theory, focuses on the interactive or combined effects of race and sex in the oppression of women of color.

V. **DIVERSE GROUPS, DIVERSE HISTORIES**
The histories of various racial and ethnic groups in the United States are similar in some ways, yet unique in others. The groups' histories are related by the common experience of White supremacy, economic exploitation, and political disenfranchisement. Members of some White ethnic groups have been the victims of prejudice and discrimination as well.

A. Native Americans
   1. At the time of the first European contacts with Native Americans in the 1640s, there was considerable linguistic, religious, governmental, and economic heterogeneity among the original 500 nations of Native Americans. Much of this tribal culture has since been destroyed.
   2. Government policies forced many Native Americans into inhospitable country, leading to starvation. Massive numbers of indigenous people were also killed by disease and wars of extermination.
   3. Today, many Native Americans, especially those living on reservations, experience abject poverty, deprivation, alcoholism, and unemployment.

B. African Americans
   1. Slaves were forcibly imported from Africa to provide free labor for sugar and tobacco plantations in the United States.
   2. Until recently, our knowledge of slavery has been distorted by its dependence on the records and observations made by White male slave owners. More recent research includes the accounts, records, and narratives of the slaves themselves.
   3. In the early part of the twentieth century, the formation of Black ghettos subjected Black Americans to grim urban conditions. However, these ghettos also encouraged the development of Black community resources, including voluntary organizations, social movements, political action groups, and artistic and cultural achievements.

C. Latinos
   Latino Americans include Chicanos and Chicanas (Mexican Americans), Puerto Ricans, Cubans, and other recent Latin American immigrants to the United States, as well as Latin Americans who have lived in the United States

for generations. There is great structural and cultural diversity among the various Hispanic groups.

1. Mexican Americans
   a. Chicanos lost claims to huge land areas (which ultimately became Texas, New Mexico, and parts of other Midwestern states) in the Mexican-American War of 1846-1848.
   b. American immigration policy in the 1920s disproportionately restricted Mexican immigration.
   c. In the early twentieth century, irrigation and its resulting year-round crop production increased the need for field labor, leading to the exploitation of migrant workers from Mexico as a cheap source of labor.

2. Puerto Ricans
   a. The Jones Act extended U.S. citizenship to Puerto Ricans in 1917, and the Commonwealth of Puerto Rico was established in 1952 with its own constitution.
   b. Unemployment in Puerto Rico became so severe that in the 1960s and 1970s, the United States government attempted to reduce the population by encouraging forms of population control, including female sterilization.

3. Cubans
   a. Cuban migration to the United States is recent in comparison to other Hispanic groups. Many of the immigrants who arrived shortly after the 1959 revolution led by Fidel Castro were middle- and upper-class professionals and land owners.
   b. The most recent wave of Cuban immigration came in 1980 when the Cuban government opened the port of Mariel to anyone who wanted to leave. The more than 125,000 Cubans who came to the U.S. at that time have been unable to achieve much social and economic mobility.

D. Asians
   Asian Americans hail from many countries and diverse cultural backgrounds.
   1. Chinese Americans began migrating to the United States during the mid-nineteenth century in response to the U.S. demand for labor. They performed much of the most difficult and dangerous work of building the Central Pacific Railroad. Ethnic antagonisms led to the establishment of several urban Chinatowns, which were ethnic enclaves that provided strength and support to residents.
   2. The first generation of Japanese immigrants, who arrived between 1890 and 1924, were generally employed in agriculture or small Japanese businesses. The second generation of Japanese Americans became better educated than their parents, lost their Japanese accents, and generally assimilated.
      a. By executive order of President Roosevelt, much of the West Coast Japanese American population had their assets frozen, their real estate confiscated by the U.S. government, and were forced to move into relocation centers during World War II.
      b. In 1987, the U.S. government offered an official apology for their actions and awarded $20,000 to each former detainee.
   3. In 1934, the Filipino Islands became a commonwealth of the U.S. and immigration quotas were imposed upon the Filipinos. Over 200,000

Filipinos immigrated to the U.S. between 1966 and 1980, most of who were professional workers with high levels of education. Demographers project that Filipinos will become the largest group of Asian Americans in the United States.

4. Korean Americans are largely concentrated in Los Angeles, California. Many Korean immigrants were professionals in Korea but have experienced downward social mobility in the United States. Conflict between African American residents and Korean business owners exists in many communities today.

5. Vietnamese people began to arrive in the United States after the fall of South Vietnam in 1975. A second wave of Vietnamese arrived after China attacked Vietnam in 1978. Despite initial discrimination in a variety of locations, at last count, 95 percent of all Vietnamese heads of households were employed full-time.

E. Middle Easterners

Immigrants from countries such as Syria, Lebanon, Egypt, and Iran speak no single language and follow no single religion, yet they are grouped together socially. Many are from working class backgrounds, but those who are professionals have not always been able to secure employment in their original occupations, leading to downward mobility.

F. White Ethnic Groups

1. White Anglo-Saxon Protestants (WASPs) who immigrated from England, Scotland, and Wales were the first ethnic group to have widespread contact with Native American Indians. WASPs dominated the newly emerging society earlier than any other White ethnic group.

   a. The original WASP immigrants were skilled workers with a strong Protestant Ethic, or desire to work and achieve wealth.

   b. WASPs began to direct prejudice and discrimination toward other European immigrants during the mid- to late-nineteenth century. The dominance of WASPs in U.S. society has declined somewhat since 1960.

2. There were two waves of immigration of White Ethnic groups in the nineteenth century, with immigrants from Northern and Western Europe arriving in the United States from 1850 to 1880 and immigrants from Eastern and Southern Europe arriving from 1890 to 1914.

3. The Irish arrived in large numbers in the mid-nineteenth century as a consequence of food shortage and massive starvation in Ireland.

4. Another large immigrant group was Jewish people. Over 40 percent of the world's Jewish population now lives in the United States.

5. In 1924, the National Origins Act imposed *ethnic quotas* that permitted immigrants to enter only in proportion to their numbers already in the United States.

VI. **PATTERNS OF RACIAL AND ETHNIC RELATIONS**

A. The Role of Minority Culture

1. By tending to ignore the strong cultural element and the occupational, educational, economic, and cultural achievements of minorities, the **victimization perspective** takes attention away from the positive actions groups have taken in response to oppression. The experience of oppression has contributed to the development of cultural strengths.

2. Racial segregation of schools was prohibited in 1954 by the famous *Brown vs. Board of Education* Supreme Court decision. This ruling

was supported by research evidence indicating that segregated schools contributed to negative self-esteem for Black children.

    3.   Today, Black and Hispanic children in both segregated and integrated schools actually have higher self-esteem on average than do Whites, because they base their self-evaluation on their own reference groups.

B.   <u>Assimilation and Pluralism</u>

    1.   The assimilation model asserts that to overcome adversity and oppression, minorities need only to imitate the dominant White culture.

    2.   Robert Park argued that there were four stages in the attainment of complete equality for a minority group.

        a.   During **accommodation**, the dominant culture allows minority immigration into the society.

        b.   During **acculturation**, the minority begins to learn the language and other elements of the dominant culture, including manners and customs.

        c.   During **assimilation**, the minority enters the economy and becomes upwardly mobile through hard work, education, and jobs.

        d.   During **amalgamation**, minority group members intermarry with the dominant group and produce interracial or interethnic offspring.

    3.   There are four problems with the assimilation model.

        a.   It does not consider the amount of time that it takes for certain groups to assimilate.

        b.   Because Blacks arrived in the U.S. involuntarily as slaves, their histories cannot be compared to Whites who came voluntarily.

        c.   Many White ethnics, despite prejudice and discrimination, entered the U.S. at a time when the economy was rapidly growing and labor was in high demand.

        d.   Assimilation is more difficult for people of color because skin color is an especially salient characteristic.

    4.   It is questionable whether a society can maintain **cultural pluralism**, defined as different groups in society maintaining their distinctive cultures while coexisting peacefully with the dominant group.

C.   <u>Colonialism</u>

    1.   Robert Blauner developed the **domestic colonialism** model and applied it to American Blacks, asserting that they are an internal colony.

    2.   Blauner identified four elements of domestic colonialism:

        a.   There is forced and involuntary entry of the dominant group.

        b.   The affairs of the colonized group are administered and determined by the colonizers (the dominant group).

        c.   Racism and stereotypes are used to explain and justify the colonizer's domination over the minority group.

        d.   The colonizers do not allow the minority group to express its culture and values.

    3.   Blauner's model is also applicable to Chicanos, Puerto Ricans, and Native Americans.

D.   <u>Segregation and the Urban Underclass</u>

    1.   **Segregation** refers to the spatial and social separation of racial and ethnic groups.

        a.   *De jure segregation*, or legal segregation, is prohibited by law.

<blockquote>

    b. *De facto segregation*, or "in fact" segregation, still exists, particularly in housing and education.

   2. Segregation has contributed to the creation of an **urban underclass**, or a grouping of people, largely minority and poor, who live at the absolute bottom of the socioeconomic ladder in urban areas.

  E. The Relative Importance of Class and Race

   1. Wilson contends that social class has become more important than race in determining Black people's access to privilege and power in the United States. He recently argued that both race and class combine to oppress not only many urban Blacks, but Whites and Hispanics as well.

   2. Blalock argues that the effects of class, the effects of race, and the effects of the statistical interaction of race and class must all be explained. Furthermore, the effects of race and class can interact with the effects of gender, which yields a *triple jeopardy effect.*

</blockquote>

VII. ATTAINING RACIAL AND ETHNIC EQUALITY: THE CHALLENGE

  A. Racial-Ethnic Conflict: A Global Problem

  Across the globe, many racial and ethnic groups have sought self-determination, or the right to choose their own leaders, politics, and lifestyles. Ethnic conflicts in the former Yugoslavia and Rwanda exemplify this process, and those conflicts have effects around the world due to globalization.

  B. Civil Rights

  The civil rights movement of the 1950s and the 1960s was the major force behind the most progressive social change in race relations in United States history. This movement culminated in the passage of the 1964 Civil Rights Act, a federal law prohibiting discrimination on the basis of race, color, national origin, religion, or sex.

  C. Radical Social Change

   1. Militant leaders grew increasingly dissatisfied with the limits and slow process of the civil rights agenda in the 1960s and 1970s.

   2. The Black Power movement saw inequality stemming from the institutional power that Whites had over Blacks.

     a. Malcolm X advocated a form of pluralism by demanding separate business establishments, banks, churches, and schools for Black Americans.

     b. Militant groups such as the Black Panthers advocated fighting oppression with armed revolution.

     c. The Black Power movement influenced the development of other groups that targeted institutional racism, including *La Raza Unida* (a Chicano organization) and the *American Indian Movement* (AIM).

  D. Affirmative Action: Race Specific versus Color-Blind Policies for Change

   1. *Color-blind policies* advocate that all groups be treated alike, with no barriers to oppression posed by race, gender, or other group differences.

   2. *Race-specific policies* recognize that racial groups occupy a unique status because of the long history of discrimination and continuing influence of institutional racism.

   3. **Affirmative action**, a heavily contested program for social change, is a race-specific policy for reducing job and educational inequality. It includes two components:

a. recruiting minorities from a wide base in order to ensure consideration of groups that have been traditionally overlooked, but without rigid quotas based on race or ethnicity.

b. using admission slots (in education) or designated contracts or jobs (in employment) to assure minority representation.

4. The Legal Defense Fund argues that Affirmative Action does not constitute discrimination against the dominant group in society; however, legal opinion on affirmative action is inconclusive.

PRACTICE TEST

MULTIPLE CHOICE QUESTIONS

1. Inequality that rests on privileges and disadvantages that accrue to persons based on their membership in a particular racial or ethnic group is (are) racial and ethnic:
   a. discrimination.
   b. achievement.
   c. stratification.
   d. formation.

2. A social category of people who share common cultural elements, such as language, religion, norms, and customs, is a(n) _____ group.
   a. racial
   b. ethnic
   c. minority
   d. dominant

3. According to sociologists, which of the following statements about race is (are) true?
   a. Race is a genetically-based category that varies little over time.
   b. Definitions of race do not vary significantly within or across groups because they are based on a universal set of physical characteristics.
   c. A race is a group of people who have been defined as distinct on the basis of certain identifiable characteristics.
   d. All of the above statements about race are true.

4. The process whereby some social category such as nationality takes on what are perceived in the society to be race characteristics is:
   a. racialization.
   b. assimiliation.
   c. aversive racism.
   d. dominative racism.

5. Any socially distinct group that presumably shares common group characteristics and is forced to occupy low status in society because of prejudice and discrimination is a(n) _____ group.
   a. majority
   b. minority
   c. racial
   d. ethnic

6. The basic premise of contact theory is that:
    a. individuals who have particular personality traits, such as tendencies toward rigidly categorizing other people, submitting to authority, and being intolerant of ambiguity, are more likely to be prejudiced.
    b. WASP's deserve to receive a greater proportion of society's rewards because they have been living and working in the U.S. longer than any other group.
    c. prejudices between Whites and Blacks can be reduced through providing ample opportunities for sustained interaction between equal members of both groups.
    d. the urban underclass developed as a result of economic and political policies designed to reduce public services (such as police patrols and garbage removal) in urban areas to save money.

7. A racial or ethnic minority group typically has which of the following characteristics?
    a. Members feel a strong sense of solidarity.
    b. Membership is usually achieved rather than ascribed.
    c. Most members share an easily identifiable characteristic.
    d. Racial and ethnic groups typically have all of the above characteristics.

8. An oversimplified set of beliefs about members of a social group or social stratum that is used to categorize individuals of that group is a(n):
    a. prejudice.
    b. stereotype.
    c. victimization.
    d. discrimination.

9. The _____ implies that we categorize people on the basis of what appears initially prominent and obvious about them, such as skin color, gender, and age.
    a. salience principle
    b. victimization perspective
    c. racial formation theory
    d. authoritarian personality model

10. Conflict theory argues that the best solution for reducing racial-ethnic inequality is to:
    a. reduce the amount of contact racial and ethnic minorities have with Whites.
    b. encourage minority groups to better assimilate into the dominant culture.
    c. establish stricter punishments for people who insult or assault minorities.
    d. reduce the degree of class inequality in society.

11. The overt negative and unequal treatment of the members of some social group solely because of their membership in that group constitutes:
    a. prejudice.
    b. discrimination.
    c. differentiation.
    d. ethnocentrism.

12. The current spatial segregation of racial and ethnic groups into different housing areas of the United States is a form of _____ segregation.
    a. de facto
    b. de jure
    c. quid pro quo
    d. in loco parentis

13.   An example of the double jeopardy effect in the United States is:
        a.   White men are passed over for job promotions in order to increase the
                representation of women and racial-ethnic minorities in upper level jobs.
        b.   Black women are given preference over White women in hiring decisions.
        c.   Black women are paid less on average for their work than are both White
                women and Black men.
        d.   Black people are separated from White people in housing through the overt and
                subtle discriminatory practices of real estate agents and bankers.

14.   The theory that argues that members of the dominant group in the U.S. have historically
        harbored frustrations in their desire to achieve social and economic success, which they
        directed toward minority group members, is the _____ theory.
        a.   assimilation
        b.   scapegoat
        c.   resentment
        d.   contact

15.   The largest community of Jewish people in the world lives in:
        a.   Israel.
        b.   Poland.
        c.   Germany.
        d.   the United States.

16.   During the mid-1800s, when the United States annexed the land that became Texas,
        which ethnic group became defined as a race who was lazy and corrupt?
        a.   Cubans
        b.   Spaniards
        c.   Mexicans
        d.   Puerto Ricans

17.   Which of the following statements about WASPs is (are) true?
        a.   WASPs immigrated primarily from Ireland and Poland.
        b.   The original WASP immigrants were skilled workers with a strong work ethic.
        c.   The dominance of WASPs in U.S. society has increased somewhat since 1960.
        d.   All of the above statements about WASPs are true.

18.   According to Robert Park, the stage at which a minority group enters the economy,
        becomes upwardly mobile through education and hard work, and thus gains greater
        social equality, is:
        a.   amalgamation.
        b.   accommodation.
        c.   acculturation.
        d.   assimilation.

19. Which of the following is **not** a feature of domestic colonialism according to Robert Blauner?
    a. The dominant group gradually enters an area and assumes control of the population's government by consent of the colonized people.
    b. The dominant group determines the agenda and administers the affairs of the colonized people.
    c. The colonizers use stereotypes to explain and justify their control over the colonized people.
    d. The colonizers suppress the colonized group's cultural values and practices.

20. The spatial and social separation of racial and ethnic groups in housing is:
    a. social accommodation.
    b. residential segregation.
    c. racial differentiation.
    d. cultural genocide.

21. The 1924 National Origins Act:
    a. allowed the U.S. to legally establish Puerto Rico as a Commonwealth.
    b. allowed an increase in immigration for groups fleeing war in their own nations.
    c. prohibited the racial segregation of public facilities such as schools and buses.
    d. imposed ethnic quotas restricting immigrants to enter the U.S. only in proportion to their representation already.

22. Demographers predict that the _____ will become the largest group of Asian immigrants to the United State within the next thirty years.
    a. Filipinos
    b. Koreans
    c. Chinese
    d. Japanese

23. Those policies that recognize the unique status of racial groups because of a long history of discrimination and the continuing influence of institutionalized racism are:
    a. domestic-based.
    b. color-blind.
    c. race-specific.
    d. culturally-oriented.

24. The majority of Cuban people who immigrated to the United States following the Cuban revolution led by Fidel Castro were:
    a. impoverished people who had little education and few job skills.
    b. working-class people who were moderately educated, skilled craftspeople.
    c. middle-class people who were highly educated professionals and land owners.
    d. None of the above groups migrated to the U.S. after the Cuban revolution because the U.S. feared retribution from Castro if it allowed refugees to enter.

25. By executive order of President Roosevelt, which of the following groups had their assets frozen, their real estate confiscated by the American government, and were ordered into relocation centers in the United States during World War II?
a. German Americans
b. Japanese Americans
c. African Americans
d. None of the above groups experienced relocation, because the United States government has never violated American citizens' rights in this way.

TRUE-FALSE QUESTIONS

1. One necessary characteristic of a minority group is that it be comprised of fewer members than are in the dominant group.

2. The minority group intermarries and produces interracial or interethnic offspring at the acculturation stage of Robert Park's model.

3. Prejudice is an individually held attitude, while discrimination is an overt behavior.

4. Aversive racism is illustrated by the situation in which a White person insults and assaults a Black person solely on the basis of their race.

5. The authoritarian personality is characterized by a tendency to challenge authority and be very tolerant of ambiguity.

6. Social psychologists argue that people with an authoritarian personality are more likely to be prejudiced.

7. Conflict theorists argue that social stability requires the assimilation of racial and ethnic minority groups.

8. Content analyses show that there have been significant improvements in the portrayal of racial and ethnic minorities in the mass media, which has led to greater equality in society.

9. The income gap between Black and Whites in the United States has remained virtually unchanged since 1967.

10. Immigrants from Middle Eastern countries such as Syria, Lebanon, and Iran are classified as a single ethnic group in the United States because they share a common language and religious affiliation.

FILL IN THE BLANK QUESTIONS

1. Prejudice is revealed in _____, or the belief that one's own group is superior to all other groups.

2. That Black students are systematically assigned to lower tracks in schools than are Whites even when they have the same test scores is an example of _____ racism.

3.	The principle of stereotype _____ holds that the same negative stereotypes are often applied to various groups who are the targets of racial or ethnic prejudice.

4.	The social majority, or _____ group, assigns particular racial and ethnic groups to subordinate status in society.

5.	During the _____ stage of Park's model, the minority group begins to learn the language and customs of the dominant group.

ESSAY QUESTIONS

1.	Compare and contrast the experiences of, and outcomes for, three minority groups in the United States based on the circumstances (such as time period and primary reason for immigrating) in which they immigrated.
2.	Explain what sociologists mean by the assertion that "race and ethnicity are socially constructed" and provide evidence supporting this position.
3.	Identify the three conditions that contact theory argues must be met to reduce prejudice between Whites and minority groups.
4.	Explain how domestic colonialism has contributed to the establishment and growth of the urban underclass in the United States.
5.	Identify the four stages in the attainment of complete equality for a minority group according to Robert Park, and explain why this model would be difficult for some racial-ethnic groups in the United States to follow.

ANSWERS TO PRACTICE TEST

Answers to Multiple Choice Questions

1.	C.	314	Inequality that rests on privileges and disadvantages that accrue to individuals based on their membership in certain racial and ethnic groups is racial and ethnic stratification. Discrimination involves the unequal treatment of groups who have lower status in society.

2.	B.	314	A social category of people who share common cultural characteristics is an ethnic group. A racial group presumably shares certain biological characteristics, such as skin color or hair type.

3.	C.	316	Race is a socially constructed category. The biological characteristics that have been used to define different racial groups vary both within and between groups, as well as over time.

4.	A.	315	The process whereby some social category such as nationality takes on what are perceived in the society to be race characteristics is racialization. An example of this process was Adolph Hitler's labeling Jews, a religious group, a race.

5.	B.	318	A minority group shares common group characteristics and is forced to occupy low status in society because of prejudice and discrimination.

6.	C.	327	Contact theory posits that prejudice can be reduced by facilitating regular, sustained interaction between members of different groups.

7.	D.	318	Sociologists identify five typical characteristics of minority groups: membership is ascribed rather than achieved, members possess characteristics that are popularly regarded as different from those of the dominant group, members suffer prejudice and discrimination, members share a strong sense of solidarity, and members usually marry within their own group.

8. B. 318 An oversimplified set of beliefs about members of a social group or social stratum that is used to categorize individuals of that group is a stereotype. Stereotypes are presumed, usually incorrectly, to describe "typical" members of a group.

9. A. 319 The salience principle implies that we categorize people on the basis of what appears initially prominent and obvious about them, such as skin color and biological sex.

10. D. 329 Conflict theory views racial and ethnic inequality as rooted in class inequality. This theory advocates actively challenging current social arrangements that are based on differences in power and access to valued resources.

11. B. 323 The overt negative and unequal treatment of the members of some social group solely because of their membership in that group is discrimination. Prejudice is an attitude, or evaluation of a group. Ethnocentrism is the belief that one's own values, norms, and practices are superior to those of other groups.

12. A. 338 De jure segregation, or legal segregation, is prohibited in the U.S., but de facto segregation persists, as illustrated by residential segregation.

13. C. 323 Women of color experience discrimination as both women and members of racial-ethnic minority groups, a condition known as double jeopardy. One example of this double discrimination is lower wages.

14. B. 327 Scapegoat theory asserts that members of the dominant group in the United States have historically harbored frustrations in their desire to achieve social and economic success, which they direct toward minority group members.

15. D. 335 The United States contains the largest population of Jews in the world.

16. C. 332 Mexicans were defined as a distinct racial-ethnic group based on geographic origin.

17. B. 335 The original WASPs were skilled workers with a strong Protestant work ethic who immigrated primarily from England and Wales. Their influence has slightly declined in recent years. Native Americans were actually the first inhabitants of the United States.

18. D. 337 According to Robert Park, minorities need only assimilate into the dominant culture to attain complete equality. At the assimilation stage, minority group members achieve greater equality through education and work.

19. A. 338 Domestic colonialism is characterized by forced and involuntary entry, the use of stereotyping to explain and justify domination, and suppression of the minority culture. Thus, the dominant group takes control of the colonized group's affairs without their consent.

20. B. 324 Residential segregation persists in the U.S. because landlords, real estate agents, mortgage officers, and homeowners engage in practices that prevent racial minority group members from viewing or selecting housing in particular neighborhoods.

21. D. 336 The National Origins Act of 1924 set ethnic quotas limiting the number of immigrants from each country to their current representation in the United States.

22. A. 334 There were about one million Filipinos in the U.S. in 1985, and

demographers predict that they will constitute the largest group of Asian Americans within the next thirty years. Many Filipino Americans are well-educated professionals.

23.	C.	343	Those policies that recognize the unique status of racial groups because of a long history of discrimination and the continuing influence of institutional racism are race-specific. Color-blind policies advocate treating members of all groups the same.
24.	C.	333	Cuban immigration is relatively recent compared to the immigration of other Hispanic groups. A majority of Cubans who fled the country after the revolution were well-educated professionals.
25.	B.	334	By executive order of President Roosevelt, Japanese Americans were forced into relocation centers after the bombing of Pearl Harbor during World War II.

Answers to True-False Questions

1.	F.	318	A minority group need not contain fewer members than the dominant group. Sociologists define minority and majority groups in terms of their social characteristics, rather than by the number of people in the groups.
2.	F.	337	According to Park's assimilation model, minority group members marry and produce offspring with majority group members during the amalgamation stage.
3.	T.	320	Prejudice is an attitude, while discrimination is a behavior.
4.	F.	324	Aversive racism occurs when members of one group avoid interaction with members of another group on the basis of racial or ethnic differences. Overt behaviors such as insults and assault constitute dominative racism.
5.	F.	327	The authoritarian personality is characterized by tendencies toward rigidly categorizing other people, submitting to authority, and being intolerant of ambiguity.
6.	T.	327	An individual who has an authoritarian personality is more likely to be prejudiced.
7	F.	328	Conflict theory views social change as emerging from the active resistance of minority groups, rather than their assimilation into the dominant culture. Functionalist theory advocates the assimilation of minority groups as the primary mechanism for reducing social inequality.
8.	F.	323	The media is a major vehicle for the communication of racial-ethnic attitudes in the United States. The change in the stereotypical portrayal of minorities on television has been minimal.
9.	T.	324	Figure 12.1 indicates that the income gap between Black and White Americans has remained virtually unchanged since 1967.
10.	F.	334	Although Middle Easterners are categorized as an ethnic group in the U.S., members do not share a single language or religious affiliation.

Answers to Fill in the Blank Questions

1.	ethnocentrism	321	4.	dominant	318
2.	institutional	326	5.	acculturation	337
3.	interchangeability	320			

CHAPTER 13
GENDER

BRIEF CHAPTER OUTLINE
Defining Sex and Gender
Sex Differences: Nature or Nurture?
      Biological Sex Identity
      Physical Sex Differences
The Sociological Construction of Gender
      The Formation of Gender Identity
      Sources of Gender Socialization
      The Price of Conformity
      Race, Gender and Identity
      Gender Socialization and Homophobia
      The Institutional Basis of Gender
Gender Stratification
      Sexism and Patriarchy
      Women's Worth: Still Unequal
      Explaining the Pay Gap
      Gender Segregation
Gender and Diversity
      The Interactions of Race, Class and Gender
      Gender in the Global Perspective
Theories of Gender
      The Frameworks of Sociology
      Feminist Theory
Gender and Social Change
      Contemporary Attitudes
      Legislative Change

QUESTIONS TO GUIDE YOUR READING
1. How and why do sociologists distinguish between the biological category of "sex" and the social category of "gender?"
2. What are the five main agents of gender socialization in the United States, and how do they influence the formation of gender identity for males and females?
3. What traits are commonly associated with the categories of "femininity" and "masculinity," and why do sociologists view these differences as socially constructed?
4. How do race, ethnicity, age, and social class intersect with gender in the labor market, and what consequences does job segregation have for women in the United States?
5. How has the legal system contributed to increased equality for women in society?

KEY TERMS (defined at page number shown and in glossary)

labor force participation rate 365
matriarchy 364
occupational segregation 367
radical feminism 367
sexism 364

liberal feminism 375
multiracial feminism 376
patriarchy 364
sex 350
socialist feminism 376

KEY PEOPLE (identified at page number shown)
Patricia Hill Collins 376
Michael Kimmel 362
Harriet Taylor Mill and John Stuart Mill 375

Heidi Hartmann 376
Catharine MacKinnon 376

CHAPTER OUTLINE

Gender affects one's physical appearance and clothing, communication style, attitudes on many social and political issues, education level, type of employment, and income.

I. **DEFINING SEX AND GENDER**
   A. **Sex** refers to one's biological identity as male or female.
   B. **Gender**, the socially learned expectation and behaviors associated with members of each sex, is viewed as a more significant concept by sociologists.
      1. From the moment of birth, gender expectations influence how boys and girls are treated.
      2. Gender roles associated with masculinity and femininity vary greatly across cultures. There can be also be substantial differences in the construction of gender across social classes or subcultures within a single society.

II. **SEX DIFFERENCES: NATURE OR NURTURE?**
   Biology is only one component of the differences between women and men. The important question for sociologists is how biology and culture interact to produce a person's gender identity. **Biological determinism** refers to explanations that attribute complex social phenomena to physical characteristics.
   A. Biological Sex Identity
      1. A person's sex identity, determined by chromosomal structure, is established at conception.
      2. **Fetal sexual differentiation** is the prenatal process by which biological differences between the sexes are established.
      3. **Hermaphroditism** is a condition produced when irregularities in chromosomal formation or fetal differentiation produce persons with mixed biological sex characteristics.
         a. Case studies of such individuals reveal the extraordinary influence of social factors in shaping the person's identity.
         b. Parents of children who are given a sex reassignment are advised to not only allow genital reconstruction, but to also give the child a new gender identity through a new name and different clothing.
      4. *Transgendered* people are those who deviate from the binary system of gender, including transsexuals and cross-dressers. Trangendered people do not fit the normative expectations of gender despite enormous pressure to do so. A person may remain genetically one sex and socially the other.

B. Physical Sex Differences
1. Physical differences between the sexes include genital differences, length and weight at birth, heart rate, blood pressure, and muscle mass and bone density.
2. Biological explanations of inequality between women and men tend to flourish during periods of rapid social change, helping to support the *status quo*, or existing social arrangements.

III. **THE SOCIAL CONSTRUCTION OF GENDER**
Through **gender socialization**, men and women learn the expectations associated with their sex. This process affects self-concept, social and political attitudes, perceptions of others, and feelings about relationships with others. Even people who set out to challenge traditional gender expectations often find themselves yielding to the powerful influence of socialization.

A. The Formation of Gender Identity
1. One result of gender socialization is the formation of **gender identity**, or one's definition of oneself as female or male.
2. Two traits commonly associated with masculine gender identity are *competition* and *dominance*. Generally, men develop a more competitive orientation than women; and males evidence more dominant behavior than women, especially in same-sex groups.
3. Some cautions are necessary when interpreting social psychological studies of gender, because research findings are highly dependent on how the researchers define the behavior being observed.

B. Sources of Gender Socialization
Gender socialization, which occurs through various *agents of gender socialization*, is reinforced whenever gender-linked behaviors receive approval or disapproval from social members.
1. Parents and Gender Socialization
   a. Parents are one of the most important sources of gender socialization. For example, gender-linked assignment of chores is less marked in families where mothers are employed outside the home and in families from higher socioeconomic levels.
   b. Gender norms appear to be applied even more strictly to boys than to girls, for example, in the choice of toys for children.
   c. Gender socialization patterns in families vary within different racial-ethnic groups and across different generations.
2. Childhood Play and Games
   a. Socialization also comes from peers. Through play, children learn patterns of social interaction, cognitive and physical development, analytical skills, values, and attitudes.
   b. Research indicates that boys' play is more likely to encourage violence, individualism, and hierarchy.
   c. Research shows that girls play more cooperatively when they are in same-sex groups than in groups with boys.
   d. Children's literature, toys, and room decorations contribute to gender socialization and stereotyping.
3. Schools and Gender Socialization
   Schools are particularly strong influences on socialization because of the amount of time children spend there. Beginning in preschool,

teachers often have different expectations for boys and girls, and teacher behavior tends to heighten boys' sense of importance.

4. Religion and Gender Socialization

   a. Religion is an often overlooked but significant source of gender socialization. Religious doctrines have a strong effect on the formation of gender identity, particularly among the most devout believers, who hold the most rigid attitudes about traditional gender roles.

   b. The major Judeo-Christian religions in the United States place strong emphasis on gender differences, with explicit affirmation of the authority of men over women.

5. The Media and Gender Socialization

   a. The mass media communicate strong gender stereotypes. Despite some changes in recent years, television, the most pervasive communication medium, continues to deliver unrealistic portrayals of women and men.

   b. Advertisements are an important outlet for the communication of gender images to the public. They disseminate idealized, sexist, and racist images of women and men.

   c. Greeting cards, CD covers, books, songs, films, comic strips, and romance novels all contain images that represent the presumed cultural ideals of womanhood and manhood.

C. The Price of Conformity

   1. A high degree of conformity to stereotypical gender expectations takes its toll on both men and women.

   2. Male socialization encourages aggression and risk-taking, which contributes to men's higher rate of early death from accidents and violence.

   3. Women report higher rates of depression, have lower self-esteem, and suffer higher rates of eating disorders than do men.

D. Race, Gender and Identity

Because the experiences of race and gender socialization affect each other, men and women from different racial groups have differing expectations regarding gender roles. For example, African American women generally hold more egalitarian views of men's and women's roles. Due to their longer history of paid employment, African American women's socialization includes an emphasis on self-sufficiency.

E. Gender Socialization and Homophobia

   1. *Homophobia* is the fear and hatred of homosexuals. It plays an important role in gender socialization because it encourages stricter conformity to traditional expectations, especially for males.

   2. Once people internalize social expectations, they do not challenge or question the status quo. This reflects the *social construction of gender*, whereby what appears to be normal or customary is only that which people have been taught is normal.

F. The Institutional Basis of Gender

   1. **Gendered institution** is the term use to identify institutions that are patterned by gender, which results in different experiences and opportunities for men and women.

   2. Gendered relations within institutions may include stereotypical expectations, interpersonal relationships, and the different placement of

men and women in the social, economic, and political hierarchies of institutions.

    3.   Women who work in organizations dominated by men report that there are subtle ways that men's importance in the organizations are communicated, often resulting in women feeling like outsiders.

IV.   GENDER STRATIFICATION

Gender Stratification refers to the hierarchical distribution of social and economic resources according to gender. For example, two-thirds of illiterate people worldwide are women, and women in Afghanistan are not permitted to leave their homes unless accompanied by a man, a system referred to as *gender apartheid*. Although gender stratification varies cross-culturally, research indicates that women are more nearly equal to men in societies where six conditions exist: 1) women's work is central to the economy; 2) women have access to education; 3) ideological or religious support for gender inequality is weak; 4) men make direct contributions to household responsibilities and child care; 5) work is not highly segregated by sex; and 6) women have access to formal power and authority in public decision-making.

    A.   <u>Sexism and Patriarchy</u>

        1.   An **ideology** is a belief system that tries to explain and justify the status quo.

        2.   **Sexism** is an ideology, but it is also a set of institutional practices and beliefs through which women are controlled because of the social significance assigned to presumed differences between the sexes.

        3.   Sexism, like racism, distorts reality by making behaviors seem natural when they are rooted in entrenched systems of power and privilege.

        4.   Sexism is part of the institutional structure of society. Patriarchies are the most common form of society around the world, whereas matriarchies are rare.

            a.   **Patriarchy** refers to a society or group in which men have power over women.

            b.   **Matriarchy** refers to a society or group in which women have power over men.

    B.   <u>Women's Worth: Still Unequal</u>

        1.   Gender stratification is especially obvious in the persistent earnings gap between women and men. Although the gap has closed somewhat since the 1960s, women who work year-round and full-time still earn, on average, only 74 percent of what men earn.

        2.   The **labor force participation rate** is the percentage of those in a given category who are employed either part-time or full-time.

        3.   The labor force participation rate among women has changed most dramatically among White women in recent years.

        4.   Changes in family patterns in contemporary society mean that more women are the sole supporters of their dependents.

    C.   <u>Explaining the Pay Gap</u>

        1.   The Equal Pay Act of 1963 was the first federal law to require that men and women receive equal pay for equal work.

        2.   **Human capital theory** explains gender differences in wages as the result of differences in the individual characteristics that workers bring to the job.

            a.   This theory assumes that the economic system is fair and competitive.

b.   *Human capital variables*, including age, prior experience, number of hours worked, marital status, and education, influence a worker's worth in the labor market.

c.   Human capital theory only explains some of the differences between men's and women's earnings.

3.   The **dual labor market theory** contends that women and may earn different amounts because they tend to work in different segments of the labor market.

a.   The dual labor market reflects the devaluation of women's work, because there are generally low wages in jobs where women are most concentrated.

b.   The labor market is organized into two different sectors.

1)   In the *primary labor market*, jobs are relatively stable, wages are good, fringe benefits are likely, and workers are afforded due process.

a)   The first tier of the primary labor market consists of high status professional and managerial jobs.

b)   The second tier is composed of working-class jobs, including clerical work and skilled and semi-skilled blue-collar work.

2)   In the *secondary labor market*, there is high job turnover, low wages, short or non-existent promotion ladders, few benefits, poor working conditions, arbitrary work rules, and capricious supervision.

c.   Women and racial-ethnic minorities are far more likely to be employed in the secondary labor market than in the primary labor market.

d.   There is an *informal sector* of the labor market where there is even greater wage inequality, no benefits, and little, if any, oversight of employment practices.

e.   **Occupational segregation**, a pattern in which different groups of workers are separated into different occupations, reflects wage differences. There is a direct association between the number of women in given occupational categories and the wages paid in those jobs. The greater the proportion of women in a given occupation, the lower the pay.

4.   **Discrimination**, or practices that single out some groups for different and unequal treatment, is a third explanation of the wage gap.

a.   Overt discrimination continues to afflict women in the workplace. The discrimination explanation of the wage gap argues that dominant groups use their position of power to perpetuate their own advantage.

b.   Examples of discriminatory practices include harassment and restricting women's and racial-ethnic minorities' access to well-paying, unionized jobs.

D.   <u>Gender Segregation</u>

Gender segregation refers to the distribution of men and women in different jobs in the labor force. It is a specific form of occupational segregation. Sociologists use a measure call the **index of dissimilarity** to measure the extent of occupational segregation. This measure indicates the number of workers who would have to change jobs to have the same occupational distribution as the comparison group.

1. The Devaluation of "Women's Work"
   a. Jobs held by women are devalued in the United States.
   b. Only a small proportion of women work in occupations traditionally thought to be men's jobs, and very few men work in occupations historically considered to be women's work.
   c. Occupational segregation reinforces the belief that there are significant differences between the sexes.

2. Gender Segregation and Gender Identity
   Perceptions of gender appropriate behavior influence the likelihood of women's success at work. When men and women cross the boundaries established by occupational segregation, they are often considered to be gender deviants. Thus, many men and women in non-traditional occupations feel pressure to assert gender-appropriate behavior.

3. Internal Gender Segregation
   Gender segregation also occurs within occupations, meaning that women not only usually work in different jobs than men, but even when they work within the same occupations, they are segregated into particular fields or job types. For example, female physicians are concentrated in the least prestigious specialties in medicine, such as pediatrics.

4. Explanations of Gender Segregation
   a. One explanation of gender segregation is that women and men are socialized differently, thus, they choose different fields.
   b. A second explanation is that structural obstacles discourage women from entering male-dominated jobs and from advancing once they are employed in those jobs. For example, the **glass ceiling** places subtle yet decisive barriers to women's advancement.
   c. Despite these difficulties, some women are moving into new areas of work and are advancing to some degree.
   d. As the participation of women in the workplace increases, they continue to hold primary responsibilities for meeting the needs of home and family. This additional burden, called the "second shift," is a source of considerable stress.

V. **GENDER AND DIVERSITY**
The experiences of women in the United States are increasingly affected by global transformations.

A. The Interaction of Race, Class and Gender
   1. The tendency to think of gender as only applicable to White women has been one of the criticisms consistently articulated by women of color.
   2. Across class and race, women have many things in common, because of the influence of gender in their lives. However, their experiences also vary, depending on many other factors, including age, sexual orientation, religion, and a variety of other social variables.

B. Gender in Global Perspective
   1. Increasingly, the economic condition of women and men in the United States is linked to the situations of people in other parts of the world. For example, American workers have become part of an international division of labor.

        a.   Multinational corporations, seeking less expensive labor, often turn to the Third World, where they find that the cheapest laborers are women and children.

        b.   Worldwide, women work as much or more than men, but receive 30 to 40 percent less pay and own only one percent of all property.

    2.   Work is not the only measure by which the status of women throughout the world is inferior to that of men. The United Nations has concluded that violence is a "global epidemic" that takes many forms, including domestic violence, rape, infanticide, and genital mutilation.

VI. THEORIES OF GENDER

    A.   <u>The Framework of Sociology</u>

        1.   Functionalist theory argues that men and women fill complementary roles that support an arrangement that works to the benefit of society.

        2.   Conflict theory views women as disadvantaged by power inequalities between women and men that are built into the social structure.

        3.   Feminist scholars have used symbolic interaction theory to develop what is known as **"doing gender,"** a theoretical perspective on gender that interprets gender as something that is accomplished through the ongoing social interactions that people have with each other.

        4.   A more recent perspective on gender is "gendered institutions" theory, which views organizations as gendered. This theory argues that gendered expectations are built into social institutions, without people necessarily recognizing the specifically gendered outcomes that result.

    B.   <u>Feminist Theory</u>

        1.   **Feminism** has many meanings, but fundamentally, it refers to beliefs and actions that support justice, fairness, and equality for all women, regardless of their race, age, class, sexual orientation, or other characteristics.

        2.   *Feminist theory* refers to analyses that seek to understand the position of women in society for the purpose of bringing about liberating social changes. The link between theory and action is critical to feminist theory.

        3.   Four major frameworks have developed in feminist theory.

            a.   **Liberal feminism** argues that inequality for women originates in past traditions that pose barriers to women's advancement. Liberal feminism emphasizes individual rights and equal opportunities as the basis for social justice and social reform.

            b.   **Socialist feminism** is a more radical perspective that defines the origins of women's oppression in the system of capitalism. Capitalists exploit women as a cheap source of labor, thus, equality for women will only come when the economic and political system is changed.

            c.   **Radical feminism** interprets patriarchy as the primary cause of women's oppression. The origin of women's oppression lies in men's control over women's bodies. Radical feminists believe that change cannot come through the existing system, because it is controlled and dominated by men.

            d.   Most recently, **multiracial feminism** has developed to emphasize the interaction of race, class, and gender. This perspective argues that there is no single, universal experience associated with being a woman, because different privileges and disadvantages accrue to women and men as a result of their location in a racially stratified and class-based society.

VII. **GENDER AND SOCIAL CHANGE**

The women's movement has changed how women's issues are perceived in the public consciousness. It also led to legal and social changes that changed women's lives.

A. Contemporary Attitudes

1. Public consciousness about sexism and its inappropriateness in a presumably fair and democratic society is probably one of the most significant results of the feminist movement.

2. Women feel increased stress when they combine the demands of family and paid work. There is heated public debate about the effects of female employment outside the home on the family.

3. People's beliefs about appropriate gender roles have evolved as women's and men's lives have changed, with younger men expressing more egalitarian views than older men.

B. Legislative Change

1. Much legislation is in place that theoretically prohibits overt discrimination against women. Past legislation created new opportunities for women in employment and education.

2. Passage of anti-discrimination policies does not guarantee their universal implementation. For example, although there has been improvement in support for women's athletics, there is a long way to go toward equality in women's sports.

3. In the workplace, a strong legal framework for gender equality is in place, yet equity has not been achieved. Some scholars suggest implementing **comparable worth**, or policies that pay women and men equivalent wages for jobs involving similar levels of skill. This policy creates job evaluation systems that assess the degree of similarity between different kinds of jobs.

4. Many victories in the fight for gender equity are now at risk, such as *affirmative action*, a method for opening opportunities to women and racial-ethnic minorities that specifically redresses past discrimination by taking proactive measures to recruit and hire previously disadvantaged groups.

5. One possible solution to the problem of gender inequality is to have more women in positions of public power.

PRACTICE TEST

MULTIPLE CHOICE QUESTIONS

1. One's biological identity of male or female is referred to as:
   a. sex.
   b. gender.
   c. sexual orientation.
   d. sexual differentiation.

2.   Sociologists who study gender assert that gender expectations influence how boys and girls are treated starting at what age?
    a.   at five years old
    b.   at three years old
    c.   at one year old
    d.   at birth

3.   Which perspective generally attributes the complex social phenomena associated with gender to differences in physical characteristics between men and women?
    a.   social constructionism
    b.   biological determinism
    c.   patriarchal domination
    d.   chromosomal geneticism

4.   The prenatal process by which biological differences between the sexes are established is:
    a.   hermaphroditism.
    b.   infant gender segregation.
    c.   chromosomal separation.
    d.   fetal sexual differentiation.

5.   Among the Navaho Indians, the *berdaches* were considered:
    a.   hermaphrodites who were forced to live as women because they were anatomically deformed.
    b.   homosexuals because they were biologically male and married other men.
    c.   ordinary men who adopted many female characteristics and lived as a third gender.
    d.   men who were born anatomically male but underwent surgery to become female because they experienced a gender identity crisis as children.

6.   Which of the following physical differences exists between males and females?
    a.   average length and weight at birth
    b.   average muscle mass and bone density in old age
    c.   average heart rate and blood pressure in adulthood
    d.   All of the above physical differences are found between males and females.

7.   The process through which individuals learn the social expectations associated with their sex is:
    a.   fetal sexual differentiation.
    b.   gender socialization.
    c.   biological training.
    d.   sex segregation.

8.   Social psychological research on gender identity indicates that compared to men, women generally:
    a.   develop a more competitive orientation, especially in mixed-sex groups.
    b.   show more concern with including others in conversation and activities.
    c.   inhibit other people in conversations by frequently interrupting.
    d.   All of the above statements about gender identity traits are true.

9. Research indicates that men who thoroughly internalize gender expectations and "overconform" to standards of masculinity are:
   a. less likely to die from suicide and heart attacks.
   b. less likely to smoke, drink alcohol, and use illegal drugs.
   c. more likely to suffer injury and early death from accidents.
   d. more likely to have closer intimate relationships with their wives.

10. The fear and hatred of homosexuals that pervades American culture is:
    a. hermaphroditism..
    b. homoeroticism.
    c. homosapiens.
    d. homophobia.

11. Janet Lever's research on childhood play suggests that gender-typed play activities:
    a. emphasize cooperation and flexibility more for boys than girls.
    b. emphasize dominance and physical competence more for boys than girls.
    c. better prepare girls than boys for employment in large corporations.
    d. better prepare boys than girls for participation in intimate couple and family relationships.

12. Research on teacher-student interaction in schools indicates that:
    a. teachers typically correct boys, but not girls, by reminding them to raise their hands when they call out answers.
    b. teachers explicitly affirm men's authority over women by always giving boys leadership roles and requiring girls to follow their male peers.
    c. boys' sense of importance is increased when teachers respond to them, regardless of whether the teacher's attention is positive or negative.
    d. None of the above are true, because teachers today do not treat their male and female students differently.

13. The hierarchical distribution of social and economic resources according to sex is referred to as gender:
    a. identity.
    b. socialization.
    c. stratification.
    d. determination.

14. Research finds that women are more nearly equal to men in societies where:
    a. work is highly segregated by sex.
    b. women's work is central to the economy.
    c. religious support for gender inequality is strong.
    d. All of the above conditions contribute to greater gender equality.

15. A(n) _____ is a belief system that tries to explain and justify the status quo, or the existing set of social arrangements.
    a. ideology
    b. identity
    c. theory
    d. index

16. The set of institutionalized practices and beliefs that distort reality by making presumed differences between men and women seem natural, even though they are rooted in social systems that distribute power unequally, is:
    a. homophobia.
    b. matriarchy.
    c. devaluation.
    d. sexism.

17. According to the _____ perspective, people "do gender" through the daily interactions they have with one another and through the interpretations they have of other's actions and appearances as consistent with "being a man" or "being a woman."
    a. functionalist
    b. human capital
    c. dual labor market
    d. symbolic interaction

18. Which perspective explains gender differences in wages as the result of differences in the individual characteristics (such as education level) that workers bring to their jobs?
    a. symbolic interaction
    b. dual labor market
    c. human capital
    d. glass ceiling

19. In the _____ labor market, there is high job turnover, short or non-existent promotion ladders, few benefits, poor working conditions, and arbitrary work rules.
    a. secondary
    b. primary
    c. singular
    d. dual

20. Occupational _____ refers to a pattern in which different groups of workers are systematically separated into different occupations that reflect different wages.
    a. worth
    b. ceiling
    c. segregation
    d. participation

21. The purpose of the federal legislation known as Title IX was to:
    a. increase the percentage of women working in traditionally male occupations by enforcing quotas that required those employers to hire more women.
    b. forbid discrimination against women in any educational program, including sports, at any school that receives government funding.
    c. redress past discrimination in education by providing government funding for colleges to recruit and retain female students in science, math, and engineering.
    d. forbid discrimination in employment practices, including hiring and promotion.

22. Which theory has asserted that men fill instrumental roles and women fill expressive roles in society, thereby creating an efficient social arrangement?
    a.   gender
    b.   conflict
    c.   feminist
    d.   functionalist

23. Women's wages as a percent of men's wages, known as the "wage gap," is the smallest in which of the following countries?
    a.   United States
    b.   Hong Kong
    c.   Turkey
    d.   Mexico

24. Which feminist framework asserts that gender is learned through traditional patterns of socialization and change can best be accomplished through legal reform aimed at eliminating formal barriers to equal opportunity in education and employment?
    a.   liberal feminism
    b.   radical feminism
    c.   socialist feminism
    d.   multiracial feminism

25. The principle of paying women and men equivalent wages for different jobs that involve similar levels of skill is:
    a.   affirmative action.
    b.   comparable worth.
    c.   doing gender.
    d.   glass ceiling.

TRUE-FALSE QUESTIONS

1. Human capital variables include factors such as one's weight, height, and heart rate.

2. Jobs in the primary labor market are relatively stable and provide good wages and benefits such as health insurance.

3. Transgendered people are those who are sexually attracted to people of the same sex.

4. Social psychological studies of gender identity indicate that males evidence more dominant behaviors while females evidence more cooperative behaviors in groups.

5. On average, women in the United States today earn sixty percent of what men earn.

6. The major Judeo-Christian religions place strong emphasis on gender equality, with explicit support for an equal division of labor and decision making between men and women in both the public and private spheres.

7. The Civil Rights Act of 1964 forbid employment discrimination on the basis of race and religion, but not on the basis of sex.

8. Research indicates that women who "overconform" to the traditional feminine gender role experience higher rates of depression and health problems than do women who occupy multiple roles.

9. Black women are generally socialized to be more self-sufficient and independent than White women.

10. Girls who choose toys defined as "masculine" or play activities associated with boys are more negatively regarded than are boys who choose "feminine" toys or activities.

FILL IN THE BLANK QUESTIONS

1. Prior to the passage of the 1964 Civil Rights Act, some employers prohibited women from working in particular jobs *because they were female*, which is an example of overt _____.

2. Jobs in the _____ labor market are characterized by high turnover, low wages, few or no benefits, and poor working conditions.

3. Sociologists use the _____ to measure the extent of occupational segregation, or the number of workers who would have to change jobs to have the same occupational distribution as the comparison group.

4. The philosophy that is based on beliefs and actions that support justice, fairness, and equity for all women, regardless of race, age, sexual orientation, and other social characteristics, is _____.

5. A society in which men have power over women is a _____.

ESSAY QUESTIONS

1. Explain how the mass media contribute to gender socialization in the United States, giving specific examples to support your points.
2. Although gender stratification varies cross-culturally, researchers have identified several common factors in societies where women are more nearly equal to men. Identify these factors and explain why they contribute to gender equality.
3. Compare and contrast human capital theory and dual labor market theory as explanations for the persistence of pay differences between women and men.
4. Identify the main assumption common to the various frameworks within feminist theory and discuss what each framework recommends as the main solution to gender inequality.
5. Provide several examples of how legislation has promoted gender equality in the United States.

ANSWERS TO PRACTICE TEST

Answers to Multiple Choice Questions

1. A. 350 Sex refers to one's biological identity as male or female, while gender refers to the socially learned expectations associated with each sex.

Sexual orientation is how individuals experience sexual arousal and pleasure.

2. D. 350 From the moment of birth, gender expectations influence how boys and girls are treated.

3. B. 351 Biological determinism refers to explanations that attribute complex social phenomena to physical characteristics. Sociologists believe that gender is socially constructed because what appears to be natural is only what people have been taught is normal through socialization.

4. D. 351 The prenatal process by which biological differences between the sexes are established is fetal sexual differentiation.

5. C. 350 Hermaphroditism is a condition produced when irregularities in chromosomal formation or fetal differentiation produce persons with mixed biological sex characteristics.

6. D. 352 Although these average physical differences exist, differences in strength are also due to training, as in the case of female athletes.

7. B. 353 Men and women learn the expectations associated with their sex through gender socialization.

8. B. 353 Gender identity refers to one's definition of oneself as female or male. It is commonly associated with competition and dominance for males and cooperation and concern for others for females.

9. C. 359 Rigid conformity to traditional gender roles is associated with risk-taking behaviors for males and higher rates of depression for females.

10. D. 361 Homophobia is the fear and hatred of homosexuals that encourages conformity to gender roles by acting as a mechanism of social control.

11. A. 356 Lever's research indicates that girls' play is more cooperative while boys' play is more individualistic and aggressive, possibly resulting in boys being better prepared than girls for later employment in large, rule-oriented, competitive organizations.

12. C. 356 Teachers have different expectations for boys and girls and treat them differently, resulting in a heightened sense of importance for boys.

13. C. 363 The hierarchical distribution of social and economic resources according to sex is gender stratification. Socialization is the process through which gender expectations are learned, and identity refers to one's sense of self.

14. B. 363 Research finds that women are more nearly equal in societies where women's work is central to the economy, work is not highly segregated by sex, men contribute to housework and childcare, women are educated, and ideology supporting gender inequality is not strong.

15. A. 364 An ideology is a belief system that tries to explain and justify the status quo. A theory is a systematic explanation of a phenomenon that may or may not support the status quo. An index is a measure of a condition, and identity refers to one's self-concept.

16. D. 364 Sexism is a set of institutionalized practices and beliefs through which women are controlled because of the significance given to the presumed differences between the sexes. A matriarchy is a society in which women have power over men. Devaluation refers to assigning lower value to work done by a particular group, resulting in lower wages and prestige being associated with that work.

17. D. 375 "Doing gender" was developed by feminist scholars using the symbolic interaction perspective to examine perceptions and social interactions.

18. C. 366 The human capital theory explains gender differences in wages as the

result of differences in the individual characteristics that workers bring to the job, such as education level and experience.

19. A. 367 Dual labor market theory contends that jobs in the secondary labor market (such as cashier) have low wages, few benefits, and poor working conditions. Jobs in the primary labor market (such as management) are relatively stable and have good wages and benefits.

20. C. 367 Occupations are segregated by race, class, and sex, with the lowest paying jobs having the highest concentration of female workers.

21. B. 379 Title IX forbid discrimination in educational activities, including sports, in schools that receive federal funding. The Civil Rights Act forbids employment discrimination on the basis of race, color, religion, national origin, or sex. Affirmative Action redresses past discrimination through intentional efforts to recruit and retain disadvantaged groups, but not by enforcing strict quota systems.

22. D. 374 Functionalist theory traditionally argued that men fill instrumental roles and women fill expressive roles, creating an efficient arrangement that benefits society. Feminist theorists have been very critical of this view.

23. C. 363 According to Figure 13.3, the wage gap is smallest in Turkey and greatest in Hong Kong.

24. A. 376 Liberal feminism is the framework that views traditional socialization practices as the main cause of women's inequality, and suggests change through the legal system. As indicated in Table 13.2, radical and socialist feminism suggest that substantial change cannot occur within the current social system because society is characterized by patriarchy and class inequality.

25. B. 378 Although used by few employers, comparable worth policy creates pay scales on the basis of job conditions rather than the sex composition of the workforce. Comparable worth is the principle of paying women and men equivalent wages for jobs involving similar levels of skill. Affirmative Action redresses past discrimination through intentional efforts to recruit and retain women and racial-ethnic minorities. The glass ceiling refers to the fact that women are substantially blocked from senior management positions in the workplace. Doing gender refers to interaction that confirms perceptions of gender roles.

Answers to True-False Questions

1. F. 366 Human capital variables include age, education level, and experience.
2. T. 367 Jobs in the primary labor market are relatively stable and have good wages and benefits.
3. F. 352 Trangendered people, such as cross-dressers, deviate from the binary categories of masculine and feminine, but are not necessarily homosexual or heterosexual, which refers to one's sexual orientation.
4. T. 353 These studies show significant differences by gender, but the findings must be interpreted with caution, because the results are influenced by how the researchers define and measure the behaviors or traits.
5. F. 365 Women who work full time, year-round earn approximately 74 percent of what men earn in the United States.
6. F. 357 Judeo-Christian religions explicitly affirm men's authority over women, which supports gender inequality in society.
7. F. 378 The Civil Rights Act of 1964 prohibited discrimination in employment

based on race, color, religion, national origin, and sex, although sex was added by conservative politicians in an attempt to *defeat* the bill.

8.   T.   359   Traditional women experience higher rates of depression and health problems, while women who balance their lives with multiple roles report greater self-esteem and more gratification.

9.   T.   359   Black women, who historically had higher rates of labor force participation than White women, are socialized to be economically self-sufficient as well as nurturing.

10.   F.   354   Gender norms about play activities appear to be more strictly applied to boys than girls, so boys who choose more "feminine" toys are more negatively regarded than girls who choose "masculine" toys.

Answers to Fill in the Blank Questions

1.   discrimination   367
2.   secondary   367
3.   index of dissimilarity   369
4.   feminism   375
5.   patriarchy   364

CHAPTER 14
AGE AND AGING

BRIEF CHAPTER OUTLINE
The Social Significance of Aging
      The Physical Process of Aging
      Social Factors in the Aging Process
      Age Stereotypes
      Age Norms
      Age and Social Structure
A Society Grows Old
Growing Up/ Growing Old: Aging and the Life Course
      Childhood
      Youth and Adolescence
      Adulthood
      Retirement
      Old Age
Death and Dying
Age, Diversity, and Inequality
      Age Groups as Minorities
      Age Prejudice and Discrimination
      Quadruple Jeopardy
      Age Seen Globally
Explaining Age Stratification

QUESTIONS TO GUIDE YOUR READING
1. Why do sociologists consider age an important feature of social stratification?
2. What social factors influence the way that different individuals experience the physical and psychological processes that accompany aging?
3. How have changes in family structure and the age composition of the population shaped social policy in the United States?
4. How do race, ethnicity, class, and gender intersect with age in producing social inequality?
5. What are the four main stages of the life course in the United States and what characteristics are associated with each stage?

KEY TERMS

CHAPTER OUTLINE
Societies differentiate people on the basis of age, thereby providing unique social experiences and different life chances for various age groups. **Age stratification** refers to the hierarchical ranking of different age groups in society. Sociologists understand that the age composition of a

society makes a difference in the social issues that society faces. For example, the *"graying of America"* refers to the increasing proportion of older people in the United States, which represents a change in population structure that poses new dilemmas for providing social services to various groups in need.

I. **THE SOCIAL SIGNIFICANCE OF AGING**

    A.   <u>The Physical Process of Aging</u>

        1.   Physical changes are an inevitable part of the aging process; however, some people appear to age much more rapidly than others.

        2.   The aging process has psychological effects that are linked to physical changes. For example, people with hearing loss may find social situations distressing.

        3.   Depression is not an inevitable consequence of aging. Experiencing stressful events and lacking inadequate social support networks are most commonly related to depression among the elderly, just as they are related to depression among other age groups.

        4.   **Dementia** is the term used to describe a variety of diseases that involve some permanent damage to the brain, usually involving mental disorientation and memory loss. **Alzheimer's disease** is a degenerative form of dementia that involves neurological changes in the brain.

            a.   Once thought to be rare, Alzheimer's disease is now known to occur in approximately ten percent of the elderly population.

            b.   Regardless of its cause, Alzheimer's disease creates numerous social strains, particularly great stress on families caring for patients with the disease.

    B.   <u>Social Factors in the Aging Process</u>

        1.   From a sociological perspective, the social dimensions of aging are critical in determining how particular people and groups experience the aging process.

        2.   Cultural understandings of events like menopause, the time when ovulation stops and women can no longer conceive children, change over time. Once silently experienced, menopause is not widely discussed in public forums.

        3.   **Life expectancy** is the probable number of years a particular group is likely to live, given aggregate statistical patterns. Life expectancy varies by gender, race, and class, with women, Whites, and upper and middle class people living longer than men, racial minorities, and lower-income people.

        4.   Aging may be an inevitable process, but how it is experienced and how long one is likely to live are social facts.

        5.   The age structure of society shapes people's opportunities, is the basis for social expectations, and plays an important part in the development of social change.

    C.   <u>Age Stereotypes</u>

        1.   Much of the meaning of growing old in the United States is embedded in social stereotypes, or oversimplified categorizations of beliefs about the characteristics of members of a group.

        2.   **Age stereotypes** are preconceived judgements about what different age groups are like. Stereotypes tend to be persistent, but they can change.

            a.   Both youths and the elderly are burdened by negative preconceptions in the United States.

         b.   Age stereotypes are reinforced by popular culture, where the elderly are commonly presented as childish, a representation called *infantilization of the elderly*.

    3.   Perceptions of aging are socially constructed; that is, people subjectively define their age in terms of how they *feel* instead of by their chronological age.

D.   Age Norms

    1.   **Age norms** are explicit and implicit rules that spell out the expectations society has for the different age strata. Age norms define what you should or should not do according to your age.

    2.   Age norms are not fixed. Like other norms, they change as society changes and people adjust to new social conditions.

    3.   Contemporary social changes have disrupted the traditional norms that have distinguished different age groups because lifestyles are more diverse than they have ever been.

    4.   Age norms differ within groups. Some racial-ethnic communities in the U.S. revere the elderly for their wisdom, whereas the dominant culture values youth.

E.   Age and Social Structure

    1.   All societies practice **age differentiation**, or the division of labor or roles in a society on the basis of age. Although differentiation of roles by age is a feature of all societies, the specific roles given to different age groups vary from society to society.

    2.   In the United States, age differentiation can be seen in the different rights and privileges people have by virtue of their age.

    3.   In addition to differentiating roles on the basis of age, societies also produce age hierarchies, or systems in which some age groups have more power and better life chance than others. *Age stratification*, the hierarchical ranking of age groups, exists because there are processes in society that ensure that people of different ages differ in their access to society's rewards, power, and privilege.

    4.   Age is an *ascribed status*, that is, age is determined by when you were born. Different from other ascribed statuses such as race and gender, which remain relatively constant over the duration of a person's life, age changes steadily throughout life.

    5.   An **age cohort** is an aggregate of people born during the same period. Within a given cohort, there is considerable diversity on many dimensions, including sexual orientation, gender, race, class, nationality, and ethnicity. However, people in the same cohort share the same historical experiences, such as wars, technological developments, and economic fluctuation.

    6.   There is a continuing interplay between age and social class. As people of different ages pass through social institutions, society itself changes.

    7.   The "graying of America" and other major demographic changes will profoundly influence the experiences of current generations, both young and old.

         a.   Racial and ethnic minorities are an increasing proportion of the older population.

         b.   The proportion of the population classified as the "oldest old" (those over age 85) will continue to grow.

        c.   Women will continue to outnumber men in old age, especially among the oldest old.

        d.   Because the educational status of the elderly is increasing rapidly, the historical gap in educational attainment between the old and the young will likely disappear by the middle of the twenty-first century.

II.   A SOCIETY GROWS OLD

Never before have so many people in the United States lived so long. Certain assumptions, or the *contract between generations*, guide the expectations and obligations that exist between generations of people. The shrinking size of families means that the proportion of elderly people is growing faster than the number of younger potential caretakers. Young people now can expect to spend more years caring for an elderly parent than raising their own children. Geographic mobility and changes in family structure, including childless couples, single-parent families, and delayed childbearing, alter the traditional patterns of intergenerational care.

The growth of the welfare state in the 20th century means that different generations now compete for the different entitlement programs that provide social and economic assistance. Public resources directed to the elderly have grown in recent years, particularly as a result of effective lobbying by older people and the groups that represent them. Currently, Social Security is one of the oldest, most successful national social policies. However, recent estimates suggest that soon after the year 2000, without significant changes in the Social Security policy, there will not be enough workers to support the number of retirees by about the year 2020.

The question of **generational equity** refers to the debate about whether one age group or generation is unfairly taxed to support the needs and interests of another generation. Sociologists have noted that the generational equity debate need not be a divisive issue.

III.   GROWING UP/GROWING OLD: AGING AND THE LIFE CHANGES

Sociologists use a **life course perspective** to examine people's experiences across the life span. The life span is divided into four phases -- childhood, youth and adolescence, adulthood, and old age. Transitions to different phases in the life span are often marked by elaborate cultural rituals called *rites of passage*, which celebrate or memorialize events in an individual's life. Without specific social markers to announce the passage from one phase of the life span to another, the distinctions between different phases are unclear. The traditional markers of adulthood (education, marriage, work) no longer clearly mark the passage from one phase of life to another.

    A.   <u>Childhood</u>

        1.   The United States is been defined as a child-centered society. This high valuation on youth is especially evident in the mass media.

        2.   Popular images of childhood depict it as a period of play, fantasy, and freedom from responsibility, which is very different from the experience of children in the past. The exploitation of child labor was so pervasive in the nineteenth century that legislation prompted dramatic social change.

        3.   Although the United States is a child-centered society, it is becoming a more dangerous place for children because violence, homelessness, poverty, sexual abuse, and drug abuse disproportionately affect children. Using the "index of social health," or a composite measure of various indicators of social problems, the social health of U.S. children and youth has seriously deteriorated in recent years.

B. Youth and Adolescence
1. Adolescence is a relatively new category in the life cycle. Until the twentieth century, children moved directly into adult roles, but adolescence came to be regarded as a separate stage of life as the period of formal education lengthened.
2. Although the boundaries of adolescence are imprecisely defined, most regard the lower boundary as the transition from elementary school (at about age 12) to junior high and high school. The term "teenager" is often used to cover the period of adolescence, whereas the notion of "pre-teen" encompasses the ages of about 9 through 12 years old.
3. Establishing a central identity is a main concern in the adolescent period. Young people typically try to mark their unique identity through the establishment of *youth subcultures*, with relatively distinct habits, customs, norms, and language that define youth in contrast to other generations.
   a. Some youth subcultures reflect the alienation that young people feel from their families and school.
   b. Elements of youth subcultures include pastimes, engagement in "escapist" entertainment, and style.
   c. Within youth subcultures, special vocabulary and manners of speaking, known as *argot,* define youth autonomy and independence from adults.

C. Adulthood
1. The role of adult carries with it more responsibility, more rights, and more privileges than any other stage in the life cycle.
2. Becoming an adult is taking longer than before because people stay in school longer, live at home longer, and delay marriage.
3. As adulthood unfolds, the traditional norms of our society suggest that both men and women, but particularly men, should have achieved most of their life goals by the time they reach middle age.
4. The *mid-life crisis* is popularly conceived as a time of trauma during which people, men in particular, become fixated on what they have failed to achieve in their work and family roles, or the things that they never attempted. However, research indicates that mid-life is actually experienced as happy and positive by most people. For many women, middle age is a period of taking on new roles, such as a new job, first job, or return to school.

D. Retirement
1. One of the most significant markers of approaching old age is retirement from work. Many adults retire in their mid-sixties.
2. The difficulties of retirement have generally been treated as men's problems, but the expanded role of women in the job market means that proportionately more women will retire in the coming years.
3. The experience of retirement varies for different social groups, and racial-ethnic minorities and women have fewer resources in retirement.

E. Old Age
1. Aging is not an entirely negative process, but there is no doubt that old age is a difficult period that is made worse by the inadequacy of social institutions for the care of the aged.

2.   Although the elderly face many problems, old age is a happy period for many people. Gove's national study found that compared to younger people, older people reported greater feelings of self-confidence, strength, intelligence, contentment, and organization.
    a.   Critics of this study argue that these results reflect a *cohort effect*, because this particular age group, or cohort, has always felt positive compared to today's youth.
    b.   A difference between the two groups more strictly dependent on age would represent a true *age effect*.
3.   Many of the perceived problems of old age, such as loss of interest in and capacity for sexual activity, are myths.
4.   Having social support through extensive friendship and familial networks helps alleviate the stress experienced by those facing the death of a spouse.
5.   Elder care in the U.S. is provided in two major ways: institutions for the elderly and private care in the home.
    a.   Older people in the U.S. are cared for mainly by families, and most care is provided by women.
    b.   Many of the elderly live alone in the homes where they once raise families.
    c.   A relatively small percentage of the elderly are placed in long-term institutional care, but women are more likely to enter nursing homes than men, largely because of differences in life expectancy and higher rates of chronic illness among women.
        1)   The cost of nursing homes varies greatly, which tends to perpetuate social class differences.
        2)   The high cost of nursing homes forces many, even from the middle class, into poverty.
        3)   On average, the elderly and their families pay 40 percent of the total cost of nursing home care. The remaining cost is paid by two governmental assistance programs -- **Medicaid**, a program for poor people, and **Medicare**, a program for the elderly.
        4)   With the expansion of Medicaid and Medicare programs, the number of privately owned nursing homes increased in comparison to those administered by charitable organizations.
6.   Physical and mental abuse of the elderly has only recently surfaced as a notable social problem. Elder abuse includes physical, sexual, and emotional abuse; financial exploitation; neglect and abandonment.

IV.   DEATH AND DYING

The behaviors and events surrounding death have a social character. For example, when people know that someone is going to die, their behavior changes. Some people engage in *anticipatory grief* by beginning to grieve before someone actually dies. Sociologists note that even death is socially structured, because patterns of stratification that reveal themselves in life are also apparent in death. For example, certain groups are more likely to die a violent death than others, and infant death rates vary by race, ethnicity, and social class.

When a person dies, s/he dies within social institutions that are organized to handle death. The social organization of death is most apparent in the funeral home industry. Prior to the twentieth century, death was usually taken care of at home, and it was largely the work of women. The **hospice movement** developed as an alternative to hospital-based, technologically controlled death to provide more personal, home-based care for dying people and their families.

V.   **AGE, DIVERSITY AND INEQUALITY**

    A.   Age Groups as Minorities

          1.   A minority group is a group with relatively less power and fewer social and economic resources than more dominant groups. Age minorities in the United States include the young and the old.

          2.   Viewing oneself as a minority group can be the basis for mobilizing for group rights, which has been a very effective strategy used by the nation's older population.

          3.   Despite certain parallels, the similarities between the aged and racial and ethnic minorities should not be overstated, because a person is in a racial or ethnic minority group for life, but is only aged for part of his or her life. Furthermore, as a group, the elderly have more political power than other minority groups and benefit from receiving far more subsidized support in the form of medical care, insurance programs, and senior discounts at private businesses.

    B.   Age Prejudice and Discrimination

          1.   **Age prejudice** refers to a negative attitude about an age group that is generalized to all people in that group. Age prejudice is manifested in negative stereotypes and myths.

          2.   **Age discrimination** is the differential and unequal treatment of people based solely on their age. Age discrimination cases have become one of the most frequently filed cases through the Equal Employment Opportunity Commission (EEOC), the federal agency set up to monitor violations of civil rights in employment.

          3.   **Ageism** is a term sociologists use to describe the institutional practice of age prejudice and discrimination. Ageism is structured into the institutional fabric of society.

    C.   Quadruple Jeopardy

          Quadruple jeopardy refers to the simultaneous effects of being old, minority, female, and poor. The effects of quadruple jeopardy can be seen in several areas, particularly the economic condition and health of some older persons.

    D.   Age Seen Globally

          1.   The treatment of the very old in society varies somewhat depending on the extent of industry in the society.

          2.   In general, the elderly have greater social status in nomadic and agrarian societies, although there are exceptions.

          3.   In industrialized societies, advances in medicine and technology tend to result in longer life expectancy; consequently, a greater proportion of the population is elderly.

          4.   One important exception to the principle that the elderly have less social status in societies that are more industrialized is Japan. The elderly in Japan are accorded very high esteem and social status.

VI.   **EXPLAINING AGE STRATIFICATION**

    A.   Functionalists argue that adulthood is functional to society because those who are adult and middle aged are seen as the group contributing the most fully to society. **Disengagement theory** predicts that as people age, they gradually withdraw from participation in society and are simultaneously relieved from responsibility.

B. Conflict theory assesses the difference between age groups not in terms of what they contribute, but in what they want. This theory argues that barring youth and the elderly from the labor market is a way of eliminating both of these groups from competition for jobs.

C. Symbolic interaction theory analyzes the different meanings attributed to age, focusing on which symbolic meanings become attached to different age groups and to what extent these meanings explain how society ranks them.

PRACTICE TEST

MULTIPLE CHOICE QUESTIONS

1. The hierarchical ranking of different age groups in society that ensures that people of different ages differ in their access to society's rewards, power, and privilege is:
   a. life chances.
   b. age stratification.
   c. cohort experience.
   d. generational differentiation.

2. Which of the following states has the largest proportion of people age 65 years and older?
   a. California
   b. Texas
   c. Florida
   d. Utah

3. Which of the following social factors tends to speed up the physical aging process?
   a. smoking cigarettes
   b. physical inactivity
   c. air pollution
   d. All of the above factors tend to speed up the physical aging process.

4. Which of the following groups has the longest life expectancy in the United States?
   a. White women
   b. White men
   c. Black women
   d. Black men

5. Age _____ refer to exaggerations or broad generalizations made about the attributes of people of different age groups.
   a. labels
   b. epithets
   c. stereotypes
   d. discrimination

6.   Which of the following is a common stereotype of elderly people in the United States?
      a.   They are adorable, innocent, and charming.
      b.   They are stubborn and lonely.
      c.   They are lazy and irresponsible.
      d.   They are careless and selfish.

7.   Age _____ are the explicit and implicit rules that spell out the expectations society has for members of different age groups.
      a.   values
      b.   norms
      c.   effects
      d.   cohorts

8.   All societies practice _____, or the division of labor and social roles on the basis of age.
      a.   age discrimination
      b.   rites of passage
      c.   age differentiation
      d.   generational categorization

9.   Depicting older people throwing tantrums or playing children's games illustrates the concept known as _____ of the elderly.
      a.   construction
      b.   infantilization
      c.   medicalization
      d.   sentimentalization

10.   Which of the following demographic trends has been predicted for the United States?
      a.   Whites will become an increasing proportion of the older population.
      b.   The proportion of people over age 85 will continue to grow.
      c.   Men will begin to outnumber women over age 65.
      d.   All of the above population trends have been predicted for the United States.

11.   Changes in family structure in the United States:
      a.   mean that the proportion of older people is growing faster than the number of younger potential caretakers.
      b.   mean that young people now can expect to spend more years caring for their own children than for an elderly parent.
      c.   have eliminated the social contract between generations.
      d.   None of the above are consequences of changes in family stucture.

12.   The concept of _____ refers to the debate about whether one age group or generation is unfairly taxed in order to support the needs and interests of another generation.
      a.   generational equity
      b.   generation gap
      c.   age jeopardy
      d.   age justice

13. Rites of passage such as weddings, christenings, and Bar Mitzvahs:
    a. are rituals that celebrate or memorialize events in an individual's life.
    b. are public affirmations of a change in an individual's social status.
    c. provide transitions to different phases of the life cycle.
    d. All of the above statements about rites of passage are true.

14. Which of the following factors is **not** a central feature of the life course perspective?
    a. the roles individuals occupy over the life span
    b. the sociohistorical context in which people grow up
    c. the personal events that individuals experience during their lifetimes
    d. the physiological consequences of disease for individuals who become ill

15. The mid-life crisis:
    a. refers to the time of trauma experience by most men and women during middle adulthood.
    b. is associated with women becoming fixated on what they have failed to achieve or the things they never attempted to do.
    c. is largely non-existent, because mid-life is actually experienced as happy and positive by most men and women.
    d. None of the above statements are true.

16. Which stage of the life course is characterized by attempts to establish autonomy and independence from authority figures while developing a coherent identity?
    a. childhood
    b. adolescence
    c. middle adulthood
    d. old age

17. Individuals in which stage of the life course have most rights and social responsibilities relative to people in other stages of the life course?
    a. children
    b. adolescents
    c. adults
    d. elderly

18. Which of the following statements is (are) true concerning the elderly who are placed in long-term institutional care?
    a. Approximately one fourth of elderly men and women in the U.S. reside in nursing homes during the later years of their lives.
    b. On average, the elderly and their families pay only ten percent of the total cost of nursing home care, because government programs pay the remainder.
    c. Men are less likely than women, and Black people are less likely than White people, to enter nursing homes during old age.
    d. All of the above statements about institutional care for the elderly are true.

19. Margaret's husband was diagnosed with terminal cancer and told he would live about three months. Margaret has started to make plans for her husband's funeral and is already beginning to mourn her loss. Sociologists refer to this as:
    a. anticipatory grief.
    b. spousal withdraw.
    c. clinical depression.
    d. financial exploitation.

20. According to functionalist theory, a manifest function of a funeral is to:
    a. dispose of the deceased person's body.
    b. provide emotional support to the bereaved.
    c. publicly acknowledge and commemorate the dead person.
    d. All of the above are manifest functions of funerals.

21. Age _____ refers to the differential and unequal treatment of people based solely on their age.
    a. discrimination
    b. stereotype
    c. prejudice
    d. jeopardy

22. Prior to the twentieth century, the preparation of a deceased person's body was a:
    a. profitable business handled by professional funeral directors.
    b. medical process, handled by licensed physicians and nurses.
    c. church matter, handled by ordained ministers and priests.
    d. family matter, handled by women in the community.

23. The simultaneous effects of being old, minority, female, and poor is referred to as:
    a. quadruple jeopardy
    b. anticipatory poverty.
    c. interactive discrimination.
    d. infantalization of the elderly.

24. Which theory argues that as people age, they gradually withdraw from participation in society and are simultaneously relieved from some responsibilities?
    a. symbolic interaction theory
    b. social uselessness theory
    c. disengagement theory
    d. life course theory

25. Which of the following theories argues that barring youths and the elderly from the labor market is a way of eliminating both of these groups from competition for jobs?
    a. conflict theory
    b. functionalist theory
    c. disengagement theory
    d. symbolic interaction theory

TRUE-FALSE QUESTIONS

1. The United States has a higher child poverty rate than any other industrialized country.

2. Depression is strongly associated with getting older because it is rooted in the inevitable deterioration of mental capacity that occurs during the aging process.

3. Although differentiation of roles by age is a feature of all societies, the specific roles given to different age groups vary from society to society.

4. The majority of elderly people have no interest in or capacity for sexual activity.

5. About half of all people over age 65 eventually develop Alzheimer's disease.

6. The number of age discrimination cases filed through the Equal Employment Opportunity Commission (EEOC), the federal agency that monitors violations of civil rights in employment, has significantly declined since the 1960s.

7. Using the "index of social health," or a composite measure of various indicators of social problems, the social health of children in the United States has significantly improved in the last 25 years.

8. Gove's national study found that when compared to younger people, older people reported less self-confidence and contentment with their lives.

9. Defining themselves as a minority group can be the basis for mobilizing for more rights, which has been done very effectively by the nation's older population.

10. Because menopause causes a variety of negative physical and emotional symptoms for women, most women dread the onset of menopause and are depressed when it occurs.

FILL IN THE BLANK QUESTIONS

1. Sociologists refer to an aggregate of people born during the same period who share the same historical experiences is a _____.

2. The _____ movement provided people who are ill with an alternative to hospital-based, technologically controlled death by providing more personalized care to dying individuals and their families within the home environment.

3. One demographic change that is profoundly affecting the United States is the aging of the Baby Boom cohort, a trend commonly referred to as the _____ of America.

4. Life _____ is the probable number of years a particular group is likely to live given aggregate statistical patterns.

5. The general term used to describe a variety of diseases that involve some damage to the brain, usually including mental disorientation and memory loss, is _____.

ESSAY QUESTIONS

1. Identify the four phases of the life span and summarize the main features of each phase.
2. Discuss how the projected demographic changes for the United States will influence caregiving demands and social policies.

3. Discuss the similarities and differences between racial-ethnic groups and the aged as minority groups.
4. Compare and contrast the perspective of aging provided by functionalist and conflict theories.
5. Explain how death is socially structured in the United States.

ANSWERS TO PRACTICE TEST

Answers to Multiple Choice Questions

1.	B.	383	Age stratification is the hierarchical ranking of different age groups in society, which results in people of different ages having different access to society's rewards and resources.
2.	C.	346	The largest proportion of elderly people is found in Florida's population.
3.	D.	385	Smoking, physical inactivity, and air pollution tend to speed up the physical aging process.
4.	A.	388	White people generally live longer than racial and ethnic minorities, and women generally live longer than men.
5.	C.	389	Age stereotypes are perceived judgements about what different age groups are like. Stereotypes are generalizations that are often false.
6.	B.	388	Elderly people are often stereotyped as lonely and stubborn. Children are perceived as adorable and innocent, while adolescents are viewed as careless, sloppy, irresponsible, and lazy.
7.	B.	390	Age norms are explicit and implicit rules that spell out the expectations society has for different age strata.
8.	C.	391	All societies practice age differentiation, or the division of labor or assignment of roles on the basis of age.
9.	B.	389	Depicting older people as stubborn or childish is referred to as infantalization of the elderly. Sentimentalization refers to viewing children as precious, rather than as economically beneficial.
10.	B.	392	The proportion of the population over age 85, classified as the "oldest old," will continue to grow. Women continue to outlive men, and Whites are declining as a proportion of the elderly population.
11.	A.	393	Changes in family structure in the U.S. mean that the proportion of the elderly is growing faster than the number of younger potential caretakers. Young people now can expect to spend more years caring for an elderly parent than raising their own children. The social contract between generations still exists, but changes in families have strained people's abilities to care for their aging parents.
12.	A.	394	The question of generational equity refers to the debate about whether one age group is unfairly taxed to support the needs of another generation. This issue is raised in discussions about Social Security.
13.	D.	395	Rites of passage are rituals that celebrate or memorialize events in an individual's life and provide transitions to different phases of the life cycle. A rite of passage such as a wedding publicly affirms a change in someone's status, for example, from single to married person.
14.	D.	395	The life course perspective examines social roles, personal experiences, and the historical context in which people live. This perspective is not useful for examining the physiological effects of illness.

15. C. 398 The mid-life crisis is largely non-existent, because mid-life is actually experienced as happy and positive by most men and women.

16. B. 396 Adolescence is characterized by attempts to form a coherent identity and establish independence from parents and other authority figures. Childhood is, ideally, a carefree period with little responsibility. During old age, many people disengage from some social roles (such as paid employment) and are relieved of responsibilities (such as childrearing).

17. B. 365 Adulthood carries with it the most rights and responsibilities.

18. C. 402 About 10 percent of elderly people reside in nursing homes, more often women than men. White people enter nursing homes more often than do Black or Hispanic people. Most elder care is provided by female relatives within the home. Elderly people and their families pay approximately 44 percent of the total cost of nursing home care.

19. A. 404 Anticipatory grief involves preparing emotionally and practically for the impending death of a loved one.

20. D. 404 The manifest functions of funerals include the clearly apparent purposes that they serve, such as disposing of the body, commemorating the deceased, and supporting the survivors.

21. A. 406 Age discrimination is the differential and unequal treatment of people based solely on their age, while prejudice is a negative attitude toward certain people. Stereotypes are generalizations made about members of different age strata.

22. C. 405 The preparation of a deceased person's body was a family matter handled by women in the community prior to industrialization. Today, death is handled by professional funeral directors.

23. A. 407 Being old, minority, female, and poor is referred to as quadruple jeopardy because each of these statuses is relatively low in society. Combined, these statuses put impoverished elderly women from racial-ethnic minorities at great risk for pronounced poverty and poor health.

24. C. 409 Disengagement theory argues that as people age, they gradually withdraw from participation in society and are simultaneously relieved from responsibility.

25. A. 409 As summarized in Table 14.3, conflict theory asserts that age intersects with race, class, and gender inequality as groups compete for valued resources such as jobs.

Answers to True-False Questions

1. T. 397 The United States has the highest rate of child poverty among industrialized nations, as indicated in Figure 14.3.

2. F. 385 Neither depression nor deterioration of mental capacity are inevitable consequences of aging.

3. T. 391 Although roles vary cross-culturally, all societies practice age differentiation.

4. F. 401 Most people retain sexual interest and capacity well into old age. That older people are not interested in or capable of sex is a myth, as indicated by Table 14.2.

5. F. 386 Alzheimer's disease is known to occur in approximately ten percent of the population age 65 and over.

6.	F.	406	Age discrimination cases are one of the most frequently filed complaints received by the EEOC. Legislation was passed in 1967 to protect people from age discrimination in employment.
7.	F.	396	According to the "index of social health," or a composite measure of various indicators of social problems such as infant mortality rate, child abuse, and suicide, the social health of American children and youth has significantly deteriorated in recent years.
8.	F.	400	Gove's national study indicates that older people are more content and self-confident than are younger people.
9.	F.	362	The elderly have formed organizations such as the AARP and the Gray Panthers to advocate for more rights and better access to resources.
10.	F.	387	Despite evidence that menopause is not related to serious depression in most women, it is still culturally depicted as a negative experience in the United States.

Answers to Fill in the Blank Questions

1.	cohort	392
2.	hospice	405
3.	graying	384
4.	expectancy	388
5.	dementia	386

CHAPTER 15
FAMILIES

BRIEF CHAPTER OUTLINE
Defining the Family
Comparing Kinship Systems
        Number of Marriage Partners
        Who Marries Whom?
        Property and Descent
        Place of Residence
        Who Holds Power?
        Extended and Nuclear Families
Sociological Theory and Families
        Functionalist Theory and the Family
        Conflict Theory and the Family
        Feminist Theory and the Family
        Symbolic Interaction Theory and the Family
Diversity Among Contemporary American Families
        Female-Headed Households
        Married Couple Families
        Stepfamilies
        Gay and Lesbian Households
        Singles
Marriage and Divorce
        Marriage
        Divorce
        Family Violence
Changing Families/Changing Society
        Global Changes in Family Life
        Families and Social Policy

QUESTIONS TO GUIDE YOUR READING

1.   Why do sociologists consider the family a social institution, and what are the main features of the family as an institution?

2.   What is the distinction between a family and a household according to the United States Census Bureau, and how does this distinction influence social policy?

3.   What are the various forms of kinship systems found in societies around the world?

4.   Why do sociologists consider the family one of the most rapidly changing social institutions in the United States, and what evidence is there of such change?

5.   How do sociologists explain the prevalence of family violence in the United States, and what suggestions do they make for addressing this serious social problem?

KEY TERMS (defined at page number shown and in glossary)

bilateral kinship system 420
egalitarian societies 420
exogamy 418
family 416
household 417
matriarchy 420
matrilocal kinship system 420
monogamy 418

cohabitation 431
endogamy 418
extended families 420
homogamy 419
kinship system 417
matrilineal kinship system 420
miscegenation 419
neolocal residence 420

CHAPTER OUTLINE

The *family ideal*, represented by a father employed as the major breadwinner and a mother at home raising children, has long been defined within dominant American culture as the family to which we should all aspire, yet few families conform to this ideal today.

Families in the United States are experiencing significant social changes that are frequently topics of heated debate. Sociologists view the family as a *social institution*, or an established social system that emerges, changes, and persists over time. Like other social institutions, families are shaped by their relationship to systems of inequality in society. For example, race, class, gender, and age stratification affect how society values certain families. These systems of stratification also influence the resources available to different families as well as the power that individual members have within families.

The family has traditionally been defined as a social unit consisting of those people related through marriage, birth, or adoption who reside together in officially sanctioned relationships and who engage in economic cooperation, socially approved sexual relations, and reproduction and childrearing. Changes in contemporary family life require some flexibility in this definition, because not all families fit these conditions. Defining the family has proven difficult for the United States Bureau of the Census, the government organization officially responsible for counting and classifying families. The Census Bureau defines a **household** as all persons occupying a housing unit who may or may not be related, whereas a family is defined as a group of two or more people related by birth, marriage, or adoption and residing together." Sociologists often define the **family** as a primary group of people, usually related by ancestry, marriage, or adoption, who form a cooperative economic unit to care for offspring and each other, and who are committed to maintaining the group over time.

I. **COMPARING KINSHIP SYSTEMS**

A **kinship system** is the pattern of relationships that define people's family relationships to one another. Kinship systems vary enormously across cultures and over time. Kinship systems are generally be characterized by these features:

* how many marital partners are permitted at one time;
* who is permitted to marry whom;
* how descent is determined and how property is passed on;
* where the family resides; and
* how power is distributed.

A. Number of Marriage Partners

1. **Polygamy** is the practice whereby men or women have multiple partners. *Polyandry*, the practice of a woman having more than one husband, is extremely rare. The more common form of polygamy is *polygyny*, where a man has more than one wife.

   a. Within the U.S., polygyny was once practiced among the Mormons, but the Church of the Latter Day Saints prohibited it in 1890. Although polygyny is most commonly associated with Mormons, other groups have also practiced this marital form.

   b. Polygyny has an economic function for families because wealthy men who can afford multiple wives are provided with a source of cheap labor.

2. **Monogamy**, the practice of forming a sexually exclusive marriage with one spouse at a time, is the most common form of marriage in the U.S.

3. Many sociologists characterize modern marriage as *serial monogamy*, in which individuals may, over a lifetime, have more than one marriage, but maintain only one spouse at a given time.

B. Who Marries Whom?

1. **Exogamy** is the practice of selecting mates from outside one's group. The group may be based on religion, territory, or racial-ethnic identity.

2. **Endogamy** is the practice of selecting mates from within one's group.

3. Even if certain forms of marriage are not explicitly outlawed, societies establish normative expectations about who is an appropriate marriage partner.

   a. The *incest taboo*, generally considered to be universal, is a cultural norm forbidding sexual relations and marriage between certain kin.

   b. Many cultures have a tradition of *arranged marriages*, in which parents or their elders make rationally calculated choices about the appropriate marriage partner for their children.

4. There is a clear pattern of homogamy in the United States, whereby people select mates with very similar social characteristics to their own.

   a. Most marriages are between members of the same racial group. Interracial marriage represents less than 3 percent of married couples; however, an increase in interracial marriage is contributing to a more multiracial, multicultural society.

   b. **Miscegenation** refers to the mixing of races through marriage. In the past, anti-miscegenation laws prohibited marriage between various racial groups. Significant not only for how they regulated marriage, but also for the importance they have had in establishing definitions of racial groups, these laws were not declared unconstitutional until 1967.

C. Property and Descent

1. Kinship systems shape the distribution of property in society, most notably by dictating how lines of descent are determined.

   a. In **patrilineal kinship systems**, family lineage or ancestry is traced through the family of the father. Offspring in such systems are typically given the name of the father.

   b. In **matrilineal kinship systems**, ancestry is traced through the mother.

2. In the United States, descent is traced through both the father and the mother, representing a **bilateral kinship system**; however, there is a patrilineal bias in that children tend to take the name of the father.

D. Place of Residence

1. In **patrilocal kinship systems**, a woman is separated from her own kinship group and resides with the husband and/or his kinship group after marriage.

2. In **matrilineal kinship systems**, a woman continues to live with her family of origin after marriage. The husband resides with the wife and her family, although he does not give up membership in his own group.

3. **Neolocal residence** is the practice of the new couple establishing their own residence, a common practice in the United States.

E.   Who Holds Power?
     1.   A **patriarchy** is a society or group where men have power over women. This is the most common form around the world.
     2.   A **matriarchy** is a society or group where women have power over men.
     3.   In **egalitarian societies**, men and women share power equally, have equal access to resources, and share decision-making. Although women and men may have different roles in egalitarian societies, they are both perceived as contributing to the common good and judged to have equal social worth.

F.   Extended and Nuclear Families
     1.   **Extended families** are those in which a group of related kin, in addition to parents and children, live together in the same household.
          a.   Extended families are common among groups who must share their labor and economic resources to survive.
               1)   Sociologists have identified *othermothers* among African-Americans, who assist bloodmothers by sharing mothering responsibilities.
               2)   Family clans in poor rural areas provide another example of extended kinship systems, as well as the system of *compandrazgo* among Chicanos.
          b.   Extended families are also found at the very top of the socio-economic scale.
     2.   The **nuclear family** is one where a married couple resides together with their children.
          a.   The origin of the nuclear family in Western society is tied to industrialization. With industrialization, paid labor was performed mostly in factories and public marketplaces, resulting in the separation of the family and the workplace.
          b.   Racial-ethnic minority families developed in the context of disruptions posed by the experiences of slavery, migration, and urban poverty.
          c.   When families are poor, they often find it necessary for the entire family to work to meet the household's economic needs.

II.   **SOCIOLOGICAL THEORY AND FAMILIES**
The complexity of family patterns makes it impossible to understand families from any single perspective. Sociologists who study the family have used four primary perspectives in their analyses: functionalist theory, conflict theory, feminist theory, and symbolic interaction theory.
A.   Functionalist Theory and The Family
     1.   Functionalist theorists view the family as fulfilling particular societal needs, including socializing the young, regulating sexual activity and procreation, providing physical care for family members, and giving psychological support and emotional security to individuals.
     2.   Marriage is conceptualized as a mutually beneficial exchange wherein women receive protection, economic support, and status in return for emotional support, sexual intimacy, household maintenance, and the production of offspring.

3.   When societies experience disruption and change, institutions like the family become disorganized, which weakens the social consensus around which institutions have formed.

4.   Functionalists note that, over time, other institutions have taken on some of the functions originally performed mainly by the family.

B.   <u>Conflict Theory and the Family</u>

1.   Conflict theorists interpret the family as a system of power relations that both reinforces and reflects the inequalities in society at large.

2.   This perspective views families as the units through which the privileges and disadvantages of race, class, and gender are acquired.

C.   <u>Feminist Theory and the Family</u>

1.   Feminist theorists contributed new ways of conceptualizing the family by focusing sociological analyses on women's experiences in the family and by making gender a central concept in the analysis of the family as a social institution. Feminist scholars assert that the family does not serve the needs of all members equally.

2.   Feminists have been especially critical of Talcott Parsons' functionalist analysis of men's and women's family roles, in which he argues that men play the *instrumental* role by being the economic providers, and women play the *expressive* role by performing caretaking and emotional support for family members.

D.   <u>Symbolic Interaction Theory and the Family</u>

1.   Symbolic interaction theorists study families using a microsociological approach that emphasizes how different people define and understand their family experiences and how people negotiate family relationships.

2.   The symbolic interaction perspective emphasizes the construction of meaning within families. Roles within families continually evolve as participants define and redefine their behavior toward each other.

III.   **DIVERSITY AMONG CONTEMPORARY AMERICAN FAMILIES**

The family is one of the most rapidly changing social institutions. Few families meet the *family ideal* of a nuclear unit with a father as head of the household, the mother at home and not employed, and two children present. Careful historical studies of families have shown how specific family forms emerge as adaptations to new societal conditions. Families are systems of social relationships that emerge in response to social conditions and that, in turn, shape the future direction of society. Compared to families in the past, families today evidence a greater diversity of lifestyles, are smaller in size, devote fewer years to childbearing and childrearing, and are more likely to experience divorce (rather than death) as the major cause of early family disruption.

A.   <u>Female-Headed Households</u>

1.   Twenty-eight percent of all children live with one parent, most of them with their mothers.

2.   The two primary causes for the growing number of women heading their own households are the *high rate of pregnancy among unmarried teens* and the *high divorce rate.*

     a.   Teenage women who become pregnant are less likely to marry now than in the past, so the number of never married mothers is higher today.

     b.   Regardless of race, teenage mothers are one among the most economically and educationally disadvantaged groups in society; and teen fathers are less likely to complete school and have lower earnings than their peers who are not parents.

    c.   Divorce contributes to the growing rate of poverty among women, partly because one-third of parents who are supposed to receive child support never do.

3.   Among African-American and Latina women, there is a high rate of female-headed households partly due to the low economic status of minority men, who face high unemployment, relatively low life expectancy, and disproportionately high rates of incarceration.

4.   Sociologists believe that the economic pressures faced by women in female-headed households puts them under great strain due to poverty, which may increase the potential for other social problems.

5.   The number of families headed by a single father is also increasing.

    a.   Male-headed households have a lower poverty rate than do female-headed households and are less likely to experience severe economic problems.

    b.   Single fathers tend to get more outside help from "mother substitutes" who perform childcare and housework.

6.   Most sociological research on single parents has focused on female-headed households because there are so many of them, but researchers are increasingly studying non-married fathers.

B.   <u>Married Couple Families</u>

1.   Among married-couple families, one of the greatest changes in recent years has been the increased participation of White, middle-class women in the paid labor force. Women of color and white working-class women have historically engaged in paid employment in addition to filling household roles.

2.   Economists estimate that after adding up the additional hours people work, in the form of more hours in the work week, more weeks worked per year, and hours worked in a second job, the average employed husband works 20 hours more per year, and the average employed wife works 14 more days per year, than they did in 1989.

3.   Women are especially likely to experience the phenomenon of the social speedup due to working a "double shift" of paid employment and unpaid work in the home.

4.   Women's labor force participation has created other changes in family life. For example, there has been an increase in the number of married couples who have commuter marriages, which is an arrangement that typically arises when work requires one partner in a dual-earner couple to reside in a different city.

C.   <u>Stepfamilies</u>

Stepfamilies have become more common in the United States. In fact, about 40 percent of marriages involve stepchildren. Both parents and children must learn new roles when they become part of a stepfamily.

D.   <u>Gay and Lesbian Households</u>

1.   The traditional heterosexual definition of the family has been challenged by the increased visibility of gay and lesbian lifestyles and a greater acceptance of gay and lesbian identity.

2.   Researchers have found that gay and lesbian couples tend to be more flexible and less gender-stereotyped in their household roles than heterosexual couples.

3. Gay and lesbian couples face unique domestic problems because the dominant culture often denies them the benefits and privileges that married heterosexual couples receive, such as shared health-care plans.

4. Although only Hawaii and Vermont legally recognize gay marriage, 40 percent of the American public believes that gay partners who make a public commitment to each other should be entitled to the same benefits as other married couples.

E. Singles

1. Single people, including those never married and those widowed and divorced, constitute 44 percent of the population today, an increase from 29 percent in 1970.

2. There has been an increase in the number of never-married persons, which is partially a statistical consequence of the fact that men and women are marrying at a later age.

3. As sexual attitudes have changed in the direction of greater permissiveness, many people find the same sexual and emotional gratification in single life as they would in marriage.

4. Among singles, Black women are likely to remain single longer than Black men or White women. Black women are more likely to expect to work to support themselves and not assume that someone else will be financially responsible for them.

5. **Cohabitation**, or living together without being married, is quite common among single people today.

6. A rising number of people are remaining in their parents' homes for longer periods of time. Known as the "boomerang generation," these young people return home in their twenties when they would normally be expected to live independently.

IV. **MARRIAGE AND DIVORCE**
The United States has the highest rate of marriage of any Western industrialized nation, but it also has a high divorce rate.

A. Marriage

1. Marital relationships involve a complex set of social dynamics, including cooperation and conflict, different patterns of resource allocation, and a division of labor.

2. Research indicates that the amount of money a person earns establishes that person's relative power within the marriage, such as the ability to influence decisions, the degree of autonomy and independence held by each partner, and the establishment of control over expectations about family life.

3. The institution of marriage is changing, with most couples now agreeing that childcare should be shared; however, men generally have more traditional expectations about marriage than do women.

4. The values of the partners and the roles they play influence their experiences of marriage. For example, women do far more work in the home and have less leisure time than do men, resulting in the *second shift* for women.

5. Despite a widespread belief that young professional couples are the most egalitarian, studies reveal that there is little difference in the amount of housework that men do across social class.

233

B.   Divorce
    1.   The United States leads the world not only in the number of people who marry, but also in the number of people who divorce.
    2.   Despite a high rate of divorce, marriage is a cultural ideal and most divorced Americans report wanting to remarry, although women are less likely than men to remarry following a divorce.
    3.   Divorce is more likely for couples that marry young, for those in second marriages, for low-income couples, for African-Americans, and for those without a high school diploma.
    4.   A number of factors contribute to the current high rate of divorce in the United States, including longer life expectancies, the American cultural orientation toward individualism and personal happiness, and changes in women's roles that have resulted in women being less financially dependent on husbands than in the past.
    5.   Although divorce is painful emotionally and potentially disastrous financially, it can be a positive alternative for people in unhappy marriages.
    6.   Studies of the effect of divorce on children have shown that a number of factors influence children's adjustment to divorce.
        a.   Where conflict between the parents is greatest (before, during, and after the divorce), the children are most likely to have ongoing difficulties as the result of the breakup.
        b.   Few children feel relieved or pleased by divorce, but most adjust reasonably well after one or two years.
        c.   In the aftermath of divorce, many fathers become distant from their children; consequently, many families receive limited or no child support from fathers after divorce.

C.   Family Violence
    1.   Family violence is a phenomenon that was hidden for many years but now receives considerable attention from researchers.
    2.   Estimates of the extent of domestic violence are extremely unreliable because the majority of cases go unreported. The American Medical Association estimates that one in three women will be physically assaulted by their husbands at some time in their married lives.
    3.   Many victims of violence stay with their abusers because they believe the abuser will change, and they find they have few other options; however, the majority of victims attempt to prevent victimization and leave the relationship.
    4.   Women's relative powerlessness in the family is at the root of high rates of violence against women. Two sociological perspectives have been developed to explain violence in families.
        a.   The *family violence approach* emphasizes that violence occurs in families because society condones violence.
        b.   The *feminist approach* places inequality between men and women at the center of analyses in the family. Arguing that because most violence in the family is directed against women, the imbalance of power between women and men in the family is the source of most domestic violence. It also emphasizes the degree to which many women are trapped in violent relationships, because they are relatively powerless within society and may not have the resources to leave the marriage.

5.   Violence within families also affects many children who are the victims of child abuse, including neglect, abandonment, and physical and sexual assault.

   a.   In 1997, there were over 3 million reported cases of child abuse, with women being the perpetrators of child abuse as often as men.

   b.   Several factors are associated with child abuse, including parent's chronic use of alcohol, unemployment, family isolation, and an absence of social supports.

   c.   One particular form of child abuse is incest, which involves sexual relations between persons who are closely related. Fathers and uncles are the most common perpetrators of incest.

V.   CHANGING FAMILIES/CHANGING SOCIETY

   A.   Global Changes in Family Life

   1.   The increasing global basis of the economy means that some people work long distances from other family members. The experience of such global mobility varies significantly by social class.

   2.   Patterns of work and migration have created a new family form, the *transnational family*, defined as families where one or both parents live and work in one country, while their children remain in their countries of origin.

   3.   The high rate of geographic mobility in the United States means that many families are geographically separated from their families of origin, which profoundly affects systems of care.

   B.   Families and Social Policy

   1.   Family social policies are the subject of intense national debate, particularly because some people claim that increasingly diverse forms of families are evidence of family collapse, which is believed to be responsible for the major social problems in the United States.

   2.   Among industrialized nations, the U.S. provides the least federal support for maternity and childcare policies. The 1993 Family and Medical Leave Act (FMLA) was the first law passed that recognized that family members need time to care for children and other dependents. This policy is of little use to people who cannot afford to take time off work without pay.

   3.   There is a pressing need for affordable childcare in the U.S., a service that consumes a large chunk of working parents' budgets.

   4.   As more women entered the paid labor market, concerns emerged about who performs the "care work" not only for children, but also for elderly people and people with disabilities.

PRACTICE TEST

MULTIPLE CHOICE QUESTIONS

1.   The U.S. Census Bureau defines a family as any group of people who:
   a.   are related by ancestry, marriage, or adoption and reside together.
   b.   are emotionally intimate and committed to caring for one another.
   c.   form a cooperative economic unit to produce and support offspring.
   d.   All of the above groups are considered families by the U.S. Census Bureau.

2. The most common marriage pattern in the United States is:
   a. polygyny.
   b. polyandry.
   c. polygymy.
   d. monogamy.

3. According to the U.S. Bureau of the Census, all persons occupying a housing unit who may or may not be related by ancestry, marriage, or adoption comprise a(n):
   a. social network.
   b. kinship system.
   c. household.
   d. family.

4. The percent of children who live with both of their parents is lowest among which racial-ethnic group?
   a. Whites
   b. Blacks
   c. Asians
   d. Hispanics

5. Which of the following is (are) features that sociologists use to categorize kinship systems?
   a. where the family resides
   b. how property is passed on
   c. how many marriage partners one has
   d. All of the above are features used to classify kinship systems.

6. Which of the following is **not** one of the features of family as a social institution?
   a. Families are regulated by government policies.
   b. Families are are organized in a socially patterned way.
   c. Families are affected by economic trends and social conditions.
   d. Families are shaped by the personalities of each individual member.

7. The practice of selecting mates from within one's own race, ethnicity, religion, or social class is:
   a. exogamy.
   b. endogamy.
   c. monogamy.
   d. polygamy.

8. The tendency for people to select mates with similar social characteristics to their own, including class, race, religion, and education level, is known as:
   a. homogamy.
   b. heterogamy.
   c. monogamy.
   d. homosexuality.

9.   Fictive kin and "othermothers" are both associated with _____ kinship systems.
       a.   bilateral
       b.   nuclear
       c.   extended
       d.   patriarchal

10.   In which type of kinship system is descent traced through the father?
       a.   bilateral
       b.   neolocal
       c.   matrilineal
       d.   patrilineal

11.   Societies in which men and women share power in families and society equally are:
       a.   endogamous.
       b.   exogamous.
       c.   egalitarian.
       d.   extinct.

12.   The practice of a newly married couple establishing their own separate household is referred to as _____ residence.
       a.   neolocal
       b.   patrilocal
       c.   matrilocal
       d.   bilateral

13.   Which racial-ethnic group experienced extreme sex imbalances in their population during the late 1800s because the United States allowed men, but not women, to immigrate?
       a.   African Americans
       b.   Chinese Americans
       c.   Korean Americans
       d.   Irish Americans

14.   Functionalist theorists view families as:
       a.   systems of power relationships that reinforce the inequalities in society at large.
       b.   organized around a harmony of interests and beneficial to all of the members.
       c.   gendered institutions that reflect the gender hierarchy in society at large.
       d.   groups in which people interact and negotiate relationships with others.

15.   Symbolic interaction theorists view families as:
       a.   systems of power relationships that reinforce the inequalities in society at large.
       b.   organized around a harmony of interests and beneficial to all of the members.
       c.   gendered institutions that reflect the gender hierarchy in society at large.
       d.   groups in which people interact and negotiate relationships with others.

16.   Which theory argues that families are sites of tension and competition characterized by power imbalances between the members?
       a.   symbolic interaction theory
       b.   functionalist theory
       c.   moral decay theory
       d.   conflict theory

17. Which of the following statements about single-parent households is (are) true?
    a. Fifty percent of all American children currently live with only one parent.
    b. A primary cause for the growing number of single-parent households in the U.S. is the high rate of divorce.
    c. About one-fourth of all single parent households in the U.S. are headed by men.
    d. All of the above statements about single-parent households are true.

18. The number of never-married mothers in the U.S. is higher today than in 1960 because:
    a. teenagers who become pregnant today are more likely to have the baby, whereas teenagers in the 1960s were more likely to have an abortion.
    b. teen mothers are easily able to complete school and be financially independent today, so they do not need any economic support from male partners.
    c. teenagers who become pregnant today are less likely to get married than they were in 1960.
    d. All of the above factors contributed to an increase in never-married mothers.

19. Which of the following factors is associated with an increased incidence of child abuse?
    a. isolation of parents from friends and relatives
    b. chronic alcohol use by a parent
    c. parental unemployment
    d. All of the above factors increase the likelihood of child abuse occurring.

20. The cultural norm, generally considered to be universal, that prohibits sexual relations and marriage between certain kin, is the:
    a. serial monogamy phenomenon.
    b. heterosexual imperative.
    c. familial dilemma.
    d. incest taboo.

21. Which of the following statements is (are) true about heterosexual couples who cohabit?
    a. The distribution of housework by gender is significantly more equal in cohabiting than married couples.
    b. More women than men in cohabiting couples expect to marry their partners.
    c. Households headed by a cohabiting couple rarely include children.
    d. All of the above statements are true.

22. Research on marriage indicates that:
    a. the majority of marital conflicts are about sex and jealousy.
    b. men do significantly more housework once the first child is born.
    c. women who contribute financially to the household have greater autonomy.
    d. All of the above statements about married couples are true.

23. The likelihood of divorce is highest for which of the following groups of people?
    a. people who marry in their late 20s or early 30s
    b. people who share household labor equally
    c. people with low levels of education
    d. people in the middle class

24. The Family and Medical Leave Act of 1993 provides twelve weeks of:
    a. free shelter to families who are homeless.
    b. free childcare to welfare recipients engaged in a job search.
    c. paid leave to most employees to manage a family emergency.
    d. unpaid leave to most employees to care for a newborn or very ill family member.

25. Which industrialized nation provides the fewest federally supported maternity programs to its citizens?
    a. United States
    b. Canada
    c. Russia
    d. Japan

TRUE-FALSE QUESTIONS

1. Antimiscegenation laws were declared unconstitutional in the United States in 1867.

2. The most common form of heterogamous marriage in the United States is marriage between people of different racial backgrounds.

3. The United States leads the world not only in the number of people who marry, but also in the number of people who divorce.

4. Research indicates that there is little difference in the amount of housework that married men do across social class.

5. More than half of all children in the U.S. will live in a single-parent family at some time before they turn 18 years old.

6. Approximately one-third of men and women in the U.S. report that they want a traditional marriage in which the husband is the sole breadwinner and the wife is a full-time homemaker.

7. Men are significantly more likely than women to commit physical abuse against children.

8. Research indicates that children raised by gay and lesbian parents experience significantly more psychological problems than do children raised by heterosexual parents.

9. Second marriages are less likely than first marriages to end in divorce.

10. The children who are most likely to have ongoing emotional difficulties as the result of their parents' divorce are those whose parents maintain joint custody.

FILL IN THE BLANK QUESTIONS

1. According to _____ theory, marriage is a mutually beneficial exchange wherein women receive protection and economic support in return for providing emotional support, household services, and childcare.

2. A rising number of people are remaining in their parent's homes for longer periods of time. Commonly referred to as the _____ generation, these young people return home in their twenties when they would normally be expected to live independently

3. In a _____ family, a married couple resides together with their children.

4. In a _____ family, one or both parents live in one country while their children remain in their countries of origin.

5. In some cultures, parents make rationally calculated choices about the appropriate marriage partner for their children, resulting in the practice of _____ marriage.

ESSAY QUESTIONS

1. Using one of the major sociological theories, explain why divorce occurs, and discuss how the consequences of divorce differ for women, men, and children.
2. Compare and contract the family violence and feminist approaches to explaining why violence occurs in families.
3. Contemporary American families are increasingly diverse. Select three lifestyles other than the "ideal family" and provide an overview of each family type using data from the text to support your summaries.
4. Identify the social conditions that have contributed to the rise in cohabitation in the United States and other industrialized nations.
5. Discuss why family social policies such as the Family and Medical Leave Act are the subject of intense national debate in the United States.

ANSWERS TO PRACTICE TEST

Answers to Multiple Choice Questions

1.	A.	417	A primary group of people who are related by ancestry, marriage or adoption and reside together is a family according to the Census.
2.	D.	418	The most common form of marriage in the U.S. is monogamy, or having only one spouse at a time.
3.	C.	417	According to the Census, all persons occupying a housing unit who may or may not be related comprise a household.
4.	B.	416	The percent of children who live with both parents is lowest for African-Americans as indicated by Figure 15.1.
5.	D.	417	Kinship systems are categorized by: place of residence, number of marriage partners and who marries whom, how descent is traced and property is passed on, and how power is distributed.
6.	D.	416	Although families are shaped by the personalities of the members, sociologists study families as social institutions, which are organized in socially patterned ways, affected by economic conditions, and regulated by government policies.

7.	B.	418	The practice of selecting mates from within one's group is endogamy.
8.	A.	419	Homogamy is the tendency for people to select mates with similar social characteristics to their own, including class, race, and education.
9.	C.	421	Extended kinship systems are common among lower-income groups because they provide a cooperative system of social and economic support. Fictive kin and othermothers are relatives and close friends who provide extensive child care and other forms of assistance in African-American communities.
10.	D.	420	Descent is traced through the father in patrilineal kinship systems.
11.	C.	420	Societies in which men and women share power equally are egalitarian.
12.	A.	420	Neolocal residence is the practice of a newly married couple establishing their own residence.
13.	B.	422	Chinese Americans experienced imbalanced sex ratios because the Chinese Exclusion Act of 1882 and the Immigration Act of 1924 prohibited Chinese women from immigrating to the United States.
14.	B.	423	Functional theorists view families as groups who reproduce and socialize children, as organized around a harmony of interests, and as experiencing "breakdown" when society undergoes rapid change.
15.	C.	425	Symbolic interaction theorists study how different people define their family experiences and negotiate family relationships. Symbolic interactionists view families as continually changing as people develop meaningful relationships and new understandings of family life.
16.	C.	424	As summarized in Table 15.1, conflict theorists view families as sites of conflict where members have diverse interests. Families reinforce and support power relations in society at large.
17.	B.	426	There has been a rise in single-parent households due to increases in the rate of divorce. Sixteen percent of these households are headed by fathers. Twenty-eight percent of children live with a single parent, and 50 percent are predicted to live in a single-parent household for some time before they reach 18 years old.
18.	C.	427	The number of never-married mothers has increased because teenagers are less likely to get married when pregnant than they were in 1960. Abortion was not legal, and therefore not as prevalent, in 1960 as it is today. Teenage mothers are less likely to complete school than their peers, and have very high rates of poverty; thus, they are not likely to be economically self-sufficient.
19.	D.	437	Child abuse is associated with unemployment, chronic alcohol use, and isolation from friends and family.
20.	D.	418	The incest taboo prohibits sexual relations and marriage between certain kin.
21.	B.	431	People who cohabit generally express more egalitarian attitudes, but develop the same gender division of labor, as married couples. More women than men expect to marry the person they cohabit with. One-fourth of all children live in a household headed by a cohabiting couple at some time, revealing how prevalent cohabitation is today.
22.	C.	432	Within marriage, women who contribute financially to the household generally have greater autonomy and decision-making power. Most marital conflicts are about finances and housework. The birth of the first child increases the gender division of labor for married couples.

23.	C.	433	Divorce is more common for people who marry in their teens or early twenties, people with low education levels, and people from lower-income groups.
24.	D.	440	The Family and Medical Leave Act of 1993 requires employers to grant full-time employees 12 weeks of unpaid leave for the birth or adoption of a child, or to care for a spouse, child, or parent who has a serious health condition.
25.	A.	439	As indicated by Table 15.2, the U.S. provides the fewest federally supported maternity programs. It is the only industrialized country that does not provide some period of *paid* leave for women who give birth.

Answers to True-False Questions

1.	F.	420	Antimiscegenation laws were not declared unconstitutional until 1967.
2.	F.	419	Most marriages in the U S. are between members of the same racial group. Interracial couples constitute 2.5 percent of married couples.
3.	T.	432	
4.	T.	432	Despite the belief that young professional couples are egalitarian, there is little difference in the amount of housework that men do across social class.
5.	T.	426	
6.	T.	431	
7.	F.	437	Women are as likely as men to be the perpetrators of child abuse.
8.	F.	429	There is no evidence that being raised by gay or lesbian parents increases the chance of developing psychological problems. Children of gay or lesbian parents may learn more flexible gender roles and learn to respect differences.
9.	F.	435	Second marriages are more likely than first marriages to end in divorce.
10.	T.	429	Research indicates that gay and lesbian couples tend to be more flexible in their household roles than are heterosexual couples.

Answers to Fill in the Blank Questions

1.	functionalist	423
2.	boomerang	431
3.	nuclear	421
4.	transnational	438
5.	arranged	418

CHAPTER 16
EDUCATION

BRIEF CHAPTER OUTLINE
Schooling and Society: Theories of Education
The Rise of Education in the United States
The Functionalist View of Education
The Conflict View of Education
The Symbolic Interactionist View of Education
Does Schooling Matter?
Effects of Education on Occupation and Income
Effects of Social Class Background on Education and Social Mobility
Education, Social Class, and Mobility Seen Globally
Analyzing Education and Mobility
Access to Higher Education
Education and Inequality
Cognitive Ability and Its Measurement
Ability and Diversity
The "Cognitive Elite" and *The Bell Curve* Debate
Tracking and Labeling Effects
Teacher Expectancy Effect
Schooling and Gender
Stereotype Vulnerability, Race, and Gender
School Reform
Reducing Unequal Funding
Back-to-Basics and Multiculturalism
The Future of American Education: New Technology in the Classroom

QUESTIONS TO GUIDE YOUR READING
1. Why did education become increasingly important in the United States over the last century?
2. What are the primary functions of the educational institution?
3. How do race, ethnicity, class, and gender influence access to, and success in, the formal educational system?
4. Why are standardized intelligence tests a source of considerable controversy?
5. What types of reforms have been proposed for managing the challenges that the educational system in the United States is currently facing?

KEY TERMS (defined at page number shown and in glossary)

KEY PEOPLE (identified at page number shown)

CHAPTER OUTLINE

Tracking, the grouping of students within the educational system using ability test scores, is a technique used to allow children to learn at a comfortable pace; however, tracking also has negative consequences. African-American males have a higher probability of dropping out of school prior to high school graduation than do White males, but a much lower probability than Hispanic males. The educational institution in the United States is capable of both lessening social inequality and perpetuating racial, ethnic, socioeconomic, and gender inequalities in society.

I.   **SCHOOLING AND SOCIETY**

Education in society is concerned with the systematic transmission of society's knowledge. **Schooling** refers to the formal, institutionalized aspects of education. Three out of ten Americans are either enrolled in some kind of educational institution or employed in the field of education as teachers, administrators, secretaries, or janitors. More money is spent on education in the United States than on any other activity or institution except for health care.

A.   The Rise of Education in the United States

1.   By 1900, compulsory education was established by law in all states except for a few in the South, where Black Americans were still largely denied formal education of any kind.

2.   College attendance increased dramatically after World War II due to the G.I. Bill, federal loan programs, and the expansion of community colleges, although the growth of community colleges slowed considerably over the last few years as federal and state aid decreased.

3.   High school and college graduation rates vary across racial and ethnic groups, with both Whites and African-Americans having higher graduation rates than Hispanics.

B.   The Functionalist View of Education

1.   All known societies have some sort of educational institution, which is generally large and highly formalized in industrialized societies such as the United States.

2.   Functionalist theory argues that education accomplishes certain functions for society.

a.   *Socialization* occurs as the cultural heritage is transmitted from one generation to another. In addition to teaching a variety of skills and knowledge, schools also inculcate values such as loyalty and punctuality.

b.   *Occupational training* is provided by schools, especially in modern industrialized societies that need a system to train people for jobs. Most jobs today require at least a high school education, and many professions require a graduate degree.

c.   *Social control* is provided by the educational institution. This indirect, non-obvious consequence of schools is called a *latent function*. One perceived benefit of compulsory education in the late 19th century was to keep kids off the streets and out of trouble as crime, overcrowding, and other problems intensified with urbanization and immigration. Additionally, education was perceived as a way to "Americanize" new immigrants in the interest of social control.

C.   The Conflict View of Education
        1.   Conflict theory emphasizes the disintegrative and disruptive aspects of education by focusing on competition between groups for power, income, and social status.
        2.   The unequal distribution of education can allow educational level to be used as a tool for discrimination through the process of **credentialism**, or the insistence upon educational credentials for their own sake, even if the credentials bear little relationship to the intended job.
        3.   Conflict theorists argue that even though most new job opportunities emerging today are less complex and less technical than jobs in the past, potential employers often continue to insist on a particular degree for a job even where there should be little expectation that education level will affect job performance.

C.   The Symbolic Interactionist View of Education
        1.   Symbolic interaction theory focuses on what emerges from the process of interaction between teachers and students, for example, during the schooling experience.
        2.   Through the operation of the *expectancy effect*, the expectations a teacher has for a student can create the very behavior that is expected, thereby affecting student test performance as well as other abilities.

II.   **DOES SCHOOLING MATTER?**
Two factors must be examined to measure the importance of schooling for individual success: how formal education ultimately affects occupation, income, and social mobility; and what effect social class *origin* has on the ultimate effects of education.

A.   Effects of Education on Occupation and Income
        1.   One way that sociologists measure a person's social class or socioeconomic status (SES) is to determine the person's amount of schooling, income, and type of occupation, which are SES *indicators*.
        2.   In the general population, there is a strong correlation between level of formal education and *occupational prestige*, or the ranking of the value of various jobs in society.
        3.   The actual, objective relationship between years of formal education and subsequent job and income is less rigid than most people think, with education having a greater effect on type of occupation than it does on income.
        4.   Income brackets are consistently higher for higher education categories, but the connection between income and education is not independent of gender. For example, the average income for women is less than the average income for men at every educational level.
        5.   **Educational deflation** refers to the declining relative economic advantage of completing college as measured in dollars. This process occurred in industrialized nations such as the U.S. as overall levels of education rose.

B.   Effects of Social Class Background on Education and Social Mobility
        1.   Education has traditionally been viewed as the principal route to upward social mobility in the United States.
        2.   Research has demonstrated that the effect of education upon a person's eventual job and income depends to a great extent upon the social class into which the person was born.

a. Among upper-class White people, social class origin is *more important than education* in determining occupation and income.
b. Among middle-class White people, education considerably improves the chance of getting a middle-class job.
c. Among lower-income people, the chances of getting a good education and a prestigious job are poor.

3. Social class origin affects occupation and income both directly and indirectly. The higher one's social class, the higher their occupational prestige and income. There is an additional, indirect effect of social class on level of educational attainment, which affects occupation and thus, income level.

C. Education, Social Class, and Mobility Seen Globally
1. Some people have argued that there is more occupational and income mobility in the U.S. than in other countries because of the American educational system, but the degree of mobility is relatively limited.
   a. Students from lower-income families have lower average scores on tests such as the Scholastic Aptitude Test (SAT) and the American College Testing Program (ACT), which diminishes their chances of getting accepted by the best colleges and universities.
   b. Women of every ethnic group score lower than their male counterparts on the quantitative sections of standardized tests.
2. In Germany and Japan, comparable examinations more rigidly determine people's subsequent educational opportunities.
3. Although the educational system in the U.S. appears to permit somewhat more social mobility than in other industrialized nations, the similarities between the U.S. and these countries tend to be more important than the differences.

D. Analyzing Education and Mobility
1. Functionalist and conflict sociologists debate the effects of education on occupational and income mobility, but both agree that education can greatly affect the life paths of individuals.
   a. Functional theorists emphasize the importance of individual merit while attributing less importance to the limits placed upon an individual by his or her social class origins.
   b. Although conflict theorists de-emphasize individual merit, they do not eliminate its role. Instead, they focus on how the social class structure has an impact on individual occupational and income attainment.
2. Symbolic interaction theorists argue that factors such as teacher expectations can have either beneficial or harmful effects on student achievement and mobility, depending on whether the teacher's expectations are favorable toward the student.

E. Access to Higher Education
College enrollment and completion are structured by race, ethnicity, and social class. In general, the higher one's family income, the greater one's chances for enrolling in college. The Black-White gap in college completion has remained about the same since 1970.

III.   EDUCATION AND INEQUALITY

To some extent, education reduced social inequalities during the twentieth century. The percentage of high school graduates has risen among Whites and minorities, both male and female, as have certain types of social mobility. The overall increase in minorities' and women's college attendance and graduation has resulted in more women and minorities holding mid-level and high-level jobs.

A.   Cognitive Ability and Its Measurement

1.   **Cognitive ability** is the capacity for abstract thinking. Educators in the United States have used **ability tests** to measure this capacity.

2.   The **unidimensional theory of** intelligence posits that intelligence is reducible to a single master capacity that humans possess. According to this view, a person who excels at one kind of mental activity, such as math, is expected to excel at other kinds, such as language skills.

3.   The **multidimensional theory of intelligence** asserts that intelligence is a matter of several distinctly different kinds of abilities. According to Howard Gardner, a leading proponent of this view, there are seven separate, independent kinds of intelligence, including: logical-mathematical, linguistic, spatial, musical, interpersonal, intrapersonal, and kinesthetic.

4.   The American system of education relies heavily upon the undimensional view of intelligence, whereby cognitive ability is gauged by the numerical results of **standardized tests**, or tests given to large populations of people and scored with respect to population averages.

   a.   There has been an attempt to reduce measurements of cognitive ability to a single number, or "intelligence quotient" (IQ).

   b.   Standardized cognitive ability tests like the SAT and ACT are presumed to measure ability much like IQ tests.

   c.   There are three major criticisms of the use of standardized tests as measures of cognitive ability.

      1)   They tend to measure only limited ranges of ability, such as quantitative or verbal aptitude, while ignoring other cognitive endowments, such as creativity.

      2)   Such tests possess degrees of *cultural bias* and *gender bias*. They tend to perpetuate social, economic, and educational inequality between different cultural or racial groups and between men and women.

      3)   The **predictive validity** of these tests, or the extent to which the tests accurately predict later college grades, is compromised for minorities and women. In fact, IQ tests and SATs do not predict school performance very well even for White students.

   d.   Ability tests are distinct from **achievement tests**, such as advanced placement (AP) exams, which are intended to measure what has actually been learned, rather than measuring ability or potential to learn.

B.   Ability and Diversity

1.   Average scores on cognitive ability tests such as the SAT differ by racial-ethnic group, social class, and gender.

2.   Overall, Whites score higher on average than minorities; men score higher than women, especially on the math portion; and the higher a person's social class, the higher the test score.
   a.   There is no evidence whatsoever that such *between-group* differences are in any way genetically inherited.
   b.   Certain *within-group* differences may reflect genetic differences among individuals within the same racial or ethnic group, but even in this category, the effects of social environment are greater than the effects of genes.

C.   The "Cognitive Elite" and *The Bell Curve* Debate
1.   *The Bell Curve*, published in 1994, created an intense debate about the nature of intelligence. Authors Herrnstein and Murray argued that not only does the distribution of intelligence in the general population closely approximate a bell-shaped curve, or *normal distribution*, but that there is one basic, fundamental kind of intelligence.
2.   The authors argue that intelligence has 70 percent *heritability*, while only 30 percent of the difference in intelligence throughout the population is determined by environment.
3.   Because intelligence is primarily inherited and different social classes differ on their average intelligence (with lower classes having lower scores), the authors argue that the lower classes are on average less endowed with genes for high intelligence, while the upper classes are relatively more endowed with high-intelligence genes.
4.   Herrnstein and Murray reason that the upper and upper-middle classes constitute a *genetically-based* **cognitive elite** in America, which consists of those with high IQs, high incomes, and prestigious jobs. The upper-class cognitive elite is comprised of a disproportionately high number of White men because of their genetic superiority.
5.   The authors have been strongly criticized for their methodology and for largely ignoring the abundant research indicating that intelligence tests and standardized ability tests do not measure intelligence and ability as accurately for some groups as for others.

D.   Tracking and Labeling Effects
1.   Approximately 80 percent of secondary schools and 60 percent of elementary schools in the U.S. currently use some kind of tracking, or ability grouping, to separate students according to some measure of cognitive ability.
2.   The basic idea behind tracking is that students will get a better education and be better prepared after high school if they are grouped according to cognitive ability.
3.   Proponents of *detracking* argue that including students of varying cognitive abilities is more beneficial because students will learn from each other. They also believe that students in lower tracks get less teacher attention, thus, they learn less than when they are included in mixed groups.
4.   Most researchers and educators who have studied tracking agree that not *all* students should be mixed together in the same classes.
5.   One of the most consistent findings from research on tracking is that students in the higher tracks receive more positive effects, but lower track students suffer more negative effects, including being taught less.

6. Both high- and low- track students are subject to the **labeling effect**, whereby students are assigned to particular tracks and thereby labeled, whether or not the label accurately reflects the student's ability.

7. Research shows that track assignment occurs on the basis of race and class as well as performance on cognitive ability tests. For example, White students are somewhat more likely to be placed in high ability tracks than minority students with the same test scores.

E. Teacher Expectancy Effect

1. The **teacher expectancy** effect refers to the influence of teacher expectations on a student's actual performance, independent of his or her actual ability. The expectations a teacher has for a student can dramatically influence how much the student will learn.

2. Through the **self-fulfilling prophecy,** merely applying a label has the effect of justifying the label.

   a. A label is attached to a student, perhaps through tracking.

   b. The teacher's perception of a particular student leads to modified behavior/expectations directed toward the student.

   c. The student reacts to the teacher's behavior.

   d. The teacher perceives the student's behavior as confirming the original label.

   e. The student accepts the label about himself or herself.

3. In the U.S. educational system, White and Asian students receive higher teacher expectations, which have a favorable effect on their performance, and they appear disproportionately in the higher tracks.

4. Black, Hispanic, and Native American students, as well as lower social class students of all races, are more likely to be assigned to lower tracks and receive lower teacher expectations. Consequently, they show lower objective performance, learn less, like school less, and like themselves less because they develop a negative self-evaluation.

F. Schooling and Gender

1. Teachers hold different expectations about boys and girls in school, which affect students' actual performance.

2. Research commissioned by the American Association of University Women (AAUW) revealed several things about gender and schooling.

   a. In general, teachers pay less attention to girls and women than boys and men, particularly in math and science classes.

   b. Women lag behind men in math ability and math and science achievement scores.

   c. Some standardized math and science tests still retain gender bias, despite the efforts of education specialists and testing organizations to weed out such bias. As a result, standardized tests in math tend to under-predict women's actual grades in mathematics.

   d. Textbooks still tend to either ignore women or stereotype them.

   e. As girls and boys approach adolescence, their self-esteem tends to drop, with the erosion of self-esteem occurring more quickly among girls than boys.

G. Stereotype Vulnerability, Race, and Gender

1. A negative stereotype about one's self can affect one's own behavior.

2. Steel identified two common **stereotypes** in the United States.

        a.   Black students must have some inherent deficiency in math and verbal skills because, on average, they perform less well on tests of math and verbal ability than do White students.

        b.   Women must have some inherent deficiency in math because, on average, they perform less well on tests of math ability than do men.

3.   When individuals internalize such stereotypes, there is a *stereotype vulnerability* effect; consequently, when Black students and female students are told in advance that a test they will take is a "genuine" test of ability, they receive lower scores than do similar groups who are given the identical test minus the misinformation about the test being a "genuine" test of ability.

4.   Likewise, an internalized positive stereotype can actually increase test performance when students are "primed" to "activate" the stereotype.

IV.   SCHOOL REFORM

School reform has been an ongoing theme in the history of U.S. education. Many challenges face the institution of education, including increasing diversity, global economic competition, inequalities among schools, and fiscal constraints.

A.   <u>Reducing Unequal Funding</u>

    1.   One of the most persistent issues for educational reform is the problem of unequal funding across different states, for different school districts within the same city, for urban versus suburban schools, and for public versus private schools.

    2.   A major problem throughout almost all states is that the electorate has become increasingly reluctant to pay for reforms that would result in increased school taxes.

B.   <u>Back-to-Basics and Multiculturalism</u>

During the 1980s and 1990s, two educational reform movements became prominent.

    1.   The **back-to-basics movement** emerged from the dissatisfaction that professional educators felt about declining student discipline, rising functional illiteracy, and teacher incompetence. This movement stresses a return to a traditional curriculum delivered with traditional methods.

        a.   A 1983 report entitled *A Nation at Risk* blamed the educational system and the curriculum for poor student performance and behavior. As a result, freedom to choose from a variety of elective courses has been somewhat reduced.

        b.   There is a push for stiffer standards in grading. The problem of "grade inflation," where an excessive number of high grades are given or where the average grade for a course is above "C," is being challenged.

        c.   Many elementary schools have discontinued "social promotion," or passing students from one grade to the next, regardless of their performance or grades.

        d.   Many states require teachers to successfully complete the standardized National Teachers Examination (NTE).

    2.   The **multiculturalism movement** is attempting to introduce more courses and educational materials concerning different cultures, subcultures, and social groups into school curricula.

        a.   The driving principle behind this movement is the belief that traditional curricula tend to stereotype women, minorities, lesbians and gays, and working-class persons, thereby giving an inaccurate picture of these groups and society.

      b.   African American Studies, Ethnic Studies, Women's Studies, Latino Studies, and Gay and Lesbian Studies have had to fight vigorously for continued support on college campuses.

C.   <u>The Future of American Education: New Technology in the Classroom</u>

    1.   Global technological changes require that the educational institution prepare students to function effectively in today's society.

    2.   There will be increased pressure on schools to adapt to the needs of a more racially and ethnically diverse population. As a result, there will be greatly increased needs for multicultural curricula and more minority teachers.

    3.   The increased use of computers in schools will have continuing consequences for both curriculum and extracurricular activities.

    4.   Current computer use is related to race and class, with more White students than Black and Hispanic students using computers in school and at home.

    5.   Gender differences in computer use at school have virtually disappeared; therefore this "digital divide" occurs mainly along the lines of race and class.

PRACTICE TEST

MULTIPLE CHOICE QUESTIONS

1.   More money is spent on education in the United States than any other activity or institution except:

    a.   welfare.
    b.   policing.
    c.   health care.
    d.   environmental conservation.

2.   Which of the following statements about high school and college enrollments is (are) true?

    a.   Black and White students drop out of high school at about the same rate.
    b.   Hispanics have a lower rate of high school and college attendance than either Whites or Blacks.
    c.   The number of people attending community college consistently decreased from the 1960s to the present.
    d.   All of the above statements are true.

3.   According to conflict theorists:

    a.   schools prepare all children for participation in society by teaching them essential skills and knowledge.
    b.   the educational institution is a tool for discrimination, because tracking practices perpetuate social inequalities.
    c.   the most important determinant of a child's success in school is how well the child gets along with his or her teachers.
    d.   schools today provide services to children that were originally fulfilled by other social institutions, such as the family.

4. According to sociologists, the best indicators of socioeconomic status in the U.S. are:
   a. education, income, and occupation.
   b. height, weight, and hair color.
   c. sex, race, and ethnicity.
   d. None of the above are good indicators of socioeconomic status in the U.S.

5. Those occupations with mid-level prestige in the United States are:
   a. doctor and physicist.
   b. waitress and hairdresser.
   c. electrician and police officer.
   d. truck driver and dock worker.

6. Which of the following is a latent function of the educational institution in the U.S.?
   a. pass on cultural heritage, including ethics and norms of the society.
   b. train adolescents for jobs as adults by transmitting knowledge and skills.
   c. inculcate values that are important to the workplace, such as punctuality.
   d. reduce juvenile delinquency by keeping youth off the streets during the day.

7. The capacity to think abstractly, which is measured by standardized IQ tests, is:
   a. cognitive ability.
   b. predictive validity.
   c. intuitive knowledge.
   d. reasoning capability.

8. In which of the following industrialized countries does the educational system seem to offer the greatest degree of social mobility relative to the other countries?
   a. Japan
   b. Russia
   c. England
   d. United States

9. According to Gardner, which kind of intelligence measures the ability to visualize three-dimensional figures?
   a. logical-mathematical
   b. linguistic
   c. musical
   d. spatial

10. The extent to which a test provides an accurate monitor of future college grades or some other criterion, such as likelihood of graduation, is:
    a. predictive validity.
    b. general accuracy.
    c. cognitive reliability.
    d. achievement potential.

11. The widely used Stanford-Binet IQ test is an example of a _____ test.
    a. achievement
    b. standardized
    c. multicultural
    d. multidimensional

12. According to Herrnstein and Murray, the authors of *The Bell Curve*, differences in test performance between Black and White students primarily result from differences in:
    a. home environments, including the availability of books and educational toys.
    b. nutritional deficiencies in infancy and early childhood.
    c. the form of the test given to each group.
    d. heredity or genetic makeup.

13. Which of the following is (are) a main criticism of the results reported in *The Bell Curve*?
    a. The authors overemphasize environmental factors and dismiss the influence of heredity, or genetic makeup, on intelligence.
    b. The authors draw too many conclusions about between-group differences from within-group results.
    c. The authors place too much emphasis on the assertion that standardized tests are not accurate measures of intelligence for racial minority groups.
    d. All of the above are criticisms of the study.

14. The idea that there are several different kinds of intelligence, rather than one basic kind, underlies the _____ theory of intelligence.
    a. multidimensional
    b. unidimensional
    c. radical
    d. elite

15. Jamie was labeled "bright" and placed in the college preparatory track in high school, where she was encouraged and praised. She therefore enjoyed school and developed high educational and occupational aspirations. This reflects the:
    a. detracking process.
    b. self-fulfilling prophecy.
    c. hidden curriculum.
    d. stereotype vulnerability effect.

16. Based on a study commissioned by the American Association of University Women (AAUW), researchers have found that:
    a. in general, teachers pay less attention to male students than female students.
    b. standardized math tests tend to over-predict women's actual grades in mathematics.
    c. girls' self-esteem erodes more quickly than boys' self-esteem as they approach adolescence.
    d. All of the above are findings from the AAUW study.

17. Which of the following is (are) an accurate example of how textbooks reinforce gender socialization?
    a. Textbooks usually portray male characters as leaders engaged in prestigious occupations such as doctor and scientist.
    b. Textbooks usually portray female characters as followers or assistants engaged in predominantly female occupations such as nurse and librarian.
    c. Male characters greatly outnumber female characters in textbooks.
    d. All of the above statements are true.

18. The _____ movement stresses a return to a traditional educational curriculum and the implementation of more stringent grading criteria in schools.
    a. multiculturalism
    b. credentialism
    c. back-to-basics
    d. deinstitutionalization

19. The _____ movement has strongly encouraged schools at all levels to offer more courses on diverse groups' perspectives and experiences.
    a. multiculturalism
    b. credentialism
    c. back-to-basics
    d. deinstitutionalization

20. Because he scored low on a standardized test given in third grade, Mark was placed in a remedial fourth grade class. This is an example of:
    a. educational deflation.
    b. detracking.
    c. tracking.
    d. justice.

21. According to symbolic interaction theorists:
    a. in terms of securing a high-paying job, the dollar value of a college degree has declined so much that getting a degree is no longer cost-effective.
    b. standardized tests are an important mechanism for eliminating certain groups from competition for coveted spaces in universities..
    c. one of the most important determinants of a child's success in school is what kind of perceptions and expectations his/her teachers have of and for him/her.
    d. contemporary schools provide many functions for children and youth that used to be the responsibility of families and religious organizations.

22. Feagin, Vera, and Nikitah's study of Black college students indicates that:
    a. racism on most college campuses has been eliminated due to the introduction of multicultural programs and diversity education.
    b. Black parents are not very supportive of their children who want to go to college because they do not recognize the importance of higher education.
    c. Black students rarely attend predominantly White colleges because they are unable to meet the stringent admission requirements at those schools.
    d. Black students often face the agonizing dilemma of trying to succeed academically while being treated as intruders at predominantly White colleges.

23. Joe failed ninth grade. When his brother Frank entered ninth grade, he was assigned the same teacher as Joe. The teacher anticipated that Frank would be a poor student and invested little effort in helping Frank learn. This is an example of:
    a. student interaction effect.
    b. teacher expectancy effect.
    c. stereotype vulnerability.
    d. educational deflation.

24. The gap in computer use in schools, known as the "digital divide," is the smallest between which groups of students in the U.S.?
   a. boys and girls
   b. Whites and Blacks
   c. upper-income and lower-income students
   d. None of the above are true, because student computer use in schools does not vary by race, class, or gender now that computers are so widely available.

25. Which of the following statements is true concerning the labeling effect?
   a. Once a student has been labeled as having a low ability level, that label can easily be altered if the student performs better on subsequent measures of his/her ability.
   b. Assigning labels to students is a fair, objective, and efficient mechanism for separating children into groups where they will be assigned material that is consistent with their ability levels.
   c. Once a label concerning ability is assigned to a student, it tends to stick, whether or not it is accurate.
   d. None of the above statements are true, because schools stopped assigning such labels to students after ending the practice of tracking.

TRUE-FALSE QUESTIONS

1. According to Howard Gardner, athletic ability is a physical talent rather than a form of intelligence.

2. The average income for women is less than the average income for men at each educational level.

3. Among White people of the upper classes, education is more important than social class origin in determining occupation and income.

4. Students from lower-income families have higher average scores than students from upper-income students on exams such as the Scholastic Aptitude Test (SAT).

5. The United States is the only industrialized nation that filters out potential university students by requiring success on standardized tests prior to college admission.

6. Fiscal constraints no longer pose a problem for schools because the United States spends more on education than virtually every other social institution.

7. Standardized intelligence tests are designed to measure seven different kinds of intelligence, including musical, spatial, interpersonal, and verbal abilities.

8. According to Herrnstein and Murray, the authors of *The Bell Curve*, intelligence in the general population is 70 percent determined by genes and 30 percent determined by environment.

9. White students are more likely to be placed in high-ability tracks than Hispanic or Black students, even when the students receive the same test scores.

10. Compulsory education was not established in most states in the U.S. until 1935.

FILL IN THE BLANK QUESTIONS

1. Educational _____ refers to the fact that the relative economic advantage of a college education has declined as far more people complete college degrees.

2. Exams that are given to large populations and scored with respect to population averages are _____ tests.

3. Proponents of _____ argue that it is more beneficial to mix students of varying cognitive abilities than to separate them, especially in high school.

4. The only racial-ethnic minority group that is well represented in higher tracks in American schools is _____.

5. The _____ theory of intelligence posits that various cognitive abilities are distinct, with no common master ability underlying them all.

ESSAY QUESTIONS

1. Compare and contrast the functionalist, conflict, and symbolic interactionist perspectives on the relative importance of individual merit on school performance.
2. Identify the functions of the educational system in industrialized nations such as the United States and discuss why formal education is so important in today's society.
3. Explain how the stereotype vulnerability effect can have both positive and negative effects on test performance for different groups of students.
4. Explain why Herrnstein and Murray's book, *The Bell Curve*, generated so much controversy in the United States.
5. Assume that you are an educator who has been asked to help develop a new curriculum for your state's school system. Your task is to prepare a statement indicating whether you are *for* or *against* your state adopting the changes recommended by the back-to-basics educational reform movement. Provide supporting evidence for your position.

ANSWERS TO PRACTICE TEST

Answers to Multiple Choice Questions

1. C. 446 The United States spends $458 billion on education at all levels each year, more than on any other institution or activity except health care.
2. B. 446 According to Figure 16.1, Hispanic students have the lowest college attendance and highest high school dropout rate.
3. B. 449 As summarized in Table 16.1, conflict theory views education as reinforcing and perpetuating inequalities in society at large.
4. A. 450 According to sociologists, the best indicators of socioeconomic status are education, income, and occupation.
5. C. 450 Occupational prestige is the subjective evaluation of the value of specific jobs to society. There is a moderate correlation between educational level needed and the occupational prestige of a job.
6. D. 448 Social control is a latent function of education. A perceived benefit of compulsory education is that it keeps young people out of trouble.

7.	A.	454	Cognitive ability is the capacity to think abstractly, which is measured by standardized IQ (intelligence quotient) tests.
8.	D.	453	The educational system in the U.S. provides relatively more social mobility than in Japan, Germany, or England, where low scores can make students ineligible for a college education.
9.	A.	455	The seven multiple intelligences proposed by Howard Gardner are: body-kinesthetic, intrapersonal, interpersonal, logical-mathematical, musical, linguistic, and spatial. Spatial intelligence refers to the ability to visualize three-dimensional figures.
10.	C.	456	The extent to which a test provides an accurate monitor of future college grades or some other criterion, such as likelihood of graduation, is predictive validity.
11.	B.	455	The Stanford-Binet IQ test is a standardized test designed to measure "general cognitive ability." Achievement tests are designed to measure what has actually been learned, rather than ability or potential.
12.	D.	457	According to the Herrnstein and Murray, the authors of *The Bell Curve*, heredity or genetic makeup determines 70 percent of intelligence. They assert that the upper classes constitute a genetically-based cognitive elite in America, consisting of those with high IQs and high incomes.
13.	B.	458	One of the criticisms of *The Bell Curve* was that the authors drew too many conclusions about between-group differences from within-group results. They also dismiss previous research that indicating that environment significantly contributes to differences in test performance, and that standardized tests do not accurately measure intelligence for all racial-ethnic or social class groups.
14.	B.	455	The unidimensional theory of intelligence asserts that there is one main kind of intelligence, which can be measured by standardized tests of cognitive ability. Gardner, a proponent of the multidimensional theory of intelligence, asserts that there are multiple kinds of intelligence.
15.	B.	459	The self-fulfilling prophecy is a powerful mechanism whereby labeling a student has the effect of justifying the label. For example, if a student is labeled bright, then s/he becomes bright because others define and treat her as if she is bright.
16.	C.	460	Both girls and boys experience a drop in self-esteem as they approach adolescence, but the erosion of self-esteem occurs more quickly for girls. In schools, teachers pay more attention to male students. Math tests tend to under-predict girls' actual grades in mathematics.
17.	D.	461	Textbooks generally present boys as leaders and girls as followers. Boys are portrayed in professions such as doctor, while girls are presented in traditionally female occupations. Male characters still outnumber female characters in textbooks.
18.	C.	464	The back-to-basics educational movement stresses a return to a traditional curriculum delivered with traditional methods, and the implementation of more stringent grading criteria.
19.	A.	465	The multiculturalism movement encourages schools at all levels to offer more courses on diverse group perspectives and experiences.
20.	C.	458	Grouping or stratifying students in school on the basis on test scores is called tracking. Tracking, is done in a majority of schools in the U.S. with the intention of better assisting students of varying abilities.
21	C.	459	Symbolic interactionists focus on the interaction between people in social groups, such as students and teachers. This perspective

recognizes that how a teacher perceives and treats a student has an effect on the student's performance.

22.	D.	464	In their book, *The Agony of Education*, Feagin and colleagues argue that the importance of education is recognized in Black communities, but Black students continue to face stereotyping and discrimination on predominantly White university campuses. The authors note that some positive changes have occurred, but many White students continue to deny that racism exists.
23.	B.	459	The teacher expectancy effect refers to the fact that the teacher's expectations affect the student's actual performance, independent of the student's actual ability.
24.	A.	446	The gap in computer use is smallest between boys and girls; in fact, it has virtually disappeared. The "digital divide" occurs mainly along the lines of race and class, with White students and higher-income students somewhat more likely than Black students and lower-income students to use computers in school and at home.
25.	C.	458	Both high- and low-track students are subject to the labeling effect. Once a label has been assigned, it tends to stick, whether or not it is accurate. These labels are not necessarily based on fair, objective, or relevant criteria for determining a student's ability.

Answers to True-False Questions

1.	F.	455	According to Gardner, athletic ability is a form of body-kinesthetic intelligence because command of one's body is fundamentally under cognitive control.
2.	T.	450	Table 16.2 summarizes income differences by gender and education.
3.	F.	451	Among White people of the upper classes, social class origin is more important than education in determining occupation and income.
4.	T.	456	Students from lower-income families have lower average scores on standardized tests such as the Scholastic Aptitude Test (SAT).
5.	F.	453	England, Germany, and Japan also require students to perform well on standardized tests to be admitted to college.
6.	F.	463	Even though the U.S. spends more money on education than virtually any other institution or activity, American schools are faced with fiscal problems. Funding for education is not distributed equally across all states or local school districts.
7.	F.	455	Standardized tests are designed to measure limited ranges of ability, such as mathematical ability.
8.	T.	457	Herrnstein and Murray assert that intelligence is determined 70 percent by genes and 30 percent by environment.
9.	T.	459	Race and ethnicity continue to influence tracking decisions in schools.
10.	F.	446	Compulsory, or mandatory, education was established in most states in the U.S., with a few exceptions in the south, by 1900.

Answers to Fill in the Blank Questions

1.	deflation	451
2.	standardized	455
3.	detracking	458
4.	Asian American	459
5.	multidimensional	455

CHAPTER 17
RELIGION

BRIEF CHAPTER OUTLINE
Defining Religion
The Significance of Religion
      The Dominance of Christianity
      Measuring Religious Faith
Forms of Religion
      Monotheism and Polytheism
      Patriarchal and Matriarchal Religion
      Exclusive and Inclusive Religious Groups
Sociological Theories of Religion
      Emile Durkheim: The Functions of Religion
      Max Weber: The Protestant Ethic and the Spirit of Capitalism
      Karl Marx: Religion, Social Conflict, and Oppression
      Symbolic Interaction: Constructing Religious Belief
Globalization: World Religions and Diversity
      Christianity
      Judaism
      Islam
      Hinduism
      Buddhism
      Confucianism
      Diversity and Religious Belief
Religious Organizations
      Churches
      Sects
      Cults
Becoming Religious
      Religion and the Family
      Religious Conversion
Social and Political Attitudes: The Impact of Religion
      Racial Prejudice
      Homophobia
      Antisemitism
Religion and Social Change
      The New Religious Conservatism
      Race, Religion, and Justice
      Women and Religion
      Religion in Decline?

QUESTIONS TO GUIDE YOUR READING
1.   Why do sociologists consider religion a social institution as well as a personal belief system?
2.   What characteristics do sociologists use to classify different forms of religion?
3.   What are the major religions found around the world, and on what principles is each of these religions founded?
4.   How do religious belief systems affect people's social and political attitudes?
5.   What influence has religion had on promoting social change in the United States?

KEY TERMS (defined at page number shown and in glossary)

antisemitism 493

charisma 489

collective consciousness 478

ethnoreligious group 486

ideology 479

matriarchal religion 477

patriarchal religion 476

profane 473

rationalization of society 498

religiosity 475

ritual 478

sects 487

secularization 498

totem 473

brainwashing thesis 490

churches 486

cults 487

exclusive religious group 477

inclusive religious group 477

monotheism 476

polytheism 476

Protestant Ethic 479

religion 472

religious socialization 489

sacred 473

secular 474

social drift theory 491

KEY PEOPLE (identified at page number shown)

Emile Durkheim 478

Max Weber 479

Karl Marx 479

CHAPTER OUTLINE

The profound effect of religion on society and human behavior is easily observed in everyday life. Sociologists study religion as both a belief system and a social institution. The belief systems of religion have a powerful hold on what people think and how they see the world. As a social institution, the patterns and practices of religion are among the most important influences on people's lives. Religious beliefs and practices are interwoven with other institutions in society, including the family, politics, and the economy.

Sociologists do not accept religion based on faith alone. Because the sociological perspective requires empirical evidence, studying religion as a sociological phenomenon requires a certain detachment and an unwillingness to take religious beliefs for granted. Sociologists assess religion in terms of what can be objectively analyzed. One can have a sociological perspective on religion and be a religious person. In developing a sociological perspective on religion, what is important is not what one believes about religion, but one's ability to be non-judgmental. The sociological observer must be willing to examine religion in its social and cultural context and to separate the practices of religion from dogma and moral tenets.

I.   **DEFINING RELIGION**

    A.   The Definition of Religion

        Sociologists define **religion** as an institutionalized system of symbols, beliefs, values, and practices through which a group of people interprets and responds to what they feel is sacred. Religion provides answers to questions of ultimate meaning.

    B.   The Elements of Religion

        1.   *Religion is institutionalized.* Religion is a pattern of social action organized around the beliefs, practices, and symbols that people develop to answer questions about the meaning of existence. Religion persists over time and has an organizational structure into which members are socialized.

        2.   *Religion is a feature of groups.* Religion is a cohesive force among believers because it is the basis for group identity and gives people a sense of belonging to a community or organization.

3. *Religions are based on beliefs that are considered sacred.*
    a. The **sacred** is that which is set apart from ordinary activity, seen as holy, and protected by special rites and rituals.
    b. The **profane** is that which is of the everyday world and is specifically not religious.
    c. Actions are considered *sacrilegious* if they desecrate or treat a sacred object in an objectionable way.
    d. A **totem** is an object or living thing that a religious group regards with special awe and reverence, such as a statue of Buddha or a crucifix.
4. *Religion establishes values and moral proscriptions for behavior.* Religion typically establishes proscriptions, or constraints, on the behavior of believers.
5. *Religion establishes norms for behavior.* Religious belief systems establish social norms, or expected patterns of behavior, about how the faithful should behave in certain situations.
6. *Religion provides answers to questions of ultimate meaning.* **Secular** beliefs, the ordinary beliefs of daily life, may be institutionalized, but they are not specifically religious. Religious beliefs often have a supernatural element.

II. **THE SIGNIFICANCE OF RELIGION**
For millions of people, religion is the strongest component of their individual and group identity, and it is often the basis of culture in societies.
    A. The Dominance of Christianity
    Despite the constitutional principle of the separation of church and state, Christian religious beliefs and practices dominate American culture. Publicly observing Christian traditions through the designation of national holidays, for example, may reveal insensitivity to the religious beliefs of other groups.
    B. Measuring Religious Faith
        1. **Religiosity** refers to the intensity and consistency of an individual's or group's faith.
        2. Sociologists measure religiosity both by asking people about their religious beliefs and by measuring membership in religious organizations and attendance at religious services.
        3. The vast majority of people in the United States identify themselves as Protestant (58 percent), Catholic (26 percent), or Jewish (2 percent), with diverse religions and those with no religious identification (6 percent) constituting the balance.
        4. The influence of religion in politics and social policy in the United States has recently increased.

III. **FORMS OF RELIGION**
Religions are categorized according to the specific characteristics of the faiths and how religious groups are organized. In different societies and among different religious groups, the form religion takes reflects differing belief systems and supports other features of society.
    A. Monotheism and Polytheism
        1. **Monotheism** is the worship of a single god. Christianity and Judaism are monotheistic.
        2. **Polytheism** is the worship of more than one deity. Most traditional Native American cultures and some Asian religions are polytheistic.

B.   Patriarchal and Matriarchal Religions
1.   **Patriarchal religions** are those in which the beliefs and practices of the religion are based on male power and authority. Christianity is a patriarchal religion.
2.   **Matriarchal religions** are based on the centrality of female goddesses, who may be seen as the source of food, nurturance, and love, or who may serve as emblems of the power of women. In societies based on matriarchal religions, women are more likely to share power with men in the society at large.

C.   Exclusive and Inclusive Religious Groups
1.   **Exclusive religious groups** are those with an easily identifiable religion and culture, including distinctive beliefs and strong moral teachings. Exclusive religious groups, such as the Black Muslims, tend to be small in membership but form coherent, close-knit communities.
2.   **Inclusive religious groups** are those with a more moderate and liberal religious orientation. These groups are more *ecumenical*, meaning that they stress interdenominational cooperation and the importance of common religious work. Inclusive groups tend to have broad-based membership and form a more diffuse religious community.

IV.   **SOCIOLOGICAL THEORIES OF RELIGION**
A.   Durkheim: The Functions of Religion
1.   Durkheim argued that religion is functional for society because it reaffirms the social bonds that people have with each other, which creates social cohesion and integration.
2.   Religious **rituals** are symbolic activities that express a group's spiritual convictions, such as a pilgrimage to Mecca.
3.   Durkheim believed that religion binds individuals to the society in which they live by establishing what he called a **collective consciousness**, or the body of beliefs that are common to a community or society and that give people a sense of belonging.
4.   Religion has a strong emotional component, both in terms of emotional expression and emotional control, which strengthens the attachment people feel to their group's way of thinking.

B.   Max Weber: The Protestant Ethic and the Spirit of Capitalism
1.   Weber argued that the Protestant faith supported the development of capitalism in the Western world because it included a belief in predestination, or the belief that one's salvation is predetermined. Material success was viewed as a gift from God, not something one earned; thus, successful people appeared to be favored by God.
2.   The key features of the **Protestant Ethic** -- hard work and self-denial -- led not only to salvation, but also to the accumulation of capital.
3.   Weber's analysis of the Protestant Ethic shows how religious beliefs continue to shape our national culture, even in its secular dimensions.

C.   Karl Marx: Religion, Social Conflict, and Oppression
1.   Religious *ethnocentrism*, or an excessive belief in the superiority of one's own group, has frequently led to the ruthless subordination of other religious groups.
2.   Marx viewed religion as a tool for class oppression because oppressed people develop religion to soothe their distress. Because religion

prevents them from rising up against oppression, it is a form of *false consciousness*.

3. To Marx, religion is an **ideology**, or a belief system that legitimates the social order and supports the ideas of the ruling class. When subordinate groups internalize the views of the dominant class, they come to believe in the legitimacy of the social order that oppresses them. This analysis of religion reveals that religion operates in ways that are not typically acknowledged.

4. It is important to note that religion can be just as much the basis for social change as it is for social continuity, as was the case in the Civil Rights Movement in the United States.

V. **GLOBALIZATION: WORLD RELIGIONS AND DIVERSITY**

Worldwide, religion is one of the most significant dimensions of culture. In some nations, religion defines the political order and shapes the other social institutions. Measured in terms of the number of followers, the largest religion in the world is Christianity, followed by Islam. The United States is one of the most religiously diverse societies in the world.

A. Christianity

In the United States, Christianity is the dominant religion, although there is considerable diversity in the different forms of Christianity worldwide.

1. Protestants form the largest religious group in the U.S., although within this group, there is further diversity.

    a. *Mainline Protestants* include 28 different denominations, all belonging to the National Council of Churches, that have a history of social activism. They have recently experienced declines in church membership and attendance due to a decrease in religious affiliation and the growth in the number of conservative Protestants.

    b. *Conservative Protestants* are also known as fundamentalists. They represent the conservative offspring of the evangelical movement. Highly organized for political action, these groups have had an enormous influence on society in recent years.

2. Roman Catholics around the world identify the Pope as the source of religious authority. Catholicism is a very hierarchical religious system, with religious values and codes of behavior mandated by the Vatican.

    a. Many Catholics hold more liberal attitudes than the official church advocates. An example of the transformation of the Catholic Church is the emergence of *liberation theology*, an inspiration of priests in Latin America who feel that the gospel of Christ commands the church to be leaders in liberating the poor and oppressed people of the world.

    b. In the United States, Catholicism has long been associated with immigrant groups such as the Italians and the Irish.

B. Judaism

Although a numerically small religious faith, Judaism has enormous world significance.

1. Over 40 percent of the world's Jewish population lives in the U.S., making this the largest community of Jewish people in the world.

2. The number of Jewish Americans is declining as the result of a low birth rate and a high rate of interfaith marriage. When Jewish men marry non-Jewish women, their offspring are not considered Jewish.

3.   There are significant differences of culture and religious practice within Judaism. Orthodox Jews adhere strictly to a traditional conception of their religious faith, Reform Jews have a more secular orientation, and Conservative Judaism falls between Orthodox and Reform in terms of strictness of observation.

C.   Islam
1.   Islam is most typically associated with Middle Eastern countries, although Islamic people are also found in parts of Africa, Asia, and increasingly in North America and Europe.
2.   Followers of Islamic religion, called Muslims, believe that Islam is the word of God, revealed in the prophet of Muhammad. The Koran is the holy book of Islam.

D.   Hinduism
1.   Hindu religion is not linked to a singular God; in fact, Hinduism rejects the idea that there is a single, powerful god.
2.   Karma is the principle in Hindu that sees all human action as having spiritual consequences, ultimately leading to a higher states of spiritual consciousness, perhaps found in the birth one experiences following death, or reincarnation.
3.   Hinduism is deeply linked to the social system of India, because the caste system in India is viewed as stemming from people's degree of commitment to Hindu principles. Those who live the most ideal forms of life are seen as part of the higher caste, with the lower caste viewed as spiritually bereft.

E.   Buddhism
Buddhism is another complex religion that does not follow a strict or singular theological god. Like Hinduism, Buddhism arises from Indian culture, is most widely practiced in Asian societies, and involves a concept of birth and re-birth through reincarnation. Buddhist view people as releasing their worldly suffering through seeking spiritual enlightenment.

F.   Confucianism
Confucianism is mostly found in China, although migration to other parts of Southeast Asia and North America brought the practice to other societies. Confucians follow the code of Confucius, a leader who promoted moral principles and a disciplined way of life.

G.   Diversity and Religious Belief
1.   Religious identification varies with a number of social factors, including age, income level, education, and political affiliation. For example, people over age 50 are most likely to say that religion is important to them.
2.   Race is one of the most significant markers when examining patterns of religious orientation. The church is a central insitution in many Black communities, where it is not only a spiritual base, but also a social and political center. Many prominent Black leaders in the United States emerged from churches or mosques.
3.   The great diversity of religious beliefs in the U.S. stems from the diverse ethnic and cultural backgrounds of the American people. Some **ethnoreligious groups**, or extreme forms of exclusive religious groups, exist in the U.S., including Hasidic Jews and the Amish.

VI. RELIGIOUS ORGANIZATIONS

A. Churches
   1. **Churches** are formal organizations that tend to see themselves, and are seen by society, as the primary and legitimate religious institutions.
   2. Churches are organized as complex bureaucracies, with a complex division of labor, different roles, and professional, full-time clergy.
   3. Church membership is renewed as children of existing members are brought up in the church, and some churches actively proselytize.

B. Sects
   Sects are groups that have broken off from an established church, typically in protest against events or beliefs within the secular world. For example, the Shakers departed from the Society of Friends (also known as Quakers).

C. Cults
   Cults, similar to sects in their intensity, are religious groups devoted to a specific cause or charismatic leader. Cults such as the Branch Davidians tend to form around leaders with great **charisma**, a quality attributed to individuals believed to have special powers.

VII. BECOMING RELIGIOUS

Regardless of affiliation, religion is often a significant part of people's social identity. The process by which one learns a particular faith, or becomes religious, is **religious socialization**. *Informal religious socialization* occurs when one observes and absorbs the religious perspective of parents and peers. *Formal religious socialization* occurs through explicit religious instruction.

A. Religion and the Family
   1. One of the strongest influences on religious socialization is the family, where members often display religious symbols and explicitly teach religious beliefs and practices to children.
   2. It is common for people who drop out of religious activities during their young adulthood to return to religious practice when they begin raising their own families.
   3. As people grow older, the family of origin's influence on religious beliefs lessens but does not disappear.

B. Religious Conversion
   1. *Conversion* is a transformation of religious identity that may be slow and gradual or dramatic. Fundamentalist Christians describe this process as being "born again."
   2. The **brainwashing thesis** claims that innocent people are tricked into religious conversion by religious cults that manipulate and coerce people into accepting their beliefs.
   3. Sociologists suggest an alternative way of understanding the process of conversion using **social drift theory**, which interprets people as gradually moving into cults when they experience personal strains or become disenchanted with their prior affiliations.
      a. The first phase typically involves an experience that leads a potential convert to perceive disruption or failure in his or her previous life, allowing the person to be open to a serious change in social environment.
      b. In the second phase of conversion, an emotional bond is created between the initiate and one or more group members.

      c.   The third phase of religious conversion is a period of intense interaction with the new group.

    4.   De-conversion involves a social process of disengagement that occurs in phases as well, including breaking the emotional attachment to the group and slowly re-integrating into society.

VIII. SOCIAL AND POLITICAL ATTITUDES: THE IMPACT OF RELIGION

Religious identification strongly influences how traditional a person's gender beliefs will be, as well as how people vote on issues such as abortion, the death penalty, and defense spending. Religion also affects people's sexual attitudes and behavior. The most religiously devout tend to be the least sexually active and the most conventional in their sexual practices.

    A.   Racial Prejudice

        1.   Not only are religious groups sometimes targeted by prejudice, but religious belief is also related to the likelihood that someone will be prejudiced.

        2.   Researchers have distinguished three patterns relating the degree of religious prejudice to the nature of religious experience.

            a.   An *extrinsic religious orientation* denotes an exclusionary and highly devout religious attitude, such as that of fundamentalist religious groups. This orientation is significantly correlated with prejudice.

            b.   An *intrinsic religious orientation*, reflected in most mainline Protestant churches, is associated with greater tolerance and openness to different forms of religious expression.

            c.   A *quest orientation* features a searching attitude toward religion, as is the case with Quakers, Unitarians, and Jews. People with this orientation tend to be tolerant of ambiguity in general and more comfortable in situations where doubt, rather than certainty, is predominant. A quest orientation is the least likely to be associated with prejudice.

    B.   Homophobia

        1.   *Homophobia*, the fear and hatred of homosexuals, has been linked to religious beliefs. Some people argue that Christianity has encouraged homophobia because the Bible has been interpreted as prohibiting same-sex sexual relations.

        2.   Some religious congregations have actively worked to encourage the participation of gays and lesbians in their congregations as well as through ordination as clergy.

    C.   Anti-Semitism

        1.   **Antisemitism**, one of the world's most persistent forms of prejudice, is the belief or behavior that defines Jewish people as inferior and targets them for stereotyping, mistreatment, and acts of hatred.

        2.   Like other forms of prejudice, antisemitism is associated with a characteristic social-psychological profile that includes being highly authoritarian and aggressive, having conventional values and a preoccupation with dominance and submission, and holding generalized hostility.

        3.   Like other forms of intolerance such as racism, sexism, and homophobia, antisemitism is expressed through the beliefs and actions of specific people, but has its origins in the social structural conditions

within society. Jewish people have often been scapegoated, or blamed for the problems that other groups may be having, such as economic difficulties.

IX. **RELIGION AND SOCIAL CHANGE**

Religion, like other social institutions, evolves over time as people adapt to changing social conditions. Religion has historically had a deep connection to other forms of social change. In recent years, the influence of conservative religious groups on the social and political agenda in the United States has increased considerably.

A. The New Religious Conservatism

1. There has been a rise in religious conservatism as evangelical groups grow in size and political influence, resulting in a dramatic shift in the influence of religion on politics.

2. There has been a dramatic increase in the number of people who say they are born-again or evangelical, with women and African Americans most likely to do so.

3. The hallmarks of evangelical religious groups are the intensity of their religious beliefs, the exclusivity of their membership, their emphasis on personal salvation through faith in Jesus, their belief that the Bible is a practical guide to everyday life, and their suspicion of religious compromise.

4. The evangelical movement consists of diverse groups. Although diffuse and consisting of small congregations, evangelicals form a tight-knit national community, which has been facilitated by the strong Christian presence on the electronic media. Christian religious media, including television, radio, and books, have become a major industry.

5. The conservative Christian movement has fueled anti-abortion activism, revived the effort to teach creationism in schools, and campaigned against women's rights and gay and lesbian rights.

B. Race, Religion, and Justice

1. Religious institutions have been a conservative force in society, often supporting prejudice and resisting social change, yet they have also been an important part of movements for social justice and human emancipation.

2. One of the central themes of African American religiosity has been liberation from oppression, and Black churches had a prominent role during the mobilization of the civil rights movement in the United States.

3. Militant Black leaders have tended to be less religiously oriented than more moderate activists. *Black nationalism* is a secular ideology that views African Americans as having a unique identity as a nation and as deserving the right to self-determination.

   a. As a political movement, Black nationalism traces its origins to the Black Muslim religious movement.

   b. Religious practice among Black Muslims involves strict regulation of dietary habits and prohibitions against many activities, such as alcohol use, drug use, and gambling.

   c. Black Muslims promote the idea of community self-control for African Americans and have established many of their own institutions, including schools.

C.   <u>Women and Religion</u>
   1.   Generally speaking, women are more religiously devout than men, yet women have long been denied the right to full participation in many churches.
   2.   Across all denominational groups, men are more supportive of female ordination than are women. In the 1990s, women received 26 percent of all seminary degrees.
   3.   African American women generally have greater equality with men in African American churches than do White women in White churches.
   4.   Traditional images of women have been the basis of many gender stereotypes; for example, that women are seductresses who lead men into temptation, as in the biblical creation story of Adam and Eve.
   5.   Religion has been the basis of liberation for many women who used their experiences within religious institutions to enrich the thinking of many strong feminist advocates. There is a growing trend toward redefining traditional religious orientations in ways that are supportive of feminist beliefs.

D.   <u>Religion in Decline?</u>
   1.   There has been a general trend in American life toward declining religious participation, reflecting **secularization**, or the process by which religious institutions, behavior, and consciousness lose their significance.
   2.   Secularization is a change in the basic organization of society. Max Weber referred to this trend as the **rationalization of society**, whereby society is increasingly organized around rational, empirical, and scientific forms of thought.
   3.   Secularization is a long-term process, reflecting the historical change from a communally based society to one based on more formal, impersonal associations. As societies become more secularized, traditional religious values lose their strength and various forms of religious experimentation usually develop.
   4.   There is little doubt that the United States has become a more secular society, but it would be inaccurate to say that religion has lost its hold. Religion may show some signs of decline, but it remains a significant social force and social institution in the contemporary United States.

PRACTICE TEST

MULTIPLE CHOICE QUESTIONS

1.   From a sociological perspective, which of the following statements about religion is false?
   a.   Religious faith provides a source of cohesion for members of society, but it also serves as a source of conflict in society.
   b.   Religion cannot be studied as a social institution because it is based on faith rather than objective principles.
   c.   A primary function of religion is to provide a sense of ultimate meaning.
   d.   Religion establishes values and norms that restrict people's behavior.

2. Religiousity refers to:
   a. the socialization mechanisms that teach people moral values and proscriptions for behavior.
   b. whether one believes in a single, powerful deity or multiple deities.
   c. the intensity and consistency of practice of a person's or group's faith.
   d. an excessive belief in the superiority of one's own values.

3. Which of the following religions does **not** follow a single, powerful god?
   a. Catholicism
   b. Hinduism
   c. Judaism
   d. Islam

4. Religions based on the centrality of female goddesses are _____ religions.
   a. monotheistic
   b. matriarchal
   c. patriarchal
   d. exclusive

5. The profane is anything that:
   a. is supernatural.
   b. excites awe and reverence.
   c. is regarded as part of the ordinary world.
   d. can be approached or handled only after ritual cleansing.

6. The Amish, an extreme form of exclusive religious group that maintains their distinctive faith by limiting interaction with the larger society is a(n): _____ group.
   a. secular
   b. legitimate
   c. ethnoreligious
   d. ecumenical

7. Religions that have easily identifiable religious culture that includes distinctive beliefs and strong moral teachings are _____ religions.
   a. exclusive
   b. informal
   c. inclusive
   d. profane

8. Symbolic activities that express a group's spiritual conviction, such as a pilgrimage to Mecca, are religious:
   a. orientations.
   b. totems.
   c. rituals.
   d. cults

9. According to Emile Durkheim, religion:
   a. is functional for society because it reaffirms the social bonds that people have with each other, which creates social cohesion and integration.
   b. is an ideology that legitimates the social order and supports the ideas of the ruling class.
   c. creates ethnocentrism that frequently leads to the subordination of other groups.
   d. is not really necessary in industrialized countries because it does not fulfill an essential function in modern societies.

10. Which theorist argued that the Protestant Ethic encouraged and supported the development of capitalism in the United States?
    a. Max Weber
    b. Confucius
    c. Karl Marx
    d. Emile Durkheim

11. The largest religion in the world, when measured in terms of followers, is:
    a. Islam.
    b. Hinduism.
    c. Buddhism.
    d. Christianity.

12. The largest religious group in the United States is:
    a. Jews.
    b. Muslims.
    c. Protestants.
    d. Roman Catholics.

13. An example of the transformation of the Catholic Church is the emergence of _____ theology, an inspiration of priests in Latin American who feel that the gospel of Christ commands the church to free the world's poor from oppression.
    a. liberation
    b. extremist
    c. revolutionary
    d. fundamentalist

14. Within Judaism, _____ Jews have a more secular orientation and offer the most flexibility in religious practices, such as offering prayers in English rather than Hebrew:
    a. Hasidic
    b. Reform
    c. Orthodox
    d. Conservative

15. Which formal organizations tend to see themselves, and are socially defined, as the primary and legitimate religious organizations in society?
    a. cults
    b. sects
    c. retreats
    d. churches

16. Karl Marx argued that religion is a form of false consciousness because:
    a. subordinate groups internalize religious ideology that justifies an oppressive social order.
    b. dominant religious ideology encourages subordinate groups to seek justice and equality by challenging oppression.
    c. religion binds individuals to each other and to society, thereby enhancing cohesion and social harmony.
    d. religious worship should take place in small, informal groups rather than in large, formal organizations such as modern churches.

17. Which theory interprets people as moving into religious cults gradually, particularly if they have experienced recent personal strains or have become disenchanted with their prior affiliations?
    a. social drift theory
    b. liberation theology
    c. brainwashing thesis
    d. deprogramming theory

18. The aspect of religious rituals that symbolic interactionists would focus on most is:
    a. why rituals reinforce a sense of social belonging.
    b. how rituals provide definitions of individual and group identity.
    c. why rituals provide legitimation for oppressive social conditions.
    d. how rituals clearly define boundaries between in-groups and out-groups.

19. The belief that Jewish people are inferior or immoral, which leads to targeting them for stereotyping, mistreatment, and acts of hatred, is:
    a. miscegenation.
    b. antisemitism.
    c. homophobia.
    d. sexism.

20. National surveys indicate that overall, American citizens have the greatest confidence in which of the following social institutions?
    a. public schools
    b. medical system
    c. organized religion
    d. criminal justice system

21. Cults tend to form around leaders with great _____, a quality attributed to individuals believed by their followers to have special powers.
    a. conservatism
    b. spirituality
    c. frustration
    d. charisma

22. Groups that have broken off from an established church, which are usually characterized by emotionally charged worship services, are:
    a. cults.
    b. sects.
    c. totems.
    d. support groups.

23.   A(n) _____ is an object or living thing, such as a statue of Buddha, that a religious group regards with special awe and reverence.
    a.   totem
    b.   trinket
    c.   ideology
    d.   theology

24.   Research on gender and religion indicates that:
    a.   women are more religiously devout than are men.
    b.   men are more supportive of female ordination than women.
    c.   people with deeper religious involvement have more traditional attitudes about gender roles.
    d.   All of the above statements are true.

25.   According to Weber, the process by which society becomes increasingly organized around empirical and scientific forms of thought is the _____ of society.
    a.   destruction
    b.   globalization
    c.   politicization
    d.   rationalization

TRUE-FALSE QUESTIONS

1.   There has been a significant decrease in the number of people in the United States who identify as born again or evangelical.

2.   There has been considerable movement toward gender equality in the religious institution, resulting in fifty percent of all seminary degrees being awarded to women.

3.   Although the number of Protestant Latinos in the United States is increasing, about seventy percent of Latinos still identify as Catholic.

4.   Exclusive religious groups such as the Black Muslims tend to be small in membership and expect members to conform strictly to religious values and behavioral norms.

5.   Marx believed that religion binds individuals to society by establishing what he called a collective consciousness, or the shared body of beliefs that give people in a community a sense of belonging.

6.   The Shakers are a cult that developed when a subgroup broke off from the established Mennonite church because followers believed that the church leaders were not strictly adhering to religious doctrine.

7.   Mainline Protestants have recently experienced considerable increases in church membership and attendance.

8.   Participation in bar mitzvah, bat mitzvah, or catechism classes is a form of informal religious socialization.

9.   Judaism has enormous world significance because it is the second largest religion in the world.

10. An extrinsic religious orientation features a searching attitude toward religion and greater tolerance of ambiguity, as is the case with Quakers.

FILL IN THE BLANK QUESTIONS

1. When someone defaces or misuses a religious object, that action is considered _____ by those who view that symbol as sacred.

2. Inclusive religious groups such as The National Council of Churches are _____, meaning that they stress interdenominational cooperation and common religious work.

3. Hinduism is a _____ religion because it is based on the belief that there are millions of gods and demons, rather than one powerful god.

4. As a society becomes increasingly complex and bureaucratized, _____ occurs, resulting in religious institutions, behavior, and consciousness losing their religious significance.

5. Christianity is categorized as a _____ religion because the beliefs and practices of this religion are based on male power and authority.

ESSAY QUESTIONS

1. Identify five major religions found around the world and indicate in which parts of the world each religion is prevalent.
2. Explain the relationship between religious ideology and prejudices such as sexism, racism, and homophobia, giving specific examples of how religious doctrine has supported social inequality.
3. Use social drift theory to explain the process that an individual undergoes during conversion to a religious cult.
4. Identify two periods in history that revived religious conservatism in the United States and discuss the effects these religious revivals had on American society.
5. Explain how African Americans have used religion to promote liberation from oppression.

ANSWERS TO PRACTICE TEST

Answers to Multiple Choice Questions

1.	D.	426	Religion is an institutionalized feature of groups that can be studied objectively using sociological theories and methods. Religion is based on beliefs that people considered sacred and that provide answers to questions of ultimate meaning. Religion can be a source of social cohesion within groups as well as a source of conflict between groups. Religion also establishes moral proscriptions for behavior.
2.	C.	475	The intensity and consistency of practice of a person's or group's faith is religiosity.
3.	B.	484	Unlike Catholicism, Protestantism, Judaism, and Islam, Hinduism rejects the idea that there is a single, powerful god. In this religion, god is not a specific entity at all.
4.	B.	477	Matriarchal religions are based on the centrality of female goddesses, while patriarchal religions are based on male power and authority.

5.	C.	473	The profane is anything that is ordinary. The sacred is set apart from the ordinary as holy and protected by special rites.
6.	C.	486	Groups such as the Amish and Hasidic Jews are ethnoreligious groups that preserve their distinctiveness by minimizing interaction with the larger society.
7.	A.	477	Exclusive religious groups are those with an easily identifiable religion and culture, including distinctive beliefs and strong moral teachings. The Black Muslims are an example of such a group. Inclusive religious groups are those with a more moderate and liberal religious orientation that stress interdenominational cooperation, such as the National Council of Churches.
8.	C.	478	Symbolic activities that express a group's spiritual conviction, such as a pilgrimage to Mecca, are religious rituals. Totems are objects or living things that religious groups regard with awe.
9.	A.	478	According to Emile Durkheim, religion is functional for society because it reaffirms the social bonds that people have with each other, which creates social cohesion and integration.
10.	A.	479	According to Max Weber, the Protestant Ethic supports hard work and self-denial, which was instrumental to the development of capitalism in the United States. The Protestant Ethic also encouraged personal accumulation of capital, which was interpreted as a sign that the individual was favored by God.
11.	D.	481	The largest religion in the world, if measured in terms of followers, is Christianity. The second largest religion is Islam.
12.	C.	482	The largest religious group in the United States is Protestants.
13.	A.	482	An example of the transformation of the Catholic Church is the emergence of liberation theology.
14.	B.	484	Within Judaism, Reform Jews are the most secular and flexible in their religious practice. Hasidic and Orthodox Jews are exclusive groups that strictly adhere to religious doctrine.
15.	D.	486	Churches are formal organizations that tend to see themselves, and are defined by society, as the primary and legitimate religious institutions. Sects are groups that have broken off from established churches, and cults are quasi-religious groups devoted to a specific cause or leader.
16.	A.	479	Marx believed that religion is a form of false consciousness because it prevents people from rising up against oppression. When subordinate groups internalize dominant religious ideology, they accept social inequality as legitimate.
17.	A.	491	The social drift theory views people as moving into religious cults gradually, particularly if they have experienced recent personal strains or have become disenchanted with their prior affiliations.
18.	B.	480	Symbolic interactionists focus on how meanings emerge through social interaction. They are concerned with how people define social phenomena and how rituals produce individual and group identity.
19.	B.	493	The belief that Jewish people are inferior or immoral is antisemitism.
20.	C.	487	As indicated in Table 17.3, Americans express the greatest confidence in organized religion.
21.	D.	489	Cults tend to form around leaders with great charisma, a quality attributed to individuals believed by their followers to have special powers.
22.	B.	487	Groups that have broken off from an established church, which are

usually characterized by emotionally charged religious services, are sects. The Shakers were an example of a sect.

23.	C.	473	A totem is an object or living thing, such as a statue of Buddha or a crucifix, that a religious group regards with reverence.
24.	D.	492	Women are generally more devout than men, and less supportive of the ordination of women. People who are more religiously devout generally have more traditional attitudes toward gender roles.
25.	D.	498	According to Max Weber, the process by which society becomes increasingly organized around rational, empirical, and scientific forms of thought is the rationalization of society. Rationalization has led to many scientific advances, but it also leaves many people feeling that they have no spiritual attachments.

Answers to True-False Questions

1.	F.	494	There has been a significant increase in the number of people who identify as born again or evangelical as the United States shifts toward greater religious conservatism.
2.	F.	497	Women earn 26 percent of all seminary degrees today, and some religions, such as the Catholic Church, still deny women ordination.
3.	T.	486	The majority of Latinos identify as Catholic.
4.	T.	477	Exclusive religious groups are those with an easily identifiable religion and culture, such as the Black Muslims..
5.	F.	479	According to Marx, a conflict theorist, religion is a form of false consciousness because it prevents people from rising up against oppression. Durkheim, a functionalist theorist, believed that religion establishes collective consciousness, which promotes social cohesion.
6.	F	487	The Shakers were a sect, or group that broke off from the established Quaker church.
7.	F.	482	Mainline Protestants have seen declines in church attendance and membership due to a drop in religious affiliation and an increase in the number of conservative Protestants, also known as fundamentalists.
8.	F.	489	Attendance at classes constitutes religious training, a type of formal religious socialization. Observing one's family and friends engaged in religious practices constitutes informal socialization.
9.	F.	483	Judaism has enormous social significance around the world despite the fact that it is a small religion in terms of the number of followers.
10.	F.	492	Religious orientation denotes patterns relating the degree of religious prejudice to the nature of religious experience. An extrinsic orientation, which characterizes fundamentalist Protestant groups, is associated with being highly devout and engaging in exclusionary practices. Groups with an intrinsic orientation, such as mainline Protestants, tend to be more tolerant. Groups with a quest orientation, such as Quakers, Unitarians, Jews, and some New Age spirituality groups, are characterized by a searching attitude and great tolerance for ambiguity.

Answers to Fill in the Blank Questions

1.	sacrilegious	473	4.	secularization	498
2.	ecumenical	477	5.	patriarchal	476
3.	polytheistic	476			

CHAPTER 18
WORK AND THE ECONOMY

BRIEF CHAPTER OUTLINE
Economy and Society
    The Industrial Revolution
    Comparing Economic Systems
The Changing Global Economy
    A More Diverse Workplace
    Deindustrialization
    Technological Change
    The Impact of Economic Restructuring
Theoretical Perspectives on Work
    Defining Work
    The Division of Labor
    Functionalism, Conflict Theory, and Symbolic Interaction
Characteristics of the Labor Force
    Who Works?
    Unemployment and Joblessness
    Work and Immigration
Diversity in the American Occupational System
    The Dual Labor Market
    Occupational Distribution
    Occupational Segregation
    Occupational Prestige
    Earnings
Power in the Workplace
    Sexual Harassment
    Gays and Lesbians in the Workplace
Worker Satisfaction and Safety
    Worker Alienation
    Occupational Health and Safety
    Disability and Work

QUESTIONS TO GUIDE YOUR READING
1. What are the three major types of economic systems found around the world, and how is each system organized?
2. Why is the concept of the global economy important in understanding how goods are produced and distributed in the modern United States?
3. What is economic restructuring and what consequences has it had for the American workforce in the last twenty years?
4. What is the division of labor and how is it structured by race, ethnicity, class, and gender in the United States?
5. What characteristics strongly influence worker satisfaction and safety?

KEY TERMS (defined at page number shown and in glossary)

alienation 530	automation 511
capitalism 505	communism 506
contingent workers 512	dual labor market 523
economic restructuring 508	economy 504
emotional labor 513	glass ceiling 526

KEY PEOPLE (identified at page number shown)

CHAPTER OUTLINE

Sociologists are interested in how work is shaped by specific economic systems, such as capitalism, socialism, and communism. A major question for sociologists is how systems of inequality influence the different jobs people secure and how well people are rewarded for their work. Another major issue for sociologists is how widespread social and economic changes influence work. Technological innovations are currently transforming work in ways that may have been unimaginable just a few years ago.

I.   **ECONOMY AND SOCIETY**

The **economy i**s the system by which goods and services are produced, distributed, and consumed in a society. How the economic structure of a society is organized makes a huge difference in how work is done and how people's lives are experienced.

A.   The Industrial Revolution

1.   The Industrial Revolution is currently giving way to the growth of post-industrial societies, which reflects development in the economic system that has far-reaching consequences for how society is organized.

2.   Historically, the development of agricultural societies followed the introduction and use of technologies that enabled people to increase the production of food from simple hunting and gathering techniques to more large-scale production.

3.   Agricultural production remains a significant part of the world economy, although it has been affected by industrialization.

4.   Although the United States is largely industrial, it is being quickly transformed into a new kind of social organization, the post-industrial society. Whereas industrial societies are primarily organized around the production of goods, post-industrial societies are organized around the provision of services.

5.   Service industry is a broad term encompassing a wide range of economic activities now common in the labor market, including banking, retail sales, hotel and restaurant work, and health care.

6.   Advanced technology forms the core of a post-industrial society because it is the mechanism through which most services are delivered and organized.

B.   Comparing Economic Systems

The three major kinds of economic systems found in the world today are capitalism, socialism, and communism. These are ideal types, because many societies have a mix of economic systems.

1.   **Capitalism** is an economic system based on the principles of market competition, private property, and the pursuit of profit.

a.   Under capitalism, the means of production are privately owned.

277

        b.   Owners keep a surplus of what is generated by the economy, which is their profit. Profit may be in the form of money, other financial assets, and other commodities.

        c.   Under capitalism, workers commonly produce the goods and provide the services, while owners disproportionately consume the goods and reap the profits.

        d.   The capitalist basis of American society shapes the character of other social institutions, such as health care and education.

2.   **Socialism** is an economic institution characterized by state ownership and management of basic industries, so that the means of production are the property of the state.

        a.   Modern socialism emerged from the work of Karl Marx, who predicted that capitalism would give way to egalitarian, state-dominated socialism, followed by a transition to stateless, classless communism.

        b.   In many nations, the global forces of capitalism mix with socialist principles.

        c.   Other world nations, such as the People's Republic of China, are more strongly socialist, although they are not immune from the penetrating influence of capitalism.

3.   **Communism** is sometimes described as socialism in its purest form. In pure communism, the state is the sole owner of the systems of production.

        a.   Communist philosophy argues that capitalism is fundamentally unjust, because powerful owners take more from laborers and society than they give, and they use their power to maintain the inequalities between the worker and owner classes.

        b.   A critical feature of communist economics has been the centralization of the economy in which administrators declare prices, quotas, and production goals for the entire country.

        c.   In Russia, communism was combined with *totalitarianism*, a political system in which powerful elites exercised total control over the population.

        d.   Since the Soviet Union dissolved itself in 1991, it has been struggling to achieve a stable economy based on combining socialism, capitalism, and remnants of communist institutions.

II.   THE CHANGING GLOBAL ECONOMY

The concept of a **global economy** acknowledges that all dimensions of the economy now cross national borders, including investment, production, management, markets, labor, information, and technology. The global economy now links the lives of millions of Americans to the experiences of other people throughout the world. **Multinational corporations** have become increasingly powerful, and an increasing number of jobs have moved from the United States to other countries.

In the global economy, the most developed countries control research and management, while assembly line work is performed in nations with less privileged positions in the global economy. The relocation of manufacturing to places where labor is cheap and management is strong has led to the emergence of the *global assembly line.* This is a new international division of labor in which research and development is conducted in the U.S., Japan, Germany, and other major world powers, while the assembly of goods (such as toys) is done primarily in poor, underdeveloped nations, mostly by women and children. Manufacturing overseas suits the interest of capitalist economies because labor in these nations is cheaper and typically non-unionized. The relative absence of state regulations governing working conditions and terms of employment make the transfer of work overseas even more attractive to profit-seeking corporations. Within the United States, the development of a global economy has created anxieties about foreign workers, particularly among the working class, who have been prone to **xenophobia**, or the fear and hatred of foreigners.

The development of a global economy is part of a broad process known as **economic restructuring**, which refers to temporary transformations in the basic structure of work that are permanently altering the workplace. This process also includes the changing composition of the workplace, deindustrialization, and the use of enhanced technology.

A.   A More Diverse Workplace
   1.   Women and racial-ethnic minorities are expected to comprise an even larger proportion of the labor force by the year 2008. The workforce will also be older than ever before with the aging of the Baby Boomers.
   2.   Changes in the social organization of work and the economy are creating a more diverse workforce than ever before, but much of the growth in the economy is projected to be in service industries where education and training are required to secure the better jobs.

B.   Deindustrialization
   1.   *Deindustrialization* refers to the transition from a predominantly goods-producing economy to one based on the provision of services.
   2.   Deindustrialization is most easily observed by looking at the number of jobs in the manufacturing sector of the U.S. economy since World War II, when the majority of workers (51 percent) were employed in manufacturing-based jobs. Today, the majority of workers (at least 70 percent) are employed in the service sector, which includes service delivery (such as food preparation) and information processing (such as banking).
   3.   **Job displacement** refers to the permanent loss of certain types of jobs that occurs when employment patterns shift.
   4.   When industries downsize, one option for workers is to leave the community altogether, although many may find it difficult to do so.
   5.   Among the areas that have been hardest hit by deindustrialization are communities that were heavily dependent on a single industry, such as steel towns or automobile-manufacturing cities.
   6.   There has been job growth in professional and administrative positions that have high educational requirements, and in some manufacturing fields that require specific technological training.
   7.   **Mismatch theory** argues that Black people are especially disadvantaged in the current labor market because of being residentially segregated in center cities, while jobs are increasingly located in suburban areas.

C.   Technological Change
   1.   Rapidly changing and developing technologies are bringing major changes in work, including how it is organized, who does it, and how much it pays.
   2.   One of the most influential technological developments of the 20th century has been the invention of the semiconductor, or computer chip.

3. Increasing reliance on the rapid transmission of electronic data has produced *electronic sweatshops*, a term referring to the back offices found in many industries where workers at computer terminals process hundreds or thousands of transactions a day.

4. **Automation** is the replacement of human labor by machines, such as robots.

5. New technology requires new workers with the skills needed to develop and use the new tools and techniques, but the number of positions developed for these workers does not nearly approximate the number of jobs eliminated by technological innovation.

6. *Deskilling* is a side effect of automation and technological progress in which the level of skill required to perform certain jobs declines over time.

    a. More women are entering the labor force, but they often lack the technological training required for the best jobs.

    b. Most job growth is in low-wage positions that have historically been race- and gender-segregated.

    c. At the bottom of the occupational hierarchy, people are stuck in low-wage jobs with few opportunities or benefits, contributing to alienation from their work.

D. The Impact of Economic Restructuring

1. Although economic restructuring creates new jobs, they are not numerous enough to replace the jobs lost in the process.

2. *Downsizing* is a term coined during the 1990s to refer to reducing the number of workers in an organization. In addition to eliminating workers, companies have downsized by reducing the layers of management, decreasing the overall number of managers, and downgrading the rank and salary of managers, thereby eliminating many of the career ladders that gave managers job mobility.

3. There is an increasing reliance on **contingent workers**, those whose employment is contracted as needed. Although these jobs offer workers flexibility and autonomy, contingent workers are paid less and are less likely to receive benefits.

III. **THEORETICAL PERSPECTIVES ON WORK**

A. Defining Work

1. Sociologists define **work** as productive human activity that creates something of value, either goods or services.

2. Some nations are far ahead of the United States in recognizing the productive labor of families. Reproductive labor refers to the care provided for both children and adults within families, including the provision of food, clothing, and nurturing. This labor makes it possible for people to engage in work outside the home.

3. Some sociologists argue that referring to only physical and mental labor as work is too narrow a definition. Arlie Hochschild introduced the concept of *emotional labor* to refer to another form of work that is common in a service-based economy.

    a. **Emotional labor** is work that is specifically intended to produce a desired state of mind in a client or consumer.

    b. Many jobs require the performance of emotional labor, including airline flight attendants and cashiers.

4. Some forms of work are more highly valued than others, both in how the work is perceived by society and how it is rewarded.

5. Judgments made about the value of different forms of work have also been turned into judgments about the value of different groups of workers. These judgments reflect the centrality of the *work ethic*, or the belief that hard work is a moral obligation in the United States.

6. Popular conceptions of work are also shaped by the assumptions we make about race, class, gender, and age in society. For example, mothers who receive welfare assistance are frequently accused of being lazy, yet full-time mothers who are supported by a husband-breadwinner are viewed as strongly committed to their families.

7. Stereotypes about the "undeserving poor" are common in American culture, and reflect the belief that people are poor because of their own failures and refusal to internalize the values of diligence and hard work.

8. Forty-three percent of the poor in the U.S. are working, and the number of *working poor* is increasing. The working poor are those whose wages for full-time work are below the federally defined poverty line.

9. Ironically, many of those people most admired in the U.S. for their presumed hard work and success actually became wealthy not through their own diligence and hard work, but from inheritance.

B. The Division of Labor
The division of labor is the systematic interrelatedness of different tasks that develops in complex societies. In the U.S., the *class division of labor* can be observed by examining the work done by those with different educational backgrounds, because education is a fairly reliable indicator of class. The *gender division of labor* refers to the different work that women and men do in society. The *racial division of labor* is seen in the pattern of people from racial and ethnic minority groups disproportionately working in the lowest paid, least prestigious, and most arduous jobs. The racial, class, and gender divisions of labor intersect, creating unique work experiences for diverse groups.

C. Functionalism, Conflict Theory, and Symbolic Interaction
1. Conflict theorists view the transformations taking place in the workplace as resulting from tensions inherent in the social system. These tensions develop because groups with unequal power are in competition for economic and social resources.

2. Functionalist theorists interpret work and the economy as functional for society. When the society changes too rapidly, due to technological developments and globalization, for example, institutions may experience social disorganization.
   a. Social disorganization often results in alienation, unemployment, and economic anxiety.
   b. According to functionalist theory, institutions will adjust to these changes over time, which will restore social stability.

3. Symbolic interaction theory is less focused on the workings of the whole society. This theory would be useful for studying the meaning of work to those who do it, as well as how interactions in the workplace support or undermine social bonds between people.

IV. **CHARACTERISTICS OF THE LABOR FORCE**
Data on the characteristics of the American labor force are typically drawn from the official statistics reported by the United States Department of Labor. In 1999, 139

million people, or 67 percent of the working-age population, were in the labor force. This represents an increase since World War II, when 59 percent were employed.

A. <u>Who Works?</u>

    1. Employment patterns vary significantly for different groups in the population. For example, women of color have historically had a high rate of employment.

    2. One of the most dramatic changes in the labor force since World War II has been the number of White women participating in the labor force.

    3. For all women, the increase in employment has been greatest for those with young children, resulting in greater demands on the workplace and society to provide childcare facilities and expanded family and medical leave policies.

    4. The Family and Medical Leave Act of 1993 resulted in increases in the number of employers who provide paternity and maternity leave; however, most of them provide only unpaid leave.

B. <u>Unemployment and Joblessness</u>

    1. The U.S. Department of Labor regularly reports data on the **unemployment rate**, or the percentage of people not working but officially defined as looking for work. These data include only those who meet the official definition of a job-seeker, which is someone who has actively sought a job during the prior four weeks and who is registered with the unemployment office.

    2. Unemployment statistics are most likely to undercount the people for whom unemployment runs the highest, including the youngest and oldest workers, women, and members of racial minority groups.

    3. **Underemployment**, or the condition of being employed at a level below what would be expected given a person's training, experience, or education, or working fewer hours than desired, is not captured by official unemployment statistics.

    4. Full employment in a society is assumed to occur when there is a 4 to 5 percent unemployment rate; thus, even in a "good" economy, large numbers of people are without paid work.

    5. Native Americans currently experience the highest unemployment rate in the U.S. As a group, Native Americans have less education and training than any other group. The form of work organization found in traditional Native American cultures is very different from the one created by a capitalist economy, making adjustments to the demands of mainstream employment difficult for Native Americans.

    6. Unemployment among African Americans, Puerto Ricans, and Mexican Americans is currently at a level associated with a major economic depression.

    7. Sociologists explain unemployment by examining structural problems in the economy, such as rapidly changing technology that reduces the need for human labor, deindustrialization, corporate downsizing, discriminatory employment practices, and the export of jobs overseas.

    8. The employment of women and minorities does not cause White male unemployment, because women are typically not employed in the same jobs as men, and racial minorities are concentrated in certain segments of the labor force.

C.   Work and Immigration
      1.   The contemporary labor force is being shaped by the employment of
            recent immigrants, the majority of whom are women.
      2.   The proportion of professionals and technicians among legal
            immigrants exceeds the proportion of professionals in the labor force as
            a whole.
      3.   Even illegal immigrants tend to have higher levels of education and
            occupational skill than typical workers in their homeland, because the
            poorest members of the population are seldom able to migrate.
      4.   Immigrants in the professions tend to enter the workforce at the bottom
            of their occupational ladder, but compared to less skilled immigrants,
            they are more likely to succeed economically.
      5.   Some immigrant groups have found work through the development of
            ethnic enclaves, which are typically urban areas in which there is a
            concentration of ethnic entrepreneurs.

V.   **DIVERSITY IN THE AMERICAN OCCUPATIONAL SYSTEM**
      A.   The Dual Labor Market
            1.   **Dual labor market theory** views the labor market as composed of two
                  major segments: the *primary labor market* and the *secondary labor
                  market*.
            2.   The primary labor market offers jobs with relatively high wages,
                  benefits, stability, good working conditions, opportunities for
                  promotion, job protection, and due process for workers, meaning that
                  workers are treated according to established rules and procedures that
                  are allegedly fairly administered.
            3.   The secondary labor market is characterized by low wages, few
                  benefits, high turnover, poor working conditions, little opportunity for
                  advancement, no job protection, and the arbitrary treatment of workers.
            4.   In addition to these two major segments, there is the *underground
                  economy*, which includes both illegal and unreported, or "under the
                  table," work.
            5.   Women and racial-ethnic minorities are the most likely groups to be
                  employed in the secondary labor market.
            6.   Some sociologists argue that the dual labor market works to the
                  advantage of capitalist owners, who find it advantageous to encourage
                  antagonism between different labor groups.
      B.   Occupational Distribution
            1.   **Occupational distribution** describes the pattern by which workers are
                  located in the labor force, which varies greatly by race, class, and
                  gender.
            2.   Work in the United States is classified into six broad categories:
                  managerial and professional; technical, sales, and administrative
                  support; service; precision production, craft, and repair; operators,
                  fabricators, and laborers; and farming, forestry, and fishing.
            3.   Several changes in occupational distribution have occurred, including a
                  decline in the number of Black women in private domestic work; an
                  increase in the number of racial minorities in professional and
                  managerial work (such as business, law, and municipal management);
                  and a slight increase in the number of women employed in working-
                  class jobs traditionally held only by men.

C.   <u>Occupational Segregation</u>

       Occupational segregation refers to the separation of workers into different occupations on the basis of social characteristics such as race and gender. Men in predominantly female occupations, such as nursing, teaching, librarianship, and social work, do not encounter the discrimination facing women who enter male-dominated professions. In fact, men in these fields actually receive advantages such as more opportunities for advancement.

D.   <u>Occupational Prestige</u>

       1.   **Occupational prestige** is the perceived social value of an occupation according to the general public.

       2.   Sociologists have found a strong correlation between occupational prestige and the race and gender of the people employed in given jobs.

           a.   The higher the socioeconomic status of the occupational group, the smaller the proportion of African American men who are employed in it.

           b.   Jobs that employ mostly women are lower in prestige than those that employ mostly men, and women receive less prestige than men for the same work.

E.   <u>Earnings</u>

       Sociologists have extensively documented that earnings from work are highly dependent on race, gender, and class, with White men earning the most. Functionalist and conflict theorists explain this disparity in earnings differently, based on the assumptions each theory makes about individual motivation and the value of different jobs in society.

VI.   POWER IN THE WORKPLACE

       Obvious factors such as level of pay and benefits influence workers' degree of satisfaction with their jobs. Less quantifiable, but nonetheless important, factors such as the valued accorded to one's job, opportunity for advancement, and degree of power in the workplace also affect levels of job satisfaction. The **glass ceiling** refers to the limits that women and minorities experience in job mobility.

A.   <u>Sexual Harassment</u>

       1.   **Sexual harassment** is defined as unwanted physical or verbal sexual behavior that occurs in the context of a relationship of unequal power and that is experienced as a threat to the victim's job or educational activities.

       2.   The law recognizes two primary forms of sexual harassment.

           a.   *Quid pro quo sexual harassment* forces sexual compliance in exchange for an employment or educational benefit.

           b.   The other form of sexual harassment is the creation of a *hostile working environment*, in which unwanted sexual behaviors are a continuing condition of work, including touching, teasing, and/or sexual comments.

       3.   The actual extent of sexual harassment is difficult to estimate because it tends to be underreported.

       4.   Although sexual harassment occurs in every kind of work setting, some organizational settings are more prone to sexual harassment than others. Women in male-dominated professions are particularly vulnerable to sexual harassment.

       5.   Some sociologists argue that sexual harassment is a mechanism men use to maintain their dominance in the workplace.

B. Gays and Lesbians in the Workplace
1. As gays and lesbians are more open about their sexuality, more attention has been given to sexual identity and workplace experiences.
2. Public opinion polls indicate that more people are now accepting of gays and lesbians in the workplace, except as teachers and clergy.
3. Any negative experience in the workplace can affect self-esteem, productivity, and economic and social well-being. Many gays and lesbians fear that they will suffer adverse career consequences if their coworkers know that they are gay.

VII. **WORKER SATISFACTION AND SAFETY**

One strong influence on worker satisfaction is the work environment. Safe and sanitary conditions, good pay, opportunities for advancement, and policies that recognize human dignity are among the foundations of worker satisfaction. The main cause of worker dissatisfaction is the absence of these workplace conditions. Women, minorities, and working class men are often the least satisfied with their jobs, which is likely a reflection of their position in the race, class, and gender hierarchies at work. Within work organizations, women tend to have less control over their workplaces than do White men. An authoritarian management style, where power is highly concentrated and blind authority to supervisors is expected, is associated with worker discontent. Some employers now provide more personal services within the workplace, such as exercise facilities and childcare centers, to help employees better manage work, family, and personal demands.

A. Worker Alienation
1. **Alienation**, a concept first developed by Karl Marx, is a feeling of powerlessness and separation from one's group or society.
2. Sociologist Robert Blauner found that worker alienation was especially intense in work such as automobile assembly lines, where workers have little control over their labor.
3. Alienation can occur in any job where workers have little control and do repetitive tasks.

B. Occupational Health and Safety
1. The most dangerous occupations are those where working-class men comprise the majority of the workforce.
2. Traffic accidents and homicides at work are the most common causes of fatal work injuries, making taxi drivers, retail clerks, and police especially prone to work-related fatalities.
3. Occupations that employ large numbers of immigrants, such as meatpacking, are especially hazardous for employees.
4. New hazards associated with the technological workplace include toxic chemicals, nuclear hazards, repetitive motion disorders, and problems associated with prolonged use of video display terminals.

C. Disability and Work
1. Sociologist Irving Zola was one of the first to suggest that people with disabilities face issues similar to minority groups. Today, those with disabilities have the same legal protections afforded to other minority groups.
    a. Federal law prohibits employers with 15 or more employees from discriminating against either job applicants who are physically disabled or current employees who become physically disabled.

b.   The Americans with Disabilities Act, passed by Congress in 1990, does not cover every person with a disability.

2.   Federal law defines pregnancy as a disability to allow pregnant workers some legal protection; however, because most women work out of economic necessity, maternity leaves are generally short.

3.   Some firms have written special policies allegedly to protect women from reproductive hazards in the workplace. One such policy is to exclude all women, pregnant or not, from occupations deemed risky. Feminists argue that an exclusionary policy is discriminatory because it targets only women, even though men also have reproductive organs that are equally vulnerable to injury or toxicological insult.

PRACTICE TEST

MULTIPLE CHOICE QUESTIONS

1.   In which economic system does the state own and manage the basic industries?
    a.   socialism
    b.   capitalism
    c.   democracy
    d.   totalitarianism

2.   Which of the following economic systems is characterized by private ownership of the means of production, profit generated by the workers' production of the goods and services, and owners' disproportionate consumption of goods and profits?
    a.   totalitarianism
    b.   communism
    c.   capitalism
    d.   socialism

3.   American workers threatened by job insecurity are particularly prone to _____, or the fear and hatred of foreigners.
    a.   alienation
    b.   xenophobia
    c.   homophobia
    d.   technophobia

4.   The United States has experienced a transition from a predominately goods-producing economy to an economy based on the provision of services, a process known as:
    a.   deindustrialization.
    b.   underemployment.
    c.   downsizing.
    d.   inflation.

5.   Middle managers in corporate settings experienced widespread job loss in the process of:
    a.   automation.
    b.   downsizing.
    c.   immigration.
    d.   welfare reform.

6. Among youth in the United States, _____ teens have the highest unemployment rate.
   a. Hispanic
   b. White
   c. Black
   d. Asian

7. Which of the following types of work is **not** included in the official measures of productivity that economists use to calculate the work output of the U.S.?
   a. volunteer activities
   b. reproductive labor
   c. housework
   d. None of the above forms of work are included in the official measure.

8. In the U.S., the Family and Medical Leave Act (FMLA) provides:
   a. eighteen weeks of paid maternity leave for employed women.
   b. twelve weeks of unpaid maternity leave for employed women.
   c. twenty-six weeks of unpaid parental leave for employed men and women.
   d. a monthly allowance for formerly employed mothers who leave the paid labor force to care for their newborns for up to one year.

9. The working poor are those who receive:
   a. no wages for their work because they perform volunteer activities in community organizations.
   b. such low wages for their work that their incomes are below the federally defined poverty line.
   c. average wages for their work but have such poor money management skills that they are unable to regularly pay their bills.
   d. government support but no wages because they are permanently unemployed due to disability or illness.

10. Conflict theorists:
    a. view recent transformations in the workplace as the result of inherent tensions in the social system that are caused by power imbalances.
    b. are primarily interested in how the workplace encourages the formation of social bonds between people.
    c. interpret work as a functional necessity for society because it integrates people within the social order.
    d. explain wage inequality as an incentive system that makes people work harder.

11. Ann, a thirty-two year old woman with a Ph.D. in philosophy, is employed part-time as a cashier at a bookstore. This is an example of:
    a. displacement.
    b. unemployment.
    c. overemployment.
    d. underemployment.

12. Occupational prestige ratings are based on the:
    a. U.S. Department of Labor's ranking of the objective value of particular jobs to society.
    b. U.S. Bureau of the Census' ranking of the average wages paid for particular jobs.
    c. U.S. Department of Commerce's ranking of the relative contribution of particular jobs to economic growth
    d. general American public's ranking of the value of particular jobs to society.

13. Which of the following jobs is categorized as a lower tier occupation in the primary labor market?
    a. firefighter
    b. bartender
    c. professor
    d. cashier

14. Which of the following statements about occupational prestige is (are) true?
    a. The higher the socioeconomic status of the job, the smaller the proportion of African American men who are employed in it.
    b. White and Asian American men generally hold the jobs with the highest prestige.
    c. Women receive less prestige for the same work as men.
    d. All of the above statements about occupational prestige are true.

15. Jane works in an auto parts store where her male coworkers hang *Playboy* magazine centerfolds in the lunchroom and tell jokes about the female body that make her very uncomfortable. Under federal law, this is an example of:
    a. *quid pro quo* harassment.
    b. *hostile environment* harassment.
    c. *emotionally abusive* harassment.
    d. This is not an example of sexual harassment under the law because Jane's coworkers never physically touched her.

16. Glen works on an automobile assembly line where he does repetitive tasks and has little autonomy or control over his labor. According to Marx, which of the following is likely to occur?
    a. Glen will be strongly motivated to return to school and earn a degree so he can pursue a more satisfying occupation.
    b. Glen will develop considerable loyalty to the company because he is so grateful to have a steady job.
    c. Glen's productivity will be low because he has little attachment to the work process or the final product of his labor.
    d. Glen's productivity will be high because he is very efficient at his assigned task due to performing it many times each day.

17. The _____ economy includes illegal and unreported work, such as drug dealing, prostitution, and undocumented domestic work.
    a. feudal
    b. primary
    c. secondary
    d. underground

18. Which of the following groups is most likely to report high job satisfaction?
    a. White working-class men
    b. White middle-class men
    c. Black women, regardless of social class
    d. White women, regardless of social class

19. Lesbian women are more likely to be open about their sexual identity in the workplace when they:
    a. work in large corporations rather than in smaller, less formal organizations.
    b. hold positions with significant supervisory responsibilities.
    c. have a female boss or supervisor.
    d. All of the above conditions increase the likelihood that a lesbian woman will be open about her sexual identity in the workplace.

20. Indonesian women earn about $2.25 per day to make Barbie dolls that are sold in the United States. This is a component of:
    a. the military industrial complex.
    b. technological displacement.
    c. the global assembly line.
    d. international automation.

21. A significant number of female immigrants to the United States are concentrated in which of the following job categories?
    a. assembly work
    b. domestic work
    c. clerical work
    d. social work

22. Which of the following is considered a disability under the Americans with Disabilities Act 0f 1990?
    a. blindness
    b. pregnancy
    c. drug addiction
    d. All of the above are considered disabilities because they impair a person's ability to work.

23. Which of the following occupations is predicted to have the greatest job growth in the first decade of 2000?
    a. professor
    b. engineer
    c. cashier
    d. lawyer

24. Research on pregnancy and employment indicates that:
    a. maternity leaves in the United States are relatively short because most women need to return to work out of economic necessity.
    b. women who work in higher-status jobs are the most likely to leave a job following the birth of a child.
    c. single mothers return to work more quickly than do married mothers.
    d. All of the above statements are true.

25. One of the most dramatic changes in the U.S. labor force since World War II has been the increase in the percentage of _____ who work full-time:
   a. Black adolescents
   b. White working-class men
   c. women with young children
   d. All of the above groups have experienced dramatic increases in full-time employment over the last fifty years.

TRUE-FALSE QUESTIONS

1. Sexual harassment was first made illegal by the 1986 Glass Ceiling Act, which identified sexual harassment as a form of employment discrimination.

2. Federal employment discrimination legislation does not cover same-sex harassment in the workplace because, by definition, sexual harassment involves men's exploitation of women.

3. National public opinion polls indicate that more than fifty percent of Americans believe that gay men and lesbians should be hired as teachers and clergy.

4. Research indicates that the interpersonal rewards women get from work contribute more to their level of job satisfaction than does their pay rate.

5. Alienation may increase the likelihood that employees will participate in organizational deviance, such as destruction of company property or theft.

6. Under the Americans with Disabilities Act of 1990, a reasonable accommodation for a student would include excusing him or her from taking exams if s/he feels that test-taking is too stressful physically or emotionally.

7. Official unemployment statistics accurately reflect the total number of people who are jobless in the United States.

8. The official unemployment rate is higher for men than for women in all racial-ethnic groups.

9. Mismatch theory posits that the primary cause of Black people's disadvantage in today's labor market is their low rate of college attendance in an economy that increasingly requires workers to have a degree.

10. Because the health care industry has been hardest hit by deindustrialization, there are dim prospects for economic recovery in communities where health care institutions are the largest employers.

FILL IN THE BLANK QUESTIONS

1. Those who do not hold regular jobs, but whose employment is dependent on demand, such as independent consultants, are _____ workers.

2.	The _____ rate reflects the percentage of people who are not working but who are actively looking for work.

3.	The concept of the _____ economy acknowledges that all dimensions of the economy now cross national borders, from research and development to assembly and distribution.

4.	Robots now perform 98 percent of the spot-welding on Ford automobiles, an example of _____, or the replacement of human labor by machines.

5.	Jobs in the _____ labor market are characterized by relatively high wages, good benefits, greater stability, and opportunities for promotion.

ESSAY QUESTIONS

1.	Identify an occupation in which emotional labor is required, and explain why emotional labor is not highly valued in the American economy.
2.	Identify the primary causes of economic restructuring in the United States and discuss the consequences of these workplace alterations for the American workforce.
3.	Explain why service workers in the primary labor market (such as police officers and firefighters) generally receive better wages and benefits than do service workers in the secondary labor market (such as maids and janitors).
4.	Explain why the back offices found in industries such as insurance firms and airlines are now referred to as electronic "sweatshops," a term originally used to refer to workplaces in the garment industry.
5.	Provide a legal definition of sexual harassment and explain why sexual harassment is considered a form of employment discrimination.

ANSWERS TO PRACTICE TEST

Answers to Multiple Choice Questions

1.	A.	505	Industries are owned and managed by the state in both socialist and communist economies. In capitalist economies, industry is privately owned and managed. Democracy and totalitarianism are political, not economic, systems.

2.	C.	505	Capitalism is an economic system in which the means of production are privately owned, profit is generated by the workers' production of goods, and owners disproportionately consume goods and profits.

3.	B.	507	American workers are particularly prone to xenophobia, the fear and hatred of foreigners. Homophobia is the fear and hatred of homosexuals, while technophobia is the fear of technology. Alienation occurs when workers have little investment in, or attachment to, the work process and the products generated.

4.	A.	509	The transition from a predominately goods-producing economy to an economy based on the provision of services is deindustrialization.

5.	B.	512	Economic restructuring, or temporary transformations in the basic structure of work, led to corporate downsizing, in which large numbers of managers were eliminated to reduce costs.

6.	C.	509	The teen unemployment rate is highest for Black youth, especially in urban areas. Figure 18.1 does not provide any statistics for Asian youth.

7. D. 513 Work is defined by sociologists as productive human activity that creates something of value, either goods or services. However, unpaid volunteer activities, reproductive labor, and housework are not counted in official measures of work.

8. B. 513 The Family and Medical Leave Act (FMLA) provides twelve weeks of unpaid leave to full-time employees to care for a newborn or newly adopted child, or a seriously ill child, spouse, or parent. New mothers in Germany receive fourteen weeks paid maternity leave. New mothers in Norway receive eighteen weeks paid maternity leave, as well as an additional twenty-six weeks leave for either parent.

9. B. 514 The working poor work's wages are below the federal poverty line despite working full-time. The working poor comprise twenty-five percent of all workers in the United States today.

10. A. 517 As summarized in Table 18.2, conflict theorists view transformations in the workplace as the result of inherent tensions in the social system caused by power differences between groups vying for economic and social resources. Symbolic interactionists focus on the formation of social bonds at work. Functionalists assert that work integrates people into society, and wage inequality acts as an incentive for people to work harder.

11. D. 520 Underemployment is the condition of being employed at a level below what would be expected given a person's training, experience, or education, or working fewer hours than desired. The unemployment rate is the percentage of those not working but looking for work.

12. D. 525 Occupational prestige ratings are based on the general public's ranking of the value of particular jobs to the United States.

13. A. 523 Dual labor market theory views the labor market as segmented into a primary labor market and a secondary labor market, with a lower tier and an upper tier in each market. As indicated in Table 18.4, firefighters are located in the lower tier of the primary market.

14. D. 525 Occupational prestige is the perceived social value of an occupation. White and Asian American men hold the jobs with the highest prestige, followed by White women. African American and Latino men are found disproportionately in jobs with the lowest prestige. Women receive less prestige for the same work (such as nursing) as men.

15. B. 527 The unwanted physical or verbal sexual behavior that occurs in the workplace is sexual harassment. There are two forms of harassment under the law. *Quid pro quo* harassment involves the exchange of sexual favors as a condition of employment. *Hostile environment* harassment occurs when the conditions of work are made uncomfortable for the worker due to verbal comments of a sexual nature and the display of sexual objects such as posters.

16. C. 530 Worker alienation, a concept first developed by Karl Marx, is highest where workers engage in repetitive tasks and have little control over their labor. It often leads to feelings of powerlessness, lack of productivity, and possibly participation in organizational deviance.

17. D. 523 Work that is illegal or not reported, such as work done under the table, is located in the underground economy. This includes drug dealing, prostitution, and unreported domestic work.

18. B. 529 Middle class white men report higher satisfaction that other groups.

They are more likely to work in safe and sanitary conditions, as well as receive higher pay and opportunities for advancement, characteristics associated with increased job satisfaction.

19.	C.	529	Lesbians are more likely to reveal their sexual identity at work when they have a female supervisor, work in predominantly female jobs and at smaller organizations, have lower pay, less supervisory responsibility, and little or no contact with children as students, clients, or patients.
20.	C.	507	The global assembly refers to the new international division of labor where research, development, and management are controlled by the most developed countries (such as the U.S., Japan, and Germany) and assembly line work is performed in the less developed, poorer countries (such as Indonesia and China), primarily by women and children.
21.	B.	522	Most immigrant women work in domestic service, the garment industry, family enterprises, and skilled services such as nursing.
22.	A.	531	Under the Americans with Disabilities Act, employers with fifteen or more employees are prohibited from discriminating against job applicants who are physically disabled or current employees who become physically disabled. A disability is defined as a condition or history of a condition that impairs a major life activity. Drug addiction and pregnancy are excluded from this federal law, but people who are blind or deaf are entitled to protection under this law.
23.	A.	510	As indicated in Table 18.1, job growth is expected in the retail industry, which includes cashiers. Job growth is also predicted in the computer networking and health care industries.
24.	A.	532	Women with higher status jobs are least likely to leave their jobs after giving birth. Women with a spouse or other adult in the household return to work after giving birth sooner than women living alone.
25.	C.	518	Women's labor force participation increased from 35 to 60 percent from 1948 to 1999, particularly for women with young children. Employment rates for White and Black working-class men have decreased. Black teenagers have the highest youth unemployment rate of all racial-ethnic groups.

Answers to True-False Questions

1.	F.	527	Sexual harassment was first made illegal by Title VII of the 1964 Civil Rights Act, and upheld as a form of employment discrimination in the 1986 Supreme Court case, *Meritor Savings Bank v. Vinson*.
2.	F.	528	Sexual harassment constitutes employment discrimination regardless of the sex of the victim or the perpetrator; therefore, same-sex harassment is illegal.
3.	T.	529	Almost two-thirds of Americans think gays should be hired as high school teachers and 54 percent of Americans think gays should be hired as elementary school teachers and clergy.
4.	F.	530	For both men and women, pay, not interpersonal rewards, increases job satisfaction.
5.	T.	530	One consequence of alienation may be organizational deviance because workers who are alienated may feel less loyalty to the company.

6.	F.	531	The Americans with Disabilities Act requires employers and schools to provide *assistance* for employees and students with designated disabilities, not to excuse them from completing their assigned work.
7.	F.	520	Unemployment statistics undercount those groups who are most likely to be unemployed. The unemployment rate does not include, for example, people who have given up looking for work and people who settled for part-time work when they could not find full-time work.
8.	F.	521	The only racial-ethnic group for whom the unemployment rate is higher for men than for women is African Americans.
9.	F.	510	Mismatch theory asserts that Black people's disadvantage in the labor market results from a combination of residential segregation in center cities and the movement of jobs to suburban areas.
10.	T.	509	Deindustrialization disproportionately affected working-class men employed in automobile manufacturing and the steel industry. The health care industry is experiencing job growth in predominantly female service occupations such as registered nurse and personal aide.

Answers to Fill in the Blank Questions

1.	contingent	512
2.	unemployment	519
3.	global	506
4.	automation	511
5.	primary	523

CHAPTER 19
POWER, POLITICS, AND AUTHORITY

BRIEF CHAPTER OUTLINE
Defining the State
> The Institutions of the State
> The State and Social Order
> Revolution
> Global Interdependence and the State

Power and Authority
> Types of Authority
> The Growth of Bureaucratic Government

Theories of Power
> The Pluralist Model
> The Power Elite Model
> The Autonomous State Model
> Feminist Theories of the State
> Comparing Theories of Power

Government: Power and Politics in a Diverse Society
> Diverse Patterns of Political Representation
> Political Power: Who's in Charge?
> Women and Minorities in Government

The Military
> The Military as a Social Institution
> Race and the Military
> Women in the Military
> Gays and Lesbians in the Military

QUESTIONS TO GUIDE YOUR READING
1. What is the purpose of the state as an institution, and what systems and organizations comprise the state?
2. What is the difference between power and authority, and how did Max Weber classify the three forms of authority that exist in societies?
3. What is a bureaucracy, and why did bureaucratic government develop and grow in modern societies?
4. What are the four main theories of power and the state, and how does each model view power relationships in the United States?
5. How do race, ethnicity, class, age, and gender structure political participation in the United States?

KEY TERMS (defined at page number shown and in glossary)

KEY PEOPLE (identified at page number shown)
Catherine MacKinnon 547   Karl Marx 544
C. Wright Mills 544   Max Weber 541

CHAPTER OUTLINE

The state regulates disputes between groups who may be well-intentioned, yet bitterly opposed to each other's wishes. The state intervenes at all levels, from arbitrating disputes between two parties, as in a lawsuit or divorce, to negotiating and defining class, race, and gender relations in society.

I. **DEFINING THE STATE**

 The **state** is the organized system of power and authority in society. It includes the government and its legal system as well as the police and the military. Theoretically, the state exists to regulate social order, although it does not always do so fairly or equitably. The state has a central role in shaping class, race, and gender relations in society and in determining the rights and privileges of different groups. Sociological analyses of the state focus on several important issues, including: the relationship between the state and inequality in society; the connections between the state and other social institutions, such as religion and the family; and the state's role in maintaining social order.

 A. The Institutions of the State

  A number of institutions comprise the state.

  1. The government creates laws and procedures that govern society.

  2. The legal system includes the courts, which punish wrongdoers and adjudicate disputes, and the prison system, which detains and punishes those who have violated the law.

  3. The police are responsible for enforcing the law and maintaining public order at the local level.

  4. The military is the branch of government responsible for defending the nation in domestic and foreign conflicts.

 B. The State and Social Order

  1. The state influences public opinion through its power to regulate the media and, in some cases, by circulating **propaganda**, or information disseminated by a group or organization that is intended to justify its power. Censorship is another means by which the state can direct public opinion.

  2. The state's role in maintaining public order is also apparent in how it manages dissent. Different states work in different ways, with some explicitly protecting the status quo, and others operating in more revolutionary or totalitarian ways.

  3. Even in a democratic state like the United States, the state typically protects the interests of those with the most power, leaving the least powerful groups in society vulnerable to oppressive state action.

 C. Revolution

  Sometimes states break down as the result of **revolution**, which is the overthrow or total transformation of state institutions. Revolution may be the result of conflict between an oppressive state and disenfranchised groups. When war or economic crisis develops, groups may have the opportunity to mobilize through social movements.

 D. Global Interdependence and the State

  1. On an international level, there are increasingly strong ties between the state and the global economy.

2. The interdependence of national economies means that political tensions in remote parts of the world, which can now be televised internationally, can have enormous economic effects across the world.

3. Some argue that increased economic interdependence will result in nations adopting similar institutions, including forms of government and laws.

4. Disagreement exists about what effects economic interdependence will have on the political structure of nations around the world.

    a. Some argue that greater interdependence will expose authoritarian regimes and create pressures for an international system of law where democratic rights are respected and human rights are protected around the world.

    b. Others argue that the strong alliance produced between economic interests, corporate power, and the state will shift global political power, favoring the most dominant nations while impoverishing and marginalizing others, whose local traditions will be destroyed.

II. POWER AND AUTHORITY

Power is the ability of one person or group to exercise influence and control over others. Sociologists are interested in how power is structured at the societal level, who has it, how it is used, and how it is built into institutionalized structures such as the state. The exercise of power may take the form of persuasion or coercion.

Authority is power that is perceived by others to be legitimate. Authority emerges not only from the exercise of power, but also from the constituents' belief that the power is legitimate. Those who accept the status quo as a legitimate system of authority perceive the guardians of the law to be exercising *legitimate authority. Coercive power* is achieved through force, often against the will of the people being forced.

A. Types of Authority

Max Weber argued that there are three types of authority in society: traditional, charismatic, and rational-legal. He believed that modern societies would be increasingly based on rational-legal authority.

1. **Traditional authority** stems from the long-established patterns that give certain people or groups legitimate power in society, such as a monarchy.

2. **Charismatic authority** is derived from the personal appeal of a leader, who is often believed to have special gifts, even magical powers, which inspire devotion and obedience. Charismatic leaders often emerge from religious movements and mobilize large numbers of people in the name of lofty ideals. Because the foundation of charismatic power rests on the qualities of a single individual, when that person leaves or dies, the movement they inspired may quickly dissipate.

3. **Rational-legal authority**, the most common form of authority in the contemporary United States, stems from rules and regulations, typically written down as laws, procedures, or codes of conduct. Under rational-legal authority, authority is gained through having been elected or appointed in accordance with society's rules.

B. The Growth of Bureaucratic Government

1. According to Weber, rational-legal authority inevitably leads to the formation of **bureaucracy**, a type of formal organization characterized by an authority hierarchy, a clear division of labor, explicit rules, and impersonality.

2. Bureaucracy has become the modern system of administration. In principle, bureaucracies are supposed to be highly efficient modes of organization, although the reality is often much different.
   a. There is a tendency within bureaucracies to proliferate rules, often to the point that the organization becomes ensnared in its own bureaucratic requirements.
   b. Within bureaucracies, administrators sometimes become so focused on rules and regulations that the actual work of the system bogs down.
3. Within bureaucracies, personal temperament and individual discretion are not supposed to influence the application of rules; however, bureaucratic workers frequently exercise discretion in applying rules and procedures.
   a. Some who encounter bureaucracies know how to "work the system," perhaps by personalizing the interaction and making a willing accomplice of the bureaucrat in dodging bureaucratic stipulations, or perhaps by using knowledge of some rules to evade others.
   b. Others without privileged relationships or information are continually disadvantaged by their inability to negotiate within the system.
   c. People may receive widely different treatment from bureaucratic workers, who may favor some people while acting prejudicially against others based on their race, gender, age, or other characteristics.

III. THEORIES OF POWER
A. The Pluralist Model
   1. The **pluralist model** interprets power in society as coming from the representation of diverse interests of different groups in society.
      a. This model assumes that in democratic societies, the system of government works to balance the different interests of groups in society.
      b. An **interest group** can be any constituency in society organized to promote its own agenda, including large, nationally-based groups such as the American Association of Retired Persons (AARP); groups organized around professional and business interests, such as the American Medical Association (AMA); or groups that concentrate on a single political or social goal, such as Greenpeace.
      c. According to the pluralist model, interest groups achieve power and influence through their organized mobilization of concerned people and groups.
   2. The pluralist model, which views the state as representative of the whole society, has its origins in functionalist theory.
      a. Groups that want to effect a change or express their point of view need only to mobilize to do so.
      b. According to this model, special interest groups are the link between the people and the government. Interest groups form when a group of people who share a belief in an issue organize themselves to get the attention of the government.

c. This model helps explain the importance of **political action committees** (PACs), groups of people who organize to support candidates they feel will represent their views.

3. Although interest groups are certainly influential in the political process, there is not as much equality between them as the pluralist model suggests.

B. The Power Elite Model

1. The **power elite model** originated in the work of Karl Marx, who argued that the dominant or "ruling" class controls all of the major institutions in society. The state is simply an instrument by which the ruling class exercises its power, rather than a representative, rational institution.

2. C. Wright Mills elaborated on Marx's work in his analysis of the power elite, arguing that the true power structure consists of people well-positioned in three areas: the economy, the government, and the military.

a. Sharing common beliefs and goals, the power elite shape political agendas and outcomes in society along the narrow lines of their own collective interests.

b. The power elite model posits a strong link between government and business, a view that is supported by the strong hand government takes in directing the economy, as well as by the role of military spending as a principal component of U.S. economic affairs.

c. This model emphasizes how power overlaps between influential groups. **Interlocking directorates** are organizational linkages created when the same people sit on the boards of directors of a number of different corporations.

3. The power elite model sees the state as part of a structure of domination, one in which the state is simply a piece of the whole. Members of the upper class need not occupy high office themselves to exert their will as long as they are in positions to influence those who are in power.

4. Two strong criticisms have been leveled against the power elite model.

a. The model too readily assumes that there is a unity of interests among elites, even though the most powerful people in society hold widely divergent views on many political issues.

b. The model fails to acknowledge how well public interest groups have been able to influence decision-making.

C. The Autonomous State Model

1. The **autonomous state model** interprets the state as its own major constituent. The state is a network of administrative and policing organizations that develops interests of its own, which it seeks to promote independent of other interests and the public that it allegedly serves.

2. Autonomous state theorists note that states tend to grow over time, possibly including expansion of their territory beyond their original boundaries.

3. An examination of the formation of the *welfare state* in the U.S. illustrates how state policies are created by independent state managers who represent their own interests. The *welfare state* consists of the vast

array of social support programs now supported by the state, including Social Security, unemployment benefits, agricultural subsidies, public assistance, and other economic interventions intended to protect citizens from the vagaries of a capitalist market system.

    4. The autonomous state model views the government as so busy tending to its own problems that it cannot competently respond to citizens' needs.

  D. Feminist Theories of the State

    1. Feminist theory begins with the premise that an understanding of power cannot be achieved without a strong analysis of gender.

    2. Feminist theory diverges from the preceding theoretical models by viewing men as a group as having the most important power in society.

      a. Some feminists argue that all state institutions reflect men's interests. They see the state as fundamentally patriarchal, with its organization embodying the fixed principle that men are more powerful than women.

      b. Despite the presence of a few powerful women, the state on the whole is devoted primarily to men's interests, and the actions of the state tend to support gender inequality. For example, the United States Congress is 87 percent male.

  E. Comparing Theories of Power

    1. The pluralist model views interest groups competing in a struggle for power. It views power emerging from the bottom up in the form of interest groups that organize to express their needs or use their votes to influence state policy.

    2. The power elite model argues that power stems from the top down, with the most powerful groups in society using the state to enforce their will.

    3. The autonomous state model argues that the power of the state feeds on itself and the state operates in its own interest, which sometimes support the interests of the people or the elites.

    4. Feminist theory argues that men hold greater power in all social institutions and elite men use the state to enforce their will.

IV. **GOVERNMENT: POWER AND POLITICS IN A DIVERSE SOCIETY**

The **government**, one of several institutions that make up the state, includes those state institutions that represent the population and make rules that govern the society. The United States government is a **democracy**, a system of government based on the principle of representing all people through the right to vote. Sociological research on political power, which concentrates on inequality in government affairs, has demonstrated large, persistent differences in the political participation and representation of different groups in society. Women, poor and working-class people, and racial-ethnic minorities are less likely to be represented by the government than are White middle- and upper-class men. .

  A. Diverse Patterns of Political Participation

    1. Among democratic nations, the United States has one of the lowest voter turnouts, with 50 percent or less of the eligible voters participating in national elections.

    2. In sociological terms, age, income, and education are the strongest predictors of whether someone will vote. The group most likely to vote is older, better educated, and financially better off than the average American citizen.

3.   There is significant variation in voting patterns by race, with African Americans being less likely to vote than Whites, a fact that reflects the disproportionate numbers of African Americans in the poor and working classes. Additionally, African Americans are generally less trusting of the political system and more alienated from politics than are their White counterparts.

4.   Sociologists have found that ethnicity can outweigh socioeconomic factors like occupation, income, and education in predicting voting patterns. African Americans and Latinos, with the exception of Cuban Americans, tend to be markedly Democratic.

5.   Gender is a major social factor influencing political attitudes and behavior. The term **gender gap** refers to the differences in women's and men's political attitudes and behavior. For example, women are more likely than men to identify and vote as Democrats and to vote more liberally on social service programs. The gender gap is widest on issues involving violence and the use of force.

B.   <u>Political Power: Who's in Charge?</u>
Most of the 535 members of Congress are well-educated White men from upper-middle- or upper-class backgrounds who have an Anglo-Saxon Protestant heritage. Simply getting into politics requires a substantial investment of money, and many of the members of Congress are millionaires.

C.   <u>Women and Minorities in Government</u>
1.   Whereas 51 percent of the population of the United States is female, only 13 percent of U.S. Senators are women. African Americans, Hispanics, Asian Americans, and Native Americans are vastly underrepresented at both the state and the federal levels of government.

2.   Researchers suggest that women and racial-ethnic minority groups continue to be underrepresented in government because of persistent public prejudices and structural barriers.

3.   The presence of women and minorities in government brings new perspectives on old issues and new attention to issues otherwise overlooked. For example, women are more likely than men to support feminist issues such as the Equal Rights Amendment and government-subsidized childcare.

V.   **THE MILITARY**
The military arm of the state is among the most powerful and influential social institutions in almost all societies. The military is the largest single employer in the United States. The pervasive influence of military goals and values throughout American culture is referred to as *militarism*.

A.   <u>The Military as a Social Institution</u>
1.   Institutions are stable systems of norms and values that fill certain functions in society. The military's function is to defend the nation against external, and sometimes internal, threats.

2.   The military is one of the most hierarchical social institutions, its hierarchy is extremely formalized, and some suggest that it is a distinctively masculine institution.

3.   There is a strong connection between the military and corporate America, as evidenced by the **military-industrial complex**, a term used to describe the linkage between business and military interests. The military supports many of the basic research and development projects in the nation.

4.   A striking feature of the military as a social institution is the diverse representation of racial minority groups and women within the armed forces, partly as a result of ending the all-male draft in 1973 and initiating an all-volunteer force in the U.S. armed services.

B.   Race and the Military
1.   African Americans have served in the military for almost as long as the U.S. armed services have been in existence. This group is the most over-represented relative to their proportion in the civilian population.
2.   For groups with limited opportunities in civilian society, joining the military seems to promise an educational and economic boost. In fact, for both Whites and racial minorities, serving in the military leads to higher earnings relative to one's non-military peers.

C.   Women in the Military
1.   There have been profound changes in the military since military academies began accepting women in 1976; however, there is still resistance to the full inclusion of women in the military, particularly in combat. The military is still a highly masculine institution in terms of personnel and policies.
2.   Gender relations in the military extend beyond just the women who serve. The experience of military wives is greatly affected by their husbands' employment as soldiers.

D.   Gays and Lesbians in the Military
According to the "*don't ask, don't tell*" policy, recruiting officers cannot ask recruits about sexual preference, and individuals who keep their sexual preference a private matter shall not be discriminated against. This controversial policy reveals continuing prejudice and discrimination against lesbian women and gay men. The longstanding policy against gays in the military has kept homosexuality in the military hidden, but not nonexistent, while disparaging comments and harassment toward gay service personnel persists.

PRACTICE TEST

MULTIPLE CHOICE QUESTIONS

1.   Which of the following state institutions is responsible for maintaining public order and enforcing laws at the local level?
a.   government
b.   military
c.   prisons
d.   police

2.   The state institution that creates laws and procedures for society is the:
a.   government.
b.   military.
c.   prisons.
d.   police.

3. According to Max Weber, _____ authority leads to the formation of bureaucracies.
   a. traditional
   b. charismatic
   c. rational-legal
   d. socioeconomic

4. A monarchy derives its legitimate right to rule from _____ authority.
   a. traditional
   b. charismatic
   c. rational-legal
   d. socioeconomic

5. The _____ model of power interprets power in society as derived from the representation of the diverse interests of different groups in society.
   a. pluralist
   b. feminist
   c. power elite
   d. autonomous state

6. Feminist theories of the state assert that:
   a. the state is fundamentally feminine in its values because decisions are based on the principle of caring for the nation's citizens.
   b. social conflict derives from the domination of the upper class elites over other groups with fewer economic resources.
   c. political power is derived from the organized activities of public interest groups
   d. all state institutions fundamentally reflect men's interests and opinions.

7. Which of the following statements reflects the gender gap in political attitudes and behavior?
   a. More men than women favor decreased gun control.
   b. More men than women favor decreased military spending.
   c. More men than women favor decreased restrictions on abortion.
   d. More men than women favor increased social service spending.

8. The _____ model of power interprets the state as its own major constituency that develops and perpetuates its own interests.
   a. pluralist
   b. power elite
   c. congressional
   d. autonomous state

9. Snipp identifies the 1960s and 1970s as a period in which the role of the U.S. government vis-à-vis American Indians was characterized by:
   a. forcible removal of Indians from their native lands.
   b. efforts to promote self-determination for Indian people through allowing American Indians to oversee their own affairs.
   c. cultural assimilation of Indians through education at boarding schools and prohibitions on traditional modes of dress and use of native languages.
   d. termination of tribal rights to ownership of reservation lands and widespread relocation of Indian populations to urban areas.

10. One way that the state directs public opinion is through _____, or the restriction of people's access to certain information, such as sexually explicit materials on the Internet.
   a. coercion
   b. revolution
   c. censorship
   d. propaganda

11. Global interdependence has led to the adoption of shared laws and economic markets among some nations. An example of one such international alliance is the:
   a. North American Monoculture.
   b. Military-industrial Complex.
   c. National Urban League.
   d. European Union

12. An example of a condition that often leads to revolution is:
   a. establishment of a new economic system.
   b. collapse of the existing economic system.
   c. political turmoil, such as war.
   d. All of the above conditions may increase the likelihood of revolution occurring.

13. According to Weber, which of the following characterize bureaucracy?
   a. shared decision-making between managers and workers
   b. clear and specific division of labor
   c. vague policies and procedures
   d. close personal relationships

14. Which of the following is a principal legal mechanism for converting money into political influence according to the pluralist model of power?
   a. lobbying
   b. propaganda
   c. campaign contributions
   d. All of the above are legal mechanisms of political influence.

15. One interesting feature of the U.S. military is that an increase in the enlistment of:
   a. Black men has led to equal representation of White and Black men as officers.
   b. women led to a reduced emphasis on competition and hierarchy in the military.
   c. women led to female participation in combat during the Persian Gulf War.
   d. None of the above have occurred because there has been a decrease, not an increase, in the enlistment of Black men and women of all races.

16. Of the following political action committees (PACs), which one contributed the largest amount of money to the Republican party in the 2000 election?
   a. At & T
   b. Service Employees Union
   c. Communication Workers of America
   d. International Brotherhood of Electrical Workers

17. The organizational linkages created when a small number of people from elite groups sit on the Board of Directors of several companies, universities, and foundations are:
    a. political action committees.
    b. interlocking directorates.
    c. marginalized parties.
    d. national alliances.

18. In the United States, the welfare state includes which of the following programs?
    a. unemployment compensation
    b. public assistance
    c. Social Security
    d. The welfare state includes all of the above programs.

19. Who is the most likely person to vote in the United States?
    a. David, a 21 year old Black college student
    b. Luis, a 31 year old Hispanic truck driver
    c. Ron, a 41 year old White lawyer
    d. All have an equal probability of voting, because race and age do not significantly influence voting behavior.

20. The composition of the U.S. Congress is representative of the American population by:
    a. Gender, but not race or education.
    b. gender and race, but not education.
    c. gender, race, and education, but not income.
    d. None of the above is true, because the U.S. Congress is not representative of the American population by gender, race, education, or income.

TRUE-FALSE QUESTIONS

1. For people of all races, serving in the military leads to higher earnings relative to their non-military peers.

2. The United States has the second highest voter turnout rate and Japan has the highest voter turnout among industrialized countries.

3. Whites are more likely to vote than their Black counterparts since they trust the political system and feel that they are an integral part of it.

4. Within bureaucracies, individual workers never exercise discretion in applying rules because bureaucracies are characterized by impersonality.

5. Latinos are the most over-represented racial-ethnic group in the military relative to their proportion in the civilian population.

6. The largest single employer in the United States is the military.

7. Disparaging comments and the harassment of gays and lesbians in the military has ceased since instituting the "don't ask, don't tell" policy.

8. In 1965, the Supreme Court declared that state supported military academies such as the Citadel could not deny women admission.

9. On an international level, ties between the state and the global economy have been weakening.

10. The primary way that the military is linked to corporate America through the military-industrial complex is that individuals enlisted in the military perform much of the assembly work needed to produce goods in manufacturing companies.

FILL IN THE BLANK QUESTIONS

1. Information disseminated by a group or organization, such as the state, to justify its power is _____.

2. The American Association of Retired Persons (AARP), a constituency organized to promote its own agenda, is an example of a(n) _____ group.

3. States may break down as the result of _____, or the overthrow of state institutions, during economic crisis or war.

4. Leaders that inspire devotion and obedience through personal appeal have _____ authority.

5. The United States is a _____, meaning that it is based on the principle of representing all people through the right to vote.

ESSAY QUESTIONS

1. Identify several ways in which official state definitions of groups determine which groups receive social support and which do not.
2. Explain why there was considerable controversy over voting methods in the 2000 Presidential election and discuss what consequences that controversy might have for future elections.
3. Explain why the increased representation of women and racial-ethnic minorities in the power elite has not really led to significant diversity in the opinions or political behavior of that group.
4. Explain how militarism affects popular culture and civilian life in the United States.
5. Discuss what consequences the "don't ask, don't tell" policy on homosexuality in the military has had for gay and lesbian solders.

ANSWERS TO PRACTICE TEST

Answers to Multiple Choice Questions

1. D. 538 The police are responsible for local law enforcement. The military defends the nation against domestic and foreign conflicts.
2. A. 538 The government creates laws and procedures, while the prison system punishes those who break the law.
3. C. 542 According to Max Weber, rational-legal authority leads to the formation of bureaucracies.

4.	A.	541	Monarchies derive their power from traditional authority, or long-established patterns of leadership.
5.	B.	547	As summarized in Table 19.2, the pluralist model interprets power in society as coming from group representation of the diverse interests in society.
6.	D.	547	As summarized in Table 19.2, feminist theories of the state view all state institutions as reflecting men's interests.
7.	A.	550	Differences in women's and men's political attitudes include men's greater likelihood of supporting decreased gun control and increased military spending, as well as women's greater likelihood of supporting increased social service spending and fewer restrictions on abortion. These differences are referred to as the gender gap.
8.	D.	546	As summarized in Table 19.2, the autonomous state model asserts that social order is maintained by an administrative system that supports the status quo.
9.	B.	539	The U.S. government practiced forcible removal, forced cultural assimilation, and termination of reservation property rights from the 1800s to the post World War II period. In the 1960s and 1970s, American Indians were granted the legal right to self-determination. Today, the U.S. government limits which Native American groups can receive benefits by restricting the definition of "Indian."
10.	C.	539	Censorship refers to the state's restriction of information to the public.
11.	D.	540	The European Union (UI) is an example of one international alliance designed to make trade easier.
12.	D.	540	Economic crisis, including collapse and the establishment of a new economic system, may lead to revolution, as can war. Groups that are dissatisfied with the political system also need opportunities to mobilize to initiate revolution.
13.	B.	542	Bureaucracies are a type of formal organization characterized by an authority hierarchy, a clear division of labor, explicit rules, and impersonality. They have a tendency to proliferate rules and alienate the people that they serve.
14.	D.	544	Interest groups such as PACs use money to legally influence the political system through lobbying, developing and disseminating propaganda, and making campaign contributions.
15.	D.	557	The increase in the percentage of women in the military has not altered the competitive, hierarchical nature of the military; but a considerable number of women participated in combat during the Persian Gulf War, which increased public support for women's right to engage in combat. Black men are under-represented as officers and discrimination against homosexuals in the military persists.
16.	A.	545	Of the $4,507,437 donated by AT&T, 61 percent went to the Republican party. Organized labor unions donated disproportionately to Democrats.
17.	B.	545	Interlocking directorates are created because people drawn from the same elite group receive most of the major government appointments and serve on the Boards of Directors of major companies, universities, and foundations.
18.	D.	546	The Welfare state is the vast array of social support programs funded by the state, including Social Security, unemployment benefits, and public assistance.

19.	C.	549	White, well educated, and older people are more likely to vote than are Black or Hispanic, less educated, and younger people. Voter participation also increases with income, so that members of the middle and upper classes are the most likely to vote.
20.	D.	551	As indicated in Figure 19.4, the U.S. Congress consists primarily of White men. Most members of Congress are well educated and have an Anglo-Saxon Protestant heritage. One-third of Congressional representatives are lawyers, and many are millionaires. Thus, Congress is not representative of the American population in terms of gender, race, education, or income.

Answers to True-False Questions

1.	T.	556	People of all racial-ethnic groups who serve in the military have higher earnings relative to their non-military peers.
2.	F.	548	As indicated in Figure 19.2, the both the U.S. and Japan have very low rates of voter turnout compared to other industrialized countries.
3.	T.	549	Blacks are less likely to vote than their White counterparts because they are less trusting of the political system and feel alienated from politics. Furthermore, people from the poor and working classes are less likely to vote than middle- and upper-class people, and Blacks are disproportionately located in the lower-income groups.
4.	F.	543	Although bureaucracies are characterized by impersonality, individual workers do exercise discretion in applying rules to the people that organizations serve.
5.	F.	556	African Americans are the most over-represented racial-ethnic group in the military today.
6.	T.	553	In the United States, the military is the largest single employer.
7.	F.	558	The "don't ask, don't tell" policy does not explicitly acknowledge the rights of homosexual soldiers, and gay or lesbian soldiers who publicly reveal their sexual identity can be expelled. The policy has not reduced discrimination and harassment against gay and lesbian soldiers.
8.	F.	556	The Supreme Court did not declare that military academies had to admit women until 1996.
9.	F.	540	There are increasingly strong ties between the state and the global economy, which means that political systems around the world are also entangled.
10.	F.	555	The military and corporate America are linked through the military-industrial complex because the military supports so many of the research and development projects undertaken by companies in the United States.

Answers to Fill in the Blank Questions

1.	propaganda	539
2.	interest	543
3.	revolution	540
4.	charismatic	541
5.	democracy	548

CHAPTER 20
HEALTH CARE

BRIEF CHAPTER OUTLINE
The Structure of Health Care in the United States
> Modern Medicine
> Gender and Modern Medicine
> Specialization in Medicine
> Medicare and Medicaid

Theoretical Perspectives on Health Care
> The Functionalist View of Health Care
> The Conflict Theory View
> Symbolic Interactionism and the Role of Perceptions

Health and Sickness in America: A Picture of Diversity
> Race and Health Care
> Social Class and Health Care
> Gender and Health Care
> Health and Sickness Globally

Attitudes Toward Health and Illness
> Sexually Transmitted Diseases
> AIDS: Illness and Stigma
> Chronic Fatigue Syndrome
> Mental Illness
> The Medicalization of Illness and Deviance

The Health Care Crisis in America
> The Fee-For-Service System
> Malpractice
> Fraud and Abuse
> A Response to the Problem: HMOs
> Alternative Medicine
> The Universal Health Care Debate

Death and Dying

QUESTIONS TO GUIDE YOUR READING
1. How is modern medicine different from traditional or holistic medicine?
2. How do social factors such as race, ethnicity, gender, class, and age influence how illness is perceived, defined, and treated?
3. Which illnesses or conditions tend to be associated with social stigma, and why?
4. What is the difference between Medicaid and Medicare, and how do these programs contribute to the health of vulnerable populations such as children, the elderly and people with disabilities?
5. How is the health care system in the United States structured, and why do sociologists consider it to be "in crisis?"

KEY TERMS (defined at page number shown and in glossary)
anabolic steroids 568
bulimia 568
defensive medicine 581
epidemiology 568
Health Maintenance Organizations 580
managed competition 582

anorexia nervosa 568
Chronic fatigue syndrome 577
deinstitutionalization movement 578
euthanasia 583
holistic medicine 581
Medicaid 566

CHAPTER OUTLINE

The health care institution in the United States is in crisis. The crisis in health care does not reside solely within health organizations, however, because individual behaviors such as smoking and drug dependency also create health problems. Although public health issues may seem like simple matters of personal responsibility or individual rights, sociologists have shown that illness in society is strongly influenced by social factors such as race, ethnicity, social class, gender, and age.

I.   **THE STRUCTURE OF HEALTH CARE IN THE UNITED STATES**

Overall, citizens of the United States are quite healthy in relation to the rest of the world; however, there are great discrepancies among Americans in terms of longevity, general health, and access to health care.

A.   Modern Medicine

In Colonial times, American physicians received their training in Europe, and mentally ill people were often perceived as possessed by evil forces. By the start of the nineteenth century, advances in biology and chemistry ignited a century of explosive growth in medical knowledge. The image of medicine as an upper-class profession was established in the late 1800's.

B.   Gender and Modern Medicine

At the outset of the twentieth century, the male-dominated medical profession vigorously opposed gender equality in medicine because only men were seen as rational and scientific. Women were seen as dominated by emotions and incapable of rigorous scientific thought. They were expected to devote their time and energy to childbearing rather than professions.

C.   Specialization in Medicine

There has been tremendous growth in the medical establishment since 1945, which includes significant increases in the number of medical professionals and the amount of money spent on health care. Along with the huge growth in medicine came increased specialization, which offers physicians increased incomes. Specialization has diminished access to general practitioners, one of the problems contributing to the crisis in health care today.

D.   Medicare and Medicaid

1.   The United States government has sought to have some form of widespread guaranteed health services, at least for certain categories of people, including veterans, the poor, and the elderly.

2.   **Medicare** is a government program that began in 1965. It provides medical care in the form of insurance that covers hospital costs for all individuals who are age 65 or older.

3.   **Medicaid** is a government program that provides medical care in the form of health insurance for poor people, people receiving welfare, and people with disabilities.

4.   The Medicare and Medicaid programs combined are as close as the United States has come to the ideal of universal health insurance.

II. **THEORETICAL PERSPECTIVES ON HEALTH CARE**

A.   The Functionalist View of Health Care

1.   Functionalist theory developed the notion of the *sick role*, defined as a pattern of expectations that society applies to someone who is ill.

2.   Functionalism argues that any institution, group, or organization can be examined by looking at its positive and negative functions in society.
        a.   Positive functions, such as the prevention and treatment of disease, contribute to the harmony and stability of society.
        b.   Negative functions contribute to disharmony and social instability. For example, there is an unequal distribution of health care in the U.S. by race-ethnicity, social class, gender, and region of the country.

B.   <u>The Conflict Theory View</u>
    1.   Conflict theory stresses the importance of social structural inequality in society. This inequality, which is inherent in capitalist society, is responsible for the unequal access to medical care.
    2.   Restricted access to health care is further exacerbated by the high costs of medical care; excessive bureaucratization, which leads to the alienation of patients; and prolonged waits in the emergency rooms of many urban hospitals in the United States.

C.   <u>Symbolic Interactionism and the Role of Perceptions</u>
    1.   Symbolic interactionists argue that illness is partly, though obviously not totally, socially constructed. The definitions of illness and wellness are culturally relative and time-dependent.
    2.   The health care system itself has a socially constructed aspect. This theory highlights several socially constructed problems, including medical practitioners' tendency to subject patients to infantilization.
    3.   The symbolic interactionist analysis of the health care system allows us to see problems more clearly and recommend relevant solutions, such as giving health care professionals more formal training in being sensitive to patients' emotional needs.

III.   HEALTH AND SICKNESS IN AMERICA: A PICTURE OF DIVERSITY

The definitions of sickness and wellness have varied greatly over time in the United States. For example, since the 1950's, a positive value has been placed on being thin. During this same time, the prevalence of eating disorders such as **anorexia nervosa** and **bulimia** increased in the population. Anorexia is characterized by compulsive dieting that may lead to starvation, while bulimia is characterized by alternate binge eating and then purging or induced vomiting. A majority of people with eating disorders are young, White women from middle- and upper-class families where parents place great pressure on their daughters to be high achievers. Some behavioral scientists have noted there is a link between eating disorders and the socially constructed ideals of beauty in American society, which are fixated on thinness.

Men are also affected by cultural standards concerning body image. Many athletes, professional and amateur, have been goaded by athletic dreams to use **anabolic steroids**, which are powerful hormones that stimulate the growth of muscle, but also have detrimental side-effects such as impotence, hair loss, heart arrhythmia, liver damage, and strokes.

Epidemiology is the study of all of the factors -- biological, social, economic, and cultural -- that are associated with disease. **Social epidemiology** is the study of the effects of social, cultural, temporal, and regional factors on disease and health.

A.   <u>Race and Health Care</u>
    1.   Health can be affected by both personal factors, such as dietary and hygienic habits, and by institutional factors, such as the structure of the

health care system and the economic health of the society's less advantaged groups.

2. Most of the factors that affect health detrimentally at either the personal or institutional level are likely to have a worse influence on the health of minorities. This is reflected in the dramatic differences in illness and life expectancies for White Americans compared to other groups.

    a. Black people are more likely than White people to fall victim to diseases such as diabetes, cancer, heart disease, and stroke.

    b. Deaths during pregnancy and childbirth are significantly higher for Black women than for White women.

    c. Although the occurrence of breast cancer is lower among Black women than White women, the *mortality rate*, or death rate, for breast cancer in Black women is considerably greater than in White women.

3. Although differences in culture, diet, and lifestyle account for some of the health differences between Black and White people it is nevertheless clear that Black women and men do not receive medical attention as early as Whites, and when they do eventually get treatment, their illnesses are further along and the treatment they receive is not of the same quality.

4. Overall, Native Americans are in very poor health relative to other Americans. The mortality rate for Native Americans is one and a half times greater than the mortality rates for the general population, and Native American babies are almost twice as likely to die in the first year of life as are babies from other racial-ethnic groups.

5. Hispanics are considerably less healthy than Whites. For example, Hispanics contract tuberculosis at a rate four times that of Whites. They are less likely than Whites to have a regular source of medical care, and when they do, it is likely to be a public health clinic or an outpatient facility. Because of language barriers and other cultural differences, Hispanics are even less likely than other minority groups to use available health services, such as hospitals, doctors' offices, and clinics.

6. One of the most infamous studies to demonstrate the connection between race and the treatment of illness in the U.S. is the **Tuskegee Syphilis Study**.

    a. A group of about 600 African American males, approximately 400 of who were affected with syphilis, was chosen for this study, the purpose of which was to advance scientific knowledge about syphilis.

    b. This study continued for forty years. Even though penicillin was discovered as an effective treatment during this period, the scientists chose not to give penicillin to the African American subjects

    c. Most commentators believe that if the individuals in the study had been middle-class Whites instead of poor African Americans, the study would have ended when penicillin was found to cure syphilis. The Tuskegee study is one of the most serious examples of ethical violations in medical and behavioral scientific research.

B. Social Class and Health Care
    1. Social class has a pronounced effect on health and the availability of health services in the United States. The lower the social class status of the person or family, the less access they have to adequate health care.
    2. The effects of social class are evident in the infant mortality and stillbirth rates as well as the distribution of diseases such as diabetes, tuberculosis, heart disease, cancer, and arthritis.
        a. The reasons for disparities in health are partly due to personal habits. For example, those of lower socioeconomic status smoke more, and smoking is the major cause of lung cancer.
        b. Social circumstances also have an effect on health. Stress due to financial difficulties, poor living conditions, elevated levels of pollution in low-income neighborhoods, and lack of access to health care facilities also contribute to the high rate of disease among lower-income people.
    3. The average number of contacts with a physician differs greatly across class strata. The lower one's social class, the less likely it is s/he will see a physician when ill.
    4. Poor people, particularly those who are Black or Hispanic, are admitted to hospitals less frequently than are more affluent people. When poor people are eventually hospitalized, they stay for longer periods, most likely because their illnesses have been allowed to progress untreated.
    5. With the exception of the elderly, whose treatment is subsidized by Medicare, low-income people remain largely outside of the mainstream private health care system.
    6. Sociologists have found that during interactions between health care providers and poor patients, especially those who are Black or Hispanic, the patients are more likely to receive health care counseling that is incorrect, incomplete, or delivered in inappropriate language that is not likely to be understood by the patient.
    7. The Medicaid program in the U.S. is imperfect, because it covers less than two-thirds of the country's poor people.
C. Gender and Health Care
    1. Even though women live longer on average than men, older women are more likely than older men to suffer from stress, hypertension, and chronic illness.
    2. The rate of death caused by infectious diseases is higher for men than women, but it has declined significantly for both since the early 1900s.
    3. Researchers cite differences in male and female roles and cultural practices to explain these differences. For example, male occupational roles call for more travel and exposure to other people, the major causes of infection. Additionally, the hard-driving lifestyle associated with men's traditional provider role tends to produce elevated levels of heart disease.
    4. Despite what tobacco executives often argue, cigarette smoking causes cancer and cardiovascular disease, which kill men more frequently than women. About 450,000 people die each year as a result of smoking. This is greater than the combined death toll from AIDS, automobile accidents, homicide, suicide, and alcohol and drug use.

5.   Varied social circumstances influence women's health. For example, women are more likely to be "tokens" in the workplace, and this experience contributes to a greater incidence of depression and anxiety than for non-tokens. Housewives have higher rates of illness than women who work outside the home, and employed women are more likely than housewives to get well quickly when sick.

6.   When measured by number of physician visits and hospital admissions, women use the health care system more often than men.

D.   <u>Health and Sickness Globally</u>

1.   In societies that are largely pastoral or horticultural, the lack of technology severely limits both the development of health care systems and the delivery of health care to the populations of these countries.

2.   Abject poverty, particularly in Third World countries and regions with extreme poverty in the U.S., reduces life expectancy to well below the seventy-plus years experienced by upper- and middle-class populations.

3.   There are few doctors and other medical personnel in impoverished areas of the world; thus, the world's poorest people, who are in dire need of medical care, may never be seen by a physician.

4.   Poverty breeds disease, which reduces the likelihood that people will be able to work, which produces more poverty, disease, and premature death.

IV.   **ATTITUDES TOWARD HEALTH AND ILLNESS**

Whereas people suffering from disease used to be regarded as victims, individuals are now believed to have some measure of control over the prevention of, and recovery from, poor health. Thus, there is a greater likelihood today that sick people are viewed as contributing to their own illnesses. This phenomenon, known as *blaming the victim*, is particularly common when the individual's illness can be traced to such activities as smoking, drinking, overeating, or having unprotected sex. Many people in the United States are now paying more attention to their health.

A.   <u>Sexually Transmitted Diseases (STDs)</u>

1.   The general attitude in the U.S. toward sex has always been one of ambivalence. Attitudes about sex have become steadily more liberal since the turn of the 20th century, yet people tend to regard sexually transmitted diseases (STDs) as not merely diseases, but also as punishments for immoral behavior.

2.   Medical experts have diagnosed approximately fifty sexually transmitted diseases. The four major STDs are syphilis, gonorrhea, genital herpes, and Acquired Immune Deficiency Syndrome (AIDS).

B.   <u>AIDS: Illness and Stigma</u>

1.   Attitudes toward people suffering from sexually transmitted diseases, particularly AIDS, represent one of the strongest examples of how stigma operates in our society.

2.   **Stigma** occurs when an individual is socially devalued because of having some malady, illness, misfortune, or similar attribute. A stigma is viewed as a relatively permanent characteristic of the individual.

3.   AIDS is the term for a category of disorders that result from a breakdown of the body's immune system.

     a.   Before 1995, AIDS was diagnosed in higher proportion among Whites than among minorities. In 1995, for the first time, there were an equal proportion of persons reported with AIDS who were Black and White.

  b. In the U.S., death rates by AIDS in 1995 were highest for African Americans, followed by Hispanics, then Whites, and finally Native Americans and Asian Americans.

 4. Much of the negative stigma carried by AIDS victims is due to beliefs about who gets AIDS and how the HIV virus is transmitted. AIDS is transmitted through the exchange of bodily fluids, particularly blood and semen. Because AIDS appeared confined to the gay male community in the early 1980s, some believed that contracting AIDS was just retribution for deviant activity. Some sympathy has since been generated for AIDS sufferers, but for the average AIDS patient, the disease continues to carry a strong negative stigma.

C. <u>Chronic Fatigue Syndrome</u>

 1. **Chronic fatigue syndrome (CFS)** is a persistent, flu-like illness that can plague its sufferers for years. Another affliction that carries a negative stigma, it is sometimes flippantly referred to as the "yuppie flu." Medical experts have had great difficulty isolating an organic cause for CFS.

 2. Compounding the difficulties for people suffering from CFS is the fact that they are frequently denied the special consideration accorded to people who are defined as sick. CFS sufferers are denied access to the sick role because they lack an official diagnosis; thus, what assistance is given is tempered with reluctance and suspicion.

 3. People suffering from serious illness usually gain social benefits when they take on the **sick role**, the patterns of behavior socially defined as appropriate for people who are officially declared ill. Like other roles, the sick role carries with it certain expectations and responsibilities. For example, people in the sick role must show that they want to be well. In return, they receive the sympathy and assistance of those around them.

 4. Symbolic interactionists note that the name of a disease influences the public perception of an illness. Surveys indicate that the label "chronic fatigue" tends to trivialize the disease, but renaming it "chronic fatigue immunodeficiency syndrome" (CFIDS) has increased its legitimacy.

D. <u>Mental Illness</u>

 1. Rosenhan's landmark study of how mentally ill people are perceived by the medical profession and the public clearly demonstrated how profoundly the definition of illness in society is subject to social construction and the effects of labeling.

 2. In the 1960s, mental health practitioners began to rethink the nature of mental illness, which resulted in the **deinstitutionalization movement**. This movement relocated many mentally ill patients to smaller, community-based facilities, or "halfway houses" that would help them lead more normal lives. By the 1990's, the number of institutionalized patients was about one-fifth of what it was 40 years ago.

E. <u>The Medicalization of Illness and Deviance</u>

 1. The **medicalization** of an illness is that process by which society, following the medical profession, assigns all aspects of health and illness an exclusively medical meaning.

 2. The *medicalization of deviance* is the process by which culturally defined deviant behavior comes to be defined as individual pathology

or sickness. One example is childhood attention deficit disorder (ADD), or the inability to concentrate on the task at hand for more than a minute or two without being distracted.

    a.   Interestingly, the diagnosis of ADD coincided with the development of a drug called *ritalin*, a strong medication that was found to decrease some hyperactivity in children.

    b.   With the new diagnosis, less blame for the behavior was attributed to the child or to the parent or teacher, because the child was seen as having less direct control over his or her behavior due to the perceived biological cause of the behavior.

V.   THE HEALTH CARE CRISIS IN AMERICA

The cost of medical care in the United States is currently more than 11 percent of the gross national product, making health care the nation's third leading industry. The U.S. tops the list of all countries in per-person expenditures for health care. There are serious issues underlying the health care crisis in the nation, including the fee-for-service system, the epidemic of malpractice suits, and fraud and abuse in the medical system.

    A.   The Fee-For-Service System

        1.   The structures in place for paying health care costs in the U.S. are in a state of chaos. The central element in the payment system is the fee-for-service principle. Under this arrangement, the patient is responsible for paying the fees charged by the physician or hospital.

        2.   Alternative approaches to the fee-for-service system are presently being examined, but the fee system still predominates, whether in the form of direct payment by the individual or indirect payment by third parties such as private insurers.

        3.   The greatest contributors to skyrocketing health care costs are the soaring costs of hospital care and the rise in fees for physician services. Another culprit is the third-party payment system, whereby patients pass on the escalating health care costs to insurance providers.

        4.   **Health Maintenance Organizations** (HMOs) are private clinical care organizations that provide medical services in exchange for a set membership fee; thus, they have direct responsibility and control over the costs incurred.

    B.   Malpractice

        1.   There has been an increase in the number of patients who sue their physicians. The American public has traditionally accorded physicians high social status and high incomes, but the recent popularity of malpractice suits suggests that the public is beginning to question the privileged status of doctors.

        2.   Several specific reasons have been suggested for client revolts against the medical profession.

            a.   Attorneys claim that the primary cause of the malpractice dilemma is a declining standard of medical care and a rising incidence of medical negligence.

            b.   Another argument is that, as a result of specialization, doctors now fail to establish old-fashioned rapport with patients, making patients less attached to their physicians than before, and more likely to turn hostile.

            c.   Another explanation is that the high cost of medical care and resentment about the outsized incomes of physicians has generated animosity in patients that is quick to manifest itself in lawsuits, especially when medical episodes have an unfortunate outcome.

      d.   Also contributing to the public's mistrust of the medical profession is the relatively high incidence of *medical errors*.

   3.   Doctors increasingly practice **defensive medicine**, which entails ordering expensive, excessively thorough tests at the least indication that something is wrong in order to protect themselves against potential malpractice suits.

C.   Fraud and Abuse

Another factor contributing to spiraling medical costs is the increasing level of fraudulent activity engaged in by some doctors, pharmacists, and patients, as well as operators of hospitals, nursing homes, laboratories, and clinics. The most common type of medical fraud involves inappropriately billing third-party insurance programs such as Medicare.

D.   A Response to the Problem: HMOs

   1.   Health maintenance organizations (HMOs) are a popular innovation in health care. People who join HMOs are assigned to a physician who administers care and, when necessary, gives referrals to specialists affiliated with the HMO.

   2.   Doctors in an HMO earn salaries rather than fees, and all services are ultimately paid for by the membership fee given by subscribers to the HMO. The elimination of both the fee-for-service system and third-party insurers drives costs down in several ways.

      a.   Physicians have an incentive to give the most economical levels of care.

      b.   The opportunity for fraud, which costs third-party insurers so much, is eliminated.

      c.   The corporate structure of HMOs presumably offers the economies of scale enjoyed by other profit-oriented corporations that are often lacking in the U.S. hospital system

   3.   HMOs are experiencing fast growth as employers and individuals grapple with rising medical costs.

E.   Alternative Medicine

   1.   People may form social movements that seek to bring about some type of desired change in society. One type of limited social movement is the *alternative movement*, so called because it attempts some form of limited, focused change in some aspect of society.

   2.   **Holistic medicine**, which emphasizes the person's entire mental and physical state as well as the person's physical and social environment, is an example of alternative medicine that developed in the late 1980s and 1990s.

   3.   Although practitioners of holistic medicine advocate the integrated treatment of the entire person, they do not completely reject the remedies of traditional medicine such as surgery and drugs.

   4.   Because practitioners of holistic medicine are concerned with how each person's physical and social environment affects his or her health, they have taken an active role in combating environmental pollution.

   5.   Practitioners attempt to decrease the patient's dependency upon the physician by shifting some responsibility from the practitioner to the patient. Thus, they advocate health-promoting behaviors involving diet and exercise.

6.	Rather than emphasizing the necessity of frequent in-office care, holistic medicine urges the increased use of patient treatment in familiar environments such as the home.

F.	The Universal Health Care Debate
1.	Between 1992 and 1994, a plan for the reorganization of the health care system was developed by the Clinton administration, which included the promise of universal health insurance for all Americans.
2.	The core of the reform was to be the conversion of the entire system to a model called **managed competition**. Under this plan, all individuals would belong to a complex of managed-care organizations that would use their collective bargaining force to drive down the cost of health insurance, while accepting responsibility for providing high-quality care and operating their own facilities in an economical manner.
3.	This plan met strong opposition from the American Medical Association and in Congress.

## V.	DEATH AND DYING

One of the most pressing problems facing the medical profession specifically and society in general is whether individuals have a right to die, or to take their own lives. This reflects a dilemma of patients' rights versus the principles of the medical profession, which dictate that all forms of medical care should be given to a patient to sustain life. As a result of several court cases, the medical profession has established two guidelines. First, the physician must clearly explain to the patient the medical options available to sustain life. If this is done, then terminally ill patients and their close family members have the right to refuse what is called "heroic" treatment. Second, the physician may honor the *living will* of the patient, which is a statement made by the patient, while still in possession of mental faculty, of whether heroic treatment should be given in the case of severe incapacity. **Euthanasia**, or the act of killing a severely ill person as an act of mercy, may involve the withholding of treatment with the knowledge that doing so will produce the death of the patient, or actively assisting the ill person in dying.

PRACTICE TEST

MULTIPLE CHOICE QUESTIONS

1.	The _____ program, begun in 1965, provides government subsidized medical insurance to cover hospital costs for all individuals who are age 65 or older.
a.	Healthwise
b.	Medicaid
c.	Medicare
d.	Edlercare

2.	Anthony is a 21 year old, unemployed man who is permanently disabled by muscular dystrophy, a genetic disease that restricts physical mobility. He is entitled to health insurance through which program?
a.	Healthwise
b.	Medicaid
c.	Medicare
d.	Unemployment Compensation

3.   Functionalists have coined the term sick _____ to refer to the pattern of expectations that society applies to a person who is ill.
      a.   role
      b.   status
      c.   stigma
      d.   identity

4.   According to _____ theory, the inequality inherent in a capitalist society is responsible for different groups having unequal access to medical care.
      a.   symbolic interaction
      b.   functionalist
      c.   feminist
      d.   conflict

5.   The theoretical perspective that recommends modifying the preparation of health care professionals to include formal training about patients' emotional needs is:
      a.   symbolic interaction theory.
      b.   functionalist theory.
      c.   sensitivity theory.
      d.   conflict theory.

6.   In the United States, health care for most citizens is paid for through the fee-for-service system. The costs for health care are therefore paid primarily by:
      a.   pharmaceutical companies.
      b.   government programs.
      c.   medical practitioners.
      d.   private citizens.

7.   The majority of individuals with eating disorders in the United States are:
      a.   elderly, African American women.
      b.   children in poor, single parent households.
      c.   White female teenagers from financially stable families.
      d.   White male teenagers who participate in organized sports.

8.   Many athletes, both professional and amateur, pursue their dreams of being successful athletes while using powerful chemicals called _____ to stimulate the growth of muscle.
      a.   anitbiotics
      b.   amphetamines
      c.   anithistamines
      d.   anabolic steroids

9.   An eating disorder characterized by alternate binge eating and purging, or induced vomiting, in order to lose weight is:
      a.   obesity.
      b.   bulimia.
      c.   anorexia nervosa.
      d.   premenstrual syndrome.

10. The study of the biological, social, economic, and cultural factors associated with disease in society is:
   a. anatomical physiology.
   b. biological psychology.
   c. social epidemiology.
   d. medical sociology.

11. Which of the following statements about social class and health care is true?
   a. Low-income people are hospitalized more often than upper-income people.
   b. Lower-income and middle-income parents are equally as likely to have their children immunized.
   c. Middle-income people are more likely to get health screenings and other preventive care than lower-income people.
   d. Middle-class people have higher rates of illness than other social class groups in the U.S. due to the stress of managing busy professional and family lives.

12. Which of the following medical conditions is often associated with social stigma?
   a. Acquired Immune Deficiency Syndrome
   b. Pneumonia
   c. Diabetes
   d. All of the above illnesses carry a stigma in the United States.

13. Chronic fatigue syndrome (CFS) can:
   a. be easily treated with rest and medication.
   b. be quickly diagnosed using a simple blood test.
   c. can plague sufferers with flu-like symptoms for years.
   d. None of the above statements about CFS is true because no such illness exists.

14. The goal of the deinstitutionalization movement of the 1960s and 1970s was to:
   a. reduce the number of criminals in American prisons.
   b. give terminally ill patients a more comfortable, personalized alternative to hospitalization.
   c. relocate mental patients to smaller, community-based facilities to give them more independence.
   d. prevent researchers from using human subjects in clinical trials for new medications with potentially dangerous side effects.

15. The process by which society, following health care professionals, assigns all aspects of health and illness an exclusively medical meaning is:
   a. privatization.
   b. medicalization.
   c. criminalization.
   d. institutionalization.

16. Which of the following statements about medical malpractice in the United States is (are) true?
    a. The number of patients who sue their physicians is decreasing.
    b. Doctors often order excessive tests for their patients to guard against malpractice claims.
    c. Lawyers are reluctant to accept malpractice cases because settlements in these cases are relatively small.
    d. All of the above statements about medical malpractice are true.

17. The type of medicine that is especially concerned with the person's entire mental and physical state, as well as the person's social environment, is _____ medicine.
    a. technological
    b. scientific
    c. holistic
    d. heroic

18. The "New Age" alternative health movement has supported the adoption of which practice as a way of improving people's well being?
    a. vegetarianism
    b. plastic surgery
    c. prescription medication
    d. weekly physician visits

19. Which of the following developments in medicine has occurred since the end of World War II in 1945?
    a. Germ theory, or the idea that microscopic organisms cause many illnesses, was developed.
    b. The American Medical Association was established, granting physicians more political power than they had previously.
    c. There was a significant increase in the number of specialists and a concurrent decrease in the number of general practitioners.
    d. All of the above developments have occurred in the U.S. since 1945.

20. Which theory stresses that the health care system contributes to the stability of society by preventing and treating disease in the population?
    a. symbolic interaction theory
    b. functionalist theory
    c. conflict theory
    d. role theory

21. Which of the following incurable sexually transmitted diseases (STDs) is most widespread in the United States?
    a. leprosy
    b. syphilis
    c. gonorrhea
    d. genital herpes

22.　The phenomenon of _____ is particularly common when an individual's illness can be traced to activities such as smoking, drinking, unprotected sex, or other behaviors perceived by the public to be within the person's control.
　　a.　blaming the doctor
　　b.　blaming the victim
　　c.　ignoring the patient
　　d.　managing the addiction

23.　Which of the following ethical violations was committed in the Tuskegee Syphilis Study?
　　a.　Medical researchers did not prescribe penicillin to hundreds of Black men who had contracted syphilis even though they knew it would cure their disease.
　　b.　Researchers purposely infected hundreds of Black men with syphilis without their consent to determine how long it takes for infected people to become ill.
　　c.　Clinic doctors who tested Black male patients who had contracted syphilis did not tell the men that they tested positive for the disease because there was no known cure and they wanted to avoid upsetting their patients.
　　d.　None of the above ethical violations ever occurred because doctors and researchers have been governed by a strict code of ethics since the 1800s.

24.　Sociologists such as Jane Sprague Zones have argued that:
　　a.　the beauty myth emphasizes appearing eternally youthful and thin.
　　b.　there is no evidence that products such as cosmetics and hair dye contribute to any physical health problems for women.
　　c.　women in Western cultures generally have higher self-esteem than women in non-Western cultures because they feel better about their appearance.
　　d.　All of the above statements about beauty and women's health are true.

25.　Of the following medical specialties, physicians who specialize in _____ earn the highest median net incomes.
　　a.　obstetrics/gynecology
　　b.　psychiatry
　　c.　pediatrics
　　d.　surgery

TRUE-FALSE QUESTIONS

1.　The Americans with Disabilities Act restricts the official definition of disability to conditions that cannot be corrected with devices or medication.

2.　Full-time housewives have lower rates of illness than do women who work outside the home.

3.　Using number of physician visits and hospital admissions as a measure, men tend to use the health care system more often than women.

4.　The occurrence of breast cancer is lower for Black women than White women, yet the mortality rate from breast cancer is considerably higher for Black women.

5. More deaths occur each year as a direct result of smoking than from the combined deaths from AIDS, automobile accidents, homicide, suicide, and alcohol and illegal drug use.

6. The rise in fees for physician services is one of the greatest contributors to skyrocketing health care costs in the United States.

7. Active euthanasia, or "mercy killing" is illegal in most states; therefore, people who participate in it can be convicted of murder.

8. People with cancer have difficulty occupying the sick role and are therefore denied the special consideration accorded to most people with serious illnesses.

9. Practitioners of holistic medicine completely reject the use of prescription medications and surgery to treat illness based on a strong belief that scientific medical practices violate fundamental religious principles.

10. One negative consequence of the deinstitutionalization movement of the 1970s was an increase in the number of homeless mentally ill people in the United States.

FILL IN THE BLANK QUESTIONS

1. Private clinical care organizations that provide medical services in exchange for a set membership fee are _____.

2. A statement made by an individual indicating whether heroic treatment should be given in case of severe incapacity is a _____.

3. The act of withholding medical treatment with the knowledge that it will result in death for a seriously ill person is _____.

4. An example of medical _____ is when pharmacists charge Medicare for expensive brand-name drugs but provide patients with cheaper generic versions of the medication.

5. Medical practitioners who treat adult patients like children by speaking to them in a condescending or patronizing manner are subjecting their patients to _____.

ESSAY QUESTIONS

1. Explain why there are dramatic differences in life expectancies among different racial-ethnic and social class groups in the United States.

2. Use symbolic interaction theory to explain the importance of labeling in the process of diagnosing and treating people with mental illness.

3. Provide a summary of the physical symptoms of Acquired Immune Deficiency Syndrome (AIDS) as well as a demographic profile of people with the illness. Discuss how race-ethnicity, social class, gender, and sexual orientation influence the perception and treatment of patients with AIDS.

4. Explain what universal health care is, and discuss why former President Clinton's plan for the reorganization of the health care system in the United States was met with strong opposition.

5. Describe the difference between active and passive euthanasia, and discuss how society defines each of these practices. Explain why you think that euthanasia should or should not be legally available to people in the United States.

ANSWERS TO PRACTICE TEST

Answers to Multiple Choice Questions

1.	C.	565	The Medicare program provides medical insurance that covers hospital costs for all individuals who are age 65 or older.
2.	B.	566	Medicaid is the governmental program that provides medical insurance for poor people and people with disabilities.
3.	A.	566	Functionalists have coined the term sick role to refer to the pattern of expectations that society applies to people who are ill. People with certain medical conditions are not afforded the privileges of the sick role. Social stigma is associated with some medical disorders, particularly those that are perceived to be the result of the patient's participation in certain activities, such as unprotected sex.
4.	D.	567	Conflict theorists view the inequality inherent in capitalist society as responsible for unequal access to medical care.
5.	A.	567	Symbolic interactionists recommend more sensitivity training for health care professionals.
6.	D.	580	Under the fee-for-service system, patients are responsible for paying for health care. Some fortunate individuals have insurance through their employers or government programs that subsidize the cost of care. In socialist economies such as Canada, all citizens are entitled to medical care, a system also known as universal health care.
7.	C.	568	Most patients with anorexia nervosa are young, White women from middle- and upper-class families where there is strong parental pressure on daughters to be high achievers.
8.	D.	568	Many athletes, both professional and amateur, have been goaded by athletic dreams to use powerful hormones called anabolic steroids to stimulate the growth of muscle.
9.	B.	568	Bulimia is an eating disorder characterized by alternate binge eating and purging to lose weight.
10.	C.	568	The study of all factors associated with disease is social epidemiology.
11.	C.	570	Personal factors, including dietary and hygienic habits, and institutional factors, such as the structure of the health care system, lead to disparities in health for members of different income groups. Low-income people are less likely to be hospitalized, regularly see a physician, and receive health screenings, immunizations, and other preventive health services.
12.	A.	575	Stigmas occur when an individual is socially devalued because of some malady, illness, misfortune, or similar attribute. People with AIDS are frequently stigmatized.
13.	C.	577	Chronic fatigue syndrome is a persistent, flu-like illness that can plague sufferers for years. There is no single diagnostic test to confirm the affliction and scientists have yet to identify a specific organic cause. Sufferers are often stigmatized and denied the special considerations of the sick role.
14.	C.	578	The deinstitutionalization movement relocated many mental patients to

smaller, community-based facilities. The movement has generated a mixed response in society.

15. B. 578 Medicalization assigns all aspects of health and illness an exclusively medical meaning. Thus, even forms of health that are normal in society may become defined as "illness," such as pregnancy.

16. B. 581 Lawyers eagerly take on malpractice suits and some recent settlements were quite large. Physicians practice defensive medicine, or the excessive use of tests, to prevent against malpractice suits. The public is increasingly mistrustful of the medical profession, which contributes to the rising number of patients who sue their physicians.

17. A. 529 Holistic medicine emphasizes the person's entire mental and physical state, plus the integration of the two, as well as the person's environment. Holistic medicine is an example of an alternative movement that cautions against the over-use of drugs and surgery associated with modern, scientific medicine.

18. A. 529 Holistic medicine is associated with New Age movements that advocate vegetarianism, meditation, and other lifestyle changes to promote physical health and overall well being. Holistic medicine attempts to reduce the patient's dependency on the physician and de-emphasizes the necessity of frequent office visits.

19. C. 565 There has been an increase in specialization and a decrease in the number of general practitioners since World War II ended. The establishment of the American Medical Association in 1847 increased physicians' power, incomes, and status.

20. B. 566 As summarized in Table 20.2, functionalism views health care as contributing to the stability of society by preventing and treating illness in the population.

21. D. 575 Genital herpes is more widespread than either syphilis or gonorrhea, affecting approximately 30 million people in the U.S. alone. There is no known cure for this sexually transmitted disease.

22. B. 575 Blaming the victim is particularly common when the individual's illness can be traced to behaviors perceived by the public to be controllable, including smoking, drinking, and overeating.

23. A. 569 The Tuskegee Syphilis study demonstrates the connection between and the treatment of illness in the United States. Hundreds of Black men with syphilis were left untreated, even though penicillin was developed as a treatment for the disease, on the grounds that treating the men would "interfere" with the research study.

24. A. 572 Zones argues that beauty ideals in Western cultures pressure women to conform to narrow standards, which generally lower women's self-esteem. Some beauty products, such as hair dyes, have been linked to health problems, and other products, such as hairspray, have negative environmental consequences.

25. D. 565 As indicated in Table 20.1, physicians specializing in surgery had a median net income of $220,000 in 1996, compared to $150,000 for all physicians.

Answers to True-False Questions

1. T. 566 In 1999, the Supreme Court restricted the definition of disability under the Americans with Disabilities Act to exclude conditions that could be

corrected with devices (such as nearsightedness) or medications (such as high blood pressure).

2.	F.	573	Women who work outside the home get sick less often and get well more quickly than do full-time housewives.
3.	F.	573	Women tend to use the health care system more often than men.
4.	T.	569	More Black women than White women die from breast cancer even though the occurrence of breast cancer is higher in White women.
5.	T.	572	About 450,000 people die each year as a result of smoking.
6.	T.	580	The increase in fees for physician services and rise in costs of hospital care are the biggest contributors to skyrocketing health care costs.
7.	F.	526	Participation in a mercy killing, also known as active euthanasia, is illegal in the United States.
8.	F.	577	People with Chronic Fatigue Syndrome (CFS) are often denied access to the sick role, because CFS sufferers are denied an official medical diagnosis, whereas people with cancer are medically and socially designated as "sick."
9.	F.	581	Holistic medical practitioners do not necessarily reject surgery and drugs, but they caution against the use of those measures alone to promote health.
10.	T.	531	The deinstitutionalization movement has generated a mixed response, with critics claiming that it was responsible for a rise in homelessness among people with mental illness.

Answers to Fill in the Blank Questions

1.	Health Maintenance Organizations (HMOs)	580
2.	living will	583
3.	euthanasia	583
4.	fraud	581
5.	infantilization	567

CHAPTER 21
POPULATION AND ENVIRONMENT

BRIEF CHAPTER OUTLINE
Demography and the U.S. Census
Diversity and the Three Basic Demographic Processes
      Birth Rate
      Death Rate
      Migration
Population Characteristics
      Sex Ratio and the Population Pyramid
      Cohorts
Theories of Population Growth Locally and Globally
      Malthusian Theory
      Demographic Transition Theory
      The "Population Bomb" and Zero Population Growth
Checking Population Growth
      Family Planning and Diversity
      Population Policy and Diversity
Urbanism
      Urbanism as a Lifestyle
      Race, Class, and the Suburbs
      The New Suburbanites
Ecology and the Environment
      Vanishing Resources
      Environmental Pollution
      Environmental Racism and Classism
      Feminism and the Environment
      Environmental Policy
Globalization: Population and Environment in the Twenty-First Century

QUESTIONS TO GUIDE YOUR READING
1. What are the main sources of data that demographers use to study the population?
2. What are the three most important variables in the study of the population and how are they measured?
3. What is an age-sex pyramid and what implications do different pyramid structures have for society?
4. How do race, ethnicity, class, and gender intersect with environmental issues?
5. What are the main concerns among environmental policy makers today?

KEY TERMS (defined at page number shown and in glossary)
age-sex pyramid 592
cohort; birth cohort 593
crude death rate 590
demography 588
ecological globalization 610
environmental racism 605
human ecology 600
immigration 589
life expectancy 590
population density 600

census 588
crude birth rate 589
demographic transition theory 595
ecological demography 609
emigration 589
greenhouse effect 603
human ecosystem 600
infant mortality rate 590
Malthusian theory 594
population replacement level 597

KEY PEOPLE (identified at page number shown)

CHAPTER OUTLINE

Population growth and density are largely responsible for many current policy issues. For example, people's childbearing decisions greatly affect the educational and occupational structure of the entire country. The population of the United States, presently over 250 million people, will reach almost 300 million people by year 2025 at the current rate of growth.

I.   **DEMOGRAPHY AND THE U.S. CENSUS**

   Demography is the scientific study of the population. This field of sociology draws on huge bodies of data generated by a variety of sources, including the United States Census Bureau. A **census** is a head count of the entire population of a country, usually done at regular intervals. In the U.S., the census is conducted every ten years as required by the Constitution. The census attempts to enumerate every individual and obtain key demographic information as well. The 1990 census is estimated to have missed or undercounted only about 2 percent of the country's population.

   The U.S. Congress and the Census Bureau have debated two issues concerning the Census. The first is whether to use the category "multiracial" (or "mixed race") along with the other racial-ethnic categories that already appear on the census questionnaire. One argument against this option is that it would subtract from the number of people indicating one or more of the other categories, thereby further undercounting African Americans, Hispanics, and Native Americans. The second issue is whether the Census Bureau should attempt to count each and every adult person in the country as it has attempted to do in the past, or whether it should be permitted to use probability sampling to estimate the total count.

   Another body of data used in demography is vital statistics. **Vital statistics** include information about births, marriages, deaths, migrations in and out of the country, and other fundamental quantitative data related to population.

II.   **DIVERSITY AND THE THREE BASIC DEMOGRAPHIC PROCESSES**

   The total number of people in society is determined by three variables: births, deaths, and migrations. These three variables show different patterns by race, ethnicity, social class, and gender. **Immigration**, or migration into a society from outside, adds to the population, while **emigration**, the departure of people from a society, reduces the population. Population grows exponentially, with an upward accelerating curve, so that an ever increasing number of people are added each year. At the present rate of growth, the world's population will double in about 40 years.

   A.   Birth Rate

      1.   The **crude birth rate** of a population is the number of babies born for every thousand members of the population each year.

      2.   The crude birth rate reflects the *fertility* of a population, which is the number of live births per number of women in the population.

3. Different countries and subgroups within a country can have dramatically different birth rates. For example, Kenya has the highest birth rate in the world, while the San Marino has the lowest.

4. Fertility is different from *fecundity*, which is the potential number of children in a population that could be born per thousand women if every woman reproduced at her maximum biological capability during the childbearing years.

5. The overall birth rate for the U.S. is about 16 per thousand people. The rate varies according to racial-ethnic group, region, socioeconomic status, and other factors such as religious affiliation.

   a. Racial-ethnic minority groups and lower-income groups tend to have somewhat higher birthrates than do White non-minority groups and middle- and upper-income groups.

   b. Religious and cultural differences are apparent in the birth rate; for example, Catholics have a higher birth rate than do non-Catholics of the same socioeconomic status.

B. Death Rate

1. The **crude death rate** of a population is the number of deaths each year per thousand people. This rate can be an important measure of the overall standard of living of a population. For example, the higher the standard of living enjoyed by a country or group within a country and the higher the quality of health care provided, the lower the death rate.

2. Another measure that tends to reflect the standard of living in a population is the **infant mortality rate**, or the number of deaths per year of infants less than one year old for every thousand live births.

   a. The overall infant mortality rate in the U.S. is about 11 deaths for every thousand live births, compared to about 35 deaths per thousand live births in developing countries such as Kenya.

   b. The lack of adequate health care and access to health facilities is one cause of high infant mortality rates; consequently, low-income people and minorities generally have higher infant mortality rates. Other conditions that contribute to higher infant mortality include the presence of toxic wastes, malnutrition of the mother, inadequate food, and outright starvation.

3. The **life expectancy** of a population or group is defined as the average number of years that members of the group can expect to live.

   a. In the U.S., life expectancy has gone from 40 years of age in 1900 to over 76 years of age today, which is still lower than the life expectancy in most other industrialized nations.

   b. Life expectancy varies by gender, race-ethnicity, and social class. On average, women live longer than men, not only in the U.S. but also throughout most of the world.

   c. African Americans, Hispanics, and Native Americans all have shorter life expectancies than Whites.

C. Migration

Migration in and out of a country is one feature of the population. Migration can occur within the boundaries of a country as well. In the 1980s, internal migration by African Americans, Hispanics, Asian Americans, and Pacific Islanders within the U.S. occurred at a rate unmatched since World War I. Among Hispanics, migration patterns have traditionally been loosely linked to the agriculture industry, but more recently, to other industries such as meatpacking and textiles as well.

## III.	POPULATION CHARACTERISTICS

The composition of a society's population can reveal a tremendous amount about the society's past, present, and future. The demographic data of a society are a record of its national history. The important data that sociologists investigate include a population's sex ratio, age composition, age-sex population pyramid, and age cohorts.

A.	Sex Ratio and the Population Pyramid

1.	The **sex ratio** is the number of males per one hundred females. A sex ratio above 100 means that there are more males than females in the population, while a ratio below 100 indicates that there are more females than males in the population.

2.	In almost all societies, there are more boys born than girls, but because males have a higher infant mortality rate and a higher death rate after infancy, there are usually more females than males in the overall population.

3.	The *age composition* of the U.S. population is currently undergoing major changes as more people are entering the 65-and-over age bracket, a trend known as the *graying of America*.

4.	The elderly will soon become the largest population category in our society. As our population ages, its older members will have more influence on national policy and a greater impact on health care, housing, and other areas where the elderly have traditionally experienced age discrimination.

5.	Sex and age data are often combined in a graphical format called an **age-sex pyramid**, which generally reflects the birth rate of a society or group.

B.	Cohorts

A birth cohort, or more simply, a **cohort**, consists of all the people born within a given period. Over time, cohorts either stay the same in size or get smaller due to deaths. The baby boom cohort, born between 1946 and 1964, now comprises about one third of the entire United States population. This cohort has had a major impact on the practices, policies, habits, preferences, and culture of American society. For example, the suburban population doubled between the 1950s and the 1970s as family size grew and more people migrated from the cities to the suburbs.

## IV.	POPULATION GROWTH LOCALLY AND GLOBALLY

A.	Malthusian Theory

1.	Like other animals, humans can survive and reproduce only when they have access to the means of *subsistence*, or the necessities of life, such as food and water.

2.	The human population has doubled many times over, and the period of doubling gets shorter and shorter.

3.	Thomas Malthus predicted disastrous population growth. His basic idea, represented by **Malthusian theory**, was that populations tend to grow faster than the subsistence needed to sustain them.

4.	Rather than adding the same number of individuals each year, populations tend to grow by *exponential increase*, in which the number of individuals added each year grows, with the larger population generating an even larger number of births with each passing year.

5.   Malthus asserted that there were three major *positive checks* on population growth: famine, disease, and war. These checks inevitably come into play when populations rise to the level of subsistence and slightly beyond.

6.   Malthusian theory actually predicted rather well the population fluctuations of many agrarian societies such as Egypt from about 500 AD through Malthus' own lifetime. However, Malthus failed to foresee three revolutionary developments that derailed his predicted cycle of growth and catastrophe.

     a.   In agriculture, technological advances have permitted farmers to work larger plots of land and grow more food per acre, resulting in higher subsistence levels than Malthus predicted.

     b.   In medicine, scientific developments have treated diseases that Malthus expected to periodically wipe out entire nations, such as the bubonic plague.

     c.   The development and widespread use of contraceptives in many countries have kept the birth rate lower than Malthus would have thought possible.

B.   Demographic Transition Theory

1.   An alternative to Malthusian theory is **demographic transition theory**, which proposes that countries pass through a consistent sequence of population patterns linked to the degree of development in the society.

2.   The three main stages of population change according to demographic transition theory are:

     a.   Stage 1: characterized by a high birth rate and high death rate.

     b.   Stage 2: characterized by a high birth rate but a low death rate, resulting in an overall population increase.

     c.   Stage 3: characterized by a low birth rate and low death rate, resulting in stabilization of the overall level of the population as medical advances continue and general cultural changes occur, such as a smaller ideal family size.

3.   Demographic transition theory has been criticized as *ethnocentric* because it is based on the experiences of heavily industrialized countries that have a mostly White population.

C.   The "Population Bomb" and Zero Population Growth

1.   In 1968, Paul Erlich stated that the sheer mathematics of population growth worldwide were sufficient to demonstrate that world population could not possibly continue to expand at its present rates.

2.   Erlich pointed out that worldwide population growth has outgrown food production, and that massive starvation must inevitably follow.

3.   Erlich was among the earliest thinkers in modern times to argue that the quality of the environment, especially the availability of clean air and water, was a critical factor in the growth and health of populations.

4.   Many of the dire predictions Erlich made have come true, including mass starvation in parts of Africa and starvation among some Black and Hispanic populations in the U.S.; increased homelessness in American cities, especially among minorities; acid rain; extinctions of plant and animal species; and the irrecoverable destruction of environments like rain forests.

5.   Erlich supports organizations like Zero Population Growth (ZPG), a group dedicated to reaching the **population replacement level**, a

condition in which the combined birth and death rate of a population simply sustains the population at a steady level.

      6.   By 1980, the U.S. had reached the replacement level of reproduction, partly due to the successful promotion of birth control techniques.

V.   CHECKING POPULATION GROWTH

By the 1980s, countries representing 95 percent of the world's population had formulated policies of some kind aimed at stemming population growth, although there is no consensus on how population growth should be controlled. Efforts to encourage the use of contraceptives, for example, have had mixed support, because some political and religious groups are opposed to the use of birth control.

    A.   <u>Family Planning and Diversity</u>

      1.   Many governments make contraceptives available to individuals and families, which is not always consistent with the beliefs and cultural practices of all groups in the society. Governmental programs that advocate contraception can only be successful if couples themselves choose smaller families over larger ones.

      2.   Birth rate and family size are correlated with the overall level of economic development of a country, as well as the economic status of certain ethnic groups within a country, as reflected in the lower birth rates and smaller average family size in more economically developed nations.

      3.   The assumed relationship between economic development and family size in demographic transition theory has been challenged. In Bangladesh, for example, the population has become receptive to birth control programs, thereby lowering the birth rate in the absence of Western-style economic development.

    B.   <u>Population Policy and Diversity</u>

      1.   Family planning programs offer great potential for achieving significant declines in birth rates. In underdeveloped, overpopulated countries where such programs can have the most effect, the demand for family planning resources surpasses the supply.

      2.   There is some cultural resistance on the part of some U.S. racial and ethnic groups to government-sponsored contraceptive programs due to fears that widespread use of contraception threatens the very survival of these groups. such governmental programs are perceived to be racist.

      3.   There are other cultural barriers against the use of contraceptive methods, such as the belief among some young men that condoms are not masculine.

VI.   URBANISM

The growth and development of cities, or centers of human activity with a high degree of population density, is a relatively recent occurrence in the course of human history. The comparative study of urban, rural, and suburban areas is the task of *urban sociology*, a specialized field of sociology that examines the social structural and cultural aspects of the city.

    A.   <u>Urbanism as a Lifestyle</u>

      1.   Georg Simmel argued that urban living had profound social psychological effects on the individual, including insensitivity to the people and events around him or her due to the intensity of city life, and discouragement of close, personal interaction.

2. Louis Wirth also argued that the city was a center of distant, cold impersonal interaction; as a result, the urban dweller experienced alienation, loneliness, and powerlessness.

3. Both Simmel and Wirth believed that city life, with its relative absence of close, restrictive ties and interactions, offered the individual a certain feeling of freedom.

4. Herbert Gans provided a contrasting view of urban life when he concluded that many city residents have strong loyalties to others and develop a sense of community. Gans classified the *urban village* as having several "modes of adaptation."

   a. *Cosmopolites* are typically students, artists, writers, and musicians who choose urban living to be near the city's cultural facilities, and together, form a tightly knit community.

   b. *Ethnic villagers* live in ethnically and racially segregated neighborhoods.

   c. The *trapped* are individuals who, similar to today's *urban underclass*, are unable to escape from the city because of extreme poverty, homelessness, unemployment, and other familiar urban problems.

B. Race, Class, and the Suburbs

1. The impact of race and class is clear in the distinction between city and suburb, as only about one-fourth of African Americans live in suburban areas today.

2. In the suburbs, one chooses one's neighbors and friends on the basis of educational and occupational similarity in addition to race. Segregation in interpersonal interaction is encouraged by practices that support residential segregation.

3. People of color, particularly African Americans, often become as segregated in suburbs as in cities due to the practices of White landlords, homeowners, and realtors, who may selectively show particular properties only to people of a certain racial group.

4. Banks that practice *redlining* make it virtually impossible for persons of color to get a mortgage loan for a specific property, further intensifying residential segregation.

C. The New Suburbanites

1. The 1924 National Origins Quota Law encouraged immigration from Northern and Western Europe while discouraging immigration from Eastern and Southern Europe.

2. Today, the most prominent immigrants in suburban neighborhoods are Hispanics and Asian Americans. Suburban Whites may perceive themselves to be in competition for jobs and housing with these new immigrant groups.

3. Current immigration has led to the *new demographic divide*, which refers to settlement that is concentrated in small cities and suburbs on the East and West coasts, with little effect on the other parts of the U.S.

VII. **ECOLOGY AND THE ENVIRONMENT**

It should be apparent that population size has an important social dimension. Social forces can cause changes in the size of a population, and population changes can transform society. **Population density** is the number of people per unit of area, usually per square mile. As population density rises to high levels, the familiar problems of urban living appear, including high rates of crime and homelessness. Interacting with these problems are crises of the physical environment, such as air and water pollution, acid rain, and the growing output of hazardous wastes.

Human ecology is the scientific study of the interdependencies between humans and their physical environment. A **human ecosystem** is any system of interdependent parts that involves human beings interacting with each other and the physical environment. Two fundamental, closely related problems confront our present ecosystems -- overpopulation and exhaustion of natural resources.

A.   Vanishing Resources

In all ecosystems, organisms depend upon each other and the physical environment for survival. The supply of many natural resources is finite, and if one element in an ecosystem is disturbed, the entire system is affected. This was exemplified by the problems that emerged in the 1940s and 1950s with the use of DDT in the United States. Whereas growing population is a problem of the developing world, shrinking resources are a problem of the industrialized world, where real estate development takes over millions of acres of farmland each year in the U.S. alone.

B.   Environmental Pollution

1.   The most threatening forms of pollution are the poisoning of the planet's air and water. The world's leading air and water polluters are the United States, Japan, Russia, and Poland.

2.   A huge portion of the pollutants released into the air comes from the exhaust pipes of private motor vehicles. On the industrial side, the Environmental Protection Agency (EPA) estimates that the hazardous and cancer-causing pollutants released into the air by industry are responsible for about 2,000 deaths a year.

3.   A daunting international issue has grown around a group of chemicals called chlorofluorocarbons (CFCs), which are used in the manufacture of plastics, as a coolant in refrigerators, and as an aerosol propellant.

4.   Related to the problem of ozone depletion is the **greenhouse effect**, which results in small changes in the average temperature of the earth that can have dramatic consequences. For example, it can cause great melting in the arctic regions, which raises the level of the sea, which can affect water, land, and weather systems worldwide.

5.   Only a very small portion of the earth's water is usable by humans. The nation's rivers and lakes have long been dumping grounds for heavy industry, yet these same industries (paper, steel, automobile and chemical) depend upon clean water for their production processes, during which they take water from the rivers and lakes and return it heated and polluted. The difference in temperature can alter aquatic habitats and kill aquatic life, earning it the name **thermal pollution**.

6.   The EPA estimates that 63 percent of rural Americans may be drinking water that is contaminated as a result of agricultural runoff and improper disposal of toxic substances in landfills. Although statutes now prohibit industry from polluting the nation's water, it continues.

7.   Many argue that of all the environmental problems facing the U.S. today, the most urgent is the dumping of hazardous wastes, if only for the sheer noxiousness of some of the materials being dumped.

C.   Environmental Racism and Classism

Toxic wastes are stored and dumped with disproportionate frequency in areas that have high concentrations of racial-ethnic minorities, a phenomenon known as **environmental racism**. *Environmental inequity* exists for various racial-ethnic groups, who suffer from greater exposure to environmental pollution, including high rates of death from cancer.

D. Feminism and the Environment

Women and men do not generally regard environmental issues equally. Women feel more vulnerable than men to risks posed by environmental problems; consequently, they tend to be more concerned with issues of environmental risk. Lack of attention on the part of local and federal governments to environmental issues can be interpreted as lack of attention to policy that differentially affects women.

E. Environmental Policy

1. Environmental policy in the U.S. has been affected by an organized environmental movement, which brought attention to environmental toxins and disasters.

2. In the past three decades, federal and local agencies have made concerted efforts to bring the problems of environmental pollution under control through stiffer antipollution laws and the encouragement of alternative technologies.

3. Industry has resisted antipollution laws because they require expensive adaptations of manufacturing processes, and unions have resisted such laws for fear that the added expense to industry would reduce jobs.

4. The development of new technologies such as emissions controls for automobile exhausts has helped reduce certain kinds of pollution.

VIII. **POPULATION AND ENVIRONMENT IN THE TWENTY-FIRST CENTURY**

Sociologists predict that the United States will continue to experience increasing suburban development, with accompanying increases in heavy industry and therefore additional pollution. Today's sociologists are concerned with both the effect that a changing planet will have upon our lifestyle, as well as the effects our lifestyle will have on the planet. Ecological concern helped stimulate the development of **ecological demography**, a field of study that combines the studies of demography and ecology.

PRACTICE TEST

MULTIPLE CHOICE QUESTIONS

1. Which of the following statements about the census is (are) true?
    a. The U.S. constitution requires that the census be conducted every ten years.
    b. The U.S. census uses probability sampling to estimate the population because counting every individual is too expensive and time-consuming.
    c. The U.S. census collects information about people's attitudes toward important social and political issues.
    d. All of the above statements about the U.S. census are true.

2. The scientific study of the size, composition, and distribution of the population is:
    a. epidemiology.
    b. urbanography.
    c. demography.
    d. ecology.

3. One of the most hotly debated issues concerning the U.S. census is whether to:
   a. stop asking people about their income because most people believe this question is an invasion of their privacy.
   b. change the official definition of a family to include unmarried, cohabiting couples.
   c. ask respondents about their sexual orientation.
   d. add a multiracial category to the survey.

4. The group most likely to be undercounted in the U.S. census is:
   a. well-educated people of all racial-ethnic groups.
   b. lower-income Hispanic people.
   c. working-class White people.
   d. middle-class Black people.

5. The measure of the potential number of children in a population that could be born per thousand women, if every woman reproduced at her maximum biological capacity during the childbearing years, is the _____ rate.
   a. fertility
   b. fecundity
   c. mortality
   d. maternalism

6. The major restructuring of the age-sex pyramid that will occur in the U.S. over the next thirty years is due to the:
   a. considerable increase in infant mortality among minority populations.
   b. significant increase in the immigration of Hispanics to the country.
   c. recent explosion in the birth rate for Whites.
   d. aging of the Baby Boom cohort.

7. Who was one of the first modern theorists to argue that the quality of the environment, particularly the availability of clean air and water, is a critical factor in the health of the population?
   a. Paul Erlich
   b. Herbert Gans
   c. Kingsley Davis
   d. Thomas Malthus

8. Which of the following industrialized nations has the lowest infant mortality rate?
   a. China
   b. Japan
   c. Russia
   d. United States

9. Which of the following factors did Malthus surmise were positive checks on population growth?
   a. immunizations
   b. abortion
   c. disease
   d. All of the above.

10. The state in which the combined birth and death rate of a population simply sustains the population at a steady level is the _____ level.
    a. positive check
    b. limited growth
    c. population explosion
    d. population replacement

11. Which of the following trends was associated with the Baby Boom cohort?
    a. increase in the sale of commodities such as baby food and diapers in the 1940s
    b. doubling of the rural population in the 1960s and 1970s
    c. decline in elementary school enrollment in the 1950s
    d. All of the above trends are associated with the Baby Boom cohort.

12. Which of the following statements about life expectancy in the U.S. is (are) true?
    a. Average life expectancy in the U.S. increased from 40 years old to 76 years old in the period between 1900 and 2000.
    b. Average life expectancy in the U.S. is higher for women than men and higher for White people than Black people.
    c. Average life expectancy is lower in the U.S. than in nearly every other industrialized country.
    d. All of the above statements about life expectancy are true.

13. The age-sex pyramid of Mexico in 1990 visually resembles which shape?
    a. horizontal rectangle
    b. vertical rectangle
    c. triangle
    d. square

14. Simmel and Wirth have both argued that urban life has what social-psychological effect(s) on individuals?
    a. feeling of liberation or freedom from restrictions
    b. heightened sensitivity to events surrounding them
    c. increased opportunity for close, personal interaction
    d. All of the above are consequences of urban living.

15. In Gans' vision of the urban village, which of the following groups choose urban living to be near the city's cultural facilities?
    a. urban underclass
    b. ethnic villagers
    c. cosmopolites
    d. the trapped

16. The examination of ecosystems has demonstrated that:
    a. the supply of natural resources is finite.
    b. humans and the physical environment are interdependent.
    c. a disturbance in one element of an ecosystem has an effect on the entire system.
    d. All of the above statements are true.

17.   According to population bomb theory, the **most** significant factor in reaching population equilibrium in the U.S., especially among the middle-class, has been:
        a.   better crop yields, leading to increased food production.
        b.   official government policies restricting family size.
        c.   increased use of birth control.
        d.   sexual abstinence.

18.   Which demographic theory is fundamentally pessimistic, predicting that the population will ultimately outstrip the food supply despite positive and preventive checks, resulting in worldwide starvation and rampant disease?
        a.   Malthusian theory
        b.   Doomsday theory
        c.   Rational Choice theory
        d.   Demographic Transition theory

19.   Stage two of the demographic transition is characterized by a:
        a.   low birth rate and low death rate.
        b.   declining birth rate and high death rate.
        c.   high birth rate and declining death rate.
        d.   high birth rate and high death rate.

20.   Which theory has been used to counter the predictions of demographic transition theory by arguing that people make conscious, purposeful decisions about how many children to have?
        a.   Population Bomb theory
        b.   Rational Choice theory
        c.   Malthusian theory
        d.   None of the above theories have been used to challenge demographic transition theory, because it is widely accepted as accurate.

TRUE-FALSE QUESTIONS

1.   Although women have higher rates of many illnesses than men, women generally live longer than men in the United States.

2.   White people are significantly more likely than Black people in the United States to die from hypertension, the flu, and Acquired Immune Deficiency Syndrome (AIDS).

3.   In almost all societies, there are more girls than boys born, resulting in a greater number of females than males in all age groups.

4.   During the great internal migration of the 1880s to the 1920s, large numbers of African Americans moved from Northern cities to rural areas in the South.

5.   The United States was in the first stage of the demographic transition during the industrialization period of the late 1800s.

6.   To reach zero population growth, the average number of children per family in a society would have to be one.

7.   The primary reason that the birthrate declined in Bangladesh in the absence of advanced economic development is the implementation of an aggressive, government-sponsored contraception program.

8.   In the suburbs, people generally choose neighbors and friends based on occupational similarity.

9.   The practice of redlining by banks contributes to racial integration in the suburbs by allocating a certain percentage of mortgages to African Americans who want to purchase housing in predominantly White neighborhoods.

10.   Those nations supplying the largest number of recent immigrants to the United States are China and Mexico.

FILL IN THE BLANK QUESTIONS

1.   The crude birth rate, or the number of babies born per year for every one thousand members of the population, reflects the _____ of a population.

2.   The departure of people from a society, or _____, results in a decrease in population.

3.   The infant _____ rate measures the number of deaths per year of infants less than one year old for every thousand live births.

4.   The group of approximately 75 million babies born in the U.S. between 1946 and 1964, which now represents nearly one-third of the population, is known as the _____.

5.   Records of births, marriages, deaths, and migrations into and out of the country are included in the _____ statistics for the nation.

ESSAY QUESTIONS

1.   Discuss how the information collected by the U.S. Census is used to determine government policies and programs.
2.   Discuss how and why life expectancy and the infant mortality rate differ by racial-ethnic and social class membership in the United States.
3.   Explain how racism and classism intersect with environmental pollution in the United States.
4.   Explain why there has been cultural resistance to government-sponsored family planning programs among certain racial-ethnic minority groups in the United States.
5.   Provide an overview of U.S. environmental policy, and discuss how successful efforts to protect the environment and the human population have been over the last 30 years.

ANSWERS TO PRACTICE TEST

Answers to Multiple Choice Questions

1.   A.   588   The U.S. census is conducted every ten years. It attempts to count every individual and collect basic demographic information such as race, marital status, and income. The Census does not ask people for their opinions on social issues.

2.	C.	588	Demography is the scientific study of the population. Epidemiology is the study of all factors associated with disease. Ecology is the study of the physical environment. Urban sociology is the study of the social structural and cultural aspects of the city.
3.	D.	588	One controversial issue concerning the U.S. Census is whether to add the category "multiracial" to the survey.
4.	C.	588	Low-income people, transient people, and members of racial-ethnic minority groups, especially new immigrants, are most likely to be undercounted by the Census; thus, lower-income Hispanic people would be more likely than the other groups listed to be undercounted.
5.	B	589	Fecundity refers to the potential number of children that could be born if every woman reproduced at her maximum capacity, while fertility is the number of live births per number of women in the population. The crude death rate is the number of deaths each year per thousand people, while the infant mortality rate refers to the number of deaths per year of infants under one year old for every thousand births.
6.	D.	592	The aging of the Baby Boom cohort, a trend called the "graying of America," has resulted in major restructuring of the age-sex pyramid.
7.	A.	597	Writing in the 1960s, Paul Erlich noted that the quality of the environment is related to the health of the population. Erlich advocates reducing population growth until the population replacement level is attained.
8.	B.	590	As indicated in Table 12.1, Japan has the lowest infant mortality rate, while China, the U.S., and Russia have the highest infant mortality rates of the industrialized nations.
9.	B.	590	Malthus argued that war, disease, and famine were positive checks on population growth. Immunizations increase population by lowering the death rate. Writing in the 1700s, Malthus could not foresee the contributions of abortion and artificial birth control to reducing population growth.
10.	D.	597	The state in which the combined birth and death rate of a population simply sustains the population at a steady level is the population replacement level.
11.	A.	593	The Baby Boom cohort has had a major impact on the practices, habits, preferences, and policies of the United States. There were increases in the sale of baby items in the 1940s, elementary school enrollments in the 1950s, and the suburban population in the 1960s and 1970s.
12.	D.	590	The average life expectancy has increased to about 76 years old in the U.S., which is considerably longer than in 1900, but lower than the average life expectancy in nearly every other industrialized nation. Within the U.S., life expectancy is lower for men, members of racial-ethnic minority groups, and lower-income people.
13.	C.	592	As depicted in Figure 21.2, the age-sex pyramid of Mexico resembles a triangle, while the age-sex pyramid of the U.S. resembles a vertical rectangle with a bulge in the middle.
14.	A.	599	Both Simmel and Wirth recognized that city life could be stimulating and liberating, but it is also characterized by cold, impersonal relationships, decreased sensitivity to one's surroundings, and feelings of alienation and powerlessness.
15.	C.	599	In Gans' vision of the urban village, cosmopolites are students, artists,

and musicians who live in the city to be near cultural facilities. Ethnic villagers live in segregated neighborhoods, or ethnic enclaves. The trapped are similar to today's urban underclass, consisting of those people who are unable to escape from the city due to poverty.

16. D. 601 The examination of ecosystems has demonstrated that the supply of many natural resources is finite, humans and the physical environment are interdependent, and a disturbance in one part of the ecosystem has an effect on the whole system.

17. C. 603 By 1980, the U.S. had reached the population replacement level of reproduction partly due to the effective use of birth control.

18. A. 594 As summarized in Table 21.2, Malthusian theory suggests that the population will eventually surpass the food supply despite positive checks on population growth.

19. C. 596 As depicted in Figure 21.3, Stage two of the demographic transition is characterized by a high birth rate and declining death rate, which increases the population.

20. B. 589 Rational choice theory has been used to counter the predictions of demographic transition theory, arguing that individuals decide how many children to have and when to have them according to their own cost-benefit analysis.

Answers to True-False Questions

1. T. 590 Although women have higher rates of some illnesses, they generally live longer than men.

2. F. 590 Black people are more likely than White people to die from the flu, hypertension, and AIDS.

3. F. 592 In almost all societies, more boys than girls are born, but boys and men have higher mortality rates, resulting in more women than men in the adult and elderly populations.

4. F. 591 During the great migration, a large number of African Americans moved from southern towns to northern cities such as Chicago, New York, Detroit, and Cleveland.

5. F. 596 The U.S. was in the first stage of the demographic transition during the Colonial period and in the second stage during Industrialization.

6. F. 597 When an average of two children are born per family, the society can reach zero population growth.

7. T. 598 Government-sponsored contraception programs have been successful in significantly reducing the birth rate in countries such as Bangladesh and China.

8. T. 600 Although race continues to be an important factor in selecting friends and neighbors in the suburbs, suburbanites rely more on social class similarity, which is reflected in education level and occupation.

9. F. 600 The practice of redlining is a form of discrimination whereby banks deny mortgages to prospective homeowners who are members of racial or ethnic minority groups, which supports continued residential segregation, particularly in the suburbs.

10. T. 600 Mexico and China, as well as Russia, have supplied the most recent immigrants to the U.S., many of whom have settled in suburban areas.

Answers to Fill in the Blank Questions

1.	fertility	589
2.	emigration	589
3.	mortality	590
4.	Baby Boomers	593
5.	vital	588

CHAPTER 22
COLLECTIVE BEHAVIOR AND SOCIAL MOVEMENTS

BRIEF CHAPTER OUTLINE
Characteristics of Collective Behavior
Crowds
       The Social Structure of Crowds
       The Influence of Social Control Agents
       Panic
Riots
       Types of Riots
       Why Do Riots Occur?
       What Stops Riots?
Collective Preoccupations
       Fads
       Fashions
       Hysterical Contagions
       Scapegoating
Social Movements
       Types of Social Movements
       Origins of Social Movements
       The Organization of Social Movements
       Strategies and Tactics
       Theories of Social Movements
Diversity, Globalization, and Social Change

QUESTIONS TO GUIDE YOUR READING

1. What are the main characteristics of collective behavior?
2. What is a crowd and how do crowds generally behave?
3. What are riots, why do they occur, and how can they be stopped?
4. What is a collective preoccupation and what forms do they take?
5. What is a social movement and what are the necessary conditions for a social movement to develop?

KEY TERMS (defined at page number shown and in glossary)

collective behavior 615
competition theory 623
emergent norm theory 619
frames 636
new social movement theory 636
political process theory 635
reactionary movements 631
resource mobilization theory 635
social change movements 628

collective preoccupations 624
convergence theory 622
expressive crowds 620
mobilization 633
personal transformation movements 628
radical movements 630
reform movements 630
scapegoating 626
social movement 627

CHAPTER OUTLINE
Sociologists are interested in the behavior of groups that are influenced by crowds or are responding to sudden and unusual situations. People think that they are acting as individuals, but, like other forms of group behavior, they are being shaped by the collective action of others.

People in crowds seem to take on a collective identity. Within a crowd, it may even be difficult to distinguish individual and group behavior.

Collective behavior is defined as behavior that occurs when usual conventions are suspended and people collectively establish new norms of behavior in response to an emerging situation. Collective behavior occurs when something out of the ordinary happens and people respond by establishing new behavioral norms. Sometimes collective behavior emerges in response to an event that never actually takes place, but people may develop new forms of behavior in response to a situation that they strongly believe will occur. For example, there are numerous examples of cults, past and present, whose members believe that spaceships will land on earth or that some other supernatural event will occur at a predictable point in time.

Types of collective behavior include crowds, riots, disasters, and social movements, as well as forms of mass action, including fads and fashion. Riots occur when groups of people band together to express a collective grievance or when groups are provoked by anger or excitement. Environmental disasters also provoke collective behavior, because blizzards, hurricanes, floods, and earthquakes all create situations in which people develop new ways of behaving in the face of unusual circumstances. **Social movements,** or groups that act with some continuity and organization to promote or resist change in society, tend to be more persistent over time more than other forms of collective behavior. Sociologists who study collective behavior are interested in how even unique and idiosyncratic events are socially structured, as well as how collective behavior generates social change.

I.   **CHARACTERISTICS OF COLLECTIVE BEHAVIOR**
        The different forms of collective behavior have some common characteristics.
        A.   Collective behavior always represents the actions of groups of people, not of individuals. It is rooted in the relationships between people and the norms governing group behavior.
        B.   Collective behavior involves new or emergent relationships that arise in unusual or unexpected circumstances. It arises when uncertainty in the environment creates the need for new forms of social action.
        C.   Because of its emergent nature, collective behavior captures the more novel, dynamic, and changing elements of society to a greater degree than other forms of action.
        D.   Collective behavior may mark the beginnings of more organized social behavior. Collective behavior often precedes the establishment of formal social organizations.
        E.   Collective behavior is patterned behavior, not the irrational behavior of crazed individuals. It is relatively coordinated among the participants.
        F.   Most forms of collective behavior appear to be highly emotional, or even volatile. However, what defines a crowd is its spontaneity, rather than its emotionality.
        G.   During collective behavior, people communicate extensively through rumors. *Rumors* are the information transmitted by participants in collective behavior as they try to make sense out of an ambiguous situation.
        H.   Collective behavior is often associated with efforts to achieve social change, whether by promoting change or resisting it.

II.   **CROWDS**
        Crowds, one of the major forms of collective behavior, share several characteristics. They involve groups of people coming together in face-to-face or visual space with each other. Crowds are transitory, volatile, and usually have a sense of urgency.

A.   The Social Structure of Crowds
1.   Although they appear to be a single entity, crowds have a discernible social structure. Each crowd is usually a particular size, participants are packed together in a particular density, and people in the crowd are more or less connected to each other. Furthermore, the boundaries of the crowd may be more or less permeable.
2.   There is no rule about how large or dense a group must be, or how connected the people need to be, to be considered a crowd.
a.   Crowds are usually "circular," surrounding the object of the crowd's attention.
a.   Where there are physical barriers, groups fill the enclosed space or form a semi-circle.
b.   The people closest to the crowd's center of interest, known as the *core* of the crowd, show the greatest focus on the object of interest.
c.   At the outer edges of the crowd, attention is less focused, and people are more likely to be talking or participating in other activities.
3.   Sociologists Ralph Turner and Lewis Killian developed emergent norm theory to describe how crowds can be both emergent and socially organized.
a.   **Emergent norm theory** postulates that when people are faced with an unusual situation, they create meanings that define and direct the situation.
b.   Group norms govern collective behavior, but the norms that are obeyed are newly created as the group responds to its new situation.
c.   Although collective behavior can sometimes appear to be without social organization, emergent norm theory emphasizes that members of the group do follow norms. They just may be created on the spot.
4.   Crowds may exhibit a division of labor and they may generate *bystander crowds*, which include both groups who are physically present, like the crowd of onlookers at a protest march, as well as groups as remote as a mass media audiences.
5.   **Expressive crowds** are those whose primary function is the release or expression of emotion. They may even instill a permanent change in the mood or behavior of participants. Expressive crowds exist where the crowd is focused on an object that is seen by participants as having deep, perhaps even religious, meaning. Although expressive crowds may be moved by any emotion, the most common are collective grief or joy.
B.   The Influence of Social Control Agents
Social control agents are present in most crowd situations, because crowds are generally believed to easily "get out of control." The ability of social control agents to shape crowd activity varies, and sometimes the behavior of social control agents may be the cause of crowd action, particularly if they overreact to crowd behavior.

C. <u>Panic</u>
1. Sometimes crowd behavior develops when there is a *panic*, or behavior that occurs when the people in a group suddenly become concerned for their safety, and seemingly spontaneous, disorganized behavior results.
2. Even in panics, there is more social structure than the popular image suggests.
3. Three main factors characterize panic-producing situations.
    a. There is a perceived threat, which may be physical, psychological, social, or a combination of these triggers.
    b. There is a sense of possible entrapment, when individuals feel that if they do not act fast, they may miss their chance to achieve some goal.
    c. There is a failure of front-to-rear communication, characterized by people at the rear of the crowd perceiving themselves to be unfairly disadvantaged in reaching their goal, and therefore exerting strong physical or psychological pressure to advance toward the goal, such as an emergency exit.

III. **RIOTS**

Sociologists view riots as a multitude of small crowd actions spread over a particular geographic area, where the crowd is directed at a particular target. There are cyclical variations in crowd activities over the course of a day, indicating that even riot behavior is linked to the daily routines of social life.

A. <u>Types of Riots</u>
There are several kinds of riots, each influenced by its historical and social context.
1. In *commodity riots*, property is the object of attack rather than people. Violence is directed at buildings or merchandise that may symbolize an object of the crowd's hatred. This was the case in the 1992 Los Angeles riots.
2. *Communal riots* are violent outbursts in which civilians riot against other civilian groups, as in the race riots that occurred in the U.S. during the 1960s.
3. *Political riots* are those in which a group rises up against a particular government policy or treatment by government officials. More recent race riots in the U.S. are examples of political riots.

B. <u>Why Do Riots Occur?</u>
1. Looters choose selected targets, often act as groups, and behave in the context of communities or social groups who give considerable support to their actions.
2. Explanations of riots that focus on individual attitudes and states of mind fall into the category of **convergence theory**, which explains riots by focusing on the participants in riots and presupposes that rioters are acting on predispositions and attitudes.
3. Sociologists have found that the demographic and structural characteristics of urban areas can make some cities more prone to riots than others.
    a. Riots are more likely to occur in cities where there is economic deprivation of racial-ethnic minority groups, including low levels of educational attainment and median income, high unemployment, and poor housing conditions.

    b.   Riots are most likely to occur in cities where grievances of the rioting group have not been addressed.

    c.   The rapid influx of new populations, through migration or immigration, is a common characteristic of cities where riots take place.

    d.   Whether a group has the resources to initiate and sustain rebellious activity also influences the development of riots.

4.   In the context of underlying social structural conditions of poverty, unemployment, and poor housing, riots are typically sparked by a precipitating event, such as a confrontation with the police.

5.   **Competition theory** views riots as developing when different groups have to compete for limited resources, such as jobs and housing.

C.   <u>What Stops Riots?</u>
Four possible explanations have been given for what brings riots to an end.

1.   The goals of the protest group may have been satisfied.

2.   The actions of social control agents may end the violence.

3.   Riots and violence may end when the political situation changes.

4.   People's discontent may be regulated by the expansion of relief services.

IV.   COLLECTIVE PREOCCUPATIONS

Collective preoccupations are forms of collective behavior wherein many people over a relatively broad social spectrum engage in similar behavior and have a shared definition of their behavior as needed to bring social change or to identify their place in the society. Collective preoccupations include fads, fashion, hysterical contagions, and scapegoating. Although collective preoccupations take on many different forms, these distinctly social phenomena share several features. They often begin with a small group of people involved in face-to-face interaction. The people are usually faced with an ambiguous situation from which they attempt to derive meaning, such as a possible UFO sighting. Groups of friends and family members may read stories in the paper about the event and come up with explanations for the UFO that was "seen." Groups of people together form a collective definition of the situation to explain the ambiguous event. Finally, the collective definition of the situation must spread beyond the initial group, which usually occurs through the mass media, pre-existing friendship networks, or organizational ties. Most of the different types of collective preoccupations provide opportunities for participants to belong to a group while differentiating themselves from other groups.

A.   <u>Fads</u>

1.   Fads represent change that has a less consequential impact than other kinds of social change. Despite their seemingly idiosyncratic nature, even fads follow certain norms.

2.   Fads are initially created within a small group who define a particular product or phrase as meaningful or desirable to possess or say. A *latent period* is followed by the *breakout period*, during which the product or activity spreads to other groups via friendship networks and the mass media. In the *peaking period*, the use of the new item is defined as a fad, and people enthusiastically adopt it. In the *decline period*, the fad quickly fades.

3.   *Crazes* are similar to fads except that they tend to represent more intense involvement for participants. Those involved in crazes tend to be highly focused on the craze behavior, seeming fanatical at times because they are devoted to the craze above all else and may endure

considerable expense and inconvenience to pursue the craze, such as
waiting in long lines or traveling long distances.

B. Fashion
    1. Fashion has traditionally been considered a form of collective behavior
        because it constantly introduces something novel into the society.
    2. Particular kinds of clothing and adornment can give people a feeling of
        acceptance, provide a sense of group identity, and differentiate groups
        from each other.
    3. Economist and sociologist Thorstein Veblen referred to the purchasing
        and displaying of goods to symbolize wealth and status as *conspicuous
        consumption*.
    4. Because fashion differentiates groups from each other, it is a means of
        marking inequality between groups in society. Likewise, apparel
        distinguishes groups within organizations, where some staff wear
        uniforms while managers wear business attire.

C. Hysterical Contagions
    1. *Hysterical contagions* involve the spread of symptoms of an illness
        among a group, usually one in close contact, when there is no
        physiological disease present.
        a. An episode of hysterical contagion usually begins with one
            person exhibiting physiological symptoms.
        b. The person receives sympathetic attention as people accept that
            the symptoms are caused by some genuine physical or
            biological agent.
        c. Soon other people begin to experience similar symptoms and
            also receive attention for their illness.
        d. Authorities attempt to locate and eliminate the source of the
            problem.
        e. When they are unable to find a biological cause for the
            outbreak, speculation begins that the episode is a case of mass
            hysteria.
    2. Hysterical contagion is most likely to occur when it provides a way of
        coping with a situation that cannot be handled in the more usual ways.
    3. During an episode of contagion, not all persons in a given place are
        necessarily participants in the contagion.
    4. Like other types of collective preoccupations, organization and
        communication networks are crucial to the spread of hysterical
        contagion.

D. Scapegoating
    1. Collective preoccupations often lead to **scapegoating**, which occurs
        when a group collectively identifies another group as a threat to the
        perceived social order and incorrectly blames the other group for
        problems they have not actually caused.
    2. Racial minority groups and other groups perceived by the dominant
        group to be a threat are commonly the victims of scapegoating. For
        example, today gays and lesbians are often blamed for undermining
        family values as the traditional family structure undergoes major
        transformation.
    3. Scapegoats may be fixed upon in small face-to-face groups where
        members collectively come to define a particular group as the cause of
        their problems.

V.   SOCIAL MOVEMENTS

A **social movement** is an organized social group that acts with some continuity and coordination to promote or resist change in society or other social unit. Social movements are the most organized form of collective behavior and they usually involve large numbers of people. Unlike a crowd, the individuals who make up a social movement are dispersed over time and place, but like crowds, social movements can give the impression that all of their members are unified around a single goal or ideology. Although movements focus on a shared goal, movements can be quite diverse internally. Even members of a given group within a movement may have divergent ideas about what the movement's goals should be and how they should be accomplished. This can lead to tensions within movements as different groups vie for dominance, but it can also lead to increased vitality, because social movements can often benefit from the diverse background, ideas, and interests of members. Within social movements, there is typically tension between spontaneity and structure.

A. Types of Social Movements

1. **Personal transformation movements** such as religious movements aim to change aspects of individuals, such as their spiritual belief systems.

2. **Social change movements** aim to change some aspect of society, such as the Civil Rights Movement.

   a. Social change movements may be *norm-focused*, by trying to change the prescribed way of doing something, or *value-focused*, by trying to change a fundamental idea or something everyone holds dear.

   b. Social movements may be either reformist or radical. **Reform movements** seek change through legal or other mainstream political means, working within existing institutions, while **radical movements** seek fundamental change in the structure of society.

3. **Reactionary movements** organize to resist change or to re-instate an earlier social order that participants perceive to be better.

B. Origins of Social Movements

At least four elements are necessary for a social movement to begin.

1. There must be a pre-existing communication network because activists need some way to communicate with the people who will become part of the new movement.

2. There must be a perceived sense of injustice among the potential participants, or a strong desire for change.

3. A precipitating factor must translate the sense of perceived grievance into action.

4. The final condition needed to get a movement started is the ability of groups to mobilize. **Mobilization** is the process by which social movements and their leaders secure and coordinate people and resources (such as money) for a movement.

C. The Organization of Social Movements

1. As movements develop, they quickly establish an organizational structure. The shape of the movement's organization may range from formal bureaucratic structures to decentralized, interpersonal, and egalitarian arrangements.

2. Many movements are large bureaucracies, including the National Organization for Women and the National Association for the Advancement of Colored People (NAACP).
3. Other social movements are often made up of organizations that are more decentralized, interpersonal, and loosely connected.
4. Links between social movements develop in several ways. Different groups may participate in joint activities, members of a group may switch to other groups or be enrolled in several organizations at once, and individuals in different groups may form friendships.
5. The advantages of informal organizations over more bureaucratic structures include greater resiliency and flexibility.
6. The disadvantages to informal organizations are that such movements cannot act rapidly as a whole, no one person can legitimately speak for the entire movement, there may be no one who can give clear direction to the movement's principles and plans, and fragmentation within the movement can lead to the movement's demise.

D. Strategies and Tactics
Social movements choose their political and social strategies based on a number of variables: the resources available to them, the constraints on their actions, the organizational structure of the movement, and the expectations the movement has about potential targets of its actions, such as the media, social control agencies, and audiences. Constraints on social movements may include values, past experiences, and expectations that groups have. The appearance of opportunities for action, the perceived response of social control agencies, and the expected effect that a group's action will have on the public all contribute to shaping the strategies the group will use.

E. Theories of Social Movements
Sociologists have developed several theories to explain the development of social movements.
1. **Resource mobilization theory** is an explanation of how social movements develop that focuses on how movements gain momentum by successfully garnering resources, competing with other movements, and mobilizing available resources, including money, communication technology, interpersonal contacts, special technical or legal knowledge, and people with organizational and leadership skills.
2. **Political process theory** posits that movements achieve success by exploiting a combination of internal factors, such as the ability of organizations to mobilize resources, and external factors, such as changes occurring in the society. Political process theory also stresses the vulnerability of the political system to social protest.
3. Resource mobilization theory and political process theory are social structural explanations, since they explain the emergence of social movements as the result of forces lying outside of individuals, such as war, demographic shifts, and economic crisis.
4. **New social movement theory conceptually** links culture, ideology, and identity conceptually to explain how new identities are forged within social movements. New social movement theorists are especially interested in how identity is socially constructed through participation in social movements. people construct new identities.
5. Other explanations of social movements focus on the importance of cultural meaning systems in mobilizing people for collective action.

a. By creating meaning systems, people create a shared identity.
b. **Frames** are schemes of interpretation that allow people in groups to perceive, identify, and label events that become the basis for collective action.
c. Cultural explanations also highlight the expressive aspects of social movements to dramatize their cause.

VI. DIVERSITY, GLOBALIZATION, AND SOCIAL CHANGE

Social movements are a major source of social change around the world as evidenced by how people have organized to protest oppressive forms of government, the absence of civil rights, or economic injustices. Sometimes collective behavior and social movements can be the basis for revolutionary events, or those that change the course of world history. Other times, the persistence of social movements gradually changes the world or a particular society. In the future, it is likely that there will be further worldwide impact from movements that originate in a particular country because modern communication systems will bring social movements in distant parts of the world closer to home. In the United States, some of the most significant social movements are those associated with the nation's diverse population, including the women's movement, the Civil Rights Movement, and the gay and lesbian movement. At the same time, those resisting expansion of the rights of these diverse populations are increasingly organizing to oppose such changes.

PRACTICE TEST

MULTIPLE CHOICE QUESTIONS

1. Which of the following is a characteristic of collective behavior?
   a. It captures and reflects the consistent, well-established elements of society.
   b. It is overly emotional, irrational behavior that follows no consistent pattern.
   c. It involves people acting collectively to establish new norms of behavior in response to an emerging situation.
   d. It only occurs in response to events that have already happened, not in anticipation of an event that may occur in the future.

2. Which theory of collective behavior asserts that when people are faced with an unusual situation, they create meanings that define and direct the situation?
   a. Scapegoat theory
   b. Emergent norm theory
   c. Relative deprivation theory
   d. Collective consciousness theory

3. Which of the following statements is (are) true about expressive crowds?
   a. The primary purpose of an expressive crowd is the release of emotion.
   b. Anger is the most common emotion that moves an expressive crowd.
   c. Expressive crowds rarely have any permanent effect on the mood or behavior of the participants.
   d. All of the above statements about expressive crowds are true.

4. In which type of riot is property, rather than people, the object of the attack?
   a. contagious riot
   b. commodity riot
   c. communal riot
   d. political riot

5. Riots are more likely to occur in areas where:
   a. there has been a rapid influx of new populations.
   b. racial-ethnic minorities experience economic deprivation.
   c. the local government is perceived as insensitive to the population's needs.
   d. All of the above conditions increase the likelihood that a riot will occur.

6. Which of the following situations does **not** generally bring a riot to an end?
   a. Social control agents take action intended to end the riot.
   b. Relief services for the deprived group are provided.
   c. The goals of the rioting group are met.
   d. The political situation remains stable.

7. Sociologists assert that people buy designer clothing with labels on the outside because:
   a. fashion is a mechanism for marking and communicating inequality between groups.
   b. purchasing and displaying expensive items is a form of conspicuous consumption.
   c. clothing symbolizes the particular identity that people wish to convey.
   d. All of the above statements about fashion are true.

8. Rumors are especially likely to develop when people:
   a. are uncomfortable in group situations.
   b. lack adequate information.
   c. do not question authority.
   d. lack higher education

9. In the breakout period of a fad,
   a. the fad quickly fades.
   b. no one knows about the fad or activity.
   c. the fad spreads through friendship networks.
   d. the new item is defined as a fad, and people enthusiastically accept it.

10. Which of the following usually occurs during a panic?
    a. People communicate extensively throughout the group.
    b. People adopt an "every man for himself" attitude.
    c. People feel a sense of entrapment.
    d. All of the above generally occur during a panic.

11. Hula hoops, Beanie Babies, and streaking are all examples of:
    a. collective preoccupations.
    b. social movements.
    c. social competitions.
    d. global linkages.

12. Which type of collective behavior is the most highly organized and tends to be sustained over time?
    a.   hysterical contagions
    b.   social movements
    c.   riots
    d.   fads

13. The process by which social movements and their leaders secure people and resources for the movement is resource:
    a.   planning.
    b.   procurement.
    c.   mobilization.
    d.   identification.

14. Gays and lesbians have often been blamed for undermining the traditional family structure in the United States. This is an example of:
    a.   rioting.
    b.   scapegoating.
    c.   social reform.
    d.   personal transformation.

15. Which theory of social movements conceptually links cultural ideology, social structure, and personal identity to explain why social movements develop?
    a.   new social movement theory
    b.   resource mobilization theory
    c.   political process theory
    d.   competition theory

16. Which theory views social movements as starting when social structural weaknesses, such as war or economic crisis, present opportunities for collective behavior to occur?
    a.   new social movement theory
    b.   resource mobilization theory
    c.   political process theory
    d.   competition theory

17. The main purpose of the Right to Life movement is to overturn the Supreme Court decision, *Roe v. Wade*, and make abortion illegal in the United States. This is an example of a _____ movement.
    a.   transformation
    b.   reactionary
    c.   expressive
    d.   rational

18. The movement against drunk driving in the U.S., led by groups such as MADD and SADD, has attempted to introduce social change through political lobbying, legal change, and other mainstream activities. This is an example of a _____ movement.
    a.   reactionary
    b.   rational
    c.   radical
    d.   reform

19. During the early period of the Civil Rights movement in the United States, Rosa Parks refused to give up her seat on a public bus in Montgomery, Alabama. This is an example of which necessary component of a social movement?
   a. preexisting communication network
   b. precipitating incident
   c. preexisting grievance
   d. ability to mobilize

20. Contemporary social movements have a tendency to become increasingly:
   a. flexible, informal, and responsive to all participants' needs.
   b. violent as access to power increases.
   c. utopian in their goals and objectives.
   d. formal, organized, and professional.

TRUE-FALSE QUESTIONS

1. People's response to a natural disaster, such as an earthquake, is a form of collective behavior.

2. The majority of Americans think that economic growth should be given priority even if the environment suffers to some extent.

3. A major contributing factor to the development of a common Asian American identity was the hatred directed toward Japanese Americans during World War II.

4. A norm-focused social movement attempts to change a fundamental idea that is prevalent in the population.

5. All social movements tend to use the same strategies and tactics to achieve their goals.

6. Even though social movements give the impression that all of their members are unified around a single goal or ideology, there are often conflicts of interest and opinions within a movement.

7. A major disadvantage of social movements made up of more informal, decentralized organizations is that they are less resilient and flexible than movements made up of large, bureaucratic organizations.

8. One example of a very successful tactic among antiabortion activists in the U.S. is to block the entrances to medical clinics, a strategy that has increased support for their position.

9. The civil rights movement of the 1960s can attribute much of its success to the ability to mobilize existing resources from Black colleges and churches.

10. Nancy Whittier's research reveals that the women's movement in the U.S. is no longer a viable social movement because feminists have reached most of their goals.

FILL IN THE BLANK QUESTIONS

1. Schemes of interpretation that allow people in groups to collectively perceive, identify, and label events within their lives are _____.

2. Fads characterized by the very intense involvement of participants, who may incur considerable expense and inconvenience in pursuit of the fad, are _____.

3. The New Age movement is a contemporary example of a _____ social movement.

4. During an episode of _____, symptoms of an illness spread among a group of people despite the absence of physiological disease.

5. During collective behavior episodes, people communicate extensively through _____, or information transmitted among participants in an attempt to make sense of an ambiguous situation.

ESSAY QUESTIONS

1. Identify the conditions in which a panic is likely to develop, and discuss how people involved in a panic generally behave.
2. Identify a contemporary fad in the United States and discuss how the fad moved through the stages of development identified by sociologists.
3. Compare and contrast the explanations offered by convergence theory and competition theory on the topic of why riots occur.
4. Using the contemporary environmental movement as an example, explain the difference between radical and reform movements.
5. Identify the four elements necessary for a social movement to begin, and give specific examples of these elements as they relate to the civil rights movement.

ANSWERS TO PRACTICE TEST

Answers to Multiple Choice Questions

1.	C.	615	Collective behavior occurs when the usual norms are suspended and people collectively establish new norms of behavior in response to an an emerging situation, or in response to the strong belief that an event will occur. Collective behavior captures the novel, dynamic, and changing elements of society and represents the actions of groups, not individuals. Although collective behavior may appear highly emotional, it is patterned and coordinated, not irrational
2.	B.	619	Emergent norm theory postulates that when people are faced with an unusual situation, they collectively create meanings that define and direct the situation.
3.	A.	620	Crowds are one of the major forms of collective behavior. The primary purpose of an expressive crowd is to release emotion. Expressive crowds are usually moved by grief or joy, and involvement in the crowd may have lasting effects on the participants' mood and behavior.
4.	B.	622	In commodity riots, property is the object of the attack.
5.	D.	623	Riots are more likely to occur where there is economic deprivation

of racial-ethnic minorities, when there has been a rapid influx of new populations, and where the grievances of the rioting group have not been addressed. Expanding relief services may regulate the discontent.

6.   D.   623   If the political situation remains stable, the riot is not likely to end. The riot may be stopped if the rioters' demands are met, relief services are provided, or social control agents take action.

7.   D.   625   Fashion has traditionally been considered a form of collective behavior because it constantly introduces something novel into the society. Fashion differentiates groups from one another, thereby communicating inequality. Economist and sociologist Thorstein Veblen referred to the purchasing and displaying of goods to symbolize wealth and status as conspicuous consumption.

8.   B.   618   Rumors are especially likely to develop when people lack adequate information, which frequently occurs during collective behavior episodes because they are emerging situations.

9.   C.   625   In the peaking period of a fad, the new item is defined as a fad, and people enthusiastically accept it. In the breakout period, the fad spreads via networks, and the fad quickly fades in the decline period.

10.   C.   620   During a panic, people become concerned for their safety due to a perceived threat. People tend to flee in groups and help others during a panic, but there is generally a failure of front-to-rear communication, which may put people at risk for injury or death from being trampled.

11.   A.   624   Collective preoccupations are forms of collective behavior wherein many people over a relatively broad spectrum engage in similar behavior and have a shared definition of their behavior as needed to bring social change or identify their place in society. Fads, such as collecting Beanie Babies, are an example of a collective preoccupation.

12.   B.   627   Social movements are the most highly organized form of collective behavior. Social movements are comprised of groups that act with some continuity and coordination to promote or resist change in society or other social units. Fads are collective preoccupations, which tend to be short-lived and have relatively little impact on society. Both riots, a form of crowd behavior, and hysterical contagions, which involve the spread of symptoms of an illness among a group of people despite the absence of physiological disease, last a relatively short time.

13.   C.   633   Mobilization is the process by which social movements and their leaders secure people and other resources for a movement.

14.   B.   626   Scapegoating occurs when one group incorrectly perceives another group for problems they have not actually caused due to a perception of that group as a threat. An example of scapegoating is blaming gays and lesbians for undermining families in the United States.

15.   A   636   New social movement theory focuses on how social structure, cultural ideology, and the personal identity of the movement's members intersect.

16.   C.   635   Political process theory asserts that movements achieve success by exploiting internal and external factors. The political system is more vulnerable to protest when there is a structural weakness, such as war.

17.   B.   631   The Right to Life movement is an example of a reactionary social movement, or a movement designed to resist social change or reinstate an earlier social order. Social change movements, such as the Civil Rights Movement, attempt to change some aspect of society, such as

race relations. Personal transformation movements, such as the New Age movement, attempt to change individuals.

18. D. 630 Social change movements may be either reformist or radical. The movement against drunk driving is an example of a reform movement, which works within existing institutions (such as the law) to achieve change. Radical movements seek fundamental changes in the structure of society.

19. B. 631 There are four elements necessary for a social movement: preexisting grievance, preexisting communication network, precipitating incident, and ability to mobilize resources. When Rosa Parks refused to give up her seat, it was the precipitating incident for the Montgomery Bus Boycott, which facilitated the goals of the Civil Rights Movement.

20. C. 633 Many of the organizations that support contemporary social movements are large bureaucracies, such as the National Organization for Women (NOW) and the National Association for the Advancement of Colored People (NAACP), which have paid, professional staffs.

Answers to True-False Questions

1. T. 616 Natural disasters are emergent events that involve collective behavior.

2. F 631 A majority of Americans report that the environment should be protected even at the risk of curbing economic growth (Figure 22.2).

3. T. 630 During World War II, fears of a "yellow peril, " or rapid growth in the Asian American population, developed, which heightened racism toward all Asian immigrant groups. According to Yen Le Espiritu, an increase in the number of American born Asian people blurred the cultural differences among Chinese, Japanese, Filipino, and Korean people, which also facilitated the development of a unified Asian identity. Finally, ethnic pride for Asian Americans has been enhanced by organized social movement activity.

4. F. 629 Norm-focused movements attempt to change the prescribed way of doing things, while value-focused movements attempt to change a fundamental idea that is prevalent in the population.

5. F. 628 There is great variety within and across social movements. For example, some organizations use more radical tactics than others. behavior.

6. T. 630 Conflicts of interests and opinions within social movements are common.

7. F. 634 Informal, decentralized organizations are more flexible and resilient than large formal organizations; however, they are at risk of fragmentation because they do not have a single leader who speaks for them and they cannot act rapidly

8. F. 635 Blocking clinic entrances is an unsuccessful strategy for antiabortion activists. This tactic backfired and support declined.

9. T. 635 The ability to mobilize existing resources contributed to the success of the Civil Rights Movement.

10. F. 629 Whittier's research indicates that feminism is an enduring social movement that has evolved with changing social conditions.

Answers to Fill in the Blank Questions

1.	frames	636
2.	crazes	625
3.	personal transformation	628
4.	hysterical contagion	626
5.	rumors	618

CHAPTER 23
SOCIAL CHANGE IN GLOBAL PERSPECTIVE

BRIEF CHAPTER OUTLINE
What is Social Change?
Theories of Social Change
       Functionalist and Evolutionary Theories
       Conflict Theories
       Cyclical Theories
The Causes of Social Change
       Collective Behavior
       Social Movements
       Cultural Diffusion
       Inequality and Change
       Technological Innovation and the Cyberspace Revolution
       War and Social Change
Modernization
       From Community and Society
       Mass Society and Bureaucracy
       Social Inequality, Powerlessness, and the Individual
Global Theories of Social Change
       Modernization Theory
       World Systems Theory
       Dependency Theory
Diversity and Social Change

QUESTIONS TO GUIDE YOUR READING

1. What is the difference between a microchange and a macrochange?
2. What are the main sources of social change?
3. What is the difference between a unidimensional and a multidimensional theory of social change?
4. What are the primary characteristics of modernization?
5. What are the basic assumptions of the three global theories of social changes?

KEY TERMS (defined at page number shown and in glossary)

core nations 656
cyclical theories 646
evolutionary social theories 644
gesellschaft 653
inner-directedness 655
mass society 654
modernization theory 656
neoevolutionary theory 644
other-directedness 655
tradition-directedness 655
world systems theory 656

cultural diffusion 648
dependency theory 657
gemeinschaft 653
globalization 656
macrochanges 642
microchanges 642
multidimensional evolutionary theory 644
noncore nations 656
social change 642
unidimensional evolutionary theory 644

KEY PEOPLE (identified at page number shown)

Peter Berger 654

Rolf Dahrendorf 654

Jurgen Habermas 655

Ralph Linton 648

Herbert Marcuse 655

Marshall McLuhan 656

Robert Reich 657

Theda Skocpol 645

Pitrim Sorokin 646

Ferdinand Toennies 653

Sherry Turkle 651

Theodore Caplow 646

Emile Durkheim 644

Gerhard Lenski 644

Karl Marx 645

William and Arlise McCord 656

William Ogburn 642

David Reisman 655

Herbert Spencer 644

Robert Farris Thompson 648

Arnold Toynbee 646

Immanuel Wallerstein 656

CHAPTER OUTLINE

Technological innovations can transform a society, but not all of these changes represent "progress." For example, technological disasters such as the Love Canal incident in New York, led to political and social changes directed at eliminating toxic wastes in the environment.

I.   **WHAT IS SOCIAL CHANGE?**

Social change is the alteration of social interactions, institutions, stratification systems, and elements of culture over time. Societies are always in a state of flux. Some changes are rapid, while others are more gradual. With increased urbanization, more rapid social change becomes possible, and new technologies circulate quickly. **Microchanges** are subtle alterations in the day-to-day interactions between people, such as fads. **Macrochanges** are gradual transformations that occur on a broad scale and affect many aspects of society. In the process of *modernization*, societies absorb the changes that develop. One trend that accompanies modernization is the increasing social differentiation of society.

Whether large or small, fast or slow, social change typically has a number of shared characteristics. Social change is uneven because the some parts of a society lag behind others in the rate of change, a principle William Ogburn referred to as *cultural lag*. The onset and consequences of social change are often unforeseen. Social change often creates conflict, particularly between women and men and among various racial-ethnic and social class groups. The direction of social change is not random and social changes cannot erase the past. Change has "direction" relative to a society's history, and as a society moves toward the future, it carries along its history, its traditions, and its institutions.

II.   **THEORIES OF SOCIAL CHANGE**

Different theories of social change emphasize different aspects of the change process.

A.   Functionalist and Evolutionary Theories

1.   Functionalist theory builds upon the belief that all societies, past and present, possess basic elements and institutions that perform certain "functions" that permit a society to survive and persist.

2.   A *function* is a consequence of some social element that contributes to the continuance of a society.

3.   According to functional theorists, societies move from structurally simple, homogeneous societies (such as foraging or pastoral societies) where members engage in largely similar tasks, to structurally more complex, heterogeneous societies (such as agricultural, industrial, and postindustrial societies) where great social differentiation exists and

there is extensive division of labor among people who perform many specialized tasks.

    4.   **Evolutionary theories** of social change are a branch of functionalist theory.

        a.   **Unidimensional evolutionary theory**, now out of favor, argued that societies follow a single evolutionary path from "simple," relatively undifferentiated societies to more complex societies, which were perceived as more "civilized."

        b.   **Multidimensional evolutionary theory**, also called **neoevolutionary theory**, argues that the structural, institutional, and cultural development of a society can follow many evolutionary paths simultaneously, with the different paths all emerging from the circumstances of the society.

            1)   The nature of social evolution in the society depends upon the interplay between the society's technology, population characteristics, extent of social differentiation, and other structural and cultural elements.

            2)   Gerhard Lenski and colleagues posit that technology has a central role in development because technological advances are significantly, although not wholly, responsible for other changes, including the nature of law, alterations in religious preference, form of government, and relations between diverse groups.

    5.   Newer functionalist theories emphasize the role of racial-ethnic, social class, and gender differences in the process of social change.

        a.   Earlier theories made the implicit assumption that European and American societies, which are predominantly White, were more evolved or advanced.

        b.   The new functionalism rejects the "primitive" versus "civilized" dichotomy and its implicit assumptions about racial groups. Rather, it regards relations between diverse social groups as an important part of any society, regardless of its stage of development or evolution.

  B.   <u>Conflict Theories</u>

    1.   The central notion of conflict theory is that conflict is built into social relations. For Marx, social conflict, particularly between the two major social classes in any society (proletariat and bourgeoisie) was the driving force behind all social change.

    2.   Sociologists now think that conflict between Whites and racial-ethnic minorities is at least partly, but not wholly, rooted in class conflict, because minorities are disproportionately represented among the less well-off classes.

    3.   Many *cultural* differences exist between Whites and Native Americans, Latinos, Whites, and Asians. There are also important cultural differences *within* broadly defined racial-ethnic groups.

    4.   A central feature of Marx's work is that revolution and dramatic social change will come about when class conflict inevitably leads to a decisive social rupture.

5. Although the worldwide revolution predicted by Marx never developed, his analysis of class-related conflict has advanced our understanding of social change.
6. Marx seems to have overemphasized the role of economics and ignored the importance of other relevant social factors in the social tensions he observed.
7. Sociologist Theda Skocpol has noted that in France, Russia, and China, countries where major revolutions have occurred, serious internal conflicts between classes were combined with major international crises that the elite classes proved unable to resolve before they were overthrown.
8. Ethnic, racial, and religious differences join social class differences as major causes of conflict within and between countries. Examples of this include recent bouts of so-called "ethnic cleansing," in which one ethnic group attempts to annihilate another.

C. Cyclical Theories
1. **Cyclical theories** of social change invoke patterns of social structure and culture that are believed to recur at more or less regular intervals.
2. Arnold Toynbee, social historian and a principal theorist of cyclical social change, argues that societies are born, mature, decay, and sometimes die.
3. Sociological theorists Pitrim Sorokin and Theodore Caplow have argued that societies proceed through three different phases or cycles.
    a. In the first phase, called *idealistic culture*, the society wrestles with the tension between the ideal and the practical.
    b. The second phase, *ideational culture*, emphasizes faith and new forms of spirituality.
    c. The third phase is *sensate culture*, which stresses practical approaches to reality, and also involves the hedonistic and the sensual ("sex, drugs, and rock and roll").

III. **THE CAUSES OF SOCIAL CHANGE**
A. Collective Behavior
Certain types of collective behavior can serve as major causes of social and cultural change. Collective preoccupations, such as fads, crazes, and fashions, can serve to initiate social change, although the magnitude of the change that results may be slight.

B. Social Movements
Social movements are highly organized and persistent forms of collective behavior with the purpose of initiating or vigorously resisting social change.

C. Cultural Diffusion
Cultural diffusion is the transmission of cultural elements from one society or cultural group to another. Diffusion of cultural elements can occur by means of trade, migration, mass communications media, and social interaction. For example, many contemporary religious practices among Black Americans are traceable back to Africa.

D. Inequality and Change
Inequalities between groups of people on the basis of sex, class, race, ethnicity, or other social structural characteristics can be a powerful spur toward social change. Culture itself can sometimes contribute to the persistence of social inequality, therefore, it may become a source of discontent for certain groups in society.

E. Technological Innovation and Cyberspace Revolution
Technological innovations can be strong catalysts of social change. The historical movement of societies from agrarian to industrialized has been tightly linked to the emergence of technological innovations. For example, the advent of the electronic computer and the subsequent development of the Internet has transformed our entire society and all of its social institutions.

F. Population and Change
Another cause of social and cultural change is changes in the population.
1. Limitations placed on the population by the natural environment can greatly influence the nature of social relationships, because crowding affects how people interact with each other.
2. Major social change can also result from shifts in the age composition of a population. For example, as the average age in the United States increases, the society must respond to the graying of America.
3. Immigration is having profound effects on the overall ethnic and racial composition of the United States. By the year 2050, it is expected that Hispanics will be 25 percent of Americans and Asians will comprise 8 percent of the U.S. population.
   a. The structure of the economy will change, as will the ethnic mix in education and jobs, and there will be an increased influence of the Hispanic culture on styles of dance, music, language, and other behaviors.
   b. Whether continuing Hispanic immigration will improve the representation of Hispanics in all job classifications will depend upon whether job discrimination declines.

G. War and Social Change
War and severe political conflict result in widescale changes for both the conquering and conquered groups. The conquerors can impose their will upon the conquered and restructure many of their institutions, or the conquerors can exercise only minimal changes.

IV. **MODERNIZATION**
Modernization is a process of social and cultural change that is initiated by industrialization and followed by increased social differentiation and division of labor. There are three general characteristics of modernization. Modernization is characterized by the decline of small, traditional communities as a society becomes more bureaucratized and interactions come to be shaped by formal organizations. There is generally a decline in the importance of the religious institution, and with the mechanization of daily life, people often feel that they have lost control of their lives.

A. From Community (Gemeinschaft) to Society (Gesellschaft)
1. The German sociologist Ferdinand Toennies viewed the process of modernization as a progressive loss of **gemeinschaft**, which is German for "community."
   a. Gemeinschaft is a state characterized by a sense of fellowship, strong personal ties and primary group memberships, and a sense of personal loyalty to one another.
   b. Toennies argued that the industrial revolution, with its emphasis on efficiency and task-oriented behavior, destroyed the sense of community and personal ties associated with an earlier rural life, substituting instead feelings of rootlessness and impersonality.

363

2. The result of industrialization and urbanization was the condition of **gesellschaft**, which is German for "society." This is a kind of social organization characterized by a high division of labor, less prominence of personal ties, the lack of a sense of community among the members of society, and the absence of a feeling of belonging.

3. One measurement of the impersonality associated with the urban gesellschaft is the effect an urban setting has on the likelihood that someone will come to the aid of a person in distress.

   a. A person in trouble on the street is more likely to be given assistance by a bystander if the event takes place in a small town than if it takes place in a large city.

   b. In a famous case in 1964, a New Yorker named Kitty Genovese was stabbed repeatedly while at least thirty-eight witnesses within the apartment complex where she lived failed to respond to her cries for help.

   c. Interestingly, research shows that when the number of people observing an emergency goes up, the likelihood that any of them will offer assistance goes down.

   d. People in a large city are more likely to merge with the crowd, or *de-individuate*, thereby failing to offer help simply because there are more people around.

B. Mass Society and Bureaucracy

   1. Modernization has produced what is called a **mass society**, or one in which industrialization and bureaucracy reach exceedingly high levels.

   2. In the mass society, the change from gemeinschaft to gesellschaft is accelerated and the breakup of primary, family, and kinship ties is particularly pronounced.

   3. In a mass society, the government expands to include tasks that were previously done by the family, such as providing care for the elderly.

   4. Dahrendorf, Berger, and other mass society theorists argue that bureaucracies have obtained virtually complete control of the individual's life.

      a. As people moved from town to city over the course of the 1900s, divisions of labor became more pronounced and social differentiation increased in the workplace, government, and other institutions.

      b. It became more common to identify people by such personal attributes as their job or gender, rather than by their kinship or their hometown, which is more commonly done in the gemeinschaft society.

      c. People became more geographically mobile and less dependent on family and kin, thereby increasing the feeling that most of the people in one's immediate environment are strangers.

      d. The rise of large government is a major part of the overall bureaucratization of social life.

C. Social Inequality, Powerlessness, and the Individual

   1. Another product of modernization is pronounced social stratification.

   2. The personal feelings of powerlessness that accompany modernization are due to social inequalities related to race, ethnicity, class, and gender stratification.

3.	Building a stable personal identity is difficult in a highly modernized society that presents the individual with complex and conflicting choices about how to live.

4.	According to Habermas, individuals in highly modernized environments are more likely than their less modernized peers to experiment with new religions, social movements, and lifestyles in search of a fit with their conception of their own "true self."

5.	Social theorist David Reisman argued that there are three main orientations of personality that can be traced to social structural conditions. Modernization tends to produce other-directedness, whereas less modernized societies tend to produce tradition-directedness.

	a.	**Other-directedness** occurs when the behavior of the individual is guided by the observed behavior of others. It is characterized by rigid conformity and attempts to "keep up with the Joneses."

	b.	**Inner-directedness** occurs when the individual is guided by internal principles and morals. It is relatively impervious to the superficialities of the social environment.

	c.	**Tradition-directedness** is characterized by a strong conformity to long-standing and time-honored norms, practices, and styles of life.

6.	The inner-directed are less likely to sway with the presence or absence of modernization. If modernization tends to produce other-directedness, then anyone who happens to be inner-directed or tradition-directed in a highly modernized and rapidly changing society, such as the United States, is likely to be seen as a deviant person.

7.	The other-directed are highly flexible, capable of rapid personal change, and more open to the influences of group pressures, changing styles, and shifting interests.

8.	The influential social theorist Herbert Marcuse argued that modernized society fails to meet people's basic needs of the people, including the need for a fulfilling identity.

	a.	The technological advances of modern society do not increase the feeling that one has control over one's own life. In fact, they reduce control and lead to feelings of powerlessness, resulting in the *alienation* of the individual from society.

	b.	This alienation is more likely to affect those who have traditionally been denied access to power, such as racial minorities, women, and the working class.

V.	**GLOBAL THEORIES OF SOCIAL CHANGE**
	Globalization refers to the increased interconnectedness and interdependence of different societies around the world. In Europe, this trend has proceeded as far as a common currency for all nations participating in the newly constructed, common economy. As societies become ever more interconnected, cultural diffusion between them creates common ground; but at the same time, cultural differences may become more important as the relationships among nations become more intimate. The different perspectives on globalization are represented by three main theories: modernization, world systems, and dependency theory.

	A.	Modernization Theory
		1.	Strongly influenced by functionalist theories of social change, **modernization theory** states that global development is a worldwide

process affecting nearly all societies that have been touched by social change.

    2.   Recent proponents of modernization theory, such as William and Arlise McCord, reject the assumption that only western European countries and the Untied States have led the process of technological globalization and its resultant homogenization. For example, Japan, Taiwan, and South Korea have also been leaders in modernization.

    3.   As a result of their involvement, Japan, with its cultural emphasis on the importance of small friendship groups in the workplace and a traditional work ethic, has profoundly influenced other countries and added to the impetus of global economic growth.

B.   <u>World Systems Theory</u>

    1.   **World systems theory**, formulated by Immanuel Wallerstein, argues that all nations are members of a worldwide system of unequal political and economic relationships that benefit the more developed, technologically advanced countries at the expense of the less developed, less technologically advanced countries.

    2.   Wallerstein divided the world system into two camps. Core nations import raw materials and cheap labor from the noncore nations, which suffer exploitation as a result.

        a.   **Core nations**, such as the United States, England, and Japan, produce goods and services both for their own consumption and for export.

        b.   **Noncore** (or peripheral) **nations**, situated in Africa, Latin America, South America, and parts of Asia, occupy lower positions in the global economy.

C.   <u>Dependency Theory</u>

    1.   Closely allied with Wallerstein's world systems theory is **dependency theory**, which maintains that highly industrialized nations tend to imprison developing nations in dependent relationships, rather than spurring the upward mobility of developing nations with transfers of technology and business acumen.

        a.   Dependency theory views the highly industrialized core nations as transferring only those narrow capabilities that it serves them to deliver.

        b.   Once these unequal relationships are forged, core nations then seek to preserve the status quo because they derive benefits in the form of cheap raw materials and labor from noncore nations.

        c.   The developing nations remain dependent upon the core nations for markets and support in keeping what industry they have acquired in working order, while at home they experience minimal social development, limited economic growth, and increased income stratification among their own population.

    2.   Trade and borrowing dependency are notable in these relationships. Robert Reich has noted that core nation have been willing to lend money to noncore nations, but often on terms that put severe economic strain on the noncore nations.

VI.   DIVERSITY AND SOCIAL CHANGE

Issues of race, class, and gender have played a major role in social change. Social change can affect the relations between societies as well as relationships among groups within a society. Diversity as a cause of change is exemplified by the effects of immigration into a country. Diversity as an effect of change is exemplified by the unequal outcomes of modernization on different ethnic groups. Modernization has the effect of making some less developed nations more dependent upon the core countries than on neighboring nations or other nations at a similar level of development.

PRACTICE TEST

MULTIPLE CHOICE QUESTIONS

1. Which invention has become a dominant force in determining the interests and habits of youth in the United States since the mid-1900s?
    a. Levi jeans
    b. jazz music
    c. television
    d. recreational drugs

2. Gradual transformations that occur on a broad scale and affect many aspects of society, such as the rise of the computer and development of digital culture, are:
    a. macrochanges.
    b. microchanges.
    c. cultural diffusions.
    d. demographic shifts.

3. Which one of the following is generally a characteristic of social change?
    a. Sociologists can accurately predict the onset and consequences of social change.
    b. Social change is a process that affects all segments of society equally and similarly.
    c. Social change often creates conflict in society.
    d. All of the above are characteristics of social change.

4. According to _____ theory, societies move from structurally simple and homogeneous to more complex and heterogeneous.
    a. symbolic interaction.
    b. functionalist
    c. conflict
    d. cyclical

5. Toynbee's assertion that all societies are born, mature, decay, and sometimes die reflects the principles of the _____ theory of social change.
    a. modernization
    b. functionalist
    c. conflict
    d. cyclical

6. Lenski argues that although other elements contribute to social change, _____ are especially important in facilitating social changes such as alterations in religious preferences, the nature of law, and the form of government in modern societies.
   a. immigration patterns
   b. technological advances
   c. changes in family structure
   d. changes in the age composition of the population

7. Sherry Turkel argues that the United States has moved to a culture of _____, in which widespread Internet use allows individuals to easily develop a new self.
   a. irresponsibility
   b. calculation
   c. simulation
   d. anonymity

8. White youth are beginning to participate in an interpersonal game called signifyin' that began in urban African American communities. This is an example of cultural:
   a. lag
   b. conflict
   c. diffusion
   d. inequality

9. A potentially negative consequence of the introduction of steel into the Yanomani Indian communities of Brazil and Venezuela is the:
   a. increase in deadly warfare.
   b. tribes' inability to continue farming efficiently.
   c. emergence of environmental pollution due to automobile emissions.
   d. All of the above have occurred since steel was introduced in these communities.

10. Because crowding is a pervasive feature of Japanese culture,
   a. close bodily contact in public places such as subway stations has strong sexual overtones.
   b. subway stations hire workers whose job is to push as many passengers as possible into each train.
   c. it is considered a violation of other people's personal space to have one's entire body pressed against a stranger.
   d. All of the above are true.

11. Which of the following is **not** a feature of modernization?
   a. decline in importance of secondary groups to social interaction
   b. decrease in the number of small, close-knit communities
   c. increase in feelings of uncertainty and powerlessness
   d. increase in the mechanization of daily life

12. According to Toennies, the kind of social organization characterized by a high division of labor, less prominence of personal ties, the lack of a sense of community among the members of society and the absence of a feeling of belonging is typically found in a(n) _____ society.
    a. agrarian
    b. gesellschaft
    c. gemeinschaft
    d. homogeneous

13. The U.S. victory over Japan and Germany in World War II resulted in an increase in the number of:
    a. men attending college.
    b. women participating in the paid labor force.
    c. Jewish people immigrating to the United States.
    d. All of the above occurred.

14. According to Dahrendorf, modernization has produced what is called a(n) _____ society, or one in which industrialization and bureaucracy reach exceedingly high levels.
    a. mass
    b. evolved
    c. depersonalized
    d. unidimensional

15. According to Sorokin's cyclical model of social change, the contemporary New Age movement represents _____ culture.
    a. utopian
    b. sensate
    c. ideational
    d. technological

16. According to David Reisman, _____ is the personality orientation whereby individuals are relatively impervious to the superficialities around them and are guided by strong internal moral principles.
    a. inner-directedness
    b. other-directedness
    c. value-directedness
    d. tradition-directedness

17. According to Marcuse, _____, or a feeling of individual powerlessness, is more likely to affect those who have traditionally been denied access to power.
    a. isolation
    b. alienation
    c. deindividuation
    d. identity disruption

18. Which theory asserts that all nations are members of a worldwide system of unequal political and economic relationships that benefit the highly developed, technologically advanced countries at the expense of the less technologically advanced, less developed countries of the world?
    a. Exploitation theory
    b. Modernization theory
    c. World Systems theory
    d. Global Network theory

19. Nations such as the U.S., England, and Japan import raw materials and cheap labor from _____ nations, which are commonly located in Africa, Latin America, and Asia.
    a. mass
    b. core
    c. noncore
    d. evolutionary

20. By the year 2050, demographers predict that Hispanics will comprise _____ percent of the total U.S. population.
    a. five
    b. twenty-five
    c. fifty
    d. seventy-five

TRUE-FALSE QUESTIONS

1. Todd Gitlin's research on the Vietnam War reveals that the percentage of college students who strongly opposed the war dramatically decreased from 1967 to 1969, when the United States was about to end American involvement in the conflict.

2. Demographers predict that by 2050, Asians will comprise 25 percent of the American population.

3. According to dependency theory, industrialized nations imprison developing nations by loaning them money at such high interest rates that they experience severe economic strain.

4. According to cyclical theory, the first phase of societal development is characterized by tension between the ideal and the practical.

5. Tradition-directedness, or strong conformity to long-standing norms, practices, and lifestyles, is the most common personality orientation found in horticultural and agricultural societies.

6. People in North American countries spend a considerably higher percentage of their household budget on food than do people in African nations.

7. People in cities are more likely than people in small towns to help individuals in need because they interact with many people and recognize the importance of group identity.

8. It is more common to identify people by personal attributes such as occupation than by kinship in a gesellschaft society.

9. The spread of bungie jumping as a form of recreation represents a macrochange.

10. With increasing modernization, there is generally a decrease in the social importance of formal religious institutions.

FILL IN THE BLANK QUESTIONS

1. The increased interconnectedness and interdependence of different societies around the world is _____.

2. Cultural _____ occurs when adjustments in nonmaterial culture, such as norms and values, take place some time after developments in material culture are introduced and adopted in society.

3. The kind of social organization characterized by the similarity of members, strong personal ties, and stable primary group memberships is _____.

4. According to Sorokin, the third phase societies pass through is _____ culture, which involves the hedonistic and sensual elements of culture.

5. According to Reisman, the personality orientation guided by rigid conformity and attempts to "keep up with the Joneses" in modern society is _____.

ESSAY QUESTIONS

1. Identify the main characteristics of social change and explain how they are manifested in the cyberspace revolution.
2. Explain why the unidimensional evolutionary theory of social change has been strongly criticized and fallen out of favor among sociologists.
3. Discuss how the graying of America is having profound effects on social relationships and social institutions in the United States.
4. Explain why Toennies was critical of the industrial revolution and the subsequent transition from a gemeinschaft to a gesellschaft society in the United States.
5. Use dependency theory to explain why developing nations cannot achieve significant mobility within the global economic system.

ANSWERS TO PRACTICE TEST

Answers to Multiple Choice Questions

1. C. 643 Technological innovations such as the television can be strong catalysts for social change.
2. A. 642 Gradual transformations that occur on a broad scale and affect many aspects of society, such as the rise of the personal computer, are macrochanges. Microchanges are subtle alternations in the daily interaction between people, such as fads. Cultural diffusion is the process of transmission of cultural elements, such as fashion, from one

			society or cultural group to another. Demographic shifts are changes in the size, composition, or distribution of the population.
3.	C.	642	Social change often creates conflict in society. Social change is uneven, affecting different parts of society to varying degrees and at different rates. The onset and consequences of social change are often unforeseen. The direction of social change is not random; rather, it occurs relative to a society's history.
4.	B.	644	As summarized in Table 23.1, functionalist theorists view societies as moving from structurally simple and homogeneous to more complex and heterogeneous. They view technology as the primary cause of social change. Conflict theorists view social change as the result of the inevitable economic conflict between social classes in capitalist societies. Cyclical theorists view social change as necessary for growth as the society moves through the phases of its life cycle.
5.	D.	646	Toynbee's ideas are associated with the cyclical theory of social change, which views societies as moving through a life cycle.
6.	B.	644	Lenski's ideas are associated with multidimensional evolutionary theory. He asserts that technological advances are centrally, although not wholly, responsible for other changes in modern societies.
7.	C.	650	According to Turkle, the Internet allows people to develop new identities and interact in a virtual world, resulting in a culture of simulation.
8.	C.	648	The participation of white youth in signifyin' is an example of cultural diffusion, in which cultural elements from one society or group are transmitted to another.
9.	A.	651	The Yanomami tribes do not use electricity or automobiles, and the introduction of steel tools generally makes farming more efficient. It appears that warlike behavior in these groups has increased as a result of contact with outsiders, or at least that warfare has become more deadly now that steel weapons are being used.
10.	B	652	Because crowding is a pervasive feature of Japanese culture, strangers are often in close contact with each other in public places such as subways. In fact, workers are hired to push as many people as possible into subway trains. This kind of close bodily contact is not considered an invasion of privacy, nor does it have sexual overtones, in Japan.
11.	A.	653	Modernization is a process of social and cultural change that is initiated by industrialization and followed by increased social differentiation and a more complex division of labor. The importance of small, traditional communities declines, as does the centrality of the religious institution to society. Feelings of uncertainty and powerlessness increase, as does the importance of secondary groups to social interaction.
12.	B.	653	According to Toennies, the kind of social organization characterized by a high division of labor, less prominence of personal ties, the lack of a sense of community among the members of society, and the absence of a feeling of belonging is typically found in a gesellschaft society. In a gemeinschaft society, there is more homogeneity, members generally feel a greater sense of belonging, and personal ties are more important to social interaction.
13.	D.	652	After World War II ended, more men attended college, women's labor force participation increased, and more Jewish people migrated to the United States.

14.   A.   654   Modernization has produced what is called a mass society, or one in which industrialization and bureaucracy reach exceedingly high levels.

15.   C.   646   According to cyclical theories of social change, the first phase is characterized by idealistic culture, in which there is tension between the ideal and practical aspects of society. In the second phase, ideational culture emerges, which emphasizes new forms of spirituality. The third phase, sensate culture, stresses practical approaches to reality and involves the hedonistic and the sensual.

16.   A.   655   According to David Reisman, other-directedness occurs when the individual's behavior is guided by the observed behavior of others. Inner-directedness occurs when the individual is guided by strong internal principles. Tradition-directedness is characterized by strong conformity to long-standing norms, practices, and lifestyles.

17.   B.   656   Marcuse argues that alienation, or a feeling of powerlessness, is more likely to affect women, racial-ethnic minorities, and the working class, groups traditionally denied access to power in society.

18.   C.   656   World systems theory argues that all nations are members of a worldwide system of unequal political and economic relationships that benefit the developed and technologically advanced countries at the expense of the less technologically advanced and less developed countries. Modernization theory states that global development is a worldwide process that affects nearly all societies. Functionalist theory views societies as evolving from structurally simple, homogeneous societies to structurally complex, more differentiated societies.

19.   C.   656   World systems theory asserts that core nations such as the U.S. import raw materials and cheap labor from noncore nations located in less developed areas of the world. Dependency theory asserts that this arrangement exploits noncore nations, imprisoning them in dependent relationships while benefiting core nations.

20.   B.   652   Demographers predict that Hispanics will comprise 25 percent of the U.S. population by 2050. The influx of Latinos into the U.S. has already resulted in profound cultural changes.

Answers to True-False Questions

1.   F.   643   Gitlin's research indicates that strong opposition to the war increased, as did the number of protests, from 1967 to 1969.

2.   F.   652   Demographers predict that Hispanics will be 25 percent and Asians will be 8 percent of the population by 2050.

3.   T.   657   Industrialized nations keep developing nations dependent through trade and borrowing practices.

4.   T.   646   The society wrestles with the tension between the ideal and the practical in the idealistic culture, which represents the first phase of societal development according to cyclical theory.

5.   T.   655   Tradition-directedness is common in less modernized gemeinschafts.

6.   F.   657   People in North American countries spend a lower percentage of their total household budgets on food than do people in African nations, as indicated in Map 23.2.

7.   F.   654   People in cities are less likely to help someone in distress than people in small towns. Furthermore, the larger the number of people observing

			an emergency, the less likely any of them will offer assistance, because individuals tend to merge with the crowd in large cities.
8.	T.	654	In gesellschafts, people are more likely to be identified by occupation, while in gemeinschafts, people are more likely to be identified by kinship group.
9.	F.	642	The spread of bungie jumping does not represent a broad social transformation, but a subtle alteration in the daily interaction between people; thus, it is an example of a microchange.
10.	T.	653	Modernization results in the decline in the importance of the religious institution as well as the prevalence of small, close-knit communities. Furthermore, the role of the government in people's lives increases, as does the importance of the mass media.

Answers to Fill in the Blank Questions

1.	globalization	656
2.	lag	642
3.	gemeinschaft	653
4.	sensate	646
5.	other-directed	655